Lecture Notes in Computer Science   **8267**

Commenced Publication in 1973
Founding and Former Series Editors:
Gerhard Goos, Juris Hartmanis, and Jan van Leeuwen

For further volumes:
http://www.springer.com/series/7410

T0212656

Yongdae Kim · Heejo Lee
Adrian Perrig (Eds.)

Information Security Applications

14th International Workshop, WISA 2013
Jeju Island, Korea, August 19–21, 2013
Revised Selected Papers

 Springer

Editors
Yongdae Kim
KAIST
Daejeon
Republic of South Korea

Adrian Perrig
ETH
Zurich
Switzerland

Heejo Lee
Korea University
Seoul
Republic of South Korea

ISSN 0302-9743
ISSN 1611-3349 (electronic)
ISBN 978-3-319-05148-2
ISBN 978-3-319-05149-9 (eBook)
DOI 10.1007/978-3-319-05149-9
Springer Cham Heidelberg New York Dordrecht London

Library of Congress Control Number: 2014933576

LNCS Sublibrary: SL 4 – Security and Cryptology

Printed on acid-free paper

Springer is part of Springer Science+Business Media (www.springer.com)

Preface

WISA 2013, the 14th International Workshop on Information Security Applications, was held during August 19–21 in the Ocean Suites Jeju Hotel, Jeju Island, Republic of Korea. The conference was hosted by the Korea Institute of Information Security and Cryptology (KIISC) and sponsored by the Ministry of Science, ICT and Future Planning (MSIP). It was also co-sponsored by the National Security Research Institute (NSRI), the Korea Internet Security Agency (KISA), and the Security Global Alliance (SGA).

We received 39 valid submissions from 16 countries, of which 15 were accepted for the full-paper track and two for the short abstract track. These proceedings contain the revised versions of the 15 full papers and two short papers. Every paper received at least three independent reviews. For the Best Paper Award, the Program Committee (PC) selected "Dynamic Surveillance: A Case Study with Enron Email Data Set" by Heesung Do, Byung Choi, and Heejo Lee. Moreover, "Bifocals: Analyzing WebView Vulnerabilities in Android Applications" by Erika Chin, and David Wagner received the Best White Hat Award. The Best SoK Paper Award was given to "SoK: Lessons Learned From SSL/TLS Attack" by Christopher Meyer, and Jorg Schwenk.

There were five invited talks, Kyoungsoo Park delivered "Building High-Performance Networked Security Systems on Low-Cost Commodity Hardware," and Wenyuan Xu spoke on "Tire Pressure Sensor vs. Utility Meters: From Good Intention to Vulnerabilities" on August 19. In addition, Seungwon Shin presented "Redesigning Network Security Applications with Software Defined Networking," and Jeonghyun Yi delivered "Deobfuscating Dexguard-Bytecode Obfuscator on Android" on August 20. Moreover, on August 21, Brent Kang spoke on "HW-Assisted Kernel Security Monitoring." We also had one keynote speech: Adrian Perrig delivered "Accountable Key Infrastructure (AKI): A Proposal for a Public-Key Validation Infrastructure." Excellent invited speeches along with a keynote speech as well as 17 regular and short paper presentations made a lof of participants stay until the last minute of the workshop. We thank all for their participation.

We would like to thank the authors of all submissions, regardless of whether their papers were accepted or not. Their work made this conference possible. We are extremely grateful to the PC members for their enormous investment of time and effort in the difficult and delicate process of review and selection. We would like to thank Jin Kwak, who was the organizing chair in charge of the local organization and finances. Special thanks go to Sungjae Hwang for providing and setting up the review software. We are most grateful to Donghoon Lee and Moti Yung, the WISA 2012 program chairs, for their timely information and replies to the host of questions we posed during the process.

August 2013

Yongdae Kim
Heejo Lee
Adrian Perrig

Organization

General Chair

Seokwoo Kim   Hansei University, Korea

Steering Committee

Bart Preneel   Katholieke University, Leuven, Belgium
Changseop Park   Dankook University, Korea
Daeho Kim   JoongBu University, Korea
Dongho Won   Sungkyunkwan University, Korea
Heungyoul Youm   Soonchunhyang University, Korea
Hideki Imai   Chuo University, Japan
Hongsub Lee   Konkuk University, Korea
Jooseok Song   Yonsei University, Korea
Kilhyun Nam   Korea National Defense University, Korea
Kwangjo Kim   KAIST, Korea
Minsub Rhee   Dankook University, Korea
Piljoong Lee   POSTECH, Korea
Sangjae Moon   Kyungpook National University, Korea
Sehun Kim   KAIST, Korea

Program Committee

Co-chairs

Yongdae Kim   KAIST, Korea
Heejo Lee   Korea University, Korea
Adrian Perrig ETH, Switzerland

Committee Members

Bo-Yin Yang   Academia Sinica, Taiwan
Brent Kang   George Mason University, USA
Byung-Gon Chun   Microsoft Research, USA
Collin Mulliner   Northeastern University, USA
Eugene Vasserman   Kansas State University, USA

Guofei Gu	Texas A&M, USA
Haibo Chen	Shanghai Jiao Tong University, China
Hiroaki Kikuchi	Meiji University, Japan
Jong Kim	Postech, Korea
Jon Oberheide	Duo security, USA
Julianor Rizzo	Independent Researcher, Argentina
Jeonghyun Yi	Soongsil University, Korea
Jung-Chan Na	ETRI, Korea
Junghwan Rhee	NEC Lab, USA
Kazuhiro Minami	Institute of Statistical Mathematics, Japan
Kiwook Sohn	NSRI, Korea
Kyoungsoo Park	KAIST, Korea
Man Ho Au	University of Wollongong, Australia
Nicholas j. Hopper	University of Minnesota -Twin Cities, USA
Nico Golde	Technical University of Berlin, Germany
Ralf-Philipp Weinmann	University of Luxembourg, Germany
Sangjin Lee	Korea University, Korea
Sang Kil Cha	CMU, USA
Seungjin Lee	Grayhash Inc., Korea
Seungjoo Kim	Korea University, Korea
Srdjan Capkun	ETH, Switzerland
Stuart Schechter	MSR, USA
Syed Ali Khayam	NUST, Pakistan
Taekyoung Kwon	Yonsei University, Korea
Taesoo Kim	MIT, USA
Tarjei Mandt	Azimuth, Norway
Thorsten Holz	Ruhr-University Bochum, Germany
Tielei Wang	Georgia Tech, USA
Wenyuan Xu	University of South Carolina, USA
Xiaobo Chen	McAfee, USA
Xiaofeng Wang	Indiana University, USA
Xuhua Ding	SMU, Singapore
Yingjiu Li	SMU, Singapore
Yoojae Won	KISA, Korea
Yuji Ukai	Fourteenforty Research Institute, Japan
Zhenkai Liang	NUS, Singapore
Zhen Ling	Southeast University, China

Organization Committee

Chair

Jin Kwak   Soonchunhyang University, Korea

Committe Members

Changhoon Lee	Seoul National University of Science & Technology
Donghoon Lee	Korea University, Korea
Hyobeom Ahn	Kongju National University, Korea
Imyoung Lee	Soonchunhyang University, Korea
Jongsung Kim	Kookmin University, Korea
Jungtaek Seo	National Security Research Institute, Korea
Kijung Ahn	Jeju National University, Korea
Kungho Lee	Korea University, Korea
Kyungho Son	KISA, Korea
Namje Park	Jeju National University, Korea
Sangsoo Yeo	Mokwon University, Kore

Contents

Looking Future

Privacy

Cryptography

LEA: A 128-Bit Block Cipher for Fast Encryption on Common Processors

Deukjo Hong[1]([✉]), Jung-Keun Lee[1], Dong-Chan Kim[1], Daesung Kwon[1], Kwon Ho Ryu[1], and Dong-Geon Lee[2]

[1] Attached Institute of ETRI, Seoul, Korea
{hongdj,jklee,dongchan,ds_kwon,jude}@ensec.re.kr
[2] Information Security & IoT Laboratory, Pusan National University, Busan, South Korea
guneez@pusan.ac.kr

Abstract. We propose a new block cipher LEA, which has 128-bit block size and 128, 192, or 256-bit key size. It provides a high-speed software encryption on general-purpose processors. Our experiments show that LEA is faster than AES on Intel, AMD, ARM, and ColdFire platforms. LEA can be also implemented to have tiny code size. Its hardware implementation has a competitive throughput per area. It is secure against all the existing attacks on block ciphers.

Keywords: LEA · Block cipher · Fast encryption

1   Introduction

CPUs and operating systems are continuously developing, and many computing devices work much better than before, with such powerful resources. For example, smart portable devices like smart phones and tablet PCs do not only replace mobile phones but also allow to enjoy various cloud computing and social network services. With those applications, the amount of the private data which people create for their business and life will be significantly increasing. Another example is a smart meter, which is a basic unit of an advanced metering infrastructure in a smart grid, recording consumption of electric energy, gathering data for remote reporting, and communicating with the utility for monitoring and billing purpose. For the convenience of management, smart meters are often implemented to perform tasks in software with small CPUs [18].

Those data mentioned in the above examples are usually important information which must be protected from various threats in networks. It implies that the wide use of software applications significantly causes the necessity of cryptographic systems on software platforms. With this consideration, we have been interested in a software encryption. Software encryptions are easier to deploy and more cost-effective than hardware ones in many cases. In particular, when a new encryption service is required for already deployed computing environments, a software encryption is more suitable than a hardware one.

Y. Kim et al. (Eds.): WISA 2013, LNCS 8267, pp. 3–27, 2014.
DOI: 10.1007/978-3-319-05149-9_1, © Springer International Publishing Switzerland 2014

A block cipher is one of the most widely used cryptographic primitives. It is applied to data encryption, message authentication, random bit generation, message hashing and so on. Presumably, the most widely used block cipher in the world is AES [27] which has been established as various international standards. AES shows good performance figures on most software and hardware platforms and is generally considered to be secure after surviving about 15 years of comprehensive cryptanalysis though some weaknesses have been found. Since AES, many block ciphers have been designed for hardware lightweight implementation. Some of them were standardized as ISO lightweight cryptography (ISO/IEC 29192-2). The main feature of the lightweight block ciphers is the efficient hardware implementation with low resource. In order to achieve that goal, most of them use simple structures with small block sizes and large number of rounds. However, those design approaches usually lead to low performance, and is far from our consideration for software encryption. Consequently, we have designed a new block cipher providing a fast encryption on common software platforms.

1.1 Contribution

We propose a new block cipher LEA. It has the block size of 128 bits and the key size of 128, 192, or 256 bits. We denote the algorithms with 128-bit, 192-bit, and 256-bit keys by LEA-128, LEA-192, and LEA-256, respectively. The structure of LEA has the following features.

1. LEA consists of only ARX (modular Addition, bitwise Rotation, and bitwise XOR) operations for 32-bit words. Those operations are well-supported and fast in many 32-bit and 64-bit platforms. Moreover, we suppose that the usage of 32-bit and 64-bit processors will grow rapidly compared to 8-bit or 16-bit ones.
2. The ARX operations contribute to the encryption and key schedule procedures in efficient and parallel way. Our arrangement of operations does not only lead to fast software encryption and small size code, but also strong resistance against the attacks using the properties of a particular operation.
3. The last round function of LEA is the same as other round functions, while many block cipher including DES and AES have special last round functions which are somewhat different from other round functions. This is for the encryption speed in both software and hardware because we think the block cipher encryption is more frequently used than decryption.
4. The key schedule of LEA has a simple structure without any interleaving between 32-bit key words. It is good for the efficiency, and does not cause any weakness.

Security. Our goal for the security of LEA is to get the resistance against all the existing attacks for block ciphers and to provide enough security margin. To achieve this goal, we firstly found the minimum number R of rounds for LEA to resist against all the known cryptanalytic techniques for each key size. Then we determined the number of rounds of LEA as around $3R/2$ to prepare for the unknown attacks to appear in future.

Efficiency. LEA provides a fast encryption on many platforms. Our experiments measuring the speed for one-block encryption on the platforms of Intel, AMD, ARM and ColdFire show that even a C level implementation of LEA is very fast. It implies that the evaluation of LEA encryption requires the light overhead to CPUs. Note that the light overhead can lead to the low power consumption which is useful for the devices based on batteries. The optimized implementation of LEA-128 for one-block encryption is faster than those of AES-128 publicly reported [25,47], on our test platforms. To objectivity, we used the announced facts for comparison instead of implementing AES.

LEA can be implemented with SIMD operations supported by Intel and AMD CPUs such that it encrypts 4 blocks simultaneously. It is useful for the highly fast encryption with ECB or CTR modes under a powerful environment like a server-based computing. Our experiments on Intel Core 2 Quad Q6600 and Intel Core i7-800 show that the speed of the 4-block SIMD implementation of LEA-128 is about 2 times and 1.7 times faster than the best records of the multi-block encryption codes of AES-128 [35], respectively.

We also found that LEA is implemented with a small code-size. The small-size implementation is useful in a memory-limited environment. LEA-128 is implemented with less than 600 and 750 bytes on the platforms of ARM926EJ-S and ColdFire MCF5213, respectively, while AES-128 is known to be implemented with around 2,400 and 960 bytes on the platforms of ARM7TDMI and ColdFire v2, respectively.

Comparison with Other Ciphers. We compare LEA to other ciphers in order to explain why it is meaningful to propose this new block cipher.

- **AES.** AES was designed based on design and analysis techniques by 2000, and cryptanalysis of block ciphers has been continuously researched and developed. Recent several attacks have pointed out some weaknesses for AES. In [11], Biryukov et al. presented a chosen-key distinguisher for full 14-round AES-256 and converted it to a key-recovery attack for a weak key class with the complexities of 2^{131} time and 2^{65} memory. In [10], Biryukov and Khovratovich presented related-key boomerang attacks on full 14-round AES-256 with $2^{99.5}$ time and data complexities and AES-192 with 2^{176} time and 2^{123} data complexities. In [14], Bogdanov et al. used biclique techniques to make key recovery attacks on full AES-128, AES-192, and AES-256 with time complexities $2^{126.1}$, $2^{189.7}$, and $2^{254.4}$, respectively. LEA is designed based on the latest design and analysis techniques and we checked that LEA is secure and has sufficient security margin against all the existing attacks.

    Furthermore, as we already mentioned, LEA provides better software encryptions in speed and size on many platforms than AES.

– **Block ciphers with ARX structure.** TEA [56] and XTEA [46] are Feistel block ciphers with simple round function and key schedule. Their encryption speeds are not fast because they have the block length of 64 bits shorter than LEA and 64 rounds more than LEA. Additionally, there are full-round attacks [37,58] on TEA and XXTEA [57], which is the third algorithm of TEA family.

At the AES competition, RC6 [49] was regarded as faster than Rijndael [21], which is the AES winner, on many software platforms. However, parallelism offered by modern CPUs is not exploited well with RC6, and the performance of recent implementation of AES exceeds that of RC6.

HIGHT [31] is a lightweight block cipher based on 8-bit ARX operations. So, it is not suitable for fast encryption on 32-bit CPUs. Recently, full-round attacks on HIGHT have been published [32,41].

Hash functions often adopt the ARX structure for the high performance on various platforms, similarly to our design goal [2,26]. Most of them have block ciphers as a component for building compression and hash functions. They are even secure against attacks for block ciphers. However, hash functions and block ciphers are different in the usage. In particular, most block ciphers in the hash functions have much larger block and key sizes than those usually required for the security and application of block ciphers.

Recently, NSA published two block cipher families SPECK and SIMON [3]. SPECK is a typical ARX cipher and SIMON consists of ANDs, rotations, and XORs. They have various parameters. The algorithms with 128-bit block are comparable with LEA. The Performance of LEA is faster than SIMON in both 32- and 64-bit processors. Since SPECK uses 64-bit addition with 128-bit block, its performance exceeds that of LEA only in 64-bit processors but LEA is more suitable for most 32-bit processors.

– **Lightweight block ciphers.** Many lightweight block ciphers like HIGHT [31], PRESENT [13], LED [30], and Piccolo [51] have short block size and large number of rounds and their software encryptions are usually not fast. Although [43] provides fast bitslice implementation of PRESENT and Piccolo, SIMD implementation of LEA is faster than them. Furthermore, a short block size is not proper for encrypting huge data because some modes of operation can allow security leakage like a ciphertext-matching attack.

KLEIN [28] is designed to be faster than AES on 8-bit and 16-bit platforms, while our targets are 32-bit and 64-bit platforms. CLEFIA [52] has the same block and key size as AES and the performance of its software encryption is close to that of AES on AMD Athlon TM Processor 4000+. However, as far as we know, it does not claim higher software performance than AES. Recently, PRINCE [16] was proposed as a low-latency block cipher which has good performance in software and hardware implementations, but its security goal is somewhat different from that for the general-purpose block ciphers.

– **Stream ciphers.** Several stream ciphers such as Salsa20 [4] are based on ARX operations, but we think the block cipher is not totally comparable to the stream cipher because they do not always have the same applications.

1.2 Organization

The remaining part is organized as follows. Section 2 describes the specification of LEA. In Sect. 3, we introduce design principles. In Sect. 4, we present the security analysis results for existing cryptanalytic techniques. In Sect. 5, we explain the implementation results. Section 6 is the conclusion of our paper.

2 Specification of LEA

LEA is a block cipher with 128-bit block. Key size is 128-bit, 192-bit, and 256-bit. The number of rounds is 24 for 128-bit keys, 28 for 192-bit keys, and 32 for 256-bit keys. In Sect. 2.1, we introduce notations which are often used in this paper. We explain how the key schedule generates round keys from the master key in Sect. 2.3. We explain how the encryption procedure converts a plaintext to a ciphertext in Sect. 2.4. We omit the description of the decryption procedure because it is simply considered as the inverse of the encryption procedure.

2.1 Notations

- P: a 128-bit plaintext, consisting of four 32-bit words $P = (P[0], P[1], P[2], P[3])$
- C: a 128-bit ciphertext, consisting of four 32-bit words $C = (C[0], C[1], C[2], C[3])$
- X_i: a 128-bit intermediate value (an input of i-th round in the encryption function), consisting of four 32-bit words $X_i = (X_i[0], X_i[1], X_i[2], X_i[3])$
- $\mathrm{Len}(x)$: the bit-length of a string x
- K: a master key. It is denoted as a concatenation of 32-bit words. $K = (K[0], K[1], K[2], K[3])$ when $\mathrm{Len}(K) = 128$; $K = (K[0], K[1], ..., K[5])$ when $\mathrm{Len}(K) = 192$; $K = (K[0], K[1], ..., K[7])$ when $\mathrm{Len}(K) = 256$
- r: the number of rounds. $r = 24$ when $\mathrm{Len}(K) = 128$; $r = 28$ when $\mathrm{Len}(K) = 192$; $r = 32$ when $\mathrm{Len}(K) = 256$
- RK: the concatenation of all round keys, defined by $RK = (RK_0, RK_1, ..., RK_{r-1})$ where RK_i is the 192-bit round key for the i-th round. Each RK_i consists of six 32-bit words $RK_i = (RK_i[0], RK_i[1], ..., RK_i[5])$
- $x \oplus y$: XOR (eXclusive OR) of bit strings x and y with same length
- $x \boxplus y$: Addition modulo 2^{32} of 32-bit strings x and y
- $\mathrm{ROL}_i(x)$: the i-bit left rotation on a 32-bit value x
- $\mathrm{ROR}_i(x)$: the i-bit right rotation on a 32-bit value x

2.2 State Representation

Let $a[0], a[1], ...$, be representation of arrays of bytes. The bytes and the bit ordering within bytes are derived from the 128-bit input sequence $input_0, input_1, ...$ as follows:

$$a[i] = \{input_{8i}, input_{8i+1}, ..., input_{8i+7}\}.$$

All the operations in the LEA algorithm are 32-bit-word-oriented. The 128-bit plaintext P of LEA is represented as an array of four 32-bit words $P[0], P[1], P[2], P[3]$. Each $P[i]$ is taken for the input bytes $a[0], a[1], ..., a[15]$ as follows:

$$P[i] = a[4i + 3] \| a[4i + 2] \| a[4i + 1] \| a[4i] \quad \text{for } 0 \leq i \leq 3.$$

The key K of LEA is also represented as an array of 32-bit words $K[0], K[1], ...,$ and taken for the input bytes in the same way. Table 1 shows how bits and bytes in the word indexed by 0 are numbered.

Table 1. Representations for words, bytes, and bits

Input bit sequence	24	$\cdots$	31	16	$\cdots$	23	8	$\cdots$	15	0	$\cdots$	7
Word number	0											
Byte number	3			2			1			0		
Bit numbers in word	31					$\cdots$						0

2.3 Key Schedule

The key schedule generates a sequence of 192-bit round keys RK_i as follows.

Constants. The key schedule uses several constants for generating round keys, which are defined as

$$\delta[0] = 0xc3efe9db, \qquad \delta[1] = 0x44626b02,$$
$$\delta[2] = 0x79e27c8a, \qquad \delta[3] = 0x78df30ec,$$
$$\delta[4] = 0x715ea49e, \qquad \delta[5] = 0xc785da0a,$$
$$\delta[6] = 0xe04ef22a, \qquad \delta[7] = 0xe5c40957.$$

They are obtained from hexadecimal expression of $\sqrt{766995}$, where 76, 69, and 95 are ASCII codes of 'L,' 'E,' and 'A.'

Key Schedule with a 128-Bit Key. Let $K = (K[0], K[1], K[2], K[3])$ be a 128-bit key. We set $T[i] = K[i]$ for $0 \leq i < 4$. Round key $RK_i = (RK_i[0], RK_i[1], ..., RK_i[5])$ for $0 \leq i < 24$ are produced through the following relations:

$$T[0] \leftarrow \text{ROL}_1(T[0] \boxplus \text{ROL}_i(\delta[i \bmod 4])),$$
$$T[1] \leftarrow \text{ROL}_3(T[1] \boxplus \text{ROL}_{i+1}(\delta[i \bmod 4])),$$
$$T[2] \leftarrow \text{ROL}_6(T[2] \boxplus \text{ROL}_{i+2}(\delta[i \bmod 4])),$$
$$T[3] \leftarrow \text{ROL}_{11}(T[3] \boxplus \text{ROL}_{i+3}(\delta[i \bmod 4])),$$
$$RK_i \leftarrow (T[0], T[1], T[2], T[1], T[3], T[1]).$$

Key Schedule with a 192-Bit Key. Let $K = (K[0], K[1], ..., K[5])$ be a 192-bit key. We set $T[i] = K[i]$ for $0 \leq i < 6$. Round key $RK_i = (RK_i[0], RK_i[1], ..., RK_i[5])$ for $0 \leq i < 28$ are produced through the following relations:

$$T[0] \leftarrow \text{ROL}_1(T[0] \boxplus \text{ROL}_i(\delta[i \bmod 6])),$$
$$T[1] \leftarrow \text{ROL}_3(T[1] \boxplus \text{ROL}_{i+1}(\delta[i \bmod 6])),$$
$$T[2] \leftarrow \text{ROL}_6(T[2] \boxplus \text{ROL}_{i+2}(\delta[i \bmod 6])),$$
$$T[3] \leftarrow \text{ROL}_{11}(T[3] \boxplus \text{ROL}_{i+3}(\delta[i \bmod 6])),$$
$$T[4] \leftarrow \text{ROL}_{13}(T[4] \boxplus \text{ROL}_{i+4}(\delta[i \bmod 6])),$$
$$T[5] \leftarrow \text{ROL}_{17}(T[5] \boxplus \text{ROL}_{i+5}(\delta[i \bmod 6])),$$
$$RK_i \leftarrow (T[0], T[1], T[2], T[3], T[4], T[5]).$$

Key Schedule with a 256-Bit Key. Let $K = (K[0], K[1], ..., K[7])$ be a 256-bit key. We set $T[i] = K[i]$ for $0 \leq i < 8$. Round key $RK_i = (RK_i[0], RK_i[1], ..., RK_i[5])$ for $0 \leq i < 32$ are produced through the following relations:

$$T[6i \bmod 8] \leftarrow \text{ROL}_1(T[6i \bmod 8] \boxplus \text{ROL}_i(\delta[i \bmod 8])),$$
$$T[6i + 1 \bmod 8] \leftarrow \text{ROL}_3(T[6i + 1 \bmod 8] \boxplus \text{ROL}_{i+1}(\delta[i \bmod 8])),$$
$$T[6i + 2 \bmod 8] \leftarrow \text{ROL}_6(T[6i + 2 \bmod 8] \boxplus \text{ROL}_{i+2}(\delta[i \bmod 8])),$$
$$T[6i + 3 \bmod 8] \leftarrow \text{ROL}_{11}(T[6i + 3 \bmod 8] \boxplus \text{ROL}_{i+3}(\delta[i \bmod 8])),$$
$$T[6i + 4 \bmod 8] \leftarrow \text{ROL}_{13}(T[6i + 4 \bmod 8] \boxplus \text{ROL}_{i+4}(\delta[i \bmod 8])),$$
$$T[6i + 5 \bmod 8] \leftarrow \text{ROL}_{17}(T[6i + 5 \bmod 8] \boxplus \text{ROL}_{i+5}(\delta[i \bmod 8])),$$
$$RK_i \leftarrow (T[6i \bmod 8], T[6i + 1 \bmod 8], T[6i + 2 \bmod 8],$$
$$T[6i + 3 \bmod 8], T[6i + 4 \bmod 8], T[6i + 5 \bmod 8]).$$

2.4   Encryption Procedure

The encryption procedure of LEA consists of 24 rounds for 128-bit keys, 28 rounds for 192-bit keys, and 32 rounds for 256-bit keys. For r rounds, it encrypts a 128-bit plaintext $P = (P[0], P[1], P[2], P[3])$ to a 128-bit ciphertext $C = (C[0], C[1], C[2], C[3])$.

Initialization. Set the 128-bit intermediate value X_0 to the plaintext P. Run the key schedule to generate r round keys.

Iterating Rounds. The 128-bit output $X_{i+1} = (X_{i+1}[0], ..., X_{i+1}[3])$ of the ith round for $0 \leq i \leq r - 1$ is computed as

$$X_{i+1}[0] \leftarrow \text{ROL}_9((X_i[0] \oplus RK_i[0]) \boxplus (X_i[1] \oplus RK_i[1])),$$
$$X_{i+1}[1] \leftarrow \text{ROR}_5((X_i[1] \oplus RK_i[2]) \boxplus (X_i[2] \oplus RK_i[3])),$$
$$X_{i+1}[2] \leftarrow \text{ROR}_3((X_i[2] \oplus RK_i[4]) \boxplus (X_i[3] \oplus RK_i[5])),$$
$$X_{i+1}[3] \leftarrow X_i[0].$$

Finalization. The ciphertext C is produced from the finally obtained X_r after round iteration in the following way:

$$C[0] \leftarrow X_r[0], \ C[1] \leftarrow X_r[1], \ C[2] \leftarrow X_r[2], \text{ and } C[3] \leftarrow X_r[3].$$

3   Design Principles

We explain the design principles for LEA (Fig. 1).

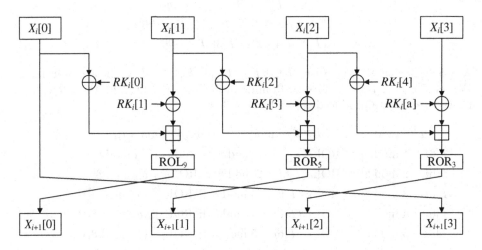

Fig. 1. ith round function

Efficient round structure with 32-bit ARX operations. The round function of LEA consists of ARX operations. Especially, we used 32-bit ARX operations instead of 8-bit ones because 32-bit operations are more popular than 8-bit ones and we think that most processors will be developed to support 32-bit operations even in resource-constrained devices. It has just three internal computation modules including two key XORs, one addition, and one bitwise rotation. We adopt the addition modulo 2^{32} as a nonlinear function with two 32-bit inputs and one 32-bit output[1]. Round key XORs are used for randomizing the inputs of the nonlinear functions, the bitwise rotations and the word-wise swap are used for diffusion. The simple and efficient structure of LEA provides both tiny-size code and high-speed code. In spite of its simplicity, it has nice nonlinearity and diffusion effect to give a proper number of rounds for good performance.

Encryption is more useful than decryption. Unexpectedly, there are not many modes of operation which need the decryption function. For example, ISO/IEC 9797-1, ISO/IEC 10116, and ISO/IEC 19772 specify 6 message authentication

---

[1] On the other hand, round key XORs and rotations work as nonlinear functions for the adversary using add-differences.

modes, 5 encryption modes, and 6 authenticated-encryption modes of block ciphers, respectively. However, only ECB, CBC, and OCB modes need both encryption and decryption functions[2]. It implies that the block cipher encryption is more widely and frequently used than the block cipher decryption. With this consideration, we did not care for the balance of the speed between encryption and decryption. Note that most block ciphers usually have the special last round different from other rounds for efficiency in the implementation of decryption, while the last round of LEA is not special but has the same structure as the other rounds for efficiency of the encryption-only modes. Nevertheless, the decryption speed of LEA is still competitive with most block ciphers.

Choice of rotations. We chose the rotations in encryption procedure such that it has the strong diffusion property. Firstly, for the parameters (a, b, c), we set the round function with input X_i, output X_{i+1}, and round key RK_i as follows.

$$X_{i+1}[0] \leftarrow \mathrm{ROL}_a((X_i[0] \oplus RK_i[0]) \boxplus (X_i[1] \oplus RK_i[1])),$$
$$X_{i+1}[1] \leftarrow \mathrm{ROL}_b((X_i[1] \oplus RK_i[2]) \boxplus (X_i[2] \oplus RK_i[3])),$$
$$X_{i+1}[2] \leftarrow \mathrm{ROL}_c((X_i[2] \oplus RK_i[4]) \boxplus (X_i[3] \oplus RK_i[5])),$$
$$X_{i+1}[3] \leftarrow X_i[0].$$

Then, we linearized the LEA encryption algorithm by replacing the additions with XORs, and searched the XOR differential characteristics (XDCs) of the linearized structure for all possible $\binom{32}{3}$ candidates of (a, b, c). Note that $\mathrm{ROL}_b = \mathrm{ROR}_{32-b}$ and $\mathrm{ROL}_c = \mathrm{ROR}_{32-c}$. One of our searching strategies is to start from a middle round with low Hamming weight of differences. As a result, we found that for each candidate of (a, b, c) there exists a 11-round XDC whose probability is not lower than 2^{-128}. The probability is estimated under the assumption that every addition is independent. Note that this assumption is not stronger than any other block ciphers because each addition can be regarded as a nonlinear function with two 32-bit inputs and a 32-bit output and because XORing subkeys with the inputs of nonlinear functions is the most popular way to combine key materials to encryption body. We found 32 candidates of (a, b, c) which have 12-round XDCs with the probability of 2^{-128} or 2^{-129} as best ones. We optimized these characteristics such that both of the first and last rounds are not linearized. We chose $(9, 27, 29)$ because it made only differential characteristics with the probability 2^{-128} as best ones, and because the number of such characteristics is fewer than any other candidates.

Additionally, we considered short characteristics for the boomerang attack, and found that the maximum number of rounds having differential characteristic with the probability greater than 2^{-32} is 7 over all (a, b, c), and so does it for the case $(a, b, c) = (9, 27, 29)$.

As a different approach for the same goal, we can also regard the linearized rounds as a linear code. So, we tried to get good differential characteristics by

---

[2] We leave the fifth mode, 'Encrypt-then-MAC' in [33] out of the discussion because it uses general notions of encryption and MAC.

applying Canteaut-Chabaud method [17] to search code words with minimum weight code words, but we could not find better differential characteristics than the first approach.

Simple key schedule. We adopt a very simple structure for the key schedule. It does not mix the words of the key and has no avalanche effect in key bits at all. Nevertheless, our security analysis show that it protects LEA from the attacks such as slide attack [12], related-key attack [5], related-key boomerang attack [10,11], biclique attack [14], rotational attack [38] and so on. The simplicity of the key schedule provides efficiency in small-size hardware and software implementations.

4   Security Analysis

We analyzed the security of LEA for existing cryptanalytic techniques by searching, constructing, or exploiting various characteristics such as differential and linear trails. For each attack, firstly, we found the maximum number N of rounds where there exists an available characteristic, and then constructed the best N-round characteristic. We determined the number of rounds making the algorithm secure against each attack, considering the difference propagation of the round function and the arrangement of the round key words, as follows.

1. If the characteristic is N-round and holds with the probability between 0 and 1, then the secure number of rounds is $N + 3$ for 128-bit keys, $N + 4$ for 192-bit keys, and $N + 5$ for 256-bit keys.
2. If the characteristic is N-round and holds with the probability 0 or 1, then the secure number of rounds is $N + 4$ for 128-bit keys, $N + 5$ for 192-bit keys, and $N + 6$ for 256-bit keys.

COSIC made an evaluation report for LEA, too, independently of us [20]. We will explain some of their security analysis results. The whole main analysis results are summarized at Table 2. We also discuss other attacks not listed in Table 2.

Table 2. Security of LEA against several main attacks

Attack type	Round # of Characteristic	Probability of Characteristic	Secure # of rounds LEA-128	LEA-192	LEA-256
Differential [9]	11	$p = 2^{-98}$	14	15	16
Truncated Differential [39]	11	$p = 2^{-91.9}$	14	15	16
Linear [44]	11	$|p - 1/2| = 2^{-62}$	14	15	16
Zero Correlation [15]	7	$|p - 1/2| = 0$	11	12	13
Boomerang [54]	14	$p^2 q^2 = 2^{-108}$	17	18	19
Impossible Differential [6]	10	$p = 0$	14	15	16
Integral [40]	6	$p = 1$	10	11	12
Differential-Linear [8]	14	$|p - 1/2| < 2^{-57}$	17	18	19

4.1 Differential Attack

As we mentioned in Sect. 3, the probability of the best 12-round differential characteristic which we have found is estimated at most as 2^{-128}. Since it is not available for the attack, we searched 11-round differential characteristic with the same way; firstly find the XOR-linearized differential characteristics with high probabilities and then optimize it by removing the linearity in the differential paths of the first and the last rounds. As a result, the best found ones of 11-round differential characteristics have the probability 2^{-98} and the following form:

- Input difference: 80000234 α0402214 β0401205 γ0400281, where $\alpha \in \{4, c\}$, $\beta \in \{4, c\}$, and $\gamma = \beta \oplus 1$,
- Output difference: η800000a 88aaa00a 220202ζ0 00200050, where $\eta \in \{4, c\}$ and $\zeta \in \{2, 6\}$.

We can apply one of these characteristics to 11 rounds from Round 0 to Round 10, and attack 12 rounds for 128-bit keys. This attack recovers 96 bits of the round key RK_{11} in the last round, Round 11 with very high signal-to-noise ratio, and requires around 2^{100} plaintexts, 2^{84} encryptions, and the memory for 2^{76} bytes. Extending it to 13-round attack is not successful because

- If one applies the 11-round characteristic to the first 11 rounds from Round 0 to Round 10 and tries to recover partial bits of RK_{12}, the round key of Round 12, he will be in trouble with the poor filtering and it leads to the bad signal-to-noise ratio.
- If one applies the 11-round characteristic to Round 1 to Round 11 and tries to recover partial bits of RK_0, the round key of Round 0 and RK_{12}, the round key of Round 12, he will face too much guessed key bits or too weak filtering to attack.

We consider the possibility of 13-round attack for 192-bit keys and 14-round attack for 256-bit keys, respectively.

Using a set of many differential characteristics with relatively high probabilities instead of a best one, we can increase the probability from 2^{-98} to $2^{-91.9}$. This is a kind of truncated differential characteristic [39], which can be used for reducing some of complexities for the above differential attack, but not be helpful for increasing the number of the attacked rounds. Analyses with other types of differences [20] have been tried but not found any critical weaknesses.

4.2 Linear Attack

A linear approximation has the following form:

$$\Gamma_P \cdot P \oplus \Gamma_C \cdot C = \Gamma_{RK} \cdot RK, \tag{1}$$

where RK is a vector composed of all round keys. We denote the probability that (1) is satisfied, by p, and let $\varepsilon = p - 1/2$. ε is called the bias of (1). A linear attack using a linear approximation has the data complexity of $O(\varepsilon^{-2})$.

It is not easy to find a good linear approximation for long rounds of LEA. Wallén's work [55] shows that in the masks of a linear approximation for modular additions the absolute value of the bias tends to decrease as the highest nonzero bit of the masks is close to the most significant. The combination of the bitwise rotations in LEA encryption significantly disturbs the appearance of linear approximations with good biases. We searched the linear approximations in such a way that the propagation of linear masks is suppressed as strong as possible. Consequently, we found 10-round linear approximation with $\varepsilon = 2^{-46}$ and 11-round linear approximation with $\varepsilon = 2^{-63}$. We can use Matsui's algorithm 1 and the 11-round linear approximation to get 1-bit information about round keys for 11 rounds with $O(2^{126})$ known plaintexts, and we can use Matsui's algorithm 2 and the 10-round linear approximation to make a 11-round key recovery attack with $O(2^{92})$ known plaintexts.

4.3   Zero Correlation Attack

Recently, the attacks using zero correlation approximations have been introduced [15], which is a counter part of the impossible differential attack in linear cryptanalysis. The best key recovery attacks in single-key setting based on zero correlation approximations have been made for TEA and XTEA. Since LEA has the use of ARX operations in common with TEA and XTEA, one may suspect the vulnerability of LEA against zero correlation attack. However, we found that a 7-round zero correlation approximation is constructed from 3-round forward and 4-round backward approximations, and it is difficult to construct much longer zero correlation approximations than 7 rounds. Based on the 7-round zero correlation approximations, we consider the possibility of 9-round attack for 128-bit keys, 10-round attack for 192-bit keys, and 11-round attack for 256-bit keys, respectively.

4.4   Boomerang Attack

The best differential probability for 7 rounds is 2^{-27}. The best 7-round one has the following differences of input and output.

- Input difference: 80000014 80400014 80400004 80400080,
- Output difference: 00001200 28000200 80800800 00000008.

We construct a 14-round boomerang characteristic from the best 7-round differential characteristic. There are some round-skip techniques maximizing the number of rounds of the boomerang characteristic [10,24], but they do not work for LEA. It is the best one which we have found ever. For 128-bit keys, we can use it to make an attack on at most 15 rounds with $2^{116.3}$ plaintexts. We could not find a proper attack on 16 rounds due to increased data complexity and worsened filtering. The amplified boomerang [36] or rectangle attacks [7] do not seem to improve our attacks significantly. We consider the possibility of 16-round attack for 192-bit keys and 17-round attack for 256-bit keys, respectively.

4.5   Impossible Differential Attack

Impossible differential attack [6] uses differential characteristics with probability of 0. They are usually constructed from miss-in-the-middle combination with forward and backward truncated differential characteristics with probability of 1. For LEA, the best impossible differential characteristics are 10 rounds, constructed with 6-round forward and 4-round backward truncated differential characteristics with probability of 1, which is reported in [20].

For 128-bit keys, we can use the 10-round impossible differential characteristics to make a 11-round attack to derive a partial information of the last round key. one may make a 12-round attack by using a set of specially chosen plaintexts or constructing a key-recovering process. We consider the possibility of 13-round attack for 192-bit keys, and 14-round attack for 256-bit keys, respectively.

4.6   Integral Attack

Integral attack [40] for LEA uses a 6-round integral characteristic, which is reported at [20]. A 6-round integral characteristic of LEA is reported at [20]. It shows that if the 3-th word $P[3]$ of the plaintext P is active, which takes all 32-bit values for one time, and other words of P are constants, then the least significant bit of the 1-th word $X[1]$ of the output X after 6 rounds is ADD-balanced. For 128-bit keys, we can use the 6-round integral characteristic to make a 9-round attack to derive a partial information of round keys. Adding rounds to the characteristic at top is impossible because it requires a code book of all plaintexts. We consider the possibility of 10-round attack for 192-bit keys, and 11-round attack for 256-bit keys, respectively. We suppose higher order differential characteristic [39] is also constructed for 6 rounds at most.

4.7   Differential-Linear Attack

Differential-linear attack [8] uses a combined characteristic from short-round differential characteristics and linear approximations. A (r_1+r_2)-round differential-linear characteristic based on one r_1-round differential characteristic with the probability p_d and two r_2-round linear approximations with same masks and the probability $p_l = 1/2+\varepsilon$ holds with the probability $p = 1/2+2p_d\varepsilon^2$. Our analysis for differential and linear attacks on LEA implies that the available differential-linear characteristics for LEA can be constructed up to 14 rounds and that the biasour searching program can find 14-round differential-linear characteristics with the bias at most 2^{-57}. However, this reasoning is based on the best results which we can find for differential and linear trails, and so we suppose that the actually found differential-linear characteristics be much shorter than 14 rounds or have the bias whose absolute value is significantly smaller than 2^{-57}.

4.8   Attacks Using Weakness of Key Schedule

Slide attack [12] uses a self-similarity in the block cipher. The key schedule of LEA obstructs it by adding the rotated constants to the key materials.

For instance, when the key size is 128 bits, $ROL_i(\delta[i \bmod 4])$ is added for the leftmost 32 bits of the i-th round key $RK_i[0]$. Although only several 32-bit constants are used, rotations depending on i make the effects of adding different round constants for every round. Therefore, there is no self-similarity which can be exploited for any attacks on LEA.

Related-key differential attack [34] and related-key boomerang attack [10,11] is the most popular ones among the attacks using related keys [5]. In the similar way to differential cryptanalysis, we searched how many rounds there exists a key difference having differential characteristics with the probability $> 2^{-128}$ up to. The best related-key differential characteristics which we found ever are 11-round one for 128-bit keys, and 12-round one for 192 and 256-bit keys. However, those characteristics cannot be used straightforwardly for any attacks because they hold with only small part of the key space.

Bogdanov et al. [14] has introduced the key recovery attacks in single-key setting, based on biclique techniques with two attack approaches. The first approach is to use the bicliques constructed from independent related-key differentials and to search the right key with partial computations based on precomputation. We checked that it is hard to construct such bicliques for more than one round of LEA for the key sizes of 128 and 192 bits and for more than two round for the key size of 256 bits, because LEA uses 192-bit round keys and all key materials are wasted in one round for 128 and 192-bit keys and in two rounds for 256-bit keys, and because all additions in the same round are active within two rounds in backward direction for any key difference. Therefore, the time complexity of the key recovery attacks based on the first approach would have a negligible difference with that of exhaustive search. The second approach is to use the bicliques constructed from interleaving related-key differential trails and to apply a basic meet-in-the-middle technique for key recovery. Such bicliques would not be constructed for more than 8 rounds because the propagation of the difference inserted at key is fast in the encryption of LEA in spite of its simple structure. Furthermore, the basic meet-in-the-middle technique of the second approach is applicable to only short rounds. So, the attack based on second approach can work for only small reduced variants with much less rounds than recommended.

4.9   Other Attacks

Recently, some kinds of meet-in-the-middle attacks have made impressive cryptanalytic results for block ciphers and hash functions. We checked that meet-in-the-middle attack techniques are not applicable to LEA very well. A basic meet-in-the-middle attack [23] is disturbed since there is no separation of long rounds. The meet-in-the-middle pseudo-preimage attack [1,50] does not work for even half rounds. The partial-matching and initial-structure techniques are not efficient in LEA.

Rotational cryptanalysis [38] is attractively available on ARX-based structures. We examined the resistance of LEA against rotational cryptanalysis for the single-key model and the related-key model in which two keys form a rotational pair. We found that key XORs in the encryption procedure and constant XORs in the key schedule prevent rotational characteristics from being constructed for long rounds.

Algebraic attack [19] forms an overdefined system of equations derived from the block cipher. Several algorithms are proposed for solving it, but they fail to find a right solution for existing block ciphers. We think they hardly work for LEA, too.

4.10 Security Margin

We have studied various existing cryptanalytic techniques for block ciphers in order to analyze the security of LEA. Although some characteristics we mentioned can be somewhat upgraded by new technologies, it is unlikely to find a new attack to improve significantly the results in Table 2, as long as we did not miss critical weakness of LEA. We determined the number of rounds for LEA-128 based on the above security analysis such that the security margin to the whole rounds ratio is greater than 30 %. For LEA-192 and LEA-256, we added 4 and 8 rounds, respectively to the rounds of LEA-128, considering the difference of key schedules and security criteria.

5 Implementation

5.1 Software Implementation

We have implemented LEA on various 32-bit and 64-bit software platforms. We have focused on LEA-128 since the speed decreases almost in proportion to the number of rounds.

On ARM platforms, we can implement LEA without register-spilling and most of the bit rotations can be processed without costing any clock cycle thanks to the barrel shifter. Thus we get remarkably high throughput compared to other block ciphers both in encryption and decryption.

On Intel/AMD platforms, we can also implement LEA without register-spilling and, due to the highly parallel structure of LEA round function, we also get high encryption speed. Moreover, by utilizing SIMD(Single Instruction Multiple Data) instructions inherent in most of recent Intel/AMD platforms, we can get even higher throughput for parallel modes of LEA.

On ARM and ColdFire platforms, we have measured the compactness of LEA. Since the round function of LEA consists of a small number ARX operations without S-box, the code size of LEA on these platforms is quite small compared to other block ciphers with the same block size.

We have also estimated the efficiency of LEA on some 8-bit platforms and confirmed that LEA has sound performance on these platforms.

ARM platforms. ARM processors are the most widely used 32-bit embedded processors. They support rotate, multiple load/store instructions as well as most arithmetic and logical ones. Comparison with the speed-optimized implementation of AES on comparable platforms is given in Table 3.

Table 4 shows the comparison with the code-size-optimized implementation of AES.

Intel and AMD Platforms. Most of recent Intel/AMD CPUs have 3 pipelines. Since LEA consists of 24 rounds and each round can be expressed as a sequence of 16 instructions, the minimal cycle cost of LEA encryption is expected to be around 128. Comparison with 32-bit implementation of AES is given in Table 5.

Table 3. Speed of LEA-128 and AES-128 on ARM platform

Algorithm	Speed (cycles/byte)	Platform
LEA-128	20.06	ARM926EJ-S
AES-128 [47]	34.00	StrongARM SA-1110

Table 4. Code size of LEA-128 and AES-128 on ARM platform

Algorithm	ROM size (bytes)	RAM size (bytes)	Speed (cycles/byte)	Platform
LEA-128	590	32	326.94	ARM926EJ-S
AES-128 [22]	2,164	304	460.50	ARM7TDMI

Decryption is slower than encryption since decryption is processed rather serially. We note that AES is faster than all other well-known block ciphers with similar block and key size on these platforms.

Most of recent Intel/AMD processors support SIMD extensions at least up to SSE2. Thus, basic 32-bit operations like XOR, ADD, SHIFT can be performed very efficiently in parallel. Moreover, the latency and throughput of SIMD instructions are close to those of corresponding 32-bit-wise instructions on recent processors. Since LEA is described as a combination of XOR, ADD, and ROTATE, it is straightforward to implement parallel modes of LEA using SSE2 to process 4 or 8 blocks simultaneously.

Comparison with SIMD implementations of AES (not using AES instruction set) is given in Table 6.

ColdFire platforms. ColdFire processors are 32-bit microprocessors targeted towards embedded systems. LEA shows lower performance here than on ARM platforms since load/store and rotate operation are performed less efficiently: They do not support rotate, multiple load/store instructions and the shift instruction can shift only by up to 8 bits. We have implemented speed-optimized and size-optimized LEA on MCF5213. Comparison with implementation of AES on comparable platform is given in Table 7. We note that LEA runs faster than hardware-accelerated AES.

8-bit and 16-bit Platforms. Though LEA is designed to achieve high performance in 32-bit platforms. We have also analyzed the performance of LEA on Advanced

Table 5. Speed (cycles/byte) of LEA-128 and AES-128 on 32-bit Intel/AMD platforms

| | LEA-128 | | AES-128 |
Platform	Encryption	Decryption	Encryption
Intel Core 2 Quad Q6600	9.29	14.83	12.20 [25]
Intel Core i5-2500	9.29	14.52	11.35 [25]
AMD Phenom II X4 965	8.85	14.50	10.35 [25]
AMD Opteron 6176 SE	8.55	14.05	N/A

Table 6. SIMD implementations of LEA-128 and AES-128

Platform	LEA CTR	AES CTR
Intel Core 2 Quad Q6600	4.51	9.32 [35]
Intel Core i7-860	4.19	6.92 [35]
AMD Opteron 6176SE	4.50	N/A

Virtual RISC(AVR), which are among the most favorable 8-bit platforms. LEA is estimated to run at around 3,040 cycles for encryption on AVR AT90USB82/162 where AES best record is 1,993 cycles [47]. We suppose that the performance of LEA is comparable to that of AES on low-end 8-bit or 16-bit platforms, both in speed and code size.

5.2 Hardware Implementation

We have implemented LEA-128 with Verilog HDL and synthesized to ASIC with fully verifying the correctness of front-end and back-end design. For HDL implementation and verification of our design, we have used Mentor Modelsim 6.5f for RTL simulation and Synopsys Design Compiler Ver. B-2008.09-SP5 for its synthesis. Our RTL level design result of LEA is synthesized to ASIC with the UMC 0.13μm standard cell library and 100 MHz operating frequency.

Since the LEA consists of the small number of simple operations such as bit XOR, rotation and 32-bit adder without complex operations such as S-box, it can be implemented with low hardware resources. The LEA can also achieve high

Table 7. Implementations of LEA-128 and AES-128 on ColdFire Platform

Algorithm	ROM size (bytes)	RAM size (bytes)	Speed (cycles/byte)	Platform
LEA-128	9,674	832	103.59	MCF5213
LEA-128	704	32	829.25	MCF5213
AES-128 [48]	7,996		1,403.51	ColdFire v2
AES-128 [48]	960		160.00	ColdFire v2 with CAU[†]

[†]Cryptographic Acceleration Unit

performance for its short critical path characteristics. The operational blocks for the round function and key scheduling are so regular that we can achieve these operations with low hardware resources by using its basic operational blocks repetitively.

Table 8 shows the hardware complexity of two different implementations of LEA-128 encryption module: One is the area-optimized and the other is the FOM-optimized (throughput/area). The area-optimized implementation of LEA has 3,826 GE and 168 clock cycles, and the FOM-optimized has 5,426 GE and 24 clock cycles. We can see that the LEA encryption algorithm has relatively lightweight key scheduling and encryption block (Round Function) from this table.

Table 9 compares our hardware implementation results of LEA-128 encryption to other 128-bit key block ciphers with view point of FOM.

Table 8. Hardware feature of LEA-128 encryption module

Block	Area(GE)	
	Area-optimized	FOM-optimized
Constants generation	970	964
Control unit	75	54
Key scheduling	400	695
State register	920	1,037
Key register	998	1,037
Round function	450	1,080
Others	23	559
Total block	3,826	5,426

Table 9. Hardware implementation of LEA-128 encryption algorithm and its comparison to that of other 128-bit key block ciphers

Algorithm	Size(bits)		Cycles	T.put[†]	Tech.	Area	FOM[‡]
	Key	block	/block		(μm)	(GE)	
LED [30]	128	64	1,872	3.42	0.18	1,265	0.26
CLEFIA [52]	128	128	328	39	0.09	2,488	1.56
PICCOLO [51]	128	64	528	12.12	0.13	758	1.59
LEA-128[1]	128	128	168	76.19	0.13	3,826	1.9
AES [45]	128	128	226	56.64	0.13	2,400	2.35
HIGHT [31]	128	64	34	188.24	0.25	3,048	6.17
TWINE [53]	128	64	36	178	0.09	1,866	9.53
LEA-128[2]	128	128	24	533.33	0.13	5,426	9.82
PRESENT [13]	128	64	32	200	0.18	1,570	12.73

[†]Throughtput@100KHz (Kbps),   [‡]FOM : (Throughput/Area)$\times 10^2$
[1] : Area-optimized implementation of LEA-128
[2] : FOM-optimized implementation of LEA-128

6   Conclusion

We have proposed a new block cipher LEA, which has 128-bit block size and 128, 192, or 256-bit key size. LEA provides a high-speed software encryption on general-purpose processors. It can be also implemented to have tiny code size. Its hardware implementation has a competitive throughput per area. It is secure against all the existing attacks. In spite of the remarkable implementation results presented in this paper, we believe that the they have room for further optimizations.

A   Differential Characteristic

Let ΔX_i be the XOR difference of X_i, and let p_i be the probability of $\Delta X_i \to \Delta X_{i+1}$. The probability p of an r-round differential characteristic is computed as $p = \prod_{i=0}^{r-1} p_i$.

Table 10 shows the 11-round differential characteristic with the probability of 2^{-98}. The differences in the table are denoted in hexadecimal.

Table 10. 11-round differential characteristic with the probability of 2^{-98}

i	ΔX_i				p_i
0	80000234	α0402214	β0401205	γ0400281	2^{-22}
1	80400080	8a000080	82000210	80000234	2^{-14}
2	80000014	80400014	80400004	80400080	2^{-9}
3	80000000	80000000	80000010	80000014	2^{-3}
4	00000000	80000000	80000000	80000000	1
5	00000100	00000000	00000000	00000000	2^{-1}
6	00020000	00000000	00000000	00000100	2^{-2}
7	04000000	00000000	00000020	00020000	2^{-4}
8	00000008	00000001	00004004	04000000	2^{-8}
9	00001200	28000200	80800800	00000008	2^{-12}
10	00200050	05440050	10100101	00001200	2^{-23}
11	η800000a	88aaa00a	220202ζ0	00200050	

The 7-round differential characteristic with the probability of 2^{-27}, discarding the first two rounds and the last two rounds is used for constructing a 14-round boomerang characteristic.

B   Linear Approximation

Let ΓX_i be the mask of X_i, and let $\varepsilon_i = p_i - 1/2$ be the bias of the linear approximation

$$\Gamma X_i \cdot X_i \oplus \Gamma X_{i+1} \cdot X_{i+1} = \Gamma K_i \cdot RK. \tag{2}$$

Table 11. 11-round linear approximation with the bias $\varepsilon = 2^{-62}$

$\Gamma X_0 =$ 0aff33f0 470032b0 735801c0	15f00080
$(\alpha_0^0, \alpha_1^0, \alpha_2^0) = $ (0a0033f0, 0f0033b0, 0a0033b0)	$\varepsilon_{\alpha^0} = 2^{-7}$
$(\beta_0^0, \beta_1^0, \beta_2^0) = $ (48000100, 6c000100, 48000180)	$\varepsilon_{\beta^0} = -2^{-4}$
$(\gamma_0^0, \gamma_1^0, \gamma_2^0) = $ (1f5800c0, 15f00080, 15500080)	$\varepsilon_{\gamma^0} = 2^{-7}$
$\Gamma X_1 =$ 00676014 0240000c 02aa0010	00ff0000
$(\alpha_0^1, \alpha_1^1, \alpha_2^1) = $ (00600014, 00400014, 0040001e)	$\varepsilon_{\alpha^1} = 2^{-4}$
$(\beta_0^1, \beta_1^1, \beta_2^1) = $ (02000018, 02000010, 03000010)	$\varepsilon_{\beta^1} = -2^{-3}$
$(\gamma_0^1, \gamma_1^1, \gamma_2^1) = $ (00aa0000, 00ff0000, 00aa0000)	$\varepsilon_{\gamma^1} = 2^{-5}$
$\Gamma X_2 =$ 80003c00 80180000 00154000	00076000
$(\alpha_0^2, \alpha_1^2, \alpha_2^2) = $ (80000000, 80000000, c0000000)	$\varepsilon_{\alpha^2} = -2^{-2}$
$(\beta_0^2, \beta_1^2, \beta_2^2) = $ (00180000, 00100000, 00100000)	$\varepsilon_{\beta^2} = 2^{-2}$
$(\gamma_0^2, \gamma_1^2, \gamma_2^2) = $ (00054000, 00076000, 0005c000)	$\varepsilon_{\gamma^3} = -2^{-4}$
$\Gamma X_3 =$ 00000180 00008000 0000b800	00003c00
$(\alpha_0^3, \alpha_1^3, \alpha_2^3) = $ (00000000, 00000000, 00000000)	$\varepsilon_{\alpha^3} = 2^{-1}$
$(\beta_0^3, \beta_1^3, \beta_2^3) = $ (00008000, 00008000, 0000c000)	$\varepsilon_{\beta^3} = -2^{-2}$
$(\gamma_0^3, \gamma_1^3, \gamma_2^3) = $ (00003800, 00003c00, 00003800)	$\varepsilon_{\gamma^3} = 2^{-3}$
$\Gamma X_4 =$ 00000000 00000600 00000700	00000180
$(\alpha_0^4, \alpha_1^4, \alpha_2^4) = $ (00000000, 00000000, 00000000)	$\varepsilon_{\alpha^4} = 2^{-1}$
$(\beta_0^4, \beta_1^4, \beta_2^4) = $ (00000600, 00000600, 00000600)	$\varepsilon_{\beta^4} = 2^{-2}$
$(\gamma_0^4, \gamma_1^4, \gamma_2^4) = $ (00000100, 00000180, 00000100)	$\varepsilon_{\gamma^4} = 2^{-2}$
$\Gamma X_5 =$ 00000000 00000030 00000020	00000000
$(\alpha_0^5, \alpha_1^5, \alpha_2^5) = $ (00000000, 00000000, 00000000)	$\varepsilon_{\alpha^5} = 2^{-1}$
$(\beta_0^5, \beta_1^5, \beta_2^5) = $ (00000030, 00000020, 00000020)	$\varepsilon_{\beta^5} = 2^{-2}$
$(\gamma_0^5, \gamma_1^5, \gamma_2^5) = $ (00000000, 00000000, 00000000)	$\varepsilon_{\gamma^5} = 2^{-1}$
$\Gamma X_6 =$ 00000000 00000001 00000000	00000000
$(\alpha_0^6, \alpha_1^6, \alpha_2^6) = $ (00000001, 00000001, 00000001)	$\varepsilon_{\alpha^6} = 2^{-1}$
$(\beta_0^6, \beta_1^6, \beta_2^6) = $ (00000000, 00000000, 00000000)	$\varepsilon_{\beta^6} = 2^{-1}$
$(\gamma_0^6, \gamma_1^6, \gamma_2^6) = $ (00000000, 00000000, 00000000)	$\varepsilon_{\gamma^6} = 2^{-1}$
$\Gamma X_7 =$ 00000200 00000000 00000000	00000001
$(\alpha_0^7, \alpha_1^7, \alpha_2^7) = $ (00000001, 00000001, 00000001)	$\varepsilon_{\alpha^7} = 2^{-1}$
$(\beta_0^7, \beta_1^7, \beta_2^7) = $ (00000001, 00000001, 00000001)	$\varepsilon_{\beta^7} = 2^{-1}$
$(\gamma_0^7, \gamma_1^7, \gamma_2^7) = $ (00000001, 00000001, 00000001)	$\varepsilon_{\gamma^7} = 2^{-1}$
$\Gamma X_8 =$ 00000200 08000000 20000000	00000201
$(\alpha_0^8, \alpha_1^8, \alpha_2^8) = $ (28000201, 38000201, 2c000301)	$\varepsilon_{\alpha^8} = 2^{-4}$
$(\beta_0^8, \beta_1^8, \beta_2^8) = $ (30000201, 20000301, 20000201)	$\varepsilon_{\beta^8} = 2^{-3}$
$(\gamma_0^8, \gamma_1^8, \gamma_2^8) = $ (00000301, 00000201, 00000201)	$\varepsilon_{\gamma^8} = 2^{-2}$
$\Gamma X_9 =$ 00060258 09000010 20000040	28000001
$(\alpha_0^9, \alpha_1^9, \alpha_2^9) = $ (01000059, 01000051, 01800071)	$\varepsilon_{\alpha^9} = 2^{-4}$
$(\beta_0^9, \beta_1^9, \beta_2^9) = $ (08000041, 0c000041, 08000061)	$\varepsilon_{\beta^9} = -2^{-3}$
$(\gamma_0^9, \gamma_1^9, \gamma_2^9) = $ (2c000001, 28000001, 38000001)	$\varepsilon_{\gamma^9} = -2^{-3}$
$\Gamma X_{10} =$ 0000e203 08400003 27000000	01060201
$(\alpha_0^{10}, \alpha_1^{10}, \alpha_2^{10}) = $ (3c660203, 3c440202, 3c440302)	$\varepsilon_{\alpha^{10}} = -2^{-7}$
$(\beta_0^{10}, \beta_1^{10}, \beta_2^{10}) = $ (34040201, 26040201, 24060301)	$\varepsilon_{\beta^{10}} = 2^{-5}$
$(\gamma_0^{10}, \gamma_1^{10}, \gamma_2^{10}) = $ (01040201, 01060201, 01840301)	$\varepsilon_{\gamma^{10}} = 2^{-4}$
$\Gamma X_{11} =$ 88060478 09203018 20308060	3c66e000

Table 12. 10-round impossible differential characteristic

	i	ΔX_i in forward direction	ΔX_i in backward direction	i
$X[0]$	0	10000000000000000000000000000000		
$X[1]$		10000000000000000000000000000000		
$X[2]$		10000000000000000000000000000000		
$X[3]$		10000000000000000000000000000000		
$X[0]$	1	00000000000000000000000000000000		
$X[1]$		00000000000000000000000000000000		
$X[2]$		00000000000000000000000000000000		
$X[3]$		10000000000000000000000000000000		
$X[0]$	2	00000000000000000000000000000000	00000000000000000000000000000000	10
$X[1]$		00000000000000000000000000000000	00000000000000000000000000000000	
$X[2]$		00010000000000000000000000000000	00010000000000000000000000000000	
$X[3]$		00000000000000000000000000000000	00000000000000000000000000000000	
$X[0]$	3	00000000000000000000000000000000	00000000000000000000000000000000	9
$X[1]$		00000xxx10000000000000000000000000	00000000000000000000000000000000	
$X[2]$		000xxx10000000000000000000000000	00000000000000000000000000000000	
$X[3]$		00000000000000000000000000000000	10000000000000000000000000000000	
$X[0]$	4	00000000000000000000000xxxxxxxxx1	10000000000000000000000000000000	8
$X[1]$		00000xxxxxxxxx10000000000000000000	10000000000000000000000000000000	
$X[2]$		000xxxxxxxxx10000000000000000000	10000000000000000000000000000000	
$X[3]$		00000000000000000000000000000000	10000000000000000000000000000000	
$X[0]$	5	xxxxxxxxxxxxxxxxxxxxxxxx1xxxxxxxxx	10000000000000000000000000000000	7
$X[1]$		00000xxxxxxxxxxxxxx10000000000000	xxxxxxxxx10000000000000000000000	
$X[2]$		000xxxxxxxxx10000000000000000000	xxxxxxxxxxxxxxxxxxxxxxxxxxx10000	
$X[3]$		00000000000000000000000xxxxxxxxx1	xxxxxxxxxxxxxxxxxxxxxxxxxxxxx100	
$X[0]$	6	xxxxxxxxxxxxxxxxxxxxxxxxxxxxxxxxx	xxxxxxxxxxxxxxxxxxxxxxxxxxxxx100	6
$X[1]$		00000xxxxxxxxxxxxxxxxxxx100000000	xxxxxxxxxxxxxxxxxxxxxxxxxxxxx100	
$X[2]$		xx1xxxxxxxxxxxxxxxxxxxxxxxxxxxxxx	xxxxxxxxxxxxxxxxxxxxxxxxxxxxxxxx	
$X[3]$		xxxxxxxxxxxxxxxxxxxxxxxx1xxxxxxxxx	xxxxxxxxxxxxxxxxxxxxxxxxxxxxxxxx	

Equation (2) is XOR-sum of the following approximations:

$$\alpha_0^i \cdot (X_i[0] \oplus RK_i[0]) \oplus \alpha_1^i \cdot (X_i[1] \oplus RK_i[1]) = \alpha_2^i \cdot ROR_9(X_{i+1}[0]),$$
$$p_{\alpha^i} = 1/2 + \varepsilon_{\alpha_i}, \tag{3}$$

$$\beta_0^i \cdot (X_i[1] \oplus RK_i[2]) \oplus \beta_1^i \cdot (X_i[2] \oplus RK_i[3]) = \beta_2^i \cdot ROL_5(X_{i+1}[1]),$$
$$p_{\beta^i} = 1/2 + \varepsilon_{\beta_i}, \tag{4}$$

$$\gamma_0^i \cdot (X_i[2] \oplus RK_i[4]) \oplus \gamma_1^i \cdot (X_i[3] \oplus RK_i[5]) = \gamma_2^i \cdot ROL_3(X_{i+1}[2]),$$
$$p_{\gamma^i} = 1/2 + \varepsilon_{\gamma_i}. \tag{5}$$

Let ε be the bias of an r-round linear approximation. Note that $\varepsilon_i = 4\varepsilon_{\alpha^i}\varepsilon_{\beta_i}\varepsilon_{\gamma^i}$ and $\varepsilon = 2^{r-1}\prod_{i=0}^{r-1}\varepsilon_i$ by Piling-Up Lemma [44].

Table 11 shows the 11-round linear approximation with the biases of 2^{-62}. The masks in the table are denoted in hexadecimal.

C   Impossible Differential Characteristic

Table 12 shows one of three 10-round impossible differential characteristic reported in [20]. '1' and '0' mean the single bits 1 and 0 in the XOR difference. 'x' means an unknown bit.

References

1. Aoki, K., Sasaki, Y.: Meet-in-the-middle preimage attacks against reduced SHA-0 and SHA-1. In: Halevi, S. (ed.) CRYPTO 2009. LNCS, vol. 5677, pp. 70–89. Springer, Heidelberg (2009)
2. Aumasson, J.P., Henzen, L., Meier, W., Phan, R.C.W.: SHA-3 proposal BLAKE. Submission to NIST (Round 3) (2010)
3. Beaulieu, R., Shors, D., Smith, J., Treatman-Clar, S., Weeks, B., Wingers, L.: The SIMON and SPECK families of lightweight block ciphers. IACR Cryptology ePrint Archive. Report 2013/404 (2013)
4. Bernstein, D.J.: The salsa20 stream cipher. In: SKEW 2005 — Symmetric Key Encryption Workshop (2005)
5. Biham, E.: New types of cryptanalytic attacks using related keys. In: Helleseth, T. (ed.) EUROCRYPT 1993. LNCS, vol. 765, pp. 398–409. Springer, Heidelberg (1994)
6. Biham, E., Biryukov, A., Shamir, A.: Cryptanalysis of skipjack reduced to 31 rounds using impossible differentials. In: Stern, J. (ed.) EUROCRYPT 1999. LNCS, vol. 1592, pp. 12–23. Springer, Heidelberg (1999)
7. Biham, E., Dunkelman, O., Keller, N.: The rectangle attack - rectangling the serpent. In: Pfitzmann, B. (ed.) EUROCRYPT 2001. LNCS, vol. 2045, pp. 340–357. Springer, Heidelberg (2001)
8. Biham, E., Dunkelman, O., Keller, N.: Enhancing differential-linear cryptanalysis. In: Zheng, Y. (ed.) ASIACRYPT 2002. LNCS, vol. 2501, pp. 254–266. Springer, Heidelberg (2002)
9. Biham, E., Shamir, A.: Differential Cryptanalysis of the Data Encryption Standard. Springer, Heidelberg (1993)
10. Biryukov, A., Khovratovich, D.: Related-key cryptanalysis of the full AES-192 and AES-256. In: Matsui, M. (ed.) ASIACRYPT 2009. LNCS, vol. 5912, pp. 1–18. Springer, Heidelberg (2009)
11. Biryukov, A., Khovratovich, D., Nikolić, I.: Distinguisher and related-key attack on the full AES-256. In: Halevi, S. (ed.) CRYPTO 2009. LNCS, vol. 5677, pp. 231–249. Springer, Heidelberg (2009)
12. Biryukov, A., Wagner, D.: Slide attacks. In: Knudsen, L.R. (ed.) FSE 1999. LNCS, vol. 1636, pp. 245–259. Springer, Heidelberg (1999)
13. Bogdanov, A.A., Knudsen, L.R., Leander, G., Paar, Ch., Poschmann, A., Robshaw, M., Seurin, Y., Vikkelsoe, C.: PRESENT: An ultra-lightweight block cipher. In: Paillier, P., Verbauwhede, I. (eds.) CHES 2007. LNCS, vol. 4727, pp. 450–466. Springer, Heidelberg (2007)
14. Bogdanov, A., Khovratovich, D., Rechberger, Ch.: Biclique cryptanalysis of the full AES. In: Lee, D.H., Wang, X. (eds.) ASIACRYPT 2011. LNCS, vol. 7073, pp. 344–371. Springer, Heidelberg (2011)
15. Bogdanov, A., Wang, M.: Zero correlation linear cryptanalysis with reduced data complexity. In: Canteaut, A. (ed.) FSE 2012. LNCS, vol. 7549, pp. 29–48. Springer, Heidelberg (2012)

16. Borghoff, J., Canteaut, A., Güneysu, T., Kavun, E.B., Knezevic, M., Knudsen, L.R., Leander, G., Nikov, V., Paar, C., Rechberger, C., Rombouts, P., Thomsen, S., Yalçın, T.: PRINCE - A low-latency block cipher for pervasive computing applications. In: Wang, X., Sako, K. (eds.) ASIACRYPT 2012. LNCS, vol. 7658, pp. 208–225. Springer, Heidelberg (2012)

17. Canteaut, A., Chabaud, F.: A new algorithm for finding minimum-weight words in a linear code: application to McEliece's cryptosystem and to narrow-sense BCH codes of length 511. IEEE Trans. Inf. Theory 44(1), 367–378 (1998)

18. Certicom White Paper Series. Critical infrastructure protection for AMI using a comprehensive security platform, Februrary 2009

19. Courtois, N.T., Pieprzyk, J.: Cryptanalysis of block ciphers with overdefined systems of equations. In: Zheng, Y. (ed.) ASIACRYPT 2002. LNCS, vol. 2501, pp. 267–287. Springer, Heidelberg (2002)

20. COSIC. Final Report: Security Evaluation of the Block Cipher LEA (2011)

21. Daemen, J., Rijmen, V.: The Design of Rijndael: AES. In: The Advanced Encryption Standard. Springer (2002)

22. Darnall, M., Kuhlman, D.: AES software implementations on ARM7TDMI. In: Barua, R., Lange, T. (eds.) INDOCRYPT 2006. LNCS, vol. 4329, pp. 424–435. Springer, Heidelberg (2006)

23. Diffie, W., Hellman, M.: Exhaustive cryptanalysis of the NBS data encryption standard. Computer 10(6), 74–84 (1977)

24. Dunkelman, O., Keller, N., Shamir, A.: A practical-time related-key attack on the KASUMI cryptosystem used in GSM and 3G telephony. In: Rabin, T. (ed.) CRYPTO 2010. LNCS, vol. 6223, pp. 393–410. Springer, Heidelberg (2010)

25. eBACS: ECRYPT Benchmarking of Cryptographic Systems, bench.cr.yp.to.

26. Ferguson, N., Lucks, S., Schneier, B., DougWhiting, Bellare, M., Tadayoshi Kohno, Callas, J., Jesse Walker, : The skein hash function family, Submission to NIST (Round 3) (2010)

27. ADVANCED ENCRYPTION STANDARD, (AES), Federal Information Processing Standards, Publication 197, 26 November 2001)

28. Gong, Z., Nikova, S., Law, Y.W.: KLEIN: A new family of lightweight block ciphers. In: Juels, A., Paar, Ch. (eds.) RFIDSec 2011. LNCS, vol. 7055, pp. 1–18. Springer, Heidelberg (2012)

29. Mukhopadhyay, D.: An improved fault based attack of the advanced encryption standard. In: Preneel, B. (ed.) AFRICACRYPT 2009. LNCS, vol. 5580, pp. 421–434. Springer, Heidelberg (2009)

30. Guo, J., Peyrin, T., Poschmann, A., Robshaw, M.: The LED block cipher. In: Preneel, B., Takagi, T. (eds.) CHES 2011. LNCS, vol. 6917, pp. 326–341. Springer, Heidelberg (2011)

31. Hong, D., Sung, J., Hong, S.H., Lim, J.-I., Lee, S.-J., Koo, B.-S., Lee, C.-H., Chang, D., Lee, J., Jeong, K., Kim, H., Kim, J.-S., Chee, S.: HIGHT: A new block cipher suitable for low-resource device. In: Goubin, L., Matsui, M. (eds.) CHES 2006. LNCS, vol. 4249, pp. 46–59. Springer, Heidelberg (2006)

32. Hong, D., Koo, B., Kwon, D.: Biclique attack on the full HIGHT. In: Kim, H. (ed.) ICISC 2011. LNCS, vol. 7259, pp. 365–374. Springer, Heidelberg (2012)

33. ISO/IEC 19772, Information technology — Security techniques — Authenticated encryption (2009)

34. Jakimoski, G., Desmedt, Y.: Related-key differential cryptanalysis of 192-bit key AES variants. In: Matsui, M., Zuccherato, R. (eds.) SAC 2004. LNCS, vol. 3006, pp. 208–221. Springer, Heidelberg (2004)

35. Käsper, E., Schwabe, P.: Faster and timing-attack resistant AES-GCM. In: Clavier, C., Gaj, K. (eds.) CHES 2009. LNCS, vol. 5747, pp. 1–27. Springer, Heidelberg (2009)

36. Kelsey, J., Kohno, T., Schneier, B.: Amplified boomerang attacks against reduced-round MARS and serpent. In: Schneier, B. (ed.) FSE 2000. LNCS, vol. 1978, pp. 75–93. Springer, Heidelberg (2001)

37. Kelsey, J., Schneier, B., Wagner, D.: Related-key cryptanalysis of 3-WAY, biham-DES, CAST, DES-X, newDES, RC2, and TEA. In: Han, Y., Quing, S. (eds.) ICICS 1997. LNCS, vol. 1334, pp. 233–246. Springer, Heidelberg (1997)

38. Khovratovich, D., Nikolić, I.: Rotational cryptanalysis of ARX. In: Hong, S., Iwata, T. (eds.) FSE 2010. LNCS, vol. 6147, pp. 333–346. Springer, Heidelberg (2010)

39. Knudsen, L.R.: Truncated and higher order differentials. In: Preneel, B. (ed.) FSE 1994. LNCS, vol. 1008, pp. 196–211. Springer, Heidelberg (1995)

40. Knudsen, L.R., Wagner, D.: Integral cryptanalysis. In: Daemen, J., Rijmen, V. (eds.) FSE 2002. LNCS, vol. 2365, pp. 112–127. Springer, Heidelberg (2002)

41. Koo, B., Hong, D., Kwon, D.: Related-key attack on the full HIGHT. In: Rhee, K.-H., Nyang, D.H. (eds.) ICISC 2010. LNCS, vol. 6829, pp. 49–67. Springer, Heidelberg (2011)

42. Lipmaa, H., Moriai, S.: Efficient algorithms for computing differential properties of addition. In: Matsui, M. (ed.) FSE 2001. LNCS, vol. 2355, pp. 336–350. Springer, Heidelberg (2002)

43. Matsuda, S., Moriai, S.: Lightweight cryptography for the cloud: exploit the power of bitslice implementation. In: Prouff, E., Schaumont, P. (eds.) CHES 2012. LNCS, vol. 7428, pp. 408–425. Springer, Heidelberg (2012)

44. Matsui, M.: Linear cryptanalysis method for DES cipher. In: Helleseth, T. (ed.) EUROCRYPT 1993. LNCS, vol. 765, pp. 386–397. Springer, Heidelberg (1994)

45. Moradi, A., Poschmann, A., Ling, S., Paar, Ch., Wang, H.: Pushing the limits: a very compact and a threshold implementation of AES. In: Paterson, K.G. (ed.) EUROCRYPT 2011. LNCS, vol. 6632, pp. 69–88. Springer, Heidelberg (2011)

46. Needham, R.M., Wheeler, D.J.: TEA extensions. computer laboratory, University of Cambridge, Technical report, October 1997

47. Osvik, D.A., Bos, J.W., Stefan, D., Canright, D.: Fast software AES encryption. In: Hong, S., Iwata, T. (eds.) FSE 2010. LNCS, vol. 6147, pp. 75–93. Springer, Heidelberg (2010)

48. https://realtimelogic.com/products/sharkssl/Coldfire-80Mhz/

49. Rivest, R.L., Robshaw, M.J.B., Sidney, R., Yin, Y.L.: Thr RC6 block cipher (1998)

50. Sasaki, Y., Aoki, K.: Finding preimages in full MD5 faster than exhaustive search. In: Joux, A. (ed.) EUROCRYPT 2009. LNCS, vol. 5479, pp. 282–296. Springer, Heidelberg (2009)

51. Shibutani, K., Isobe, T., Hiwatari, H., Mitsuda, A., Akishita, T., Shirai, T.: Piccolo: an ultra-lightweight blockcipher. In: Preneel, B., Takagi, T. (eds.) CHES 2011. LNCS, vol. 6917, pp. 342–357. Springer, Heidelberg (2011)

52. Shirai, T., Shibutani, K., Akishita, T., Moriai, S., Iwata, T.: The 128-bit blockcipher CLEFIA (Extended abstract). In: Biryukov, A. (ed.) FSE 2007. LNCS, vol. 4593, pp. 181–195. Springer, Heidelberg (2007)

53. Suzaki, T., Minematsu, K., Morioka, S., Kobayasi, E.: Twine: A lightweight, versatile block cipher. In: Proceedings of ECRYPT Workshop on Lightweight Cryptography (2011)

54. Wagner, D.: The boomerang attack. In: Knudsen, L.R. (ed.) FSE 1999. LNCS, vol. 1636, pp. 156–170. Springer, Heidelberg (1999)

55. Wallén, J.: On the differential and linear properties of addition, Master's thesis, Helsinki University of Technology, Laboratory for Theoretical Computer Science, November 2003
56. Wheeler, D.J., Needham, R.M.: TEA, a tiny encryption algorithm. In: Preneel, B. (ed.) FSE 1994. LNCS, vol. 1008, pp. 363–366. Springer, Heidelberg (1995)
57. Wheeler, D.J., Needham, R.M.: Correction of XTEA. Computer Laborarory, University of Cambridge, Technical report (October 1998)
58. Yarrkov, E.: Cryptanalysis of XXTEA, IACR Cryptology ePrint Archive 2010/254 (2010)

Some New Weaknesses
in the RC4 Stream Cipher

Jing Lv[1(✉)], Bin Zhang[1], and Dongdai Lin[2]

[1] Laboratory of Trusted Computing and Information Assurance, Institute
of Software, Chinese Academy of Sciences, 100190 Beijing, China
[2] State Key Laboratory of Information Security, Institute of Information
Engineering, Chinese Academy of Sciences, Beijing, China
{lvjing,zhangbin}@tca.iscas.ac.cn,
ddlin@iie.ac.cn

Abstract. In FSE 2011, Maitra and Paul observed that there exists
negative bias in the first byte of the RC4 keystream towards 0. In this
paper, we give our theoretical proof of this bias. This bias immediately
provide distinguisher for RC4, and ciphertext only attack on broadcast
RC4. Additionally, we discover some new weaknesses of the keystream
bytes even after the first N rounds of the PRGA, where N is the size
of the RC4 permutation, generally, $N = 256$. The weaknesses in turn
provide us with certain state information from the keystream bytes no
matter how many initial bytes are thrown away.

Keywords: RC4 · Broadcast RC4 · Ciphertext only attack · Distinguishing attack · State recovery attack.

1 Introduction

RC4, designed by Ron Rivest in 1987, is the most widely deployed stream cipher
in practical applications. Due to its simplicity and extremely fast software performance, RC4 has been integrated into TLS/SSL and WEP applications. RC4
takes an interesting design approach which is quite different from that of LFSR-
based stream ciphers. This implies that many of the analysis methods known
for such ciphers cannot be applied. The internal state of RC4 consists of a table
of $N = 2^n$ n-bit words and two n-bit pointers, where n is a parameter (for the
nominal version, $n = 8$). The table varies slowly in time under the control of
itself. When $n = 8$, RC4 has a huge state of $(2^8)^2 * log_2 2^8!$, approximately 1,700
bits. It is thus impractical to guess even a small part of this state, or to use
standard time/memory/data tradeoff attacks. In addition, the state evolves in
a complex non-linear way, and thus it is difficult to combine partial information about states which are far away in round. Consequently, all the techniques
developed to attack stream ciphers based on linear feedback shift registers seem
to be inapplicable to RC4.

Y. Kim et al. (Eds.): WISA 2013, LNCS 8267, pp. 28–38, 2014.
DOI: 10.1007/978-3-319-05149-9_2, © Springer International Publishing Switzerland 2014

The initial bytes(the first N outputs) of RC4 have been thoroughly analyzed in a large amount of papers. In FSE 2011, Matrai and Paul proved that the initial 3–255 bytes of the keystream are positive biased to 0 which are in accordance with the experiment. The experiment also showed that the first keystream byte is negative biased to 0, the proof of the bias was posed as an open problem, see [10]. In this paper, we provide a satisfied proof of this bias, this bias immediately provide distinguisher for RC4, and it can be used for plaintext recovery attack in the broadcast RC4.

In FSE 2013, Alfardan, Bernstein etc. reported their result of all the biases in the first N bytes of the RC4 keystream without theoretical proofs. However, the keystream bytes produced after round N of the PRGA haven't been adequately studied in the last decades, most of previous attacks will fail when the first N bytes of the keystream are dumped. In our paper, we give out some weaknesses exit in all rounds, which will in turn provide us with certain information form any keystream byte and improve the state recovery attack [1,7].

This paper will be organized as follows. In Sect. 2, we introduce the RC4 cipher and the notations we use throughout this paper. We give our theoretical proof of the open problem in [10] in Sect. 3, what's more, the corresponding distinguishing attack and ciphertext only attack were presented. Section 4 details some weaknesses exit in all PRGA rounds of RC4. Finally, we conclude in Sect. 5.

2   Description of RC4

RC4 runs in two phases, the key scheduling phase KSA and the output keystream generation phase PRGA. The description is as follows.

```
1   KSA
2   for i ← 0 to N − 1
3        do s[i] ← i
4   j ← 0
5   for i ← 0 to N − 1
6        do j ← j + s[i] + k[i mod l]
7            swap (s[i], s[j])
8   PRGA
9   i, j ← 0
10  while i ≥ 0
11       do i ← i + 1
12          j ← j + s[i]
13          swap (s[i], s[j])
14          output s[s[i] + s[j]]
```

The KSA swaps N pairs of the array $\{0, 1, 2, \ldots, N-1\}$, depending on the value of the secret key, where l is the word length of the secret key. At the end of KSA, we reach an initial state for PRGA phase, which generates keystream words of $\log_2 N$ bits. Note that the symbol $'+'$ denotes the addition modular N.

Notations. Let s_t, i_t, j_t, z_t denote the state, index i, index j and the keystream byte respectively, after $t(t \geqslant 0)$ rounds of PRGA have been performed. Specially, s_0 is the state just before the PRGA starts, i.e, right after the KSA ends. $'+'('-')$ denotes addition(substraction) modular by N when applying to the algorithm of RC4, where $N = 256$.

3 z_1 Is Negative Biased to 0

In this section, we give the theoretical proof of the negative bias. We state our result by the following theorem.

Theorem 1. *The probability that the first RC4 keystream byte is equal to 0 is* $Pr(z_1 = 0) \approx 0.003877$.

During the proof of our theorem, we shall require the following well known result in RC4 crytanalysis from the existing literature. This appears in [5], and we restate the result as follows.

Lemma 1. *At the end of KSA, for* $0 \leqslant u \leqslant N - 1, 0 \leqslant v \leqslant N - 1$,

$$Pr(s_0[u] = v) = \begin{cases} \frac{1}{N}[(\frac{N-1}{N})^v + (1 - (\frac{N-1}{N})^v)(\frac{N-1}{N})^{N-u-1}] & if v \leqslant u; \\ \frac{1}{N}[(\frac{N-1}{N})^{N-u-1} + (\frac{N-1}{N})^v] & if v > u. \end{cases}$$

We denote the probability $Pr(s_0[u] = v)$ *as* $p_{u,v}$ *in the following part of the paper.*

We also need the following probability formula through our proof.

Lemma 2. *Let* A, B *be two events with* $Pr(B) \neq 0$, $\{C_i\}_{i=1}^n$ *be a sequence of events satisfied* $Pr(\cup C_i) = 1$ *and* $\cap C_i = \emptyset$. *Then* $Pr(A|B) = \sum_i Pr(A|C_i, B) Pr(C_i|B)$.

Proof.

$$Pr(A|B) = \sum_i Pr(A, C_i|B) = \sum_i \frac{Pr(A, C_i, B)}{Pr(B)}$$

$$= \sum_i \frac{Pr(A|C_i, B)Pr(C_i, B)}{Pr(B)} = \sum_i Pr(A|C_i, B)Pr(C_i|B).$$

Now we will prove Theorem 1 with the lemmas.

The proof of Theorem 1

We prove the result by decomposing the event $z_1 = 0$ into two mutually exclusive and exhaustive cases as follows.

$$Pr(z_1 = 0)$$
$$= Pr(z_1 = 0|s_0[1] = 1)Pr(s_0[1] = 1) + Pr(z_1 = 0|s_0[1] \neq 1)Pr(s_0[1] \neq 1)$$
$$= p_{1,1}Pr(z_1 = 0|s_0[1] = 1) + (1 - p_{1,1})Pr(z_1 = 0|s_0[1] \neq 1) \tag{1}$$

Now we consider the events $z_1 = 0|s_0[1] = 1$ and $z_1 = 0|s_0[1] \neq 1$ individually to calculate their probabilities. Note that $z_1 = s_1[s_1[1] + s_1[j_1]] = s_1[s_0[j_1] + s_0[1]] = s_1[s_0[s_0[1]] + s_0[1]]$.

Calculation of $Pr(z_1 = 0|s_0[1] = 1)$. In this case, $j_1 = s_0[1] = 1 = i_1$, and thus s_1 is the same permutation as s_0. Then we have the probability

$$Pr(z_1 = 0|s_0[1] = 1) = Pr(s_1[s_0[s_0[1]] + s_0[1]] = 0|s_0[1] = 1)$$

$$= Pr(s_1[2] = 0|s_0[1] = 1) = \frac{1}{N-1} \qquad (2)$$

In fact, we infer from Lemma 1 that $Pr(s_0[a] = 0)$ is uniformly distributed ($v=0$), with a trivial probability of $\frac{1}{N}$. Also, considering $s_0[2] \neq 1$ when $s_0[1] = 1$. It is reasonable to estimate $Pr(s_0[2] = 0|s_0[1] = 1)$ as $\frac{1}{N-1}$. Generally, we estimate $Pr(s_0[a] = x|s_0[b] = y)$ as $\frac{N}{N-1}p_{a,x}$ when $x \neq y$, $a \neq b$.

Calculation of $Pr(z_1 = 0|s_0[1] \neq 1)$. By Lemma 2,

$$Pr(z_1 = 0|s_0[1] \neq 1)$$
$$= Pr(z_1 = 0|s_0[s_0[1]] = 0, s_0[1] \neq 1)Pr(s_0[s_0[1]] = 0|s_0[1] \neq 1)$$
$$+ Pr(z_1 = 0|s_0[s_0[1]] = 1 - s_0[1], s_0[1] \neq 1)Pr(s_0[s_0[1]] = 1 - s_0[1]|s_0[1] \neq 1)$$
$$+ Pr(z_1 = 0|s_0[s_0[1]] \neq 0, 1 - s_0[1], s_0[1] \neq 1)Pr(s_0[s_0[1]] \neq 0, 1 - s_0[1]|s_0[1] \neq 1)$$

Now we consider the three parts of the equation separately.

For $Pr(z_1 = 0|s_0[s_0[1]] = 0, s_0[1] \neq 1)$, since $s_0[1] \neq 1$, $0 = s_0[s_0[1]] \neq s_0[1]$, thus we get $z_1 = s_1[s_0[1] + s_0[s_0[1]]] = s_1[s_0[1]] = s_0[1] \neq 0$. Therefore, $Pr(z_1 = 0|s_0[s_0[1]] = 0, s_0[1] \neq 1) = 0$.

For $Pr(z_1 = 0|s_0[s_0[1]] = 1 - s_0[1], s_0[1] \neq 1)$, since $s_0[1] \neq 1$, $s_0[s_0[1]] = 1 - s_0[1] \neq 0$, thus we get $z_1 = s_1[s_0[s_0[1]] + s_0[1]] = s_1[1] = s_0[s_0[1]] \neq 0$. Therefore $Pr(z_1 = 0|s_0[s_0[1]] = 1 - s_0[1], s_0[1] \neq 1)=0$.

For $Pr(z_1 = 0|s_0[s_0[1]] \neq 1 - s_0[1], s_0[1] \neq 1)$, since $s_0[s_0[1]] + s_0[1] \neq 1, s_0[1]$. $z_1 = s_1[s_0[s_0[1]] + s_0[1]] = s_0[s_0[s_0[1]] + s_0[1]]$. Thus we get

$$Pr(z_1 = 0|s_0[s_0[1]] \neq 0, 1 - s_0[1], s_0[1] \neq 1)$$
$$= Pr(s_0[s_0[s_0[1]] + s_0[1]] = 0|s_0[s_0[1]] \neq 0, 1 - s_0[1], s_0[1] \neq 1)$$

the value of s_0 at $s_0[1]+s_0[s_0[1]]$ are independent of the value at $s_0[1]$, 1, because of the randomness of $s_0[1]$. Through a similar analysis with (2), we get

$$Pr(z_1 = 0|s_0[s_0[1]] \neq 0, 1 - s_0[1], s_0[1] \neq 1) = \frac{1}{N-1}$$

Combine these results, we get

$$Pr(z_1 = 0|s_0[1] \neq 1)$$
$$= \frac{1}{N-1}Pr(s_0[s_0[1]] \neq 0, 1 - s_0[1]|s_0[1] \neq 1)$$
$$= \frac{1}{N-1}\sum_{x=0}^{N-1} Pr(s_0[s_0[1]] \neq 0, 1 - s_0[1]|s_0[1] = x, s_0[1] \neq 1) Pr(s_0[1] = x|s_0[1] \neq 1)$$

$$= \frac{1}{N-1} \sum_{x \neq 1} \Pr(s_0[x] \neq 0, 1 - x | s_0[1] = x) \Pr(s_0[1] = x | s_0[1] \neq 1)$$

$$= \frac{1}{N-1} \sum_{x \neq 1} [1 - \Pr(s_0[x] = 0 | s_0[1] = x) - \Pr(s_0[x] = 1 - x | s_0[1] = x)] p_{1,x} * \frac{N}{N-1}$$

$$= \frac{N}{(N-1)^2} \left(\sum_{x \neq 1} p_{1,x} - \sum_{x=2}^{N-1} \frac{1}{N-1} p_{1,x} - \frac{N}{N-1} \sum_{x \neq 1} p_{x,1-x} p_{1,x} \right) \tag{3}$$

Combining the probabilities from Eqs. (2) and (3) into (1), we obtain the following

$$Pr(z_1 = 0)$$

$$= \frac{1}{N-1} p_{1,1} + \frac{N}{(N-1)^2} \left(\sum_{x \neq 1} p_{1,x} - \sum_{x=2}^{N-1} \frac{1}{N-1} p_{1,x} - \frac{N}{N-1} \sum_{x \neq 1} p_{x,1-x} p_{1,x} \right) (1 - p_{1,1})$$

Now, substituting the values of $p_{m,n}$ from Lemma 1, we obtain

$$Pr(z_1 = 0) \approx 0.003877. \tag{4}$$

We run the RC4 algorithm 1 billion times, each with a randomly generated 16 byte key, and obtain z_1. The probability of $z_1 = 0$ is 0.003896, which is slightly larger than our theoretical result, this may due to the approximation of the probability $Pr(s_0[a] = x | s_0[b] = y)$.

3.1 A New Distinguisher

Theorem 1 immediately give a new distinguisher. In [3], it is proved that if an event e happens with probabilities p and $p(1 + q)$ in distributions X and Y respectively, then for p and q with small magnitude, $O(p^{-1} q^{-2})$ samples suffice to distinguish X from Y with a constant probability of success.

   In our setting, let X and Y denote the distributions corresponding to random stream and RC4 keystream respectively, and e denotes the event $z_1 = 0$. From Eq. (4), we have $Pr(z_1 = 0) \approx \frac{1}{N}(1 - 0.007488)$, thus $p = \frac{1}{N}$, $q = 0.007488$. Therefore, to distinguishing RC4 keystream from random stream, based on the event $z_1 = 0$, one would need number of samples of the order of $\left(\frac{1}{N}\right)^{-1} * 0.007488^{-2} \sim O(N^3)$. We list the distinguishers of the form $z_t = 0$ in Table 1.

Table 1. Distinguishers of the form $z_t = 0$.

Round number t	Data complexity	Reference
1	$O(N^3)$	Our
2	$O(N)$	[3]
3–255	$O(N^3)$	[10]

3.2   A Ciphertext-Only Attack on Broadcast RC4

A broadcast cipher is a multi-round protocol in which each general broadcasts the same message to all the other generals, where each copy is encrypted under a different key agreed in advance between any two generals. For example, many users send the same email message to multiple recipients(encrypted under different keys), and many groupware applications enable multiple users to synchronize their documents by broadcasting encrypted modification lists to all the other group members. By using RC4, the generals will succeed in reading coordinated decisions, however, an enemy will probably collects all the ciphertext and recover the first plaintext.

Theorem 2. *Let M be a plaintext, and let $C_1 \cdots C_k$ be the RC4 encryptions of M under k uniformly distributed keys. Then if $k = O(N^3)$, the first byte of M can be reliably extracted from $C_1 \cdots C_k$.*

Proof. Recall from Theorem 1 that $Pr(z_1 = 0) \approx 0.003877$. Thus, for each encryption key chosen during broadcast, the first plaintext byte M[1] has probability 0.003877 to be XOR-ed with 0.

Due to the bias of z_1 towards 0, 0.003877 fraction of the first ciphertext byte will have the same value as the first plaintext byte, with a lower probability. When $k = O(N^3)$, the attacker can identify the less frequent character in $C_1[1] \cdots C_k[1]$ with probability 0.003877 as M[1] with constant probability of success.

Experiment. We generate k 16 byte keys, and obtain k keystreams, these keystreams are used to encrypt the same message. When $k = 2^{27}$, the success probability is only 16 %, and it reaches 70 % when $k = 2^{30}$. The reason for higher data complexity is that the probabilities $Pr(z_1 = 253)$, $Pr(z_1 = 254)$, $Pr(z_1 = 255)$ are only slightly larger than the probability $Pr(z_1 = 0)$, which we can see from the experiment result of [2]. Thus we need more keystreams to distinguishing them.

In [3,10], there are plaintext recovery attack on $M[2]$ to $M[N-1]$, together with our recovery on $M[1]$, one can consist a plaintext recovery attack on the first N bytes of RC4. What's more, if we apply the biased sequence of the form ABSAB in [4] to recover the bytes after round N as well, a full plaintext recovery attack is possible.

4   Some New Weaknesses of RC4

When we take a closer look at the proofs of our bias on $z_1 = 0$ and other biases exit in the first N bytes mentioned in [3,6,10], we will find that most of the biases are due to the non-uniformly distributed s_0. That means the initialization of RC4 is weak. However, all these attacks become infeasible when the first N bytes of the keystream are dumped, in fact, when the round number t is large enough, the permutation s_t is uniformly distributed. In this section, we present two general weaknesses of RC4, these weaknesses exit no matter how many keystream bytes are dumped.

4.1   The Weakness about $z_t = 0$

We express the first weakness by the following theorem.

Theorem 3. *When the round number $t \geqslant 1$, if $s_{t-1}[t+1] = 0$, $j_{t-1} = 0$ and $s_{t-1}[t] \neq t+1$, then $z_{t+1} = 0$.[1]*

Proof. The proof comes from the execution process of the cipher. At the tth round, j_t is updated by $j_t = j_{t-1} + s_{t-1}[t] = s_{t-1}[t] \neq t+1$, together with $i_t = t \neq t+1$, we get $s_t[t+1] = s_{t-1}[t+1] = 0$. During the $(t+1)$th round, j_{t+1} is updated by $j_{t+1} = j_t + s_t[t+1] = j_t$, therefore we swap $s_t[t+1]$ and $s_t[j_t]$ to update the state s_{t+1}. From above, we obtain

$$
\begin{aligned}
z_{t+1} &= s_{t+1}[s_{t+1}[t+1] + s_{t+1}[j_t]] = s_{t+1}[s_t[j_t] + s_t[t+1]] \\
&= s_{t+1}[s_{t-1}[t]] = s_{t+1}[j_t] = s_t[t+1] = 0.
\end{aligned}
$$

As we know, the non-randomness of $z_{t+1} = 0$ will give new distinguishers. We denote E_{int} the event $s_{t-1}[t+1] = 0$, $j_{t-1} = 0$ and $s_{t-1}[t] \neq t+1$, then it follows immediately from Theorem 3 that $Pr(z_{t+1} = 0 | E_{int}) = 1$. If we assume that when E_{int} does not occur, $z_{t+1} = 0$ happens with probability $\frac{1}{N}$, then the probability of $z_{t+1} = 0$ is computed as follows

$$
\begin{aligned}
Pr(z_{t+1} = 0) &= Pr(z_{t+1} = 0 | E_{int}) Pr(E_{int}) + Pr(z_{t+1} = 0 | \overline{E_{int}}) Pr(\overline{E_{int}}) \\
&= Pr(E_{int}) + \frac{1}{N}(1 - Pr(E_{int}))
\end{aligned}
\tag{5}
$$

When t is large, s_t and j_t are expected to be uniformly distributed, thus $Pr(E_{int}) = \frac{1}{N^2}(1 - \frac{1}{N})$. We substitute this probability to (5) and get when t is large,

$$
Pr(z_{t+1} = 0) = \frac{1}{N}(1 + \frac{1}{N}(1 - \frac{1}{N})^2)
\tag{6}
$$

Equation (6) implies a large bias. Unfortunately, experiment shows that when t is large, z_{t+1} is only a little positive biased towards 0. The bias is not so large as (6) claims, thus hard to detective. By carefully analyzing this situation one can show that though the event E_{int} is correctly computed, the probability $Pr(z_{t+1} = 0 | E_{int})$ is slightly negative biased, i.e, smaller than $\frac{1}{N}$, thus cancels the positive bias. Therefore, we can still estimate the probability of $Pr(z_{t+1} = 0)$ by $\frac{1}{N}$. However, we can detect inner state from the keystream by this theorem. The event $z_{t+1} = 0$ is an external event in the keystream which we can obtain, while the event E_{int} an internal event of the inner state which is non-visible. By Theorem 3, $Pr(z_{t+1} | E_{int}) = 1$. We are more interested in the event $E_{int} | z_{t+1}$, since it means detecting the inner state from the known keystream.

Theorem 4. *When $z_{t+1} = 0$, the event $s_{t-1}[t+1] = 0$ and $j_{t-1} = 0$ happens with a probability larger than $\frac{1}{N} - \frac{1}{N^2}$, which is greatly larger than the random case of $\frac{1}{N^2}$.*

---

[1] All the operation '$+$' and '$-$' applying to the algorithm of RC4 are modular by N, and the notation $s_t[t_1]$ means $s_t[t_1 mod N]$.

Proof. We denote E_{int} as mentioned above. Applying Bayes formula we can derive the following.

$$Pr(s_{t-1}[t+1] = 0, j_{t-1} = 0 | z_{t+1} = 0)$$
$$\geqslant Pr(E_{int} | z_{t+1}) = \frac{Pr(z_{t+1} | E_{int}) Pr(E_{int})}{Pr(z_{t+1})}$$
$$= \frac{\frac{1}{N^2}(1 - \frac{1}{N})}{\frac{1}{N}} = \frac{1}{N}(1 - \frac{1}{N})$$

From Theorem 4, one can guess j_{t-1} and $s_{t-1}[t+1]$ for more than the probability of a random guess of $\frac{1}{N^2}$, every time we obtain $z_{t+1} = 0$ in the RC4 keystream.

Experiment. In Fig. 1, we plot the experiment values observed by running the RC4 algorithm 1 billion times each with a randomly selected 16 byte key, the initial $51 * N - 1$ rounds of keystream bytes are thrown away, we start from the $51 * N$th round. We can see from the figure that most of the probability are around $\frac{1}{N}$, all of them are much greater than $\frac{1}{N^2} \approx 0.000015$. But some of them are lower than $\frac{1}{N} - \frac{1}{N^2} \approx 0.00389099$, this may due to the probability of $Pr(z_{t+1} = 0)$ is slightly positive biased at some ts.

4.2   The Weakness about $z_t = z_{t+1}$

We will introduce another general weakness of RC4 in this subsection.

Theorem 5. *When $t \geqslant 1$ and $t \neq -2 (mod\ N)$, if $j_{t-1} = 0$, $s_{t-1}[t] = t+1$, then we have $z_t \neq z_{t+1}$.*

Proof. At the tth round, j_t is updated by $j_t = j_{t-1} + s_{t-1}[t] = t + 1$, together with $i_t = t$, we get $s_t[t+1] = s_{t-1}[t] = t + 1$, $s_t[t] = s_{t-1}[t+1]$. And the output is

$$z_t = s_t[s_t[t+1] + s_t[t]] = s_t[s_t[t] + t + 1].$$

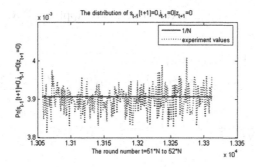

Fig. 1. The probability of $Pr(s_{t-1}[t+1] = 0, j_{t-1} = 0 | z_{t+1} = 0)$ at $51 * N$ to $52 * N$ rounds

During the $(t+1)$th round, j_{t+1} is updated by $j_{t+1} = j_t + s_t[t+1] = 2t+2$, therefore we swap $s_t[t+1]$ and $s_t[2t+2]$, i.e, $s_{t+1}[t+1] = s_t[2t+2]$, $s_{t+1}[2t+2] = s_t[t+1] = t+1$. And the output is

$$z_{t+1} = s_{t+1}[s_{t+1}[t+1] + s_{t+1}[2t+2]] = s_{t+1}[s_t[2t+2] + t + 1].$$

We derive from $t \neq -2$ that $s_t[t] \neq s_t[2t+2]$, thus the indices of z_t and z_{t+1} are unequal. Therefore if $z_t = z_{t+1}$, the indices of z_t and z_{t+1} are both the exchange indices at round $t+1$, there are two cases

$$s_t[t] + t + 1 = t + 1, s_t[2t+2] + t + 1 = 2t + 2 \tag{7}$$

or

$$s_t[t] + t + 1 = 2t + 2, s_t[2t+2] + t + 1 = t + 1 \tag{8}$$

For (7), $s_t[2t+2] = t+1 = s_t[t+1]$, thus $t = -1,(\text{mod}N)$. Substitute the value of t to (7), we get $s_{-1}[-1] = s_{-1}[0] = 0$. This contradicts to the fact that s_{-1} is a permutation. Equation(8) implies $s_t[t] = t+1 = s_t[t+1]$, this is also impossible.

In [8,9], S.Paul and B.Preneel gave their discovery about the non-randomness of the event $z_1 = z_2$. However, there hasn't been much research on the distribution of the events $z_t = z_{t+1}$ when $t > 1$. Similar to the analysis of the event $z_t = 0$, when applying to the first N bytes, the non-uniformly distributed s_0 has big influence on the event $z_t = z_{t+1}$, while to the round number t is large enough, the state s_t is expected to be uniformly distributed, we plot the distribution of $Pr(z_t = z_{t+1})$ in Fig. 2, also, we run the RC4 algorithm 1 billion times, each with a randomly selected 16 byte key. We conclude from the figure that when the round number t is small, the probability is lower than random case of $\frac{1}{N}$, and when t is large enough, it is uniformly distributed. The same as the weakness mentioned in Sect. 4.1, it will leads to information leakage when t is large enough.

Theorem 6. *When $z_t \neq z_{t+1}$ and $t \neq -2$, the event $j_{t-1} = 0$, $s_{t-1}[t] = t+1$ happens with probability of $\frac{1}{N^2-N}$, which is larger than $\frac{1}{N^2}$.*

Proof. When $t \neq -2$, using Theorem 5 as well as applying Bayes formula we can derive the following.

$$Pr(s_{t-1}[t] = t+1, j_{t-1} = 0 | z_t \neq z_{t+1})$$
$$= \frac{Pr(z_t \neq z_{t+1} | s_{t-1}[t] = t+1, j_{t-1} = 0)Pr(s_{t-1}[t] = t+1, j_{t-1} = 0)}{Pr(z_t \neq z_{t+1})}$$

$$= \frac{\frac{1}{N^2}}{1 - \frac{1}{N}} = \frac{1}{N^2 - N}$$

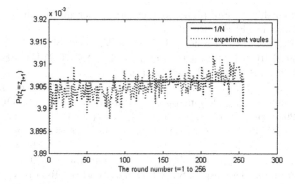

Fig. 2. The probability of $Pr(z_t = z_{t+1})$ at the first N rounds

5   Conclusion

In this paper, we give out the theoretical proof of the negative bias of z_1 towards 0, which is an open problem proposed in [10]. This bias can distinguish RC4 keystream reliably from a random stream of bytes. Further, the bias can be exploited to mount an attack against broadcast RC4. In addition to the 2th to 255th plaintext bytes recovery in [3,10], we are able to recover the first N bytes.

Further, we propose some weaknesses in the whole PRGA phase, contrary to the previous work, the weaknesses still exists even though the first N bytes are dumped, and will lead to the leakage of the state information. We would like to make a small note on a related observation, the probability of $Pr(z_{t+1} = 0 | \overline{s_{t-1}[t+1] = 0, j_{t-1} = 0, s_{t-1}[t+1] \neq t+1})$ is smaller than $\frac{1}{N}$, i.e, slightly negative biased, where $\bar{A}$ denotes the complement event of A. But we haven't found the reason, we would like to pose this as an open problem.

Acknowledgment. This work was supported by the National Basic Research 973 Program of China under Grant NO.2013CB338002. The authors would like to thank the anonymous reviewers for their helpful suggestions.

References

1. Maximov, A., Khovratovich, D.: New state recovery attack on RC4. In: Wagner, D. (ed.) CRYPTO 2008. LNCS, vol. 5157, pp. 297–316. Springer, Heidelberg (2008)
2. Bernstein, D.: Failures of secret-key cryptography. Fast Software Encryption-FSE'2013, inviting talk. http://fse2013.spms.ntu.edu.sg/slides/slides07.pdf
3. Mantin, I., Shamir, A.: A practical attack on broadcast RC4. In: Matsui, M. (ed.) FSE 2001. LNCS, vol. 2355, pp. 152–164. Springer, Heidelberg (2002)
4. Mantin, I.: Predicting and distinguishing attacks on RC4 keystream generator. In: Cramer, R. (ed.) EUROCRYPT 2005. LNCS, vol. 3494, pp. 491–506. Springer, Heidelberg (2005)
5. Mantin, I.: Analysis of the stream cipher RC4. Master's Thesis, The Weizmann Institute of Science, Israel (2001)

6. Isobe, T., Ohigashi, T.: Full plaintext recovery attack on broadcast RC4. In: Fast Software Encryption-FSE'2013 (2013)
7. Knudsen, L.R., Meier, W., Preneel, B., Rijmen, V., Verdoolaege, S.: Analysis methods for (alleged) RC4. In: Ohta, K., Pei, D. (eds.) ASIACRYPT 1998. LNCS, vol. 1514, pp. 327–341. Springer, Heidelberg (1998)
8. Paul, S., Preneel, B.: Analysis of non-fortuitous predictive states of the RC4 keystream generator. In: Johansson, T., Maitra, S. (eds.) INDOCRYPT 2003. LNCS, vol. 2904, pp. 52–67. Springer, Heidelberg (2003)
9. Paul, S., Preneel, B.: A new weakness in the RC4 keystream generator and an approach to improve the security of the cipher. In: Roy, B., Meier, W. (eds.) FSE 2004. LNCS, vol. 3017, pp. 245–259. Springer, Heidelberg (2004)
10. Maitra, S., Paul, G., Sen Gupta, S.: Attack on Broadcast RC4 Revisited. In: Joux, A. (ed.) FSE 2011. LNCS, vol. 6733, pp. 199–217. Springer, Heidelberg (2011)

Improvements on Reductions among Different Variants of SVP and CVP

Gengran Hu$^{(\boxtimes)}$ and Yanbin Pan

Key Laboratory of Mathematics Mechanization, NCMIS, Academy of Mathematics and Systems Science, Chinese Academy of Sciences, 100190 Beijing, China
hudiran10@mails.ucas.ac.cn, panyanbin@amss.ac.cn

Abstract. It is well known that Search SVP is equivalent to Optimization SVP. However, the classical reduction from Search SVP to Optimization SVP by Kannan needs polynomial times of calls to the oracle that solves Optimization SVP. In this paper, a new rank-preserving reduction is presented with only one call to the Optimization SVP oracle. The idea also leads to a similar direct reduction from Search CVP to Optimization CVP with only one call to the corresponding oracle. Both of the reductions above can be generalized for l_p norm with $p \in \mathbb{Z}^+$.

On the other hand, whether the search and optimization variants of approximate SVP are computationally equivalent is an outstanding open problem. Recently, Cheng gave a reduction from Search SVP$_\gamma$ to Optimization SVP$_{\gamma'}$, where $\gamma' = \gamma^{\frac{1}{n(n-1)\log_2 \gamma n}}$ is much smaller than γ. We slightly improve the reduction by making $\gamma' = \gamma^{\frac{O(\log_2 n)}{n(n-1)\log_2 \gamma n}}$. In addition, a reduction from Search CVP$_\gamma$ to Optimization CVP$_{\gamma'}$ with $\gamma' = \gamma^{\frac{1}{n\lceil n/2+\log_2 \gamma \cdot \text{dist}(t, \mathcal{L}(B))\rceil}}$ is also presented.

Keywords: Search SVP · Optimization SVP · GapSVP · Lattice · Reduction

1 Introduction

Lattices have many important applications in cryptographic constructions due to the seminal work of Ajtai [1] in 1996 which first connected the average-case complexity of lattice problems to their complexity in the worst case. Many lattice-based public-key cryptosystems have been proposed since then like the well-known Ajtai-Dwork cryptosystem [2], Regev's LWE-based cryptosystem [18], the GPV system [6] and the famous NTRU [7]. Moreover, a lot of other lattice-based cryptographic primitives have been also presented, such as the hash function [1,12,14,16], the digital signatures schemes NTRUSign [8] and the fully homomorphic encryption [5]. Usually, the securities of these schemes can be

This work was supported in part by the NNSF of China (No.11071285, No.11201458, and No.61121062), in part by 973 Project (No. 2011CB302401) and in part by the National Center for Mathematics and Interdisciplinary Sciences, CAS.

Y. Kim et al. (Eds.): WISA 2013, LNCS 8267, pp. 39–51, 2014.
DOI: 10.1007/978-3-319-05149-9_3, © Springer International Publishing Switzerland 2014

based on the hardness of some lattice problems, such as SVP and CVP. SVP (the shortest vector problem) and CVP (the closest vector problem) are two of the most famous computational problems of lattice. SVP refers to finding a shortest non-zero vector in a given lattice, whereas CVP asks to find a lattice vector closest to a given target vector.

Depending on whether we have to actually find a shortest vector, find its length, or just decide if it is shorter than some given number, there are three different variants of SVP: Search SVP, Optimization SVP and Decisional SVP (See Sect. 2 for the definitions).

It has been proved that the three problems of SVP are equivalent to each other (see [15]). It is easy to check that Decisional SVP is as hard as Optimization SVP and the optimization variant can be reduced to the search variant.

In 1987, Kannan [11] showed that the search variant can be reduced to the optimization variant. The basic idea of his reduction is to recover the integer coefficients of some shortest vector under the given lattice basis by introducing small errors to the original lattice basis. However, his reduction is a bit complex. It needs to call Optimization SVP oracle polynomial times, since it could not determine the signs of the shortest vector's entries at one time. It also needs an oracle to solve Optimization SVP for some lattices with lower rank along with the same rank as the original lattice.

In this paper, we propose a new rank-preserving reduction which can solve Search SVP with only one call to the given Optimization SVP oracle. It is obvious that there is no reduction with less calls than ours. For the new reduction, we try to construct a new lattice by adding small errors to the original lattice basis such that the integer coefficients of the new lattice's shortest vector under the new basis are the same as the integer coefficients of some shortest vector in the original lattice under the original lattice basis. Moreover, by the Optimization SVP oracle, we can recover the integer coefficients.

A similar direct reduction from Search CVP to Optimization CVP with only one call also holds whereas some popular reductions [15, 17] usually take Decisional CVP to bridge Search CVP and Optimization CVP. The former reduction from Decisional CVP to Optimization CVP needs one call to the Optimization CVP oracle, but it needs polynomial times of calls to reduce Search CVP to Decisional CVP.

Both of our two reductions can be generalized to the case for any l_p-norm $(p \in \mathbb{Z}^+)$.

Since there exists efficient reduction from Search SVP to Optimization SVP, we want to obtain similar results for the approximate version. In fact, one open problem on the complexity of lattice problems is whether the search and optimization variants of approximate SVP are computationally equivalent. As pointed out in [13], once there exists an efficient reduction from Search SVP$_\gamma$ to Optimization SVP$_\gamma$, almost all the lattice problems used in cryptography, such as uSVP (unique SVP), BDD (Bounded Distance Decoding), SIVP (the shortest independent vector problem), GapSVP (Decisional SVP), SVP, CVP, are equivalent up to polynomial factors.

It seems difficult to generalize our idea above to solve the problem, for our new reduction is sensitive to the error. However, Cheng [9] recently gave a reduction from Search SVP$_\gamma$ to Optimization SVP$_{\gamma'}$ with $\gamma' = \gamma^{\frac{1}{n(n-1)\log_2 \gamma n}}$. His reduction uses the framework in [13] but shrinks the factor γ too much.

We slightly improve this result to $\gamma' = \gamma^{\frac{O(\log_2 n)}{n(n-1)(n+\log_2(\gamma n))}}$, but we have to point out that it is still far away to be useful to give some meaningful result about the complexity of some lattice problems because the approximation factor is still shrunk exponentially.

Finally, enlightened by the idea in the above reduction, we present a new reduction from Search CVP$_\gamma$ to Optimization CVP$_{\gamma'}$ where $\gamma' = \gamma^{\frac{1}{n\lceil n/2 + \log_2 \gamma \cdot \text{dist}(t, \mathcal{L}(B))\rceil}}$. This is the first reduction from Search CVP$_\gamma$ to Optimization CVP$_{\gamma'}$ although γ' is also much smaller than γ.

The remainder of the paper is organized as follows. In Sect. 2, we give some preliminaries needed. In Sect. 3, we describe the new reduction from Search SVP to Optimization SVP. In Sect. 4, an improved reduction from Search SVP$_\gamma$ to Optimization SVP$_{\gamma'}$ with $\gamma' = \gamma^{\frac{O(\log_2 n)}{n(n-1)(n+\log_2(\gamma n))}}$ is given. Our reduction from Search CVP$_\gamma$ to Optimization CVP$_{\gamma'}$ can be found in Sect. 5. Finally, we give a short conclusion in Sect. 6.

2 Preliminaries

Given a matrix $B = (b_{ij}) \in \mathbb{R}^{m \times n}$ with rank n, the lattice $\mathcal{L}(B)$ spanned by the columns of B is

$$\mathcal{L}(B) = \{Bx = \sum_{i=1}^{n} x_i b_i | x_i \in \mathbb{Z}\},$$

where b_i is the i-th column of B. We call m the dimension of $\mathcal{L}(B)$ and n its rank. The determinant of $\mathcal{L}(B)$, say $\det(\mathcal{L}(B))$, is defined as $\sqrt{\det(B^T B)}$. It is easy to see when B is full-rank $(n = m)$, its determinant becomes $|\det(B)|$.

A sublattice of $\mathcal{L}(B)$ is a lattice whose elements are all in $\mathcal{L}(B)$. The space spanned by B is defined as $span(B) = \{By | y \in \mathbb{R}^n\}$. The dual lattice $\mathcal{L}(D)$ of $\mathcal{L}(B)$ is defined as $\mathcal{L}(D) = \{z \in span(B) | \forall y \in \mathcal{L}(B), y^T z \in \mathbb{Z}\}$. Moreover, a basis of $\mathcal{L}(D)$ is given by $B(B^T B)^{-1}$, and $\det(\mathcal{L}(D)) = \det(\mathcal{L}(B))^{-1}$.

The first minima of lattice $\mathcal{L}(B)$ is defined as

$$\lambda_1(\mathcal{L}(B)) = \min_{0 \neq v \in \mathcal{L}(B)} \|v\|,$$

where $\|v\|$ is the l_2 norm of vector v. Minkowski's first theorem tells us that for any lattice $\mathcal{L}(B)$ with rank n,

$$\lambda_1(\mathcal{L}(B)) \leq \sqrt{n} \cdot \det(\mathcal{L}(B))^{1/n}.$$

SVP usually refers to finding a vector in $\mathcal{L}(B)$ with length $\lambda_1(\mathcal{L}(B))$. It has the following three variants:

- Search SVP: Given a lattice basis $B \in \mathbb{Z}^{m \times n}$, find $v \in \mathcal{L}(B)$ such that $\|v\| = \lambda_1(\mathcal{L}(B))$.
- Optimization SVP: Given a lattice basis $B \in \mathbb{Z}^{m \times n}$, find $\lambda_1(\mathcal{L}(B))$.
- Decisional SVP: Given a lattice basis $B \in \mathbb{Z}^{m \times n}$ and a rational $r \in \mathbb{Q}$, decide whether $\lambda_1(\mathcal{L}(B)) \leq r$ or not.

Notice that we restrict the lattice basis to be integer vectors instead of arbitrary real vectors. The purpose is to make the input representable in finite bits so we can view it as a standard computation problem.

Since SVP is proved to be NP-hard under randomized reductions (see [3]), its approximate versions are attracting more attention. With approximate factor $\gamma \geq 1$, the corresponding variants of approximate SVP are:

- Search SVP$_\gamma$: Given a lattice basis $B \in \mathbb{Z}^{m \times n}$, find $v \in \mathcal{L}(B)$ such that $\|v\| \leq \gamma \cdot \lambda_1(\mathcal{L}(B))$.
- Optimization SVP$_\gamma$: Given a lattice basis $B \in \mathbb{Z}^{m \times n}$, find d such that $d \leq \lambda_1(\mathcal{L}(B)) \leq \gamma \cdot d$.
- Decisional SVP$_\gamma$: Given a lattice basis $B \in \mathbb{Z}^{m \times n}$ and a rational $r \in \mathbb{Q}$, decide $\lambda_1(\mathcal{L}(B)) \leq r$ or $\lambda_1(\mathcal{L}(B)) > \gamma \cdot r$.

For the Search SVP$_\gamma$, the famous LLL algorithm [10] tells us a basis $b_1, b_2, \ldots, b_n$ can be found in polynomial time such that

$$\|b_1\| \leq 2^{(n-1)/2} \lambda_1(\mathcal{L}(B)).$$

The Decisional SVP$_\gamma$ is usually denoted by GapSVP$_\gamma$. This is a promise problem defined by two disjoint sets: the YES instances ($\lambda_1(\mathcal{L}(B)) \leq r$) and the NO instances ($\lambda_1(\mathcal{L}(B)) > \gamma \cdot r$). We have to decide which set the input lattice is taken from.

Given any $t \in \mathbb{R}^m$, the distance of t to $\mathcal{L}(B)$ is defined as

$$\mathrm{dist}(t, \mathcal{L}(B)) = \min_{v \in \mathcal{L}(B)} \|t - v\|.$$

In the same way, for approximate factor $\gamma \geq 1$, CVP$_\gamma$ also has three variants:

- Search CVP$_\gamma$: Given a lattice basis $B \in \mathbb{Z}^{m \times n}$ and a target $t \in \mathbb{Q}^m$, find $v \in \mathcal{L}(B)$ such that $\|t - v\| \leq \gamma \cdot \mathrm{dist}(t, \mathcal{L}(B))$.
- Optimization CVP$_\gamma$: Given a lattice basis $B \in \mathbb{Z}^{m \times n}$ and a target $t \in \mathbb{Q}^m$, find d such that $d \leq \mathrm{dist}(t, \mathcal{L}(B)) \leq \gamma \cdot d$.
- GapCVP$_\gamma$: Given a lattice basis $B \in \mathbb{Z}^{m \times n}$, a target $t \in \mathbb{Q}^m$ and a rational $r \in \mathbb{Q}$. In YES instances, $\mathrm{dist}(t, \mathcal{L}(B)) \leq r$. In NO instances, $\mathrm{dist}(t, \mathcal{L}(B)) > \gamma \cdot r$.

For the Search CVP$_\gamma$, Babai's Nearest Plane Algorithm [4] says a lattice vector v can be found in polynomial time such that

$$\|t - v\| \leq 2^{(n-1)/2} \cdot \mathrm{dist}(t, \mathcal{L}(B)).$$

Notice that when $\gamma = 1$, these problems will become exact variants of CVP.

3 The New Reduction from Search SVP to Optimization SVP

For simplicity, we just give the new reduction for the full rank lattice, i.e., $n = m$, as in [11], with l_2 norm. It is easy to generalize the new reduction for the lattices with rank $n < m$ and l_p norm ($p \in \mathbb{Z}^+$).

3.1 Some Notations

Given a lattice basis $B = (b_{ij}) \in \mathbb{Z}^{n \times m}$, let $M(B) = \max |b_{ij}|$. For lattice $\mathcal{L}(B)$, we define its SVP solution set S_B as:

$$S_B = \{x \in \mathbb{Z}^n \,|\, \|Bx\| = \lambda_1(\mathcal{L}(B))\}.$$

S_B is nonempty and might contain more than one element.

We denote by $poly(n)$ the polynomial in n. More generally, the polynomial in the variables $n_1, n_2, \ldots, n_p$ is denoted by $poly(n_1, n_2, \ldots, n_p)$.

3.2 Some Lemmas and Corollaries

We need some lemmas and corollaries to prove our main theorem.

Lemma 1. *Given a fixed positive integer p, then for every positive integer $n \geq p$, there exist n positive integers $a_1 < a_2 < \cdots < a_n$ s.t. all the $a_{i_1} + \cdots + a_{i_p} (i_1 \leq \ldots \leq i_p)$'s are distinct (up to a permutation) and a_n is bounded by $poly(n)$.*

Proof. We can take

$$a_i = \sum_{k=0}^{p} (p(n+1)^p)^{(p-k)} i^k,$$

for $i = 1, 2, \ldots, n$. Suppose

$$a_{i_1} + a_{i_2} + \cdots + a_{i_p} = a_{j_1} + a_{j_2} + \cdots + a_{j_p},$$

for some $i_1, \ldots, i_p, j_1, \ldots, j_p$.

Let $\sigma_k(i) = \sum_{t=1}^{p} (i_t)^k$ and $\sigma_k(j) = \sum_{t=1}^{p} (j_t)^k$, then the former equality turns to

$$\sum_{k=0}^{p} (p(n+1)^p)^{(p-k)} \sigma_k(i) = \sum_{k=0}^{p} (p(n+1)^p)^{(p-k)} \sigma_k(j).$$

Notice that $\sigma_k(i), \sigma_k(j) < p(n+1)^p$ for $k = 1, 2, \ldots, p$, then by taking both sides modulo $p(n+1)^p$, we get

$$\sigma_p(i) = \sigma_p(j),$$

which leads to

$$\sum_{k=0}^{p-1} (p(n+1)^p)^{(p-k-1)} \sigma_k(i) = \sum_{k=0}^{p-1} (p(n+1)^p)^{(p-k-1)} \sigma_k(j).$$

Again taking both sides modulo $p(n+1)^p$, we get

$$\sigma_{p-1}(i) = \sigma_{p-1}(j).$$

Similarly, we repeat this procedure to obtain

$$\sigma_k(i) = \sigma_k(j),$$

for $k = 1, 2, \ldots, p$. Thus by the property of the symmetric polynomials, we know that $i_1, \ldots, i_p$ and $j_1, \ldots, j_p$ are both exactly all the roots of a same polynomial, which implies $i_1, \ldots, i_p$ and $j_1, \ldots, j_p$ are equal up to a permutation. Hence all the $a_{i_1} + \cdots + a_{i_p} (i_1 \leq \cdots \leq i_p)$'s are distinct. Since p is a fixed positive integer, then by our choice, a_n is bounded by $poly(n)$.

Corollary 1. *For every positive integer $n > 1$, there exist n positive integers $a_1 < a_2 < \cdots < a_n$ s.t. all the $a_i + a_j (i \leq j)$'s are distinct and a_n is bounded by $poly(n)$.*

Lemma 2. *Given a positive odd integer $q > 2$, and any positive integer n, which satisfies $n = \sum_{i=0}^{k} n_i q^i$ where $|n_i| \leq \lfloor q/2 \rfloor$, then we can recover the coefficients n_i's in $\lceil \log_q n \rceil$ steps.*

Proof. We can recover n_0 by computing $a \equiv n \bmod q$ and choose a in the interval from $-\lfloor q/2 \rfloor$ to $\lfloor q/2 \rfloor$. After obtaining n_0, we get another integer $(n - n_0 * q^0)/q$. Recursively in $\lceil \log_q n \rceil$ steps, we can recover all the coefficients.

Lemma 3. *For bivariate polynomial $f(x, y) = xy$, given any lattice basis matrix $B \in \mathbb{Z}^{n \times n}$, $\lambda_1(\mathcal{L}(B))$ has an upper bound $f(M, n)$, where $M = M(B)$. What's more, for every $x \in S_B$, $|x_i|$ $(i = 1, \ldots, n)$ has an upper bound $f(M^n, n^n)$.*

Proof. The length of any column of B is an upper bound of $\lambda_1(L(B))$, so $\lambda_1(L(B)) \leq n^{1/2} M \leq nM$.

For $x \in S_B$, we let $y = Bx$, then $\|y\| = \lambda_1(L(B)) \leq \sqrt{n}M$. By Cramer's rule, we know that

$$x_i = \frac{\det(B^{(i)})}{\det(B)},$$

where $B^{(i)}$ is formed by replacing the ith column of B by y. By Hadamard's inequality, $|\det(B^{(i)})| \leq n^{n/2} M^n \leq n^n M^n$. We know $|\det(B)| \geq 1$ since $\det(B)$ is a non-zero integer. Hence $|x_i| \leq n^n M^n$.

3.3　The Main Theorem

Theorem 1. *Assume there exists an oracle $\mathcal{O}$ that can solve Optimization SVP for any lattice $L(B')$ with basis $B' \in \mathbb{Z}^{n \times n}$, then there is an algorithm that can solve Search SVP for any lattice $L(B)$ with basis $B \in \mathbb{Z}^{n \times n}$ with only one call to $\mathcal{O}$ in $poly(\log_2 M, n, \log_2 n)$ time, where $M = M(B)$.*

Proof. The main steps of the reduction are as below:

(1) Constructing a new lattice $L = L(B_\epsilon)$.

We construct B_ϵ from the original lattice basis B:

$$B_\epsilon = \epsilon_{n+1} B + \begin{pmatrix} \epsilon_1 & \epsilon_2 & \dots & \epsilon_n \\ 0 & 0 & \dots & 0 \\ \vdots & \vdots & & \vdots \\ 0 & 0 & \dots & 0 \end{pmatrix},$$

where the ϵ_i will be determined as below.

For any $x \in \mathbb{Z}^n$, we define

$$c(x) = \sum_{i=1}^{n} b_{1i} x_i,$$

for $x \in S_B$. By Lemma 3, $|x_i|$ has an upper bound $f(M^n, n^n)$. Let $M_1 = 2f((M+1)^n, n^n)$. In addition, $\|Bx\| = \lambda_1(L(B))$ is bounded by $f(M, n)$. Let $M_2 = f(M+1, n)$. since $|c(x)| \leq \|Bx\|$, $|c(x)|$ is also bounded by M_2. We let

$$R = 2 * \max\left\{M_2^2, 2M_1 M_2, 2M_1^2\right\} + 1.$$

By Corollary 1, we can choose $n + 1$ positive integers $a_1 < a_2 < \dots < a_{n+1}$, such that all the $a_i + a_j (i \leq j)$'s are distinct where a_{n+1} is bounded by *poly(n)*. Let

$$\epsilon_i = R^{a_i}.$$

We claim that

$$S_{B_\epsilon} \subseteq S_B.$$

Since $S_{B_\epsilon} = S_{\frac{1}{\epsilon_{n+1}} B_\epsilon}$ by scaling, it is enough to prove $S_{\frac{1}{\epsilon_{n+1}} B_\epsilon} \subseteq S_B$.

We first show that $\left| \det\left(\frac{1}{\epsilon_{n+1}} B_\epsilon\right) \right| \geq \frac{1}{2}$. Notice that

$$\det\left(\frac{1}{\epsilon_{n+1}} B_\epsilon\right) = \det(B) + \sum_{i=1}^{n} \alpha_i \frac{\epsilon_i}{\epsilon_{n+1}},$$

where α_i is the cofactor of b_{1i} in B. Since $\frac{\epsilon_i}{\epsilon_{n+1}} \leq \frac{1}{R^2}$ and $|\alpha_i| \leq M^{n-1}(n-1)^{n-1}$ by Hadamard's inequality, $\left| \sum_{i=1}^{n} \alpha_i \frac{\epsilon_i}{\epsilon_{n+1}} \right| \leq \frac{1}{R^2} M^{n-1} n^n < \frac{1}{2}$. Notice that $\det(B)$ is a non-zero integer, we get $\left| \det\left(\frac{1}{\epsilon_{n+1}} B_\epsilon\right) \right| \geq \frac{1}{2}$.

For any $x \in S_{\frac{1}{\epsilon_{n+1}} B_\epsilon}$, by the proof of Lemma 3 and the fact that $\left| \det\left(\frac{1}{\epsilon_{n+1}} B_\epsilon\right) \right| \geq \frac{1}{2}$, we know that $|x_i| \leq M_1$, $|c(x)| \leq M_2$. By the choice of R, we have $x_i^2, 2c(x)x_i, 2x_i x_j$ are in the interval $[-\lfloor R/2 \rfloor, \lfloor R/2 \rfloor]$.

Next, we prove $S_{\frac{1}{\epsilon_{n+1}} B_\epsilon} \subseteq S_B$. Suppose there exists $x \in S_{\frac{1}{\epsilon_{n+1}} B_\epsilon}$ but $x \notin S_B$, then

$$\|Bx\|^2 \geq \lambda_1(L(B))^2 + 1.$$

Taking $y \in S_B$, we get $\frac{1}{\epsilon_{n+1}} B_\epsilon y \in L(\frac{1}{\epsilon_{n+1}} B_\epsilon)$. Noticing $\epsilon_{n+1} > R^2 \epsilon_n$, $\frac{\epsilon_i \epsilon_j}{\epsilon_{n+1}^2} (i \leq j)$'s are different powers of R (by our choice of ϵ_i and Corollary 1), and y_i^2, $2c(y)y_i, 2y_iy_j$ are in the interval $[-\lfloor R/2 \rfloor, \lfloor R/2 \rfloor]$ by the choice of R, we have

$$
\begin{aligned}
\|\tfrac{1}{\epsilon_{n+1}} B_\epsilon y\|^2 &= \|By\|^2 + \sum_{i=1}^n y_i^2 (\tfrac{\epsilon_i}{\epsilon_{n+1}})^2 + \sum_{i=1}^n 2c(y)y_i \tfrac{\epsilon_i}{\epsilon_{n+1}} + \sum_{i<j} 2y_iy_j \tfrac{\epsilon_i\epsilon_j}{\epsilon_{n+1}^2} \\
&< \lambda_1(L(B))^2 + (\lfloor R/2 \rfloor + 1)\tfrac{\epsilon_n}{\epsilon_{n+1}} \\
&\leq \|Bx\|^2 - (1 - (\lfloor R/2 \rfloor + 1)\tfrac{\epsilon_n}{\epsilon_{n+1}}) \\
&< \|Bx\|^2 - (\lfloor R/2 \rfloor + 1)\tfrac{\epsilon_n}{\epsilon_{n+1}} \\
&\leq \|Bx\|^2 + \sum_{i=1}^n x_i^2 (\tfrac{\epsilon_i}{\epsilon_{n+1}})^2 + \sum_{i=1}^n 2c(x)x_i \tfrac{\epsilon_i}{\epsilon_{n+1}} + \sum_{i<j} 2x_ix_j \tfrac{\epsilon_i\epsilon_j}{\epsilon_{n+1}^2} \\
&= \lambda_1(L(\tfrac{1}{\epsilon_{n+1}} B_\epsilon))^2,
\end{aligned}
$$

which is a contradiction. Hence $S_{B_\epsilon} \subseteq S_B$.

(2) Querying the oracle $\mathcal{O}$ with B_ϵ once, we get $\lambda_1(\mathcal{L}(B_\epsilon))$.

So there exists $x = (x_1, \ldots, x_n)^{\mathrm{T}} \in S_{B_\epsilon} \subseteq S_B$, such that

$$
\|Bx\|^2 \epsilon_{n+1}^2 + \sum_{i=1}^n x_i^2 \epsilon_i^2 + \sum_{i=1}^n 2c(x)x_i \epsilon_{n+1}\epsilon_i + \sum_{i<j} 2x_ix_j \epsilon_i \epsilon_j = \lambda_1(\mathcal{L}(B_\epsilon))^2.
$$

(3) Recovering all the x_i's and output Bx.

Since $x \in S_B$, every coefficient $\|Bx\|^2, x_i^2, 2c(x)x_i, 2x_ix_j$ is in the interval $[-\lfloor R/2 \rfloor, \lfloor R/2 \rfloor]$ and $\epsilon_i\epsilon_j \ (i \leq j)$'s are different powers of R. Hence, $\log_2(\lambda_1(\mathcal{L}(B_\epsilon)))$ is bounded by $poly(\log_2 M, n, \log_2 n)$. Furthermore, by Lemma 2, we can recover all the coefficients in $poly(\log_2 M, n, \log_2 n)$ time. Especially, we can recover all x_i^2 and $x_ix_j (i \neq j)$. Let $k = \min\{i | x_i \neq 0\}$. We fix $x_k = \sqrt{x_k^2} > 0$, and can recover all the remaining $x_j = sign(x_kx_j)\sqrt{x_j^2}$ according to x_j^2 and $x_kx_j(k \neq j)$.

It is easy to check that the time and space complexity of every step is bounded by $poly(\log_2 M, n, \log_2 n)$.

Remark 1. Notice that the norm in our main theorem is the most common l_2-norm. In fact, our result can be easily generalized to the case for l_p-norm $(p \in \mathbb{Z}^+)$ by Lemma 1.

Remark 2. For any Search CVP instance (B, t), given an oracle which can solve the Optimization CVP, we can call the oracle with $(B_\epsilon, \epsilon_{n+1}t)$ only once to solve the Search CVP similarly.

4   Improved Reduction from Search SVP$_\gamma$ to Optimization SVP$_{\gamma'}$

In [9], Cheng gave a reduction from Search SVP$_\gamma$ to Optimization SVP$_{\gamma'}$ where $\gamma' = \gamma^{\frac{1}{n(n-1)(n+\log_2(\gamma n))}}$. We slightly improve the result to $\gamma' = \gamma^{\frac{O(\log_2 n)}{n(n-1)(n+\log_2(\gamma n))}}$. As in [9] (Theorem 1), the main idea is to obtain lower rank sublattice of $\mathcal{L}(B)$

which still contains an approximate shortest lattice vector of $\mathcal{L}(B)$. After lowering the rank for several $(n-1)$ times, we finally obtain a rank-one sublattice of $\mathcal{L}(B)$ containing a short vector. Since it is easy to find the shortest vector in a lattice with rank one (its basis), we can find an approximate shortest lattice vector of $\mathcal{L}(B)$. Below we will give a self-contained proof.

Theorem 2. *For any $\gamma \geq 1$, Search SVP_γ can be polynomially reduced to Optimization $SVP_{\gamma'}$ where $\gamma' = \gamma^{\frac{O(\log_2 n)}{n(n-1)(n+\log_2(\gamma n))}}$.*

Proof. Given the input instance $B = (b_1, b_2, \ldots, b_n)$, we intend to find $v \in \mathcal{L}(B)$ such that $\|v\| \leq \gamma \cdot \lambda_1(\mathcal{L}(B))$.

First, for $k = O(\log_2 n)$, we consider $2^{k+1} - 1$ sublattices of $\mathcal{L}(B)$ where their respective bases are $B_{i,j} = (2^i b_1 + j b_2, 2^{k-i} b_2, b_3, \ldots, b_m)(i = 1, 2 \ldots, k, 0 \leq j < 2^{k-i})$. Notice for every $B_{i,j}$, $\det(\mathcal{L}(B_{i,j})) = 2^k \det(\mathcal{L}(B))$. We claim that

$$\mathcal{L}(B) = \bigcup_{i,j} \mathcal{L}(B_{i,j}).$$

For any $w = x_1 b_1 + x_2 b_2 + \cdots + x_n b_n$ in $\mathcal{L}(B)$, $x_1 \in \mathbb{Z}$ can be written as $x_1 = 2^r s$, where s is odd. If $r \geq k$, then $w \in \mathcal{L}(B_{k,0}) = \mathcal{L}(2^k b_1, b_2, \ldots b_m)$. Otherwise, we assume $r < k$. There exist integers p, q such that $sp + 2^{k-r}q = 1$ since $(s, 2^{k-r}) = 1$, which implies $spx_2 + 2^{k-r}qx_2 = x_2$. We take $i = r, j = px_2$ mod 2^{k-r}, then $s(2^i b_1 + j b_2) + (qx_2 + s\frac{px_2 - j}{2^{k-r}})2^{k-r}b_2 = x_1 b_1 + x_2 b_2$. So $w \in \mathcal{L}(B_{i,j})$, thus $\mathcal{L}(B) \subseteq \bigcup_{i,j} \mathcal{L}(B_{i,j})$. On the other hand, since all the $\mathcal{L}(B_{i,j})$'s are sublattices of $\mathcal{L}(B)$, our claim follows.

Secondly, we want to find a good sublattice $\mathcal{L}(B_{i,j})$ of the original lattice $\mathcal{L}(B)$ still containing a short lattice vector. We query the Optimization $SVP_{\gamma'}$ oracle for 2^{k+1} (which is $ploy(n)$ by the choice of k) times with these $B_{i,j}$ and get the output intervals $I_{i,j} = [r_{i,j}, \gamma' \cdot r_{i,j})$ containing $\lambda_1(\mathcal{L}(B_{i,j}))$ respectively. Specially, we can invoke the $SVP_{\gamma'}$ oracle for B to obtain an interval $I = [r, \gamma' \cdot r)$ containing $\lambda_1(\mathcal{L}(B))$. By our claim, a shortest lattice vector in $\mathcal{L}(B)$ must lie in some $\mathcal{L}(B_{i,j})$ which means I must intersect some $I_{i,j}$'s. We take I_{i_0,j_0} that has the smallest left endpoint from these $I_{i,j}$'s. We claim

$$\lambda_1(\mathcal{L}(B_{i_0,j_0})) \leq \gamma' \cdot \lambda_1(\mathcal{L}(B)).$$

Let $I_{i',j'}$ be the interval where a shortest lattice vector in $\mathcal{L}(B)$ lies. Then by the choice of $I_{i,j}$, $\lambda_1(\mathcal{L}(B_{i_0,j_0})) \leq \gamma' \cdot r_{i_0,j_0} \leq \gamma' \cdot r_{i',j'} \leq \gamma' \cdot \lambda_1(\mathcal{L}(B))$.

Thirdly, we repeat this procedure by replacing the input B with the B_{i_0,j_0}. After $t = \frac{n(n+\log_2(\gamma n))}{O(\log_2 n)}$ steps, we obtain a sublattice $\mathcal{L}(B')$ of $\mathcal{L}(B)$ such that

$$\lambda_1(\mathcal{L}(B')) \leq (\gamma')^t \cdot \lambda_1(\mathcal{L}(B)),$$

where $\det(\mathcal{L}(B')) = 2^{kt} \det(\mathcal{L}(B)) \geq 2^{n(n+\log_2 \gamma n)} \det(\mathcal{L}(B))$.

According to Minkowski's bound, we have $\lambda_1(\mathcal{L}(B)) \le \sqrt{n}\det(\mathcal{L}(B))^{1/n}$. Denote by u' a shortest lattice vector in $\mathcal{L}(B')$, then

$$\|u'\| \le (\gamma')^t \sqrt{n}\det(\mathcal{L}(B))^{1/n}.$$

Assume $\mathcal{L}(D)$ is the dual lattice of $\mathcal{L}(B')$. Then $\det(\mathcal{L}(D)) \le 1/(2^{n(n+\log_2 \gamma n)} \det(\mathcal{L}(B)))$. By the LLL Algorithm [10], we can find a vector $u \in \mathcal{L}(D)$ such that

$$\|u\| < 2^n \sqrt{n}\det(\mathcal{L}(D))^{1/n} \le \sqrt{n}2^n/(2^{(n+\log_2 \gamma n)}\det(\mathcal{L}(B))^{1/n})$$
$$= 1/(\gamma\sqrt{n}\det(\mathcal{L}(B))^{1/n}).$$

By Cauchy–Schwarz inequality, we have

$$|\langle u', u\rangle| \le \|u'\| \cdot \|u\| < (\gamma')^t/\gamma \le 1.$$

Since $u' \in \mathcal{L}(B'), u \in \mathcal{L}(D)$, $\langle u', u\rangle$ is an integer, which means $\langle u', u\rangle = 0$. Hence u' lies in the sublattice of $\mathcal{L}(B')$ orthogonal to u. Denote this sublattice by $\mathcal{L}(B_1)$ and notice that its rank is $n - 1$. Therefore, we can efficiently find a lower rank sublattice $\mathcal{L}(B_1) \subseteq \mathcal{L}(B)$ such that $\lambda_1(\mathcal{L}(B_1)) \le (\gamma')^t\lambda_1(\mathcal{L}(B))$.

Finally, after repeating $n - 1$ times of the above procedures, we obtain a sublattice $\mathcal{L}(B_{n-1})$ of rank one with

$$\lambda_1(\mathcal{L}(B_{n-1})) \le (\gamma')^{(n-1)t}\lambda_1(\mathcal{L}(B)).$$

Since a lattice basis is already the shortest lattice vector in any 1-rank lattice and $(\gamma')^{(n-1)t} = \gamma$, we can find a lattice vector in $\mathcal{L}(B)$ of length $\lambda_1(\mathcal{L}(B_{n-1})) \le \gamma\lambda_1(\mathcal{L}(B))$. This completes our proof.

Remark 3. The above reduction is for l_2-norm. Using the fact that for any $v \in \mathbb{R}^n$ and any $p \ge 1$, $\|v\|_2/\sqrt{n} \le \|v\|_p \le n^{1/p}\|v\|_2$, we can generalize our reduction to the case for any l_p-norm, where $\gamma' = \gamma^{\frac{O(\log_2 n)}{n(n-1)(n+\log_2(\gamma n^{3/2+1/p}))}}$.

5   Our Reduction from Search CVP$_\gamma$ to Optimization CVP$_{\gamma'}$

In this section, we present our reduction from Search CVP$_\gamma$ to Optimization CVP$_{\gamma'}$ where $\gamma' = \gamma^{\frac{1}{n\lceil n/2+\log_2 \gamma \cdot \mathrm{dist}(t,\mathcal{L}(B))\rceil}}$. We have to point out that the relationship between two approximate factors γ and γ' is still waiting to be improved.

Theorem 3. *For any $\gamma' \ge 1$ and $n \ge 4$, Search CVP$_\gamma$ can be solved in polynomial time given an oracle solving Optimization CVP$_{\gamma'}$ where $\gamma' = \gamma^{\frac{1}{n\lceil n/2+\log_2 \gamma \cdot \mathrm{dist}(t,\mathcal{L}(B))\rceil}}$.*

Proof. Given the input lattice basis $B = (b_1, b_2, \ldots, b_n) \in \mathbb{Z}^{m \times n}$ and a target $t \in \mathbb{Q}^n$, we call the Optimization $\text{CVP}_{\gamma'}$ oracle to obtain an interval $[r, \gamma' \cdot r)$ containing $\text{dist}(t, \mathcal{L}(B)) \triangleq d$. Our goal is to find a $v \in \mathcal{L}(B)$ s.t. $\|v - t\| \le \gamma \cdot \text{dist}(t, \mathcal{L}(B))$.

Firstly, a sequence of instance $(B_i, t_i)(i = 0, 1, \ldots, k$, where $k = \lceil n/2 + \log_2 \gamma \cdot d \rceil)$ is constructed in the following way.

Let $B_0 = B$, $t_0 = t$ and $B_i = (2^i b_1, b_2, \ldots, b_n)$. We want to construct t_{i+1} from t_i, B_i and B_{i+1}. Given (B_i, t_i), we call the Optimization $\text{CVP}_{\gamma'}$ oracle on the three inputs (B_i, t_i), (B_{i+1}, t_i) and $(B_{i+1}, t_i - 2^i b_1)$ to get three interval $I_0 = [r_0, \gamma \cdot r_0)$, $I_1 = [r_1, \gamma \cdot r_1)$ and $I_2 = [r_2, \gamma \cdot r_2)$ containing $\text{dist}(t_i, \mathcal{L}(B_i)) \triangleq d_0$, $\text{dist}(t_i, \mathcal{L}(B_{i+1})) \triangleq d_1$ and $\text{dist}(t_i - 2^i b_1, \mathcal{L}(B_{i+1})) \triangleq d_2$ respectively. Notice that

$$\mathcal{L}(B_i) = \mathcal{L}(B_{i+1}) \cup (\mathcal{L}(B_{i+1}) + 2^i b_1),$$

meaning $d_1 = d_0$ or $d_2 = d_0$. So I_0 must intersect at least one of I_1 and I_2. Similar to that in the proof of Theorem 2, let I_{i_0} be the interval having the smallest left endpoint in these I_i's that intersect I_0. Then we set t_{i+1}:

$$t_{i+1} = \begin{cases} t_i & (i_0 = 1) \\ t_i - 2^i b_1 & (i_0 = 2). \end{cases} \tag{1}$$

We can also prove that

$$\text{dist}(t_{i+1}, \mathcal{L}(B_{i+1})) \le \gamma' \cdot \text{dist}(t_i, \mathcal{L}(B_i)).$$

Hence we can find $(B_k = (2^k b_1, b_2, \ldots b_n), t_k)$ such that $\text{dist}(t_k, \mathcal{L}(B_k)) \le (\gamma')^k \cdot \text{dist}(t, \mathcal{L}(B))$.

Secondly, by repeating this procedure for other lattice basis vector $b_2, \ldots, b_n$, we obtain $(B_{nk} = (2^k b_1, 2^k b_2, \ldots, 2^k b_n), t_{nk})$ s.t.

$$\text{dist}(t_{nk}, \mathcal{L}(B_{nk})) \le (\gamma')^{nk} \cdot \text{dist}(t, \mathcal{L}(B)) = \gamma \cdot \text{dist}(t, \mathcal{L}(B)) = \gamma \cdot d,$$

where t_{nk} is of the form $t + u$ ($u \in \mathcal{L}(B)$ is known). We denote $\text{dist}(t_{nk}, \mathcal{L}(B_{nk}))$ by d_{nk}.

Notice that the new lattice $\mathcal{L}(B_{nk}) = 2^k \mathcal{L}(B)$ is sparse enough with $\lambda_1(\mathcal{L}(B_{nk})) = 2^k \lambda_1(\mathcal{L}(B)) \ge 2^k \cdot 1 = 2^k$. For the choice of k,

$$\lambda_1(\mathcal{L}(B_{nk})) \ge 2^k \ge 2^{n/2} \gamma d \ge 2^{n/2} d_{nk}.$$

By Babai's Nearest Plane Algorithm [4] on input (B_{nk}, t_{nk}), we can find a lattice vector $v \in \mathcal{L}(B_{nk})$ s.t. $\|v - t_{nk}\| \le 2^{\frac{n-1}{2}} \cdot d_{nk}$. We claim that v is the lattice vector closest to t_{nk} in $\mathcal{L}(B_{nk})$. Let v' be the lattice vector closest to t_{nk} in $\mathcal{L}(B_{nk})$, then $\|v' - t_{nk}\| = d_{nk}$. We will show $v = v'$. For any $w \ne v' \in \mathcal{L}(B_{nk})$, we have

$$\|w - t_{nk}\| \ge \|w - v'\| - \|v' - t_{nk}\| \ge \lambda_1(\mathcal{L}(B_{nk})) - d_{nk} \ge 2^{n/2} d_{nk} - d_{nk} > 2^{\frac{n-1}{2}} d_{nk},$$

where the last inequality comes from $n \geq 4$. Together with $\|v - t_{nk}\| \leq 2^{\frac{n-1}{2}} \cdot d_{nk}$, we have v is actually the lattice vector closest to t_{nk} in $\mathcal{L}(B_{nk})$. Thus we have

$$\|v - t_{nk}\| = \text{dist}(t_{nk}, \mathcal{L}(B_{nk})) \leq \gamma \cdot \text{dist}(t, \mathcal{L}(B)).$$

Finally, as v is in $\mathcal{L}(B)$, we subtract the known u from v to get our Search CVP$_\gamma$ solution $v - u$.

Remark 4. The above reduction can also be generalized to the case for any l_p-norm, where $\gamma' = \gamma^{\frac{1}{n\lceil n/2 + \log_2 \gamma n^{1/p} \cdot \text{dist}(t, \mathcal{L}(B)) \rceil}}$.

6 Conclusions

In this paper, we give a new reduction from Search SVP to Optimization SVP with only one call, which is the least, to the Optimization SVP oracle. A similar result for CVP also holds. When it goes to approximate version, inspired by the idea in [9], we get an improved result on reduction from Search SVP$_\gamma$ to Optimization SVP$_{\gamma'}$ and a reduction from Search CVP$_\gamma$ to Optimization CVP$_{\gamma'}$.

Acknowledgements. We thank the anonymous referees for their suggestions on how to improve the presentation of this paper.

References

1. Ajtai, M.: Generating hard instances of lattice problems. In: Annual Symposium on the theory of Computing (STOC), pp. 99–108. ACM Press, New York (1996)
2. Ajtai, M., Dwork, C.: A public-key cryptosystem with worst-case/average-case equivalence. In: Annual Symposium on the theory of Computing (STOC) (1997) (An improved version is described in ECCC 2007)
3. Ajtai, M.: The shortest vector problem in L2 is NP-hard for randomized reductions (extended abstract). In: Proceedings of the 30th Annual ACM Symposium on Theory of Computing, pp. 266–275 (1998)
4. Babai, L.: On Lovasz' lattice reduction and the nearest lattice point problem. Combinatorica **6**(1), 1–13 (1986)
5. Gentry, C.: Fully homomorphic encryption using ideal lattices. In: Proceedings of the 41st Annual ACM Symposium on Theory of Computing (STOC09), New York, pp. 169–178 (2009)
6. Gentry, C., Peikert, C., Vaikuntanathan, V.: Trapdoors for hard lattices and new cryptographic constructions. In: Annual Symposium on the theory of Computing (STOC), pp. 197–206 (2008)
7. Hoffstein, J., Pipher, J., Silverman, J.H.: NTRU: a ring-based public key cryptosystem. In: Buhler, J.P. (ed.) ANTS 1998. LNCS, vol. 1423, pp. 267–288. Springer, Heidelberg (1998)
8. Hoffstein, J., Howgrave-Graham, N., Pipher, J., Silverman, J.H., Whyte, W.: NTRUSIGN: Digital signatures using the NTRU lattice. In: Joye, M. (ed.) CT-RSA 2003. LNCS, vol. 2612, pp. 122–140. Springer, Heidelberg (2003)

9. Cheng K.: Some complexity results and bit unpredictable for short vector problem. https://eprint.iacr.org/2013/052.pdf
10. Lenstra, A.K., Lenstra Jr, H.W., Lovasz, L.: Factoring polynomials with rational coefficients. Math. Ann. **261**, 513–534 (1982)
11. Kannan, R.: Minkowski's convex body theorem and integer programming. Math. Oper. Res. **12**(3), 415–440 (1987)
12. Lyubashevsky, V., Micciancio, D.: Generalized compact knapsacks are collision resistant. In: Bugliesi, M., Preneel, B., Sassone, V., Wegener, I. (eds.) ICALP 2006. LNCS, vol. 4052, pp. 144–155. Springer, Heidelberg (2006)
13. Lyubashevsky, V., Micciancio, D.: On bounded distance decoding, unique shortest vectors, and the minimum distance problem. In: Halevi, S. (ed.) CRYPTO 2009. LNCS, vol. 5677, pp. 577–594. Springer, Heidelberg (2009)
14. Lyubashevsky, V., Micciancio, D., Peikert, C., Rosen, A.: Swifft: A modest proposal for fft hashing. Fast Software Encryption (FSE) 2008. LNCS, vol. 5086, pp. 54–72. Springer, Heidelberg (2008)
15. Micciancio, D., Goldwasser, S.: Complexity of Lattice Problems: A Cryptography Perspective. Kluwer Academic Publishers, Boston (2002)
16. Peikert, C., Rosen, A.: Efficient collision-resistant hashing from worst-case assumptions on cyclic lattices. In: Halevi, S., Rabin, T. (eds.) TCC 2006. LNCS, vol. 3876, pp. 145–156. Springer, Heidelberg (2006)
17. Regev, O.: Lattices in computer science. Lecture notes of a course given in Tel Aviv University (2004)
18. Regev, O.: On lattices, learning with errors, random linear codes, and cryptography. In: Annual Symposium on Theory of Computing (STOC) (2005)

A General Method to Evaluate the Correlation of Randomness Tests

Limin Fan[✉], Hua Chen, and Si Gao

Trusted Computing and Information Assurance Laboratory, Institute of Software,
Chinese Academy of Sciences, 100190 Beijing, China
{fanlimin,chenhua,Gaosi}@tca.iscas.ac.cn

Abstract. This paper discusses the correlation of the randomness tests. In this paper, we propose a new general method to evaluate the correlation of randomness tests. Firstly, we deduce the distribution that independent randomness tests should obey, then evaluate whether the randomness tests are independent or not based on hypothesis test. Using this method, we research the correlation of some statistical tests included in the NIST SP 800-22 suits, which is a collection of tests for the evaluation of both true random and pseudorandom number generators for cryptographic applications. Our experiment results show that some correlations of dependent exist among the randomness tests, which is different from the declaration that the randomness tests are independent by NIST. Moreover, the method we proposed also can be used in the study of parameter selection in randomness tests.

Keywords: Statistical test · Correlation of randomness tests · Hypothesis test · NIST SP 800-22

1 Introduction

Random numbers play an important role in many cryptographic applications such as key generation, authentication protocols, digital signature schemes, zero-knowledge protocols, etc. Using weak random numbers may result in an adversary ability to break the cryptosystem. The word "random" can be defined as the result of the flips of an unbiased "fair" coin [1] with sides that are labeled by "0" or "1". The flips are independent of each other and each flip has a probability of exactly 1/2 of producing a "0" or "1". All elements of the sequence are generated independently of each other regardless of the number of elements produced. Obviously, the use of unbiased coins for cryptographic purposes is impractical. But the unbiased coins can serve as a benchmark for the evaluation of true random number generators (TRNGs) and pseudorandom number generators (PRNGs), which are two basic types of generators used to produce random number sequence in practical application.

The best way to generate unpredictable random numbers is to use physical processes. But generating random numbers by physical processes often is

Y. Kim et al. (Eds.): WISA 2013, LNCS 8267, pp. 52–62, 2014.
DOI: 10.1007/978-3-319-05149-9_4, © Springer International Publishing Switzerland 2014

inefficient. So, most systems use PRNGs based on deterministic algorithms. Desired properties of PRNGs are [2]:

(i) good randomness properties of the output sequence;
(ii) reproducibility;
(iii) speed or efficiency;
(iv) large period.

A theoretical proof for the randomness of a generator is hard to give, so statistical inference based on observed sample sequences produced by the generator seems to be a good option. Considering the properties of binary random sequences, various statistical tests can be designed to evaluate the assertion that the sequence is generated by a perfectly random source. Statistical test is a classical approach to evaluate the random number generator through testing whether an experimental set of data, output of the generator, fits with a given hypothesis. The famous statistical test suites for randomness are NIST (National Institute of Standards and Technology, America) test suite [3] (also noted as NIST SP 800-22), The BSI (Bundesamt fr Sicherheit in der Informationstechnik) test suite [4,5], Marsaglia's DIEHARD test suite [6], Crypt-X statistical test suite [7] and so on. Each test suite defines a collection of randomness test algorithms to evaluate randomness of generators extensively. Among them, the NIST SP 800-22 is one of the best known statistical test suite. There are many research results about this test suite [8–10] and the latest version of the suite consists of fifteen randomness tests.

To have more confidence in the randomness of generators, coverage of test suite should be as high as possible. On the other hand, as Soto stated in [3], to achieve reliable results, the statistical tests in a suite should be independent. There are some research results on independency of randomness test report that there exist some dependency relation between the randomness tests. In [11], the relation between approximate entropy, overlapping serial and universal test is analyzed and highly correlated results are obtained using defective sources. In [2] the concept of sensitivity is defined, and frequency, overlapping template, longest run of ones, random walk height and maximum order complexity tests are correlated for short sequences. Reference [12] gives the relation between autocorrelation and binary derivation test, the result shows that autocorrelation test is equal with binary derivation test in some specific parameters. Most of the research achievements at present are aimed at the specific randomness test, and the efficient and general method to evaluate the dependence between the randomness test is still seldom.

In this paper, we propose a new general method to evaluate the relation between randomness test. We deduce the distribution that two independent randomness test should obey firstly, and then give a test algorithm to judge the relation between randomness test based on hypothesis test. Using this method, we research the correlation of some statistical tests. The experiment results show that there are some correlations of dependent among the randomness tests used in NIST test suite, which is different from the declaration that all the randomness tests of SP 800-22 are independent by NIST.

The organization of this paper is as follows. In Sect. 2, basic background information about randomness tests is presented. In Sect. 3, a general method to evaluate the relation between randomness test is proposed. In Sect. 4, we give some experiment results. In the last section, we give some concluding remarks and possible future work directions.

2   Randomness Test

Randomness test is a classical approach used to evaluate whether an experimental set of data fits with given hypothesis (the null hypothesis, usually indicated with H_0). For each test, a relevant randomness statistic must be chosen and used to determine the acceptance or rejection of the null hypothesis. Under an assumption of randomness, such a statistic has a distribution of possible values.

The basic procedure of a randomness test can be described as following:

(i) Firstly, giving a null hypothesis and an alternative hypothesis,

Null hypothesis H_0: the statistics of sequence follow the reference distribution.

And the alternative hypothesis H_α: otherwise, the statistics of sequence doesn't follow the reference distribution.

(ii) Secondly, a test statistic value is computed on the sequence being tested.

(iii) Finally, compare the test statistic value and the critical value, which is computed differently based on the null hypothesis. If the random assumption is true, the test statistic value will have a very low probability of exceeding the critical value. In the other words, if the test statistic value exceeds the critical value, the null hypothesis for randomness is rejected.

There are several methods to compare the test statistic value and critical value. The most popular method is $p-value$ method. $P-value$ is the probability that a perfect random number generator would have produced a sequence less random than the tested sequence. If a $p-value$ for a test is determined to be equal to 1, then the sequence appears to have perfect randomness. A $p-value$ of zero indicates that the sequence is completely non-random. A significance level α can be chosen for the test. If $p-value >= \alpha$, then the null hypothesis is accepted. If $p-value < \alpha$, then the null hypothesis is rejected. The significance level usually is a very small real number, for example, α is 0.01 or α is 0.001.

In practical test, a set of data will be tested and a set of $p-values$ will be achieved. There are many ways to interpret the empirical results. For the interpretation of empirical results, NIST adopts two evaluation approaches:

(i) proportion of sequence passing.

Given the empirical results for a particular statistical test, compute the proportion of sequences that passing the test. The range of acceptable proportions is determined using the confidence interval defined as

$$(1 - \alpha) - 3\sqrt{\alpha(1 - \alpha)/m} \tag{1}$$

Here, α is the significance level, and m is the sample size.

(ii) uniform distribution of $p - values$.

Besides, the distribution of $p - values$ is examined to ensure uniformity. The interval between 0 and 1 is divided into ten sub-intervals, and the $p - values$ in each sub-interval maybe approximately same. Uniformity may be determined via an application of a test and the determination of a $p-value$ corresponding to the Goodness-of-Fit distribution test on the $p - value$ obtained for an arbitrary statistical test (that is a $p - value$ of $p - values$).

Our research in this paper is related to the two evaluation approaches.

3   A General Method to Evaluate the Relation Between Randomness Tests

In this section, firstly, we deduce the distribution of the $p - values$ difference if two randomness tests are independent. And then propose a general algorithm to test the relation of randomness tests.

3.1   The $p - value$ Distribution of Two Independent Randomness Tests

When a sequence is tested by two different statistical tests, the results of them will not influence each other if the statistical tests are independent. We denote the two different randomness tests as TX and TY. The distribution of $p - values$ for random data set tested by TX is X, which probability density is $f(x)$. The distribution of $p - values$ for random data set tested by TY is Y, which probability density is $f(y)$.

Next, we deduce the distribution of $Z = X - Y$ when TX and TY are independent.

For random sequences, the distribution X of TX will follow the uniform distribution of real number between 0 and 1. So, the probability density $f(x)$ of X is formula (2)

$$f(x) = \begin{cases} 0, & x < 0 \\ 1, & 0 \le x \le 1 \\ 0, & x > 1 \end{cases} \qquad (2)$$

Similarly, the probability density $f(y)$ of Y is formula (3)

$$f(y) = \begin{cases} 0, & y < 0 \\ 1, & 0 \le y \le 1 \\ 0, & y > 1 \end{cases} \qquad (3)$$

The probability density $f(w)$ of $W = -Y$ will follow formula (4)

$$f(w) = \begin{cases} 0, & w > 0 \\ 1, & -1 \le w \le 0 \\ 0, & w < -1 \end{cases} \qquad (4)$$

The distribution of $p - values$ of randomness tests would be independent if TX is independent with TY. That means random variables X and Y are independent. And because W is linear with Y, So random variables X and W are independent too. The probability density of the random variable $Z = X - Y = X + W$ is formula (5)

$$f(z) = f_X * f_W = \int_{-\infty}^{\infty} f_X(x) * f_W(z - x)dx \tag{5}$$

Using the formulas (2) and (4), we can achieve formula (6) from (5):

$$f(z) = \begin{cases} 0, & z < -1 \\ z + 1, & -1 \leq z \leq 0 \\ -z + 1, & 0 \leq z \leq 1 \\ 0, & z > 1 \end{cases} \tag{6}$$

The derivation procedure above shows that, if the randomness test TX and TY are independent, the distribution of difference of $p - values$ for the two randomness test should follow the distribution with probability density $f(z)$. The distribution function noted as $F(z)$. Then we can judge whether any two randomness tests are independent or not based on hypothesis test. Next sub-section we should introduce the algorithm based on hypothesis test in details.

3.2   The Algorithm for Testing the Relation of Randomness Tests

Based on the derivation result of above sub-section, we propose a new hypothesis testing method to test whether two randomness tests are independent or not.

First, we construct the null hypothesis as follows:

H_0 : the distribution of difference of $p - values$ conforms to the distribution function $F(z)$;

Accordingly, the alterative hypothesis is:

H_α : the distribution of difference of $p - values$ does not conform to the distribution function $F(z)$.

Because every $p - value$ is a real number between 0 and 1, so the difference of two $p - values$ is a real number between -1 and 1. The interval between -1 and 1 is divided into k sub-intervals, then the ith sub-interval is formula (7),

$$\begin{cases} \left[-1 + \frac{2*(k-1)}{k}, -1 + \frac{-1+2*i}{k} \right], i = 1 \\ \left(-1 + \frac{2*(k-1)}{k}, -1 + \frac{-1+2*k}{k} \right], 1 < i \leq k \end{cases} \tag{7}$$

The probability of difference of $p - value$ falling in the ith sub-interval is formula (8)

$$P_i = \int_{-1+\frac{2*(i-1)}{k}}^{1+\frac{2*i}{k}} f(z)dz \tag{8}$$

There are S samples, the number of them falling in ith sub-interval is S_i, we construct the statistic value as formula (9)

$$V = \sum_{i=1}^{t} \frac{(S_i - S * P_i)^2}{S * P_i} \tag{9}$$

If the null hypothesis is true, the value of V would be very small. The distribution of V should follow chi-square distribution with freedom $k - 1$ according to Pearson chi-squared test. That is V follows χ^2 distribution with freedom $k - 1$.

Next, we give the pseudo-code of the test algorithm. Our algorithm is divided into two parts listed as $CT - single$ and $CT - total$.

$CT - single$:

$Input$:

$seq_n[]$: the sequence with length of n bits, and the number of sequences is S;

TX, TY: Two randomness tests to be tested whether they are independent;

α_T : Significance level;

K : The interval between -1 and 1 is divided into K sub-intervals.

$Output$:

If the result is 1 then TX and TY is independent for this test.

CT-single: Single-Sample-Test($TX, TY, seq_n[], S, \alpha_T, K$)

Step1. for the ith $(0 < i < S)$sequence in $seq_n[]$ do:

    step1.1. test the sequence using TX ;

        $PvalueX[i] := TX(Seq_n[i])$;

    step1.2. test the sequence using TY ;

        $PvalueY[i] := TY(Seq_n[i])$

    step1.3. Compute the distance of pvalue;

        $\Delta P = PvalueX[i] - PvalueY[i]$;

    step1.4. if $-1 \leq \Delta P \leq -1 + 2/K$ then $S_1 + +$

        else if $-1 + 2(i-1)/K < \Delta P \leq -1 + 2i/K$

        then $S_i + +$

step2. compute $V = \sum_{i=1}^{K} \frac{(S_i - S*P_i)^2}{S*P_i}$;

step3. compute $P_T = Igamc((k-1)/2, V/2)$;

        Here Igamc is incomplete Gamma function used to compute $p - value$

step4. if $P_T > \alpha_T$ then return 1;

    else return 0.

Accepting the null assumption H_0 or not is a probability incident because the test is a hypothesis statistical test. In other words, the $CT - single$ is a probability method. We reduced the error by multiple tests. And using the percentage of passing to evaluate whether the randomness tests are independent or not. We repeat t times $CT - single$ in order to reduce the error rate.

$CT - total$:

$Input$:

$seq_n[]$: the sequence with length of n,and the number of sequences is $S * t$;

TX, TY: Two randomness test to be tested whether they are independent;
α_T : Significance level;
K : The interval between -1 and 1 is divided into K sub-intervals;
t : repeat the $CT - single$ t times;
Output :
Percentage of the success of $CT - single$.

CT-total: Independence-Statistics-Test($TX, TY, seq_n[], S, \alpha_T, K, t$)

Step1. Set passnum=0;
Step2. For $i = 1$ to t do
　　Apply CT-single ($TX, TY, seq_n[], S, \alpha_T, K$);
　　here, the sequences $seq_n[]$ are from $(i - 1) * S$ to $i * S$;
　　If the result of CT-single is 1 then $passnum + +$;
Step3. Compute the success percentage $sucper$
　　　　　$sucper = 100 * passnum/t$;
Step4. return $sucper$.

3.3 Algorithm Complexity Analysis

In this subsection, we analysis the complexity of our method.

For CT-single algorithm, in *Step1* TX and TY are called S times respectively. Here, TX and TY are different randomness test algorithms. In *Step3*, the incomplete Gamma function $Igamc$ is called one time. The total execution time is the summation of S times TX, S times TY, one time $Igmac$ function and S times real number subtraction and integer addition. So the execution time is related with the specific randomness test algorithm TX and TY. We denote C_a and C_b as the complexity of TX and TY, So the the complexity of CT-single is approximately O(S*max[C_a, C_b]).

CT-total algorithm is implemented by multiple(t times) calling CT-single. So the complexity of our method is O(S*t*max[C_a, C_b]).

4 Correlation Analysis on the NIST SP 800-22

In this section, we study the relations among some randomness tests included in NIST test suite using the proposed method in above section.

4.1 Experiment Procedure

The randomness test items studied are listed in Table 1.

Here, the interval from -1 to 1 is divided into 10 sub-intervals. And the probability of each sub-interval listed in Table 2 can be computed by formula (8).

Our experiment procedure can be described as follows:

Table 1. The ID of randomness test in our experiment

Randomness test	Test id	Randomness test	Test id
Monobit	1	Universal statistical	7
Block frequency	2	Approximate entropy	8
Cusum	3	Serial	9
Runs	4	Linear complexity	10
Long runs of ones	5	Spectral DFT	11
Rank	6		

Table 2. The probability of each sub-interval

Subinterval	[-1,-0.8)	[-0.8,-0.6)	[-0.6,-0.4)	[-0.4,-0.2)
Probability	0.02	0.06	0.1	0.14
Subinterval	[-0.2,0)	[0,0.2)	[0.2,0.4)	([0.4,0.6)
Probability	0.18	0.18	0.14	0.1
Subinterval	[0.6,0.8)	[0.8,1.0]		
Probability	0.06	0.02		

(a) Producing a set of data as samples using random number generators. Noted that, the base of our method is that the data source is perfect random sequences. In this section, we choose some well-known good pseudorandom number generators such as G-DES, G-BBS, G-ANSI and G-SHA-1. In our experiment, we generate 100 sets of data by each randomness generator. Each set include 300 binary sequences and the length of each sequence is 1,000,000 bits.

(b) For any two different randomness tests TX and TY listed in Table 2, the relations are computed by $CT - single$ and $CT - total$. For each data source of each random number generator, do (b.1) and (b.2)

(b.1) For each set of 300 binary sequences, compute the result of $CT - single$, if the result is 1, then TX and TY is independent in this test.

(b.2) Repeat (b.1) 100 times and computer the success percentage using $CT - total$;

(c) Record the percentage result to form the relations of randomness test.

4.2   Correlation Analysis

From the experiment results we find that the dependency relation of randomness test is not relate to the different random number generators. And we find that there are some dependency between the randomness tests used in NIST SP 800-22. Here, we only give the results of G-BBS as a representative in this section taking into account too many results and limited space. Table 3 is the experiment result by random number generator G-BBS.

Table 3. Pass rate of independent test by sequences from G-BBS

test item ID	1	2	3	4	5	6	7	8	9	10	11
1	0	100	0	100	100	100	100	0	100	100	100
2	100	0	100	100	100	100	100	100	100	100	99
3	0	100	0	100	100	100	99	31	100	100	100
4	100	100	100	0	97	100	99	37	46	97	99
5	100	100	100	97	0	100	100	100	100	99	100
6	100	100	100	100	100	0	99	100	100	100	99
7	100	100	99	99	100	99	0	100	99	100	100
8	0	100	31	37	100	100	100	0	1	100	100
9	100	100	100	46	100	100	99	1	0	100	100
10	100	100	100	97	99	100	100	100	100	0	100
11	100	99	100	99	100	99	100	100	100	100	0

Table 4. Test result of the dependent randomness tests

Randomness test	related randomness test
Monobit	cusum, approximate entropy
Runs	approximate entropy,serial
Approximate entropy	monobit, cusum, runs, serial
Serial	runs, approximate entropy

Table 3 shows that there are some related randomness test marked by gray column. For example, momobit test is not independent with cusum test and approximate entropy test. Serial test is dependent with several randomness tests, which are monobit test, cusum test, autocorrelation test and runs test, etc. The dependent randomness test listed in Table 4.

Next, we analysis the experiment results in details.

The interval [-1,1] is divided into 10 sub-intervals equally. In each test, we record the number of sequences falling into each sub-interval and the number of total sequence is 300. The result of each test form a line and the 100 lines is the result of Fig. 1. The expected number of sequences falling into each sub-interval should be 6, 18, 30, 42, 54, 54, 42, 30, 18, 6 individually by tabled 2. But the experiments result deviated the expected number severely. For example in the eighth, ninth and tenth sub-internals the experiment result almost are 0. And in the sixth sub-interval the expected number should be 54. But the experiment result in each time almost than 100. So, there are some relations between the p-values of monobit test and cusum test and we can give the conclusion that the two randomness tests are not independent with each other. The Fig. 2 shows the similar result of the dependency between monobit test and entropy test.

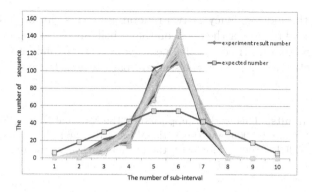

Fig. 1. Experiment result of monobit test and cusum test

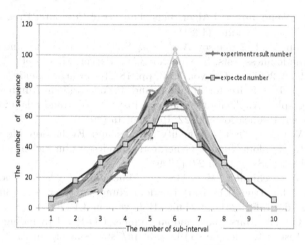

Fig. 2. Experiment result of monobit test and approximation entropy test

5 Conclusion

There are many randomness tests at present and how to choose a proper randomness test set in practical is a practical question. There are some research about the independence of randomness test. Most of the research achievements are aimed at the specific randomness test, and there are still not a very powerful general method that can be used to evaluate the dependence between the randomness test. In this paper, we propose a new general method to evaluate the relation between randomness tests. Firstly, we deduce the distribution that two independent randomness test should obey, then we give a test algorithm to judge the relation between randomness test based on hypothesis test. Using this method, we find some dependency in the randomness tests used in NIST test suite, which is different from the declaration that the randomness tests are independent by NIST.

Although the independency of two randomness tests can be judged by our method, it is hard to answer the question that which one is more powerful, which is the main problem we tried to solve next. Moreover, the method we proposed in this paper also can be used in the study of parameter selection in randomness test.

Acknowledgements. This work is supported by the National Natural Science Foundation of China (No.91118006) and the National Basic Research Program of China (973 Program, No.2013CB338002). Moreover, the authors are very grateful to the anonymous referees for their comments and editorial suggestions.

References

1. Knuth, D.E.: Seminumerical Algorithms. The Art of Computer Programming, vol. 2. Addison-Wesley, Reading (1981)
2. Sönmez Turan, M., Doğanaksoy, A., Boztaş, S.: On independence and sensitivity of statistical randomness tests. In: Golomb, S.W., Parker, M.G., Pott, A., Winterhof, A. (eds.) SETA 2008. LNCS, vol. 5203, pp. 18–29. Springer, Heidelberg (2008)
3. A Statistical Test Suite for Random and Pseudorandom Number Generators for Cryptographic Applications, National Institute of Standards and Technology (NIST) Special Publication 800–22, Revision 1a (2010)
4. Schindler, W.: AIS 20: Functionality Classes and Evaluation Methodology for Deterministic Random Number Generators, Bundesamt fur Sicherheit in der Informationstechnik (BSI) version 2.0 (1999)
5. Killmann, W., Schindler, W.: AIS 31: Functionality Classes and Evaluation Methodology for True (Physical) Random Number Generators, Bundesamt fur Sicherheit in der Informationstechnik (BSI) version 3.1 (2001)
6. Marsaglia, G.: The Marsaglia Random Number CD-ROM Including the DieHard Battery of Test of Randomness (1995). http://stat.fsu.edu/pub/diehard/
7. Caelli, W., Dawson, E., Nielsen, L., Gustafson, H.: CRYPTCX Statistical Package Manual, Measuring the Strength of Stream and Block ciphers (1992)
8. Hamano, K., Satoh, F., Ishikawa, M.: Randomness test using discrete Fourier transform, Technical Report 6841. Technical Research and Development Institute, Japan Defense Agency (2003)
9. Hamano, K.: The distribution of the spectrum for the discrete Fourier transform test included in SP800-22. IEICE Trans. Fundam. **E88–A**(1), 67–73 (2005)
10. Hamano, K.: Correction of overlapping template matching test included in NIST randomness test suite. ICICE Trans. Fundam. **E90–A**(9), 1788–1792 (2007)
11. Hellekalek, P., Wegenkittl, S.: Empirical evidence concerning AES. ACM Trans. Model. Comput. Simul. (TOMACS) **13**(04), 322–333 (2003)
12. Fan, L., Feng, D., Chen, H.: On the relativity of binary derivation and autocorrelation randomness test. J. Comput. Res. Dev. **45**(6), 956–961 (2009)

Social Network Security

Improving Social Network-Based Sybil Defenses by Rewiring and Augmenting Social Graphs

Aziz Mohaisen$^{(\boxtimes)}$ and Scott Hollenbeck

Verisign Labs, Reston, VA 20190, USA
amohaisen@verisign.com

Abstract. Recent solutions to defend against the Sybil attack, in which a node generates multiple identities, using social networks. In these solutions, social networks are assumed to be fast mixing, and Sybil nodes—which disrupt the fast mixing property of social networks—are detected. Little is known about the cause of the mixing quality in social graphs, and how to improve it in slow mixing ones. In this work we relate the mixing time of social graphs to graph degeneracy, which captures cohesiveness of the graph. We experimentally show that fast-mixing graphs tend to have a larger single core whereas slow-mixing graphs tend to have smaller multiple cores. We then propose several heuristics to improve the mixing of slow-mixing graphs using their topological structures by augmenting them. We show that our heuristics greatly improve Sybil defenses.

Keywords: Sybil attacks and defenses · Social networks · Mixing time

1 Introduction

The Sybil attack is a very challenging security threat in distributed systems. In this attack, a single malicious node claims multiple identities with the intention of disrupting the normal operation of the distributed system by acting as if she is multiple nodes [6]. To defend against this attack, there are two schools of thoughts: centralized [3,4,6,30] and decentralized solutions [13,24,28,29]. In the centralized solutions, a centralized authority is used to provide digital credentials, such as cryptographic keys, and to bind them to the identity of participating nodes in the system. These credentials are then used to hold nodes accountable to their actions. While effective, those solutions are expensive: (1) they require an online authority that is hard to bring in distributed systems, (2) the authority would rely on privacy-sensitive information, like an identification number, physical address, and the like, and that would scare users away from using the system, (3) the existence of the centralized authority is very challenging to the scalability and security of the distributed system in general; an adversary would target that authority with attacks making it a potential bottleneck. Accordingly, centralized solutions are impractical in largely distributed systems.

Y. Kim et al. (Eds.): WISA 2013, LNCS 8267, pp. 65–80, 2014.
DOI: 10.1007/978-3-319-05149-9_5, © Springer International Publishing Switzerland 2014

Decentralized solutions replace the centralized authority with decentralized mechanisms. Nodes in distributed systems oftentimes have physical resources that are limited in nature, such as processing capabilities, memory, addresses, and geographical location, and these can be verified by other nodes in the distributed system to establish the identity of that node. Solutions that rely on those credentials overcome several of the shortcomings of the decentralized solutions: no single point of failure, and (mostly) no privacy concerns associated with the solution. However, these solutions work effectively on the premise that the adversary has a user-level resources: a powerful adversary can easily surpass such assumptions and gain control over more resources, thus bypassing the detection mechanism and introducing more Sybil identities in the system.

Recent solutions to the problem use social networks and their fabric of trust [4,10,15,17,28,29]. In such solutions, nodes are limited by their resources; the number of edges they create with others. To make such identities well enmeshed into the social graph, the adversary needs to create many edges between himself and the rest of the social graph, collectively representing honest users, which is associated with a high cost. Informally, many social network-based designs to defend against the Sybil attack rely on the mixing characteristics of social graphs for their operation. These designs assume that social networks are fast mixing, meaning that a short random walk from any node in the graph after a small number of steps will end up on a node that is randomly selected from the entire graph. The introduction of large number of Sybil identities hidden behind a few nodes that are connected by a few edges with the rest of the graph would violate this property: the honest and dishonest parts of the graphs are slow mixing. More formally, the prior literature on defending against the Sybil attack makes the assumption that a random walk of $O(\log n)$ steps, where n is the number of nodes in the social graph, is enough to obtain a sample that is driven from a distribution close to the stationary distribution of the random walk. The theoretical guarantees of Sybil defenses and their practicality rely greatly on such parameters: the number of tolerable Sybil identities per an attack edge, an edge connects an honest node with a malicious node, is proportional to the random walk length that is considered the mixing time.

Researchers recently demonstrated that the mixing time of social graphs is slower mixing used in the literature, and showed several immediate findings [22]. First, the theoretical guarantees that make use of certain qualities of the mixing time of social graphs are inaccurate, since the property does not hold in these graphs as being assumed. Second, although the mixing time is larger than expected, Sybil defenses still work fairly reasonably on many of the graphs with the relatively large mixing time, indicating that a more relaxed property than the one used in the theoretical reasoning about the operation of Sybil defenses. Finally, different graphs have different quality of the mixing time, and in certain graphs—which are mostly the result of face-to-face interactions—the slow mixing prohibits the applicability of Sybil defenses on them [17,22].

The main intuition behind the quality of the mixing time is hypothesized to be the community structure in them: whereas face-to-face graphs have slower mixing characteristics because of their clear community structure, online social networks have faster mixing times because they are likely subject to noise and weak social ties, resulting in flat and less clear community structures. However, no prior work tested this intuition to show its validity in social networks used for building such applications. Yet more importantly, no prior work used the inherent properties of slower mixing social graphs to improve their mixing time, and make them more suitable for such applications as Sybil defenses. To this end, we set out to investigate the reasons why certain graphs are slower mixing than others. We use our findings on why certain social graphs are slower mixing to improve their mixing time, and thus improve the security of social network-based systems when operated on top of them.

▶ **Contributions.** Motivated by the lack of prior work on understanding the mixing time of social graphs, our contribution is two-fold. First, we explore understanding the mixing time of social graphs by identifying why some social graphs are fast mixing whereas others are slow mixing. We relate the quality of the mixing characteristics of social graphs to the degeneracy (coreness) of graphs: we find that whereas slow mixing graphs have multiple small cores, fast mixing graphs have a single large core. Second, we use this observation to propose several heuristics that utilize the structure of slow mixing social graphs to augment them and to improve their mixing characteristics. We show that the improvement in the mixing time affects Sybil defenses built on top of social graphs. In one particular heuristics, we are able to reduce the overhead of operating SybilLimit by more than 55 % and the security by more than 70 %.

▶ **Organization.** The rest of this paper is organized as follows. In Sect. 3, we review preliminaries used in this work; including the graph model and the formal definition of the mixing time, as long as the k-coreness, the main metric used for understanding the mixing time. In Sect. 4, we present measurements on relating the mixing time of social graphs to core structure followed by heuristics to improve the mixing time in Sect. 5. Conclusion is in Sect. 6.

2   Related Work

To the best of our knowledge, there is no prior work on understanding the mixing time, improving the mixing time of slow mixing social graphs, and studying the impact of that on the operation of Sybil defenses, except for our preliminary work in [19] which is limited to the first part. Concurrent to this work, rewiring of social graphs to improve the mixing time is proposed in [31], without identify reasons why some social graphs are slow mixing, and without considering the context of Sybil defenses for the improvement. The rest of the related work can be broadly classified into three veins: wok that investigated improving Sybil defenses, although in different ways than our approach, related work on measuring the mixing time, and work on building new Sybil defenses.

Our prior work in [17] improves the performance of Sybil defenses by accounting for trust, not the underlying honest social graphs: selection on nodes and edges in Sybil defenses are biased based on differential trust. Measuring the mixing time and testing whether assumptions widely used for building Sybil defenses are valid or not is studied in [22] and independently in [5], although findings and conclusions of both studies are at odd. Looking into building tools to measure the mixing time of directed graphs and the security implications on the operation of Sybil defenses, as well as anonymous communication systems built on top of social networks and using the mixing time, is done in [21]. Finally, mathematical tools and theoretical bounds that characterize the mixing time and are used for measuring it are proposed in [8, 25].

As pointed out in the introduction, there has been several works on the design of defenses that make use of the mixing time of social networks, some of which use it directly and require some strict quality for their theoretical guarantees to be achieved while others merely require it as a crude property to conceptually capture an identifying and distinguishing characteristic between Sybil and honest nodes. Those works include [3,4,11,16,17,22,28,29], among others—an interesting survey of such works is provided in [27]. Our findings in this paper, although test on SybilLimit, are easily extendable to other designs. Indeed, our heuristics provided in this paper do not alter the operation of SybilLimit, but rather the underlying social graph to improve its mixing characteristics. To this end, we expect that one can easily extend the results and findings on improving the operation of other Sybil defenses using the same mechanisms.

3 Preliminaries

3.1 Graph Model

Let $G = (V, E)$ be an undirected and unweighted graph over n vertices and m edges, where the set of vertices $V = \{v_1, v_2, \ldots, v_n\}$ and the set of edges $E = \{e_{ij}\}$ for every $v_i \sim v_j$ (v_i is adjacent to v_j). For G, let $P = [p_{ij}]^{n \times n}$ be a transition probability matrix s.t. $p_{ij} = 1/\deg(v_i)$ if $v_i \sim v_j$ (i.e., if $e_{ij} \in E$) and 0 otherwise. k_x denotes a fully connected graph on x vertices.

▶ **The mixing time.** Informally, the mixing time is the length of a random walk to reach a constant distance from the stationary distribution of that walk, when starting from any node in the graph. The stationary distribution is defined as a probability distribution for any node to be selected as the final node in a random walk after an infinite number of steps. For the same graph defined above, the stationary distribution is defined as $\pi = [\pi_i]^{1 \times n}$, where $\pi_i = [\deg(v_i)/2m]$ for $1 \leq i \leq n$. Formally, the mixing time is defined as

$$T(\epsilon) = \max_j \min_t \{t : ||\pi - \pi^{(j)} P^t|| < \epsilon\}, \tag{1}$$

where $\pi^{(j)}$ is the delta distribution (also known as the Kronecker delta function) concentrated on the j-th position in that vector. This is, $\pi^{(j)}$ is defined as $\pi^{(j)} = \delta[x]$ where $\delta[x] = 0$ if $x \neq j$ and 1 otherwise, and the norm $||\cdot||$ in (1) is defined as $||\pi - \pi^{(j)}|| = \frac{1}{2} \sum_{i=1}^{n} |\pi_i - \pi_i^{(j)}|$.

In the literature, two methods are used for measuring the mixing time of social graphs. The first method uses the definition in (1); given that the mixing time converges as the sample of the starting distribution increases, and because the property of interest in many social network-based Sybil defenses is the distribution over ϵ, rather than a fixed ϵ as defined for the largest t in (1), one can start from a random set of nodes and obtain different values of ϵ as t increases. The different values of ϵ can be used to measure its distribution and characterize the mixing time of social networks. On the other hand, the second method for measuring the mixing time makes use of the second largest eigenvalue of the the matrix P defined above, and only provides an upper and lower bound on the mixing time as defined in (1).

Graphs are either fast or slow mixing depending on how quickly walks on them reach the stationary distribution [22] (i.e., how large is t for a given ϵ in the model in (1)). It has been claimed that the mixing time does not relate to any of the graph structural properties, making the mixing time interesting in its own right [5]. We re-examine this claim, and find that mixing characteristics of a graph are closely related to the core structure, which captures graph cohesiveness. We show that fast mixing graphs have large *single* core, whereas slower mixing graphs have multiple small cores and use that observation to propose several herustics to improve the mixing time.

3.2   *k*-Coreness

For the undirected graph G we defined in Sect. 3.1, let k be a parameter such that $k \geq 1$. We define the graph $G_k = (V_k, E_k)$, where $V_k = \{v_k^i, \ldots, v_k^{n_k}\}$, and $E_k = \{e_{ij}\}$ for all $v_k^i \sim v_k^j \in V_k$, to be a subgraph in G such that $|V_k| = n_k$, $\min\{\deg(v_k^i)\} \geq k$ for all $v_k^i \in V_k$. The subgraph G_k is said to be a k-core of G if it satisfies the above degree condition, it is maximal in size, and it is a connected graph. By relaxing the connectivity condition, we obtain a set of cores (potentially more than one), each of which satisfies the degree condition. For such k-core, we define the normalized size as $s_k = n_k/n$. Formally, G_k consists of $t_k \geq 1$ components denoted as $\{G_k^1, G_k^2, \ldots, G_k^{t_k}\}$. We denote nodes that are in G_k^i as $v_k^{i1}, \ldots, v_k^{i|V_k^i|}$. We refer to the largest connected G_k^i as the major core and others for a given k as minor cores.

An example illustrating the definition stated above is shown in Fig. 1 of a graph over 11 nodes and 14 edges, with a lowest degree of 1 and highest degree of

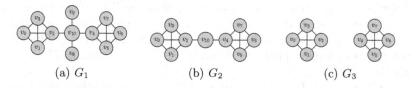

(a) G_1　　　　　　(b) G_2　　　　　　(c) G_3

Fig. 1. An illustration of the $k-$core decomposition of the graph. The original graph $G = G_1$ is shown in 1(a). Notice that G_4 is an empty graph, which results from trimming nodes in G_3, which is shown in Fig. 1(c), with degrees ≤ 3.

3, thus the k−core number of the graph is less than or equal to 3. By recursively omitting nodes in G with degree less than or equal to 1, we get G_2, shown in Fig. 1(b). Similarly, omitting nodes with degree less than or equal to 2 in Fig. 1(b) produces G_3 shown in Fig. 1(c), which consists of two components, each of which is a fully connected graph defined over 4 nodes. Given that they are equal in size, either of the components can be considered as the major component, and the other is considered as the minor component. Given that the highest degree in G_3 is 3 as well, the original graph has a maximum k of 3, and this dissolves entirely when omitting nodes with degree less than or equal to 3. Computing the k-cores of a graph for any k is done efficiently using off-the-shelf algorithms. An efficient algorithm for decomposing a simple graph on m edges and n nodes to its k−cores by iteratively pruning nodes with degree less than k has the complexity of $O(m)$ [2]. To this end, the overall complexity of running algorithms described in the rest of this paper is linear in both the maximum k value and the number of edges in the graph G. Finally, notice that the definition of k-core [14] is related to k-coloring [7], and thus can be naturally connected to the connectivity of the graph.

4   Measurements and Results

▶ **Datasets.** We use the datasets in Table 1 in our measurements. All of these datasets are widely used as benchmarking graphs in the literature [3,12,18,19, 21]. The datasets DBLP, Physics 1, and Physics 2 are scientific collaboration graphs, and can be considered of the same type, while Slashdot is a blog following graph, and Wiki-vote is wikipedia's admin voting graph. In DBLP, nodes represent authors while edges indicate that two authors have a co-authored paper among them. The Slashdot dataset consists of users and as nodes and an edge between two nodes indicates that the first node follows an article by the second node (we omit directions as below). Finally, Wiki-vote is the wikipedia administrators voting dataset in which the first node has voted for the promotion of the second node to become an administrator. Some of these datasets are directed (i.e., Slashdot and Wiki-vote), so we follow the literature [3,12] and convert the directed graphs to undirected ones, by considering an edge between two nodes in the undirected graph if it exists in either direction in the directed one.

▶ **Measuring the mixing time.** We use the definition in (1) to compute ϵ for a varying t when starting walks from different nodes in the graph. For feasibility, we sample the initial distributions of the walks: we start from 1000 uniformly distributed nodes in each graph and compute the mixing time as per the definition in (1) and the average ϵ for each walk length. The mixing characteristics of these graphs are shown in Fig. 2—maximum in Fig. 2(a) and average in Fig. 2(b).

For each graph in Table 1, we use an off-the-shelf linear-time algorithm [2] to compute the k−core. As k increases to its ultimate value at which the graph diminishes, we compute the following: (1) the number of cores in each k-core, (2) the normalized size of each k-core. Results are shown in Fig. 3. Notice that

Table 1. Datasets used in experimentation and validation.

Dataset	# nodes	# edges
DBLP	769, 641	3, 051, 127
Slashdot	70, 355	459, 620
Physics 2	11, 204	117, 619
Physics 1	4, 158	13, 422
Wiki-vote	1, 300	36, 529

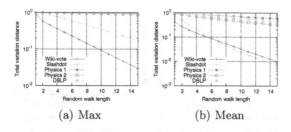

(a) Max   (b) Mean

Fig. 2. Mixing time measurement of graphs in Table 1.

graphs in Figs. 3(a)-(b) are slow mixing and graphs in Figs. 3(c)-(d) are fast mixing, as demonstrated in Fig. 2 for both the maximum and average mixing time cases.

By comparing Figs. 3(a),(c),(d), we observe that slow mixing graphs are less cohesive whereas fast mixing graphs are more cohesive. This observation is reflected in the number of cores in the k-core of each graph as we increase k until the graph is dissolved entirely. Also, whereas slow mixing graphs—shown in Figs. 3(a) and (b)—are decomposed into multiple cores as we increase k, fast mixing graphs resist this decomposition and remain cohesive as k increases, even for larger k than in the slower mixing graphs.

Second, even though slow mixing graphs are decomposed into multiple cores, these cores are relatively small in size and the graph dissolves quickly as k increases. Fast mixing graphs on the other hand remain in a single core, which is relatively larger in size than the counterpart core in slow mixing graphs.

5 Improving the Mixing Time and Sybil Defenses

With a different motivation, there has been several attempts in the literature to design algorithms that improve the mixing time of random walks on social graphs [1,9]. The main motivation of these designs is to provide a better method for sampling large graphs and to obtain representative samples of the large population in these graphs [9,18,23]. However, these solutions fall short in providing the desirable features for Sybil defenses. For example, existing solutions that improve the mixing characteristics of social graphs by providing uniform teleportation probability to any node in the graph at any step in the random walk

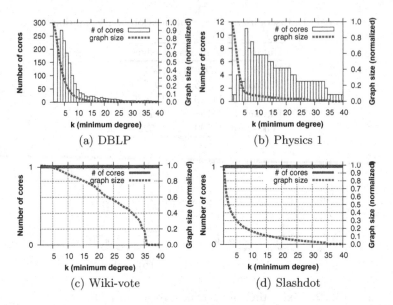

Fig. 3. The core structure of slow mixing (3(a) and (b)) versus fast mixing (3(c) and (d)) graphs. The slow mixing graph dissolves into multiple cores as k, the minimum degree in the $k-$core algorithm increases, unlike fast mixing graphs which consist of a single large core.

are expensive [1], since they require each node to know the entire social graph. More importantly, these designs are impractical for Sybil defenses, which use the mixing time for their operation. This impracticality comes from the fact that these algorithms will ultimately improve the mixing characteristics of both honest and dishonest nodes arbitrarily, since the probability of choosing an honest and a Sybil node in the graph as a next step of the random walk due to the teleportation is equal, even when the algorithm is performed in a centralized fashion. Notice the latter shortcoming can be prevented if the label of destination is known in advance. However, deviation based on the label would of the nodes will reduce the effectiveness of the algorithm by not achieving the claimed improvement in the mixing time in aforementioned work.

As we have shown in the previous section, the mixing characteristics of social graphs, which influences the operation of Sybil defenses on top of social networks, depend on the core structure of these graphs. Slower mixing graphs tend to have multiple cores as the parameter k increases, whereas fast mixing graphs resist dissolution and consist of a single core as k increases. Using this observation, we proceed to describe several heuristics to improve the mixing time, and ultimately improve the operation of Sybil defenses on top social networks. The main goal of these heuristics is to prevent the dissolution of social graphs into multiple cores, thus improving its connectivity in a meaningful way. Our work is different in both objective and tools we use, and is tailored for random walks on social graphs.

5.1 Heuristics to Improve the Mixing Time

From our previous measurements we observe that as k increases the graph dissolves into multiple cores, particularly in slow mixing social graphs. Accordingly, we refer to the largest core for a given k value as the *main core*, and other cores as *minor cores*. In each of the following heuristics we aim to improve the mixing time by preventing the creation of multiple cores as k increases using auxiliary edges. We call this process of adding edges as *core wiring*. We introduce these heuristics with sybil defenses in mind as potential applications.

Heuristic X-1-C. The intuition here is to add edges so that only prevent the dissolution of the graph into multiple cores as k increases. Accordingly, for $G_k = \{G_k^1, \ldots, G_k^{t_k}\}$ ($k \geq 1$ and $t_k > 1$), where G_k^1 is the main core and G_k^i for $i \geq 2$ is a minor core, we add an edge between only one random node v_k^{ij} in the minor core G_k^i (where j is chosen at random) and v_k^{1l} in the major core G_k^1. We repeat that process as k increases to its ultimate value upon which the whole graph diminishes. The total number of added edges in the original graph G is $[(\sum_{k=1}^{k_{max}} t_k) - k_{max}]$, where k_{max} is the largest k of a core in G.

Heuristic X-A-C. An illustration of the operation of the heuristic is highlighted in Fig. 4. As k increases, for $k = 1$ and $k = 2$, the resulting graph is a single component, so no edges are added to it. However, when $k = 3$, the graph dissolves into two components, as shown in Fig. 1(c). Thus, two nodes are randomly selected; one from each component (i.e., one is from the major and the other is the minor component, which these labels used interchangeably for the graph in G_3). Then an edge is created between the two selected nodes, which is the dotted edge in Fig. 4, created between node v_5 and v_2.

Unlike in the previous heuristic where only dissolution prevent measure is taken to improve the connectivity of the graph, in this heuristic we aim to further improve the connectivity by adding multiple edges that would improve resilience of the graph to the removal of edges in between of different components. The heuristic accordingly adds multiple edges between each component in the k-core graph, as k increases. This is, for $G_k = \{G_k^1, \ldots, G_k^{t_k}\}$ ($k \geq 1$ and $t_k > 1$), where G_k^1 is the main core and G_k^i for $i \geq 2$ is a minor core, we add an edge between every node v_k^{ij} in the minor core G_k^i and random nodes v_k^{1l} in the major core G_k^1. We repeat that process as k increases to its ultimate value upon which the whole graph diminishes. The total number of added edges in the original graph G is $[(\sum_{k=1}^{k_{max}} t_k) - k]$.

An illustration of this heuristic is applied to the graph in Fig. 5. In this example, and without losing generality, recall that only G_3 dissolves into multiple components, and requires addition of edges to prevent such dissolution, as shown in Fig. 1(c), according to the heuristic X-A-C. Also, without losing generality, let $G^1_3 = (V^1_3, E^1_3)$ where $V_3^1 = \{v_4, v_5, v_6, v_7\}$ be the minor core and let $G^2_3 = (V^2_3, E^2_3)$ where $V_3^2 = \{v_0, v_1, v_2, v_3\}$ be the major core. In this heuristic, every node in G_3^2 is associated with a node in the major core G_3^2, where the latter node need not to be unique.

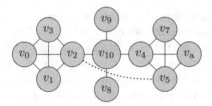

Fig. 4. An illustration of how the $k-$core decomposition of the graph is used to improve graph connectivity using X-1-C.

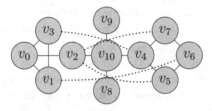

Fig. 5. An illustration of how the $k-$core decomposition of the graph is used to improve graph connectivity using X-A-C.

▶ **Heuristic X-A-A.** In this heuristic, we aim to further enmesh nodes in different cores together by adding edges across cores, not only between nodes in the major and the minor cores. To this end, we wire all nodes in a minor core to other cores in the graph, including both minor and major cores. The number of auxiliary edges is bounded by the *order* of the number of nodes in each k-core. However, to avoid undesirable complexity in the operation of the heuristic, we first sort all components in a given graph G_k, for any valid k, with respect to their size (the number of nodes each component has). Then, we wire nodes in the smaller component with nodes in the bigger component only.

▶**Heuristic X-A-A$^+$.** As we have seen in the previous proposed heuristics, additional edges are added to the graph in order to prevent its dissolution as k increases. These added edges can be viewed as a cost associated with the operation of these heuristics, and it is desirable to reduce this cost. Indeed, one desirable modification to the previous heuristic is graph rewiring. At each time an edge is added between two nodes in two different components, an edge is removed from either component (for that, we remove edges from the minor component, or the component with the smaller size when the number of minor components is greater than one). Desirably, we remove edges that constitute triangles within that component, and stop the process of rewiring the graph when we exhaust all triangles in that component. This approach is similar to the concurrent work in [31], although the strategy used for rewiring edges is different. Notice that this heuristic preserves the number of edges in the original graph, and would rewire nodes instead of adding edges. This heuristic provides the highest improvement, which suggests that adapting this strategy to other earlier heuristics will also improve them.

5.2   Practical Considerations

Two issues have a great influence on the operation of the proposed heuristics in this paper that could possibly limit their practicality. In the following, we raise these issues as questions and subsequently answer them. First, what is the rationale of using such edges, particularly when the number of edges is large? Second, what is the guarantee that edges are not going to be created between good nodes and Sybil nodes, thus improving the mixing time not only for the honest region of the graph, the region that includes honest nodes only, but also the dishonest region of the graph as well?

We address the first issue by pointing out two practical considerations. First, such edges can be made as a part of the natural evolution of the underlying social graph; by incorporating them into a link recommendation system where that is possible. Ultimately, not all links will be added to the graph, but some of them that would be created and such links would be of great importance to the connectivity of the graph. Second, since the operation of Sybil defenses on top of social networks does not require a real existence of links between nodes, but rather the flow of the walk on these links—which makes these edges virtual, we claim that such edges can be created virtually, but not in reality. This is, when a random walk is originated from a node on the graph, the random walk would deviate at that point from the one done on the original graph by assigning transition probability to the walk towards nodes connected via the virtual edges.

This part of practical consideration of our approach is in a sense similar to the prior work that adds a random teleportation probability of the random walk to improve the mixing time [1,9]. However, our approach will limit the number of nodes this teleportation would be assigned to (bounded by the number of the added edges a node in the graph would be a part of), thus no prior knowledge of the entire graph is done. However, the probability assigned to each node that is not connected to a given node have to be given in advance to that node. These probabilities (practically, they will be identifiers of nodes to which random walks are then propagated) can be distributed in the initialization phase of the Sybil defense, which can be done in a centralized manner.

To address the second issue, we use the existing reasoning in the literature which considers pre-existing labels of nodes in social graph to operate social network-based Sybil defenses [3,17,26]. For example, some of the prior work in the literature has assumed a predetermined labels of honest and Sybil nodes to improve the operation of Sybil defenses by incorporating weights on existing edges between some nodes in a more favorable way than others [17]. On the other hand, some work has indeed used a pre-determined list of labeled honest nodes to start the operation of the Sybil defense and to rank other nodes as either honest or Sybil [3,26]. To address the second issue, we claim that one can create edges, or add the transition probability as described previously for virtual edges, between only previously labeled honest nodes, thus improving the mixing time of the honest region of the graph but not the Sybil one.

In conclusion, auxiliary edges added in our heuristics can be made part of the evolution of the social graph through link recommendation. Alternatively, when

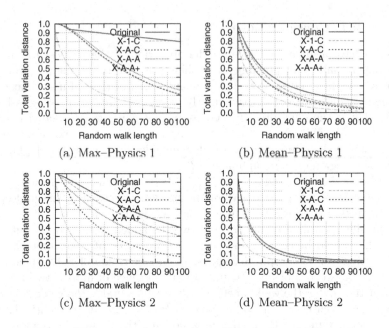

Fig. 6. Mixing time measurement of Physics 1 and Physics 2.

centralized initialization is viable, these edges can be virtually created among honest nodes only if some of the nodes are labeled, as used previously.

5.3   Results and Discussion

We select Physics 1 and Physics 2, two of the slow-mixing and relatively small social graphs to explore the potential of our heuristics in improving the mixing time for slow-mixing social graphs. We emphasize that the main reason to choose those social networks is their size, which enabled us to compute the mixing time using the definition in (1) from all nodes in each of the graphs. The results of measuring the mixing time after applying the heuristics in Sect. 5.1 for all possible initial distributions are in Fig. 6; Figure 6(a) and (b) are for the Physics 1 dataset whereas Fig. 6(c) and (d) are for Physics 2. The total number of edges before and after wiring graphs using the different methods explained earlier is shown in Table 2. Notice that the total number of nodes is still the same as in Table 1, and the number of edges in X-A-A$^+$ is preserved as in the original graph. In the following we elaborate on how the different heuristics affect the mixing time and the performance of Sybil defenses on top of them.

Heuristics Impact on the Mixing Time. By comparing the different plots in Fig. 6, it is obvious to see that the heuristics improve the mixing time, and in some cases greatly, for both the average and the minimum time. Particular, we first observe that our simplest heuristic (X-1-C), which produces minimal effect on the graph density—only 122 edges are added to Physics 1—significantly improves the mixing time according to its definition as the *maximal* walk length for a given total variational distance.

Second, the extent to which additional edges improve the mixing time differs and depends on the initial mixing characteristics of the graph. For example, X-1-C adds 68 edges to Physics 2 graph, which exhibits almost no effect on the mixing time, as shown in Fig. 6(d). The original graph already mixes better than Physics 1 dataset on average, and the addition of these edges, although improves the slowest mixing sources, does not improve a lot on average. Finally, by considering the number of added edges in X-A-A in both social graphs and the measured mixing time after adding these edges, we observe that the addition of a lot of edges—despite improving the density of the graph—does not improve the mixing time significantly (sometimes yields worse mixing as in Fig. 6(c)). This last remark tells us that auxiliary edges need to be placed wisely in graph in order to improve the mixing time.

This is further made clear by observing how rewiring the graph in X-A-A$^+$ improves the mixing time, despite maintaining the same number of edges as in the original graph. We attribute that effect on the performance to the inherent changes added on the graph to enmesh nodes in it, and reduce the number of loops within community (core) that would diverge the random walks.

5.4   Heuristics Impact on Sybil Defenses

We implement and run SybilLimit [28] over the augmented social graphs, according to the heuristics described earlier, in order to improve their mixing characteristics. In the following, we use describe SybilLimit, then provide our results and findings.

▶ **SybilLimit.** In SybilLimit, each node samples r edges in the graph as "witnesses", where $r = r_0 \sqrt{m}$, by running r independent instances of random walks each of length $w = O(\log n)$, which is the mixing time of the social graph. Accordingly, there is an overwhelming probability that the sampled subsets of honest nodes in the social graph will have a non-empty intersection, which would be used for suspect verification. Formally, if the social graph is fast mixing—i.e., has a mixing time of $O(\log n)$—then probability of the last node/edge visited in a walk of length $O(\log n)$ drawn from the edge/node stationary distribution is at least $1 - \frac{1}{n}$. Accordingly, by setting r_0 properly, one can use the birthday paradox to make sure that the intersection between two sampled subsets of edges (by two honest nodes) is non-empty with an overwhelming probability. Furthermore, given that the social graph is fast mixing, and the number of attack edges—edges that connect Sybil with honest nodes—is limited, the probability for random walks originated from honest region ending up to the dishonest region is limited. Chances of dishonest nodes being accepted by sampling honest edges is limited, and bounded by the number of attack edges.

▶ **Results.** To evaluate the performance of SybilLimit when operated on the original and modified graph, we use both the number of accepted honest suspects by honest verifiers when using a fixed walk length and varying number of

Table 2. Datasets used in this study.

Dataset	Number of edges (total)			
	Orig.	X-1-C	X-A-C	X-A-A
Physics 1	13,422	13,544	16,482	25,064
Physics 2	117,619	117,687	119,082	121,169

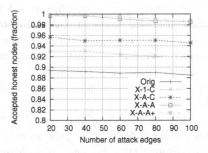

Fig. 7. Accepted honest nodes for varying attack edges.

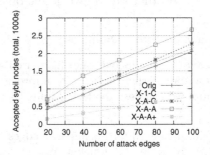

Fig. 8. The performance of SybilLimit: accepted sybils under varying number of attack edges.

attack edges, and the number of accepted Sybil nodes introduced in total for the same settings as earlier. We used a random walk length of 16 for the first two heuristics, and notice that a walk length of 38 on the original graph is sufficient to accept 97 % of the honest suspects by honest verifiers [22]. Because X-A-A$^+$ improves the mixing time significantly more than other heuristics, we measure the proper walk length that makes more than 99 % honest nodes accepted by honest verifiers, and find that to be a walk length of 7 which we use for that experiment only. Results are shown in Figs. 7 and 8, where Fig. 7 shows the number of accepted honest nodes by honest verifiers while varying the number of attack edges, and Fig. 8 shows the number of accepted Sybils while varying the number of attack edges for the different heuristics on the original graph.

In this measurement we observe that (among the first three heuristics) X-A-A accepted the most honest users followed by X-A-C and X-1-C, which is anticipated given their consistent order with respect to their modified density as shown in Table 2 and the mixing characteristics as in Fig. 6. However, and as anticipated given the theoretical interplay of the mixing characteristics and security guarantees of Sybil defenses, X-A-A also accepted significantly more Sybil nodes than others, given its improved mixing time. Interestingly, until the number of attack edges is 40, X-1-C does not increase the number of accepted Sybil nodes, while increasing the number of accepted honest nodes by honest verifiers by around 3.5%. Comparing the Sybil defense when using the three different heuristics, and that of X-A-A$^+$, we find that the latter heuristic outperforms them all by accepting most honest nodes and the least of Sybils.

6 Conclusion

In this work we explored understanding and improving the mixing characteristics of social graphs. We pointed out that the mixing characteristics of social graphs are related to the core structure, and used that to improve the mixing time. Using a running example, we demonstrated that the improved mixing time affects Sybil defenses, such as SybilLimit, although findings can be applied to other defenses. In the future, we will also look at measures to identify wider range of the quality of the mixing characteristics, as opposed to both extremes of the maximum and average explained in this work.

Acknowledgement. Part of this work appears in our unpublished prior study in [20]. The first author would like to thank Y. Kim, N. Hopper, and H. Tran for their help with the prior work.

References

1. Avrachenkov, K., Ribeiro, B., Towsley, D.: Improving random walk estimation accuracy with uniform restarts. In: Kumar, R., Sivakumar, D. (eds.) WAW 2010. LNCS, vol. 6516, pp. 98–109. Springer, Heidelberg (2010)
2. Batagelj, V., Zaversnik, M.: An $O(m)$ algorithm for cores decomposition of networks. Arxiv, preprint cs/0310049 (2003)
3. Cai, Z., Jermaine, C.: The latent community model for detecting sybil attacks in social networks. In: NDSS (2012)
4. Danezis, G., Mittal, P.: SybilInfer: detecting sybil nodes using social networks. In: NDSS (2009)
5. Dellamico, M., Roudier, Y.: A measurement of mixing time in social networks. In: IWSTM (2009)
6. Douceur, John R.: The sybil attack. In: Druschel, Peter, Kaashoek, MFrans, Rowstron, Antony (eds.) IPTPS 2002. LNCS, vol. 2429, pp. 251–260. Springer, Heidelberg (2002)
7. Erdős, P., Hajnal, A.: On chromatic number of graphs and set-systems. Acta Math. Hung. **17**(1), 61–99 (1966)
8. Jerrum, M., Sinclair, A.: Conductance and the rapid mixing property for markov chains: the approximation of the permanent resolved. In: STOC, pp. 235–244. ACM (1988)

9. Lee, C.-H., Xu, X., Eun, D.Y.: Beyond random walk and metropolis-hastings samplers: why you should not backtrack for unbiased graph sampling. In: Harrison, P.G., Arlitt, M.F., Casale, G. (eds) SIGMETRICS, pp. 319–330. ACM (2012)

10. Lesniewski-Laas, C.: A Sybil-proof one-hop DHT. In: Proceedings of the 1st Workshop on SNS, pp. 19–24. ACM (2008)

11. Lesniewski-Laas, C.: Design and applications of a secure and decentralized distributed hash table. Ph.D thesis, Massachusetts Institute of Technology (2010)

12. Lesniewski-Lass, C., Kaashoek, M.F.: Whānau: a sybil-proof distributed hash table. In: NSDI, pp. 3–17 (2010)

13. Li, F., Mittal, P., Caesar, M., Borisov, N.: Sybilcontrol: practical sybil defense with computational puzzles. In: Proceedings of the Seventh ACM Workshop on Scalable Trusted Computing, pp. 67–78. ACM (2012)

14. Lick, D., White, A.: k-Degenerate graphs. Can. J. Math. **22**, 1082–1096 (1970)

15. Mittal, P., Caesar, M., Borisov, N.: X-Vine: secure and pseudonymous routing using social networks. In: NDSS (2012)

16. Mohaisen, A., Hopper, N., Kim, Y.: Designs to account for trust in social network-based sybil defenses. In: ACM CCS (2010)

17. Mohaisen, A., Hopper, N., Kim, Y.: Keep your friends close: Incorporating trust in social network-based sybil defenses. In: INFOCOM (2011)

18. Mohaisen, A., Luo, P., Li, Y., Kim, Y., Zhang, Z.: Measuring bias in the mixing time of social graphs due to graph sampling. In: MILCOM (2012)

19. Mohaisen, A., Tran, H., Hopper, N., Kim, Y: Understanding social network properties for trustworthy computing, In: SIMPLEX (2011)

20. Mohaisen, A., Tran, H., Hopper, N., Kim, Y.: Understanding the mixing patterns of social networks. Technical report, UMN (2011)

21. Mohaisen, A., Tran, H., Hopper, N., Kim, Y.: On the mixing time of directed social graphs and implications. In: ACM ASIACCS (2012)

22. Mohaisen, A., Yun, A., Kim, Y.: Measuring the mixing time of social graphs. In: IMC, pp. 383–389. ACM (2010)

23. Ribeiro, B.F., Towsley, D.F.: Estimating and sampling graphs with multidimensional random walks. In: IMC (2010)

24. Shi, L., Yu, S., Lou, W., Hou, Y.T.: Sybilshield: an agent-aided social network-based sybil defense among multiple communities. In: INFOCOM (2013)

25. Sinclair, A.: Improved bounds for mixing rates of mc and multicommodity flow. Comb., Prob. & Comp. **1**, 351–370 (1992)

26. Yang, C., Harkreader, R.C., Zhang, J., Shin, S., Gu, G.: Analyzing spammers' social networks for fun and profit: a case study of cyber criminal ecosystem on twitter. In: WWW (2012)

27. Yu, H.: Sybil defenses via social networks: a tutorial and survey. SIGACT News **42**(3), 80–101 (2011)

28. Yu, H., Gibbons, P.B., Kaminsky, M., Xiao, F.: SybilLimit: a near-optimal social net defense against sybil attacks. In: S&P (2008)

29. Yu, H., Kaminsky, M., Gibbons, P.B., Flaxman, A.: SybilGuard: defending against sybil attacks via social networks. In: SIGCOMM (2006)

30. Yu, H., Shi, C., Kaminsky, M., Gibbons, P.B., Xiao, F.: Dsybil: optimal sybil-resistance for recommendation systems. In: IEEE Symposium on Security and Privacy (2009)

31. Zhou, Z., Zhang, N., Gong, Z., Das, G.: Faster random walks by rewiring online social networks on-the-fly. In: ICDE (2013)

Dynamic Surveillance: A Case Study
with Enron Email Data Set

Heesung Do[1]([✉]), Peter Choi[2], and Heejo Lee[3]

[1] Wantreez Music Inc., Seoul, Korea
heesung@wantreez.com
[2] Akamai Technologies Inc., 8 Cambridge Center, Cambridge, MA 02142, USA
peter.bkchoi@akamai.com
[3] Division of Computer and Communication Engineering,
Korea University, Seoul, Korea
heejo@korea.ac.kr

Abstract. Surveillance is a critical measure to break anonymity. While surveillance with unlimited resources is often assumed as a means, against which, to design stronger anonymity algorithms, this paper addresses the general impact of limited resource on surveillance efficiency. The general impact of limited resource on identifying a hidden group is experimentally studied; the task of identification is only done by following communications between suspects, i.e., the information of whos talking to whom. The surveillance uses simple but intuitive algorithms to return more intelligence with limited resource. The surveillance subject used in this work is the publicly available Enron email data set, an actual trace of human interaction. The initial expectation was that, even with limited resource, intuitive surveillance algorithms would return the higher intelligence than a random approach by exploiting the general properties of power law-style communication map. To the contrary, the impact of limited resource was found large to the extent that intuitive algorithms do not return significantly higher intelligence than a random approach.

Keywords: Surveillanc · Budget · Anonymity · Email data set

1 Introduction

One of the popular models of observer in the anonymity research is the one with unlimited resource and computing power such that the observer can monitor every single communication occurrence between any entities and exploit any possible derived information from the observation. Anonymity algorithms that can confuse such a powerful observer are regarded highly effective.

To understand the mighty power of the observer from a different perspective, one can ask this simple question, "what happens with limited resource?" This is the motivation of this paper. However, a glimpse of the anonymity research reveals the vast space of exploration to answer the question in a comprehensive manner. Different anonymity systems will cause different impact on

Y. Kim et al. (Eds.): WISA 2013, LNCS 8267, pp. 81–99, 2014.
DOI: 10.1007/978-3-319-05149-9_6, © Springer International Publishing Switzerland 2014

resource-limited surveillance. This paper takes one small step to obtain insights into the impact of limited resource on surveillance.

The model for this work involves a simple anonymity group and simple surveillance algorithms; the anonymity group is the target for the surveillance to find. The target group does not employ sophisticated anonymity algorithms but encryption. The surveillance uses only the information of communication relationship (whos talking to whom) to find the entire target group.

The limited resource can be implemented in many different ways. In this paper, it is represented as the "budget", which is loosely defined as the unit of resource to monitor one subject (potential or identified hidden group member). So the number of subjects under surveillance is linearly proportional to the budget.

One consequence with the budget is that the surveillance has to make a decision at some points whether to continue to monitor the subjects currently under surveillance or replace the subject with another potentially more promising one. By "promising" it is meant that the new subject would likely be to reveal more members of the hidden group. Note that surveillance with unlimited resource would not need to change the monitoring subject. That kind of surveillance would just keep adding more subjects. This is the point where the attribute "dynamic" is introduced to better characterize the nature of surveillance with limited budget; the critical decision is made dynamically at points in time.

This dynamism creates the two parameters; period and selection algorithms. The period is some time amount, at the end of which, the surveillance makes a strategic decision to select more promising subjects for next surveillance period. The selection algorithms assign a priority to each candidate subject. Top priority subjects, as many as the budget allows, will be selected for next surveillance period.

The selection algorithms in this experiment are high-degree-first (HDF), high-traffic-first (HTF), and random (RAND). The "degree" means the number of edges from the node in the communication map. There is one-to-one relationship between the node in the communication map and one subject in the real world. The HDF assigns priority based on the degree; higher degree receives higher priority. Likewise, in HTF, higher traffic (higher communication occurrences) nodes receive higher priorities. Lastly, the RAND assigns priority in a random fashion. It is chosen as the baseline against which the performances of HDF and HTF are compared.

This paper uses the publicly available email data set of once American energy company Enron, as a trace of actual human communication. The process of identifying the target group is performed by following the communication of a selected target. The experiments show the general impact of limited resource on the intelligence obtained by the surveillance. The intelligence is measured by the number of Enron employees as the hidden group and the number of third parties who have communicated with any employee of Enron.

With the well known power-law phenomenon in social graph, where a few nodes are connected to a large portion of the entire nodes while a large portion of the nodes is connected only to a few other nodes, it may be natural to expect a maximum intelligence return from the surveillance by following the largest degree or largest traffic volume subjects.

Surprisingly, the simulated surveillance shows the opposite. Both HDF and HTF do not return noticeably higher intelligence than RAND. In other words, the impact of limited resource can be larger than expected.

The paper is organized as follows. A brief survey on related work and background information are given in Sect. 2. The surveillance model, simulation overview and simulation data are described in Sect. 3. Section 4 details the impact of limited resource by showing the returning intelligence from HDF, HTF, and RAND with various periods and budgets. The concluding remarks and future work are provided in Sect. 5.

2 Related Work

In a broad sense, this paper belongs to the other side of the general idea of anonymity research (for example, [2,3,9,13,16]). While the general goal of anonymity research is to hide the communication relationships and the participants identities, the goal of surveillance is to reveal such information.

There is one research work addressing the efficiency of surveillance at an abstract level [7]. The focus of the work of [7] is different from that of this paper, however. The former investigates the impact that the revelation of one single member of the target group brings to the discovery of the entire target group. Surprisingly, one single member revelation is found to divulge about 50 other members of the same target group. So, carefully planned surveillance would need to monitor only one fiftieth of the estimated target group population.

This paper, in comparison, treats each target subject individually. It does not take the clustering coefficient (relationships existing among members of the same group) into account. From the perspective of [7], this work can be said to investigate an extreme case, where each and every group has only one member. From some distance, this work seems to be related to the existing surveillance systems such as Carnivore [17] and NarusInsight [12]. The details of the systems are not known to the authors, however.

A number of research works have utilized the publicly available Enron email data set. Shetty et al. [14] created a MySql database from raw Enron email corpus, analyzed the statistics of the data set, and derived a social network graph. Keila et al. [11] explored the structure of the data set and analyzed the relationships among individuals by using the word use frequency. In addition to the study of analyzing the Enron email data set itself, some work [1,4,15] use the data set as a testbed for the applied research. In relation to this paper, one of them investigates the communication map of the email data set in great detail [8]. To the best of the authors knowledge, this paper is the first attempt to utilize the data set to investigate surveillance efficiency issues with limited resource.

3   Surveillance Model

3.1   Simulation Overview

The goal of this paper is to obtain insights into the impact of limited resource on the intelligence returned by surveillance. The intelligence in this experiment is to identify firstly the target (hidden) group and secondly the group of third parties who have communicated with any surveillance subject.

The target group is assumed unaware of the surveillance. It does not take any measure against the surveillance. So, whatever seen by the surveillance is the actual communication in this model.

The process of identifying the target group is performed by following the communication map drawn from observation of communication between one known subject and another subject. The content of the communication is assumed properly encrypted so that decipherment of the message is not practical. However, the identity of communicating subject is assumed to be decode-able by some means.

Since the surveillance finds more unidentified subjects anyway as time progresses, the communication map grows accordingly. However, the communication map adds only newly identified subjects. Otherwise, it adds more edges or increase traffic volumes. As the resource is limited, the communication map is always a subset of what has happened in the real world.

At the end of each monitoring time window, within the limited budget, the surveillance has to make a decision about which discovered subjects will be under next round surveillance. The selected subjects will determine the quality of next round surveillance because any new discovery will be done by identified communications with any of those subjects. The three algorithms for the target selection in this work are HDF, HTF, and RAND.

By identifying each subject this way the surveillance will eventually identify and establish the entire target group if time and budget allow. The simulated surveillance is done when the communication is exhausted, i.e., all the input data is exhausted. Different intelligence will be returned at the end of one simulation run with a different set of period, selection algorithms, and budget. This surveillance process is simulated by the software designed for the purposes.

To obtain one point in the figures in what follows the simulation is performed as follows.

1. A simulation data set is given, which is a trace of actual human interactions.
   (a) Each communication occurrence of the data set is associated with the time of occurrence and the sender and receiver.
   (b) so, the entire data set is a collection of communications on the time line from the beginning to the ending time points.
2. Set the surveillance period, subject selection algorithm, budget.
3. Read the first time slice of the simulation data set based on the period.
4. At the beginning of the first period,
   (a) Select some subjects from the slice randomly as many as the budget.
   (b) Put those under surveillance.

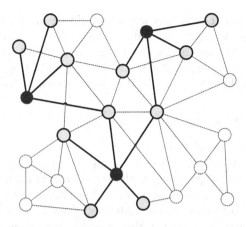

Fig. 1. Illustration of the surveillance model under limited budget. This example shows budget 3, so that only three nodes (3 red nodes) can be put under surveillance.

    (c) Run surveillance.
        i. Observe the communication chronologically.
        ii. Create the communication map accordingly.
5. At the end of the first period, run the subject selection algorithm.
    (a) Select the top priority subjects as many as the budget.
    (b) Put those under surveillance.
6. Read the next time slice of the simulation data set based on the period.
    (a) Run the surveillance with the subjects selected at the end of the previous round.
        i. Observe the communications with the selected subjects chronologically.
        ii. Update the communication map accordingly.
7. At the end of the current period, run the subject selection algorithm.
    (a) Select the top priority subjects as many as the budget.
    (b) Put those under surveillance.
8. Repeat the above two steps (6, 7) until the input data set is exhausted.
9. At the end of the run report the intelligence.
    (a) The identified subjects of the hidden group.
    (b) The identified third party subjects, who have communicated with one of the identified subject of the hidden group.
    (c) Other information as desired.
10. Repeat the entire procedure above 30 times with the same set of period, selection algorithm, and budget.
11. Obtain the averaged intelligence of the 30 runs.

The averaged intelligence should not be affected by the seed subjects, which are randomly selected from the first time slice of the simulation data set.

Illustration of Limited Resource. Figure 1 shows an example of surveillance under a limited budget. The graph represents a communication map among subjects from a period. The budget is set to 3. There are 23 nodes in the communication map. However, the surveillance can only identify 14 nodes; 3 red (or dark in black-and-white) nodes and 11 grey nodes. The rest 9 nodes cannot be observed by the surveillance due to the limited budget. In other words, the surveillance returns the intelligence of the 11 discovered nodes.

3.2 Simulation Data

The input data to the simulation is the Enron email data set. So, in this work, each unique email address is treated as an unique individual or a possible surveillance subject. The target group is the set of unique email addresses which are in the form of "somename@enron.com". Identifying the target group then becomes identifying all unique email addresses which end with "@enron.com". The third parties are identified when their communication with any known subject is identified by the surveillance.

The first public release of the Enron email data set was done in May 2002 by the Federal Energy Regulatory Commission [6]. Since the public release, several groups have subsequently processed and used the data set for a range of different research purposes. As a result, there are a few different versions available now. In this paper, the ISI (Information Sciences Institute) MySql version [10] of the data set is used. The ISI version was originally based on the CMU (Carnegie Mellon University) version [5].

The CMU version contains 517,431 messages from 151 employees. By removing meaningless messages from the CMU version, the ISI version now holds 252,759 messages from 151 employees, about half of the CMU version. This work slightly improves the ISI version in terms of message validity for surveillance purposes. As a result, the MySql file size changes from 740 Mbytes (ISI version)

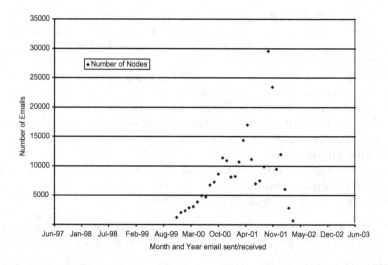

Fig. 2. Distribution of email messages in time [14]

to 667 Mbytes in this work. The data set used in this work has 252,692 email messages, 75,529 unique email addresses from Jan. 4, 1998 through Dec. 21, 2002.

So, the simulated surveillance is to identify all the 151 employees (someone@enron.com) and other third parties who communicated with one of the employees. Figure 2 shows the message distribution for the 5-year time period. The message volume peaks around Oct. 2001.

4 Experimental Results

4.1 Simulation Specifics

Surveillance time window. The two types of window are used in this work; time based and message based. In the time based, the entire data set is divided by a time period. Each window has the same time span. Some windows see a large number of email messages while some others do not. In the message based, the entire data set is divided by a number of messages. Each window has the same number of messages. Some windows take a large time span while some others take a short time span. Once the simulation started, each window is fetched from the MySql database in sequence, and, is given to the simulation software for surveillance processing.

Target selection scope. The target nodes in the communication map are the subjects, with which the simulated surveillance runs for the next time window. This work uses three simple strategies for target selection; HDF, HTF, and RAND at the end of each surveillance period. In the process of target selection, the surveillance needs to see the pool of candidates. The pool can be formed in two ways; local and global. The local pool is formed by the nodes observed in the current window of communication map. The global pool is formed by the entire nodes observed from the beginning up to the current window included. The local pool has fewer candidates while the global pool has an increasingly large number of candidates. Depending on the setting of the target selection, the three strategies (HDF, HTF, and RAND) select the target nodes either from the local or from the global scope.

Eligibility of Re-selection

1. *Rule 1:*
   A target node in this work is not allowed to be selected again to be one of the target nodes for the immediately following window. A target node however can be selected again as one of the target nodes for the window, which is at least two window-hops away. Two neighboring windows are one window-hop away from each other. This is different from the target selection scope. The target selection scope defines the pool of candidates. This rule defines the eligibility of re-selection.

2. *Rule 2:*
   One assumption of the simulation is that the target nodes will communicate with unknown parties during the next surveillance window so that the

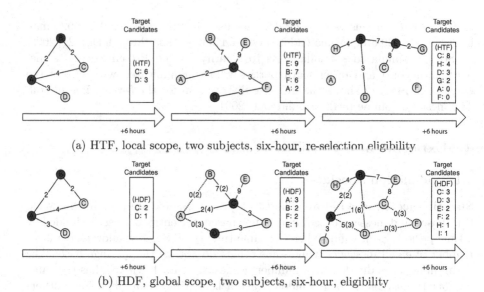

(a) HTF, local scope, two subjects, six-hour, re-selection eligibility

(b) HDF, global scope, two subjects, six-hour, eligibility

Fig. 3. Illustration of surveillance example (target selection strategy, target selection scope, budget, window, re-selection eligibility)

surveillance will identify more suspect nodes. A question arises when the target nodes do not exhibit communication with any unknown parties. The two choices are available in this case for selecting target nodes;

(a) Select one of the target nodes from the past for the next window, or,

(b) Use the target nodes of the current window for the next window because no new candidates are available from the current window.

This work uses the second choice. This "continued status of the target node over two neighboring windows" is one exceptional case to the "Rule 1" of eligibility of re-selection.

Illustration of Simulation Specifics. Figure 3 shows an illustration how the surveillance works with different target selection strategies and scopes with the same simulation data set for the same time windows and the same re-selection eligibility rules; (a) shows HTF in the local scope in the three consecutive windows, (b) shows HDF in the global scope in the same three consecutive windows. The setting includes a time window of 6 hours, budget 2. The red (or dark in black-and-white) nodes are the target nodes. The edge represents the identified communication between nodes. The weight of the edge is the communication volume; the number of email messages exchanged by the pair of nodes.

In the first window of the Fig. 3(a), there are two target nodes (A, B). Through the target nodes, the surveillance observes the communication between A and B, A and C, A and D, and, B and C. In terms of HTF, A is still the highest traffic node with 9 communications. However, since there are other unknown nodes, C and D, A is not allowed to be selected to be a target node for the next window. Accordingly, C and D are selected as the target nodes for the next window of 6 h. In the second window of (a), C is the highest traffic node. Again, however, other new so-far unknown nodes are selected as the target nodes for the third window; E and B.

The same rules are applied in Fig. 3(b). The differences are the target selection strategy and scope; HDF in the global scope. The target nodes of the first window are A and B. At the end of the first window, A and B are still the highest degree nodes. Due to the "eligibility of re-selection", however, C and D are selected as the target nodes for the second window. The global scope of the second window is represented by the solid and dotted lines between nodes. The solid line is the communication occurred in the current window. The dotted line is the communication observed in previous windows. Likewise, the number in the parenthesis on the edge is the cumulative communications between the pair of nodes up to the immediately preceding window, while the number out of the parenthesis represents the communications observed in the current window.

In Fig. 3(b), both B and F have the same degree, 2, at the end of the second window. The tie is broken in this work in favor of higher traffic; B has $7(2) + 0(2)$, while F has $3 + 3$. Eventually A and B are selected as the target nodes for the third window. Note that A and B were the target nodes for the first window. Both A and B are eligible to be a target node for third window because the first and third windows are two window-hops apart. Note that the two communication maps made by HDF and HTF grow differently with the same simulation data set. Both communication maps are incomplete anyway due to the limited resource.

4.2 Dynamic Surveillance with Limited Budget

In the figures below, the "suspects" are the unique email addresses of 151 Enron employees. The "nodes" are the unique addresses, which are either suspects or any other addresses, which have communicated with the employees at least once during the surveillance.

Figure 4 shows six graphs which differ from each other in the window type and target selection scope. The first column (a, c, e) shows the node discovery, and, the second column (b, d, f) shows the suspect discovery. The first 4 graphs (a, b, c, d) are obtained using the target selection from the local scope, while the last two (e, f) are obtained by the global scope target selection. The X-axis shows the surveillance window size in either message or time and its corresponding percentage of the entire surveillance period (5 years). Note that the X-axis is not a time line. One simulation run produces a value at one point of the curve. The Y-axis show the averaged intelligence either node or suspect discovery percentage against the entire data set size with the given budget, window, target selection strategy, and target selection scope.

The first two (a, b) use time windows while the last four (c, d, e, f) use message windows. Each graph has five sets of curves; each set represents the budget 4, 16, 64, 256, and 1024. Each set of the graph in turn shows the performance of the three target selection strategies; HDF, HTF and RAND under the

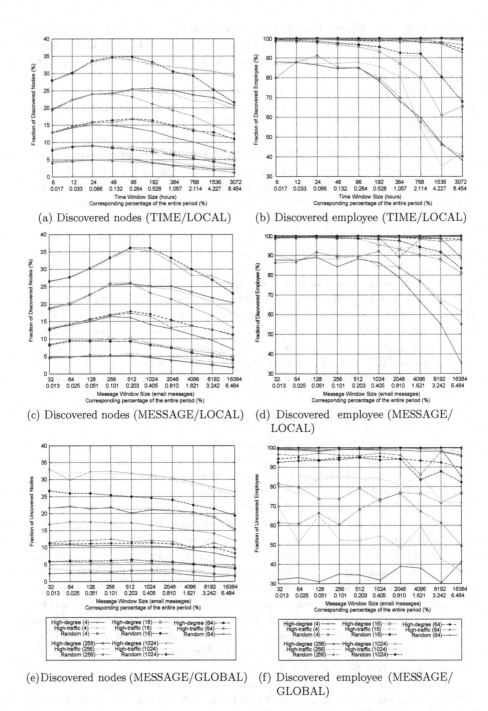

(a) Discovered nodes (TIME/LOCAL) (b) Discovered employee (TIME/LOCAL)

(c) Discovered nodes (MESSAGE/LOCAL) (d) Discovered employee (MESSAGE/LOCAL)

(e) Discovered nodes (MESSAGE/GLOBAL) (f) Discovered employee (MESSAGE/GLOBAL)

Fig. 4. Node discovery of dynamic surveillance

same conditions of budget and window. Each graph has fifteen curves in total, therefore.

Each point is obtained by the average value of 30 simulation runs with the same simulation setting but different seed nodes. For example, in (a), both HDF and HTF with the window of 96 h and budget 256 produce the node discovery ratio of about 25 %. This is the averaged value of 30 simulation runs. So each graph is a collection of averaged values from a set of independent simulation runs. Simulation runs higher than 30 do not produce noticeable difference. The best possible node discovery in this experiment as seen in the figure is about 35 % or 36 % of the entire nodes when the email data set is exhausted.

Global vs. Local Scopes. The last two graphs (e, f) use the global target selection scope while the first four (a, b, c, d) graphs use the local scope. One can expect that the global scope would return higher intelligence because the larger pool of candidates. To the contrary, the results are the opposite. The node discovery rates of (e) are lower than those of (a) and (c). Similarly, the performance of (f) is lower than (b) and (d). The reason is in the limited budget. The global scope tend to select the same target nodes again in later windows due to their accumulated higher degrees and traffic volumes. This trend prevents other new more promising nodes from being selected. The local scope, however, has to select the target nodes from the new local pool at each window.

Budget vs. Discovery Rates. With the increasing budgets, the 151 suspect nodes (employee addresses) are 100 % discovered. As can be seen from (b), (d) and (f), the complete suspect (employee) discovery is achieved with the budgets 256 and 1,024. So, budgets higher than 1,024 are not experimented. The graphs (a), (c) and (e) show that higher budgets yield higher discovery of nodes. However, while the budget is increased by 4 times at each step, the discovery ratio increases only sub-linearly.

The ratio of discovery to budget is found only to decrease. With this kind of sub-linearity, an absurdly large budget would be required to discover higher nodes than shown in (a) and (c). Further, the return intelligence is found increasingly marginal from each multiplicatively higher budget investment.

Time vs. Message-Based Window. In this experiment, as can be seen in Fig. 4(a) and (c) or (b) and (d), no big performance difference is found between the two different kinds of surveillance period; time and message windows. This is somewhat counter intuitive because the number of communication occurrences in the time window is likely to be different for each period. The logical explanation to this is that the variation of the message volume in the time window was not to the extent, where performance degradation would be seen. As seen later, both windows find new nodes at a rather constant rate.

HDF, HTF vs. RAND. In (a) and (c), the set of curves seems to have a mild peak. Interestingly, the three selection strategies do not show much performance difference until that point. After the peak, RAND shows the lowest performance while HTF is only slightly lower than HDF. Throughout the range of budgets,

HDF and HTF do not show noticeable difference. One possible logical explanation to these results is that, up to some window sizes and budgets, for example, 512 messages or 48 to 96 h and 64 or higher budgets, intuitive algorithms do not necessarily perform better than a random approach. In other words, the windows and budgets up to the peak point may not be large enough for the intuitive algorithms to exploit some patterns in the communication maps.

Peak. Interestingly, in (a) and (c), there tends to be a peak in the node discovery ratio. For example, in (a), the node discovery reaches about a little more than 35 % with the budget 1024, the window of 48 h regardless of the strategy. Similarly, in (c), the ratio reaches about 36 % with the budget 1024, the window of 512 messages, again, regardless of the strategies. The peak becomes more recognizable with higher budgets. In this work, the peak is interpreted that budgets larger than certain percentage of the entire nodes may have some optimal range of windows to maximize the return intelligence.

The peak is clearer in the message windows in (c) although the overall performances are not much different from those of time windows in (a). This is because the number of message appearing in each window is constant in (c), while it is necessarily fluctuating in the time windows in (a). The even distribution of messages in (b) must have helped manifest the optimal range of windows.

The performance degradation of (a) and (c) after the peak point is also interpreted due to the larger window. The peak point is effectively the turning point where the window size becomes sufficiently large to create the global scope effect for target selection. By the same argument, the global scope also produces flat curves in (e),

Another side effect of the global scope is the larger gap between RAND and the other two (HDF, HTF) with large budgets (256, 1,024). In (a) and (c), the gap between RAND and the other two becomes visible only with large budgets and large windows. Statistically RAND has higher probability to choose worse nodes in the global scope than in the local scope. The wider variety of the global scope contributes to the poor target node selection of RAND. In the local scope, since it is always created by the most promising nodes from the previous window, RAND has lower probability to choose low performing nodes.

4.3   Variations of Dynamic Surveillance

Strategically Uneven Budget Allocation. So far, the budget is evenly allocated to each window. This is to reflect the general situation that the dynamic surveillance would not know when more new nodes would appear in the surveillance. Without knowing the future information, the strategy of even budget allocation would be a reasonable choice.

The general question is whether there would be a better way of budget allocation in an effort to improve node discovery. To be fair, the total amount of budget needs to be assumed fixed. The total amount of budget is defined as the average budget per window multiplied by the number of windows of the entire surveillance period, 5 years.

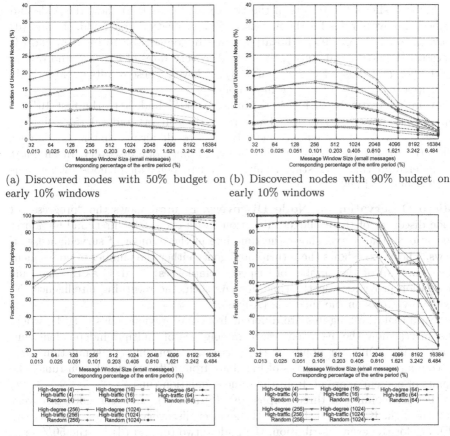

(a) Discovered nodes with 50% budget on early 10% windows

(b) Discovered nodes with 90% budget on early 10% windows

(c) Discovered employee with 50% budget on early 10% windows

(d) Discovered employee with 90% budget on early 10% windows

Fig. 5. Node discovery with variable budget distribution in before-event surveillance (message window based)

One immediate way is to allocate a relatively large portion of budget to the early stage of surveillance. The idea is to exploit the general pattern of communication map that a small percentage of nodes are connected to most of the nodes.

The hope is that if such small percentage of nodes would be discovered at an early stage, the node discovery would be more effective for the rest of the surveillance even with less amount of budget to the following windows. Therefore, the two variations of budget allocation are experimented here: firstly 50 % of the total budget to the early 10 % of the surveillance period, secondly 90 % of the total budget to the early 10 % of the surveillance period. The rest of surveillance windows receive the even distribution of the remaining budget in both cases.

Figure 5 shows the results of the two cases; (a) and (c) show the node and suspect discovery rates for the first case (50 % allocation first), and, (b) and (d) show the second case (90 % allocation first). In comparison to Fig. 4(c) and (d) (message window, local scope), the node discovery rates of Fig. 5(a) and (c) are not higher, and those of Fig. 5(b) and (d) are lower. These results apparently do not support the hope of finding more node.

More interestingly, in Fig. 5, (b) and (d) (90 % budget to the first 10 % of surveillance period) show even lower rates than in (a) and (c) (50 % budget to the first 10 % of surveillance period). This result means that higher budget allocation to the early stage results in even lower node discovery. In an effort to understand this interesting result, the micro behavior of node discovery is further analyzed next.

Micro Observation of Node Discovery. Figure 6 shows the "progress" of node discovery of three budget allocation cases; even, 50 % first, and 90 % first allocations. The X-axis shows the time line in the number of surveillance windows. The Y-axis shows the return intelligence either the number of nodes identified (a, c, e) or the number of suspects (employees) (b, d, f) as the one time simulation progresses on the time line. As such, the returning intelligence (Y-axis) only grows on the time line (X-axis).

Note that these figures are different from the previous ones (Fig. 4), where the curves show the averaged return intelligence of multiple independent simulation runs. Different points of the curve are from different simulation runs. In comparison, different curves of Fig. 6 are from different simulation runs. The points of one curve are all from the same simulation runs.

The left column of three graphs, (a), (c) and (e), show the node discovery and the right three (b, d, f) show the suspect discovery. The first row, (a) and (b), are for the even distribution, the middle two (c) and (d) for the 50 % first, and, the bottom two (e) and (f) are for the 90 % first.

The highlight of this figure is the growing rate of the returning intelligence. In (a), the even distribution of budget, the node discovery grows almost linearly and eventually tops around 27,000 nodes, which is about 35 % of the entire nodes.

In (c) the discovery grow rapidly for the first 10 % surveillance period and the growth rate goes down immediately after the first 10 % surveillance period. This phenomenon stands out more distinctively in (e). This trend remains the same even in the suspect discovery rates in (d) and (f).

Interestingly, in (e), the 90 % first does not boost the node discovery rate even for the early 10 % of surveillance period in comparison to (c). Evidently, this tells that more than 50 % budget allocation to the early 10 % of surveillance would not result any more intelligence return in this case study.

From a slightly different angle, this also suggests that the higher budget allocation to the early 10 % of surveillance was not much effective because the possible pattern (power-law, for example) of communication map was not fully recognizable in the early stage even by the temporarily large budgets. So, in this case study, choosing the even budget distribution seems favorable for the two selection algorithms, HDF and HTF.

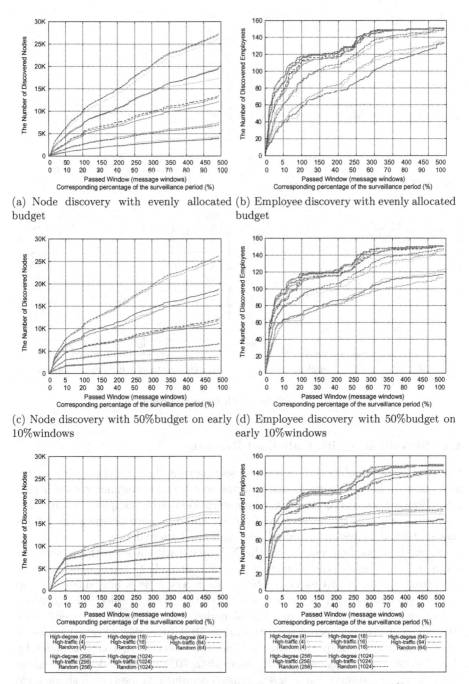

(a) Node discovery with evenly allocated budget

(b) Employee discovery with evenly allocated budget

(c) Node discovery with 50%budget on early 10%windows

(d) Employee discovery with 50%budget on early 10%windows

(e) Node discovery with 90%budget on early 10%windows

(f) Employee discovery with 90%budget on early 10%windows

Fig. 6. Progress of node discovery with various budget allocation cases

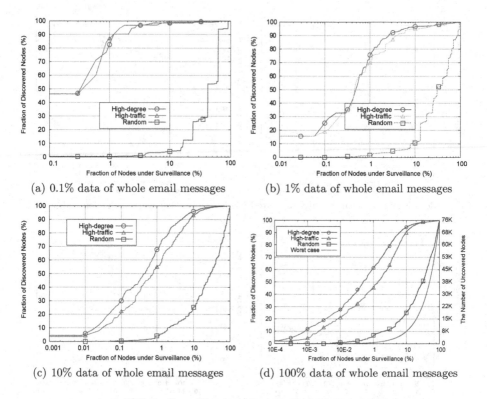

(a) 0.1% data of whole email messages

(b) 1% data of whole email messages

(c) 10% data of whole email messages

(d) 100% data of whole email messages

Fig. 7. Surveillance with unlimited resource

4.4   Surveillance with Unlimited Resource

Using the same simulation data set, this section runs the simulation with unlimited resource, i.e., the surveillance monitors every single communication occurrence between any two nodes. The communication map is complete at any given moment, therefore. The motivation is to see the difference between the intelligence returned by resource-limited and -unlimited surveillance.

Figure 7 shows four graphs on the X-Y plane with a logarithmic scale on the X axis. As before, the Y-value is the ratio of node (unique email address: both employee and third party combined) discovery. The X axis shows the top percentage of nodes with the priorities assigned by the target selection algorithm.

For example, in (b), the top 1 % of nodes selected (on X-axis) either by HDF or HTF are connected with the other 70 % or higher (Y-axis) nodes of the communication map. This means that the selection of top 1 % nodes by the selection algorithms can identify more than 70 % of the nodes at the given moment. Since the surveillance has unlimited computing power, each single node or communication addition causes a new complete computation of the entire communication map. This allows the algorithm to assign the priority based on the exact global and complete view at any moment.

The four graphs are obtained as follows. First, take the first 0.1 %, 1 %, 10 %, and 100 % portion of the simulation data set from the time line. (Remember that the simulation data set is a chronologically ordered communication occurrences among subjects.) Second, sort out the selected portion using the three algorithms; HDF, HTF, and RAND. Here, all the nodes, which ever communicated with any of the selected nodes are considered discovered. Third, create a curve for each selection algorithm for the four different sets.

Since the four first portions (0.1 %, 1 %, 10 %, and 100 %) are different in size from each other, the connectivity of the top percentage of the first portion to the rest of the first portion is different from each other, too. For example, the node discovery by top 1 % is more than 80 % in (a), more than 70 % in (b), more than 50 % in (c), and lastly more than 40 % in (d). The larger the first portion, the smaller the top percentage nodes connectivity.

Note that Fig. 7 cannot be directly compared to Fig. 4, where the X-axis was a time line while it is the top percentage of priority by the chosen target selection algorithm.

One convenient way to interpret the four graphs is to regard each one (a, b, c, d) as the snapshot of the surveillance with unlimited resource at the moments where the communication map reaches the first 0.1 %, 1 %, 10 %, and eventually 100 % of the entire nodes. Because it is resource limitation-free, the surveillance knows exactly what has happened. The current communication map itself reveals 100 % discovery at any time. This is the big difference between the resource-limited and -unlimited surveillance.

With the always complete Communication map a few interesting observations are readily available.

1. As the surveillance progresses, HDF returns higher intelligence than HTF,
2. RAND returns constantly poor intelligence.
3. The curve patterns do not seem to change regardless of the size of the early portion of data set.

Considering these observations, it can be said that there maybe some patterns in the complete communication map, and, the HDF seems to exploit the patterns most effectively. It indirectly shows that the pattern may be a power law-style. Since RAND does not utilize any pattern, it should return the worst intelligence.

There is an interesting observation with the sizes of window. Figure 4 uses a range of window sizes. For example, the largest window size in Fig 4(c) is 16,384 messages, which corresponds to about 6.5 % of the entire data set. This window size is actually larger than those of Fig. 7(a) and (b). The largest window of Fig. 4(a) is 3,072 h, corresponding to about 8.5 % of the entire surveillance period. Interestingly even these large window sizes do not make the node discovery higher than 40 % in Fig. 4(a) and (c).

Again, the major contributor to this interesting result is the incompleteness of the communication map due to the limited budget. The incomplete map constantly leads a sub-optimal selection of target nodes for next surveillance round. This phenomenon continues even with considerably large window sizes.

Lastly, the lowest curve in Fig. 7(d), is a hypothetical case, in which the target group uses an anonymity system such that the node discovery is perfectly linearly proportional to the surveillance budget. So, in order to find out X number of subjects of the target group, the budget of X should be invested. Finding the existence of such an anonymity system is out of the scope. This case, however, gives the lower bound to the surveillance performance. Even RAND performs better than this imaginary case.

5   Conclusions

The motivation of this work is to obtain insights into the impact of limited resource on the intelligence returned by surveillance. This work takes an experimental method in an effort to approach the right answer. The experiment was done in a form of simulated surveillance using a publicly available Enron email data set. The data set does not contain a complicated anonymity algorithms except data encryption. So the target selection algorithms were simple for the surveillance. However, the nature of the data set, a reflection of human interactions as a real trace, gives some credit on the actuality of the data set.

The experiment was done firstly with limited resource and followed by another form of surveillance with unlimited resource for comparison. As seen in the two strikingly different graphs (Figs. 4, 7), the impact of limited resource can be larger than expected. As seen in Fig. 4, the idea of exploiting some intuitive patterns (high degree or high traffic) on the communication map was not effective with limited budgets. After the peak points, larger budgets and larger window sizes produced worse intelligence. Although both HDF and HTF perform much better that RAND after the peak, the intelligence returned by both was monotonically decreasing with considerably larger budgets and window sizes.

By comparing the two surveillance cases (resource limited vs. unlimited), even though this work is about only one single case study with Enron email data set, some conclusions can be drawn that:

- Surveillance with limited resource may have some optimal points in terms of the combination of budget and window size that can maximize the quality of intelligence returned by the surveillance.
- Even allocation of budgets throughout the surveillance may work better than strategically uneven allocations.
- The incompleteness of the communication map seems to be maintained throughout the surveillance. This may be the major contributor to the observation that both HDF and HTF do not return significantly higher intelligence than RAND.

This work, although the generality is limited due to the scope of single case study, solicits further work, including but not limited to, on the optimal combination of budget and window size while the hidden group size is still unknown (with possible estimates of the group size), and, on the minimum size of communication map that is yet large enough to show some patterns to be utilized.

References

1. Akoglu, L., McGlohon, M., Faloutsos, C.: Anomaly detection in large graphs. In: CMU-CS-09-173 Technical report (2009)
2. Bansod, N., Malgi, A., Choi, B.K., Mayo, J.: Muon: epidemic based mutual anonymity in unstructured p2p networks. Comput. Netw. **52**(5), 915–934 (2008)
3. Berthold, O., Federrath, H., Köpsell, S.: Web mixes: a system for anonymous and unobservable internet access. In: Workshop on Design Issues in Anonymity and Unobservability, pp. 115–129 (2000)
4. Chapanond, A., Krishnamoorthy, M.S., Yener, B.: Graph theoretic and spectral analysis of enron email data. Comput. Math. Organ. Theor. **11**(3), 265–281 (2005)
5. CMU. Enron email dataset. http://www.cs.cmu.edu/enron
6. F. E. R. Commission. Enron investigation. http://www.ferc.gov/industries/electric/indus-act/wec/enron/info-release.asp
7. Danezis, G., Wittneben, B.: The economics of mass surveillance and the questionable value of anonymous communications. In: Anderson, R., (eds.) Proceedings of the Fifth Workshop on the Economics of Information Security (WEIS 2006), Cambridge, UK, June 2006
8. Diesner, J., Frantz, T.L., Carley, K.M.: Communication networks from the enron email corpus "it's always about the people. Enron is no different". Comput. Math. Organ. Theor. **11**(3), 201–228 (2005)
9. Goldschlag, D.M., Reed, M.G., Syverson, P.F.: Onion routing. Commun. ACM **42**(2), 39–41 (1999)
10. ISI. Enron dataset. http://www.isi.edu/adibi/Enron/Enron.htm
11. Keila, P.S., Skillicorn, D.B.: Structure in the enron email dataset. Comput. Math. Organ. Theor. **11**(3), 183–199 (2005)
12. NarusInsight. Narusinsight solutions for traffic intelligence. http://www.narus.com/index.php/product
13. Sherwood, R., Bhattacharjee, B., Srinivasan, A.: P^5: a protocol for scalable anonymous communication. J. Comput. Secur. **13**(6), 839–876 (2005)
14. Shetty, J., Adibi, J.: The enron email dataset database schema and brief statistical report (2004)
15. Shetty, J., Adibi, J.: Discovering important nodes through graph entropy the case of enron email database. In: Proceedings of the 3rd International Workshop on Link Discovery, LinkKDD '05, pp. 74–81, ACM, New York (2005)
16. Shields, C., Levine, B.N.: A protocol for anonymous communication over the internet. In: ACM Conference on Computer and Communications Security, pp. 33–42 (2000)
17. Ventura, H.E., Miller, J.M., Deflem, M.: Governmentality and the war on terror: Fbi project carnivore and the diffusion of disciplinary power. Crit. Criminol. **13**, 55–70 (2005)

Mobile Security

Towards Elimination of Cross-Site Scripting on Mobile Versions of Web Applications

Ashar Javed[✉] and Jörg Schwenk

Chair for Network and Data Security, Horst Görtz Institute for IT-Security,
Ruhr-University Bochum, Bochum, Germany
{ashar.javed,joerg.schwenk}@rub.de

Abstract. In this paper, we address the overlooked problem of
Cross-Site Scripting (XSS) on mobile versions of web applications. We
have surveyed 100 popular mobile versions of web applications and
detected XSS vulnerabilities in 81 of them. The inspected sites present
a simplified version of the desktop web application for mobile devices;
the survey includes sites by Nokia, Intel, MailChimp, Dictionary, Ebay,
Pinterest, Statcounter and Slashdot. Our investigations indicate that a
significantly larger percentage (81 % vs. 53 %) of mobile web applications
are vulnerable to XSS, although their functionality is drastically reduced
in comparison to the corresponding desktop web application.

To mitigate XSS attacks for mobile devices, this paper presents a
light-weight, black-list and regular expressions based XSS filter for the
detection of XSS on mobile versions of web applications, which can be
deployed on client or server side. We have tested our implementation
against five different publicly available XSS attack vector lists; none
of these vectors were able to bypass our filter. We have also evaluated
our filter in the client-side scenario by adding support in 2 open source
mobile applications (WordPress and Drupal); our experimental results
show reasonably low overhead incurred due to the small size of the filter
and computationally fast regular expressions. We have contributed an
implementation of our XSS detection rules to the ModSecurity firewall
engine, and the filter is now part of OWASP ModSecurity Core Rule Set
(CRS)   https://github.com/SpiderLabs/owasp-modsecurity-crs/blob/
master/base_rules/modsecurity_crs_41_xss_attacks.conf.

Keywords: XSS, Mobile web, Regular expression, Client-side filter

1 Introduction

Cross-Site Scripting (XSS) [3] is one of the most prevalent security issue in web
applications: according to a recent report by WhiteHat, 53 % of websites have
XSS vulnerabilities [4]. An attacker can exploit an XSS vulnerability to steal
users' credentials, spread worms and deface websites. Researchers have proposed
different mitigation against XSS ranging from purely client or server side methods to hybrid solutions [22,23,25,27–29,31–33]. However, the field which still
lacks research is mobile versions of web applications.

Y. Kim et al. (Eds.): WISA 2013, LNCS 8267, pp. 103–123, 2014.
DOI: 10.1007/978-3-319-05149-9_7, © Springer International Publishing Switzerland 2014

Characterization of Mobile Web Applications. In mobile web applications, functionality and user interaction is adapted to the small touchscreens of modern smartphones. The URLs of mobile web applications often start with the letter "m", or end in the words "mobi" or "mobile". Sites automatically present a simple and optimized version of their web application to mobile browsers, e.g., Etsy (a popular handmade items' marketplace) website[1]. These *stripped-down* versions of web applications contain significantly less or no AJAX-style interactions, thus the attack surface for XSS should (at first glance) be reduced.

We found that mobile sites have approximately 69% less HTML code as compared to desktop versions (see Sect. 2.3). *Only one* mobile site (http://www.jobmail.co.za/mobile/) is using Modernizr[2] – a JavaScript library that detects HTML5 and CSS3 features in the user's browser – which indicates that these novel features are rarely used. According to [5]:

"... *In mobile interfaces, set of navigation options is usually presented one at a time; for example, with iPhone-style sliding drill-down menu panels.* ..."

A usability study of hundreds of sites conducted by Nielsen Norman Group [6] states:

"*Good mobile user experience requires a different design (cut features, cut content and enlarge interface elements) than what's needed to satisfy desktop users. The desktop user interface platform differs from the mobile user interface platform in many ways, including interaction techniques, how people read, context of use, and the plain number of things that can be grasped at a glance.*"

XSS Vulnerabilities in Mobile Web Applications. We found XSS vulnerabilities in 81 of the 100 surveyed applications (see Sect. 2) which shows (when compared to the 53% from the WhiteHat study [4]) that a significantly higher percentage of these applications are affected by XSS. This result is surprising, since the reduced functionality of the mobile versions should facilitate protection against such attacks. According to OWASP Top 10 Mobile Risks, client-side injection is ranked as number four [17].

Mitigation against XSS. For the simple and optimized mobile versions of web applications, we need a simple and light-weight solution that incurs reasonably low run-time overhead for the application (both on client and server side) and at the same time requires little effort or knowledge from the developers.

Filtering malicious content is the most commonly used method for the prevention of XSS on web applications and sites normally use filtering as a first line of defense. The main goal of filtering is to remove malicious contents from the user-supplied input, while still allowing the non-malicious parts to be processed. A recent paper [16] has also argued in favor that mobile applications can learn from the web experience.

Since removing malicious content from user-supplied input is a complicated and error-prone task, we take the stricter *blocking* approach to keep our filter

---

[1] "*Type Etsy.com into your mobile browser on your phone and you'll find a simple and optimized version of the Etsy site* http://www.etsy.com/".

[2] http://modernizr.com/

simple: Whenever we detect malicious content, the whole request is blocked, and only an error message is returned.

Related Work. The idea of using client-side filter to mitigate XSS is not new. Engin Kirda et al. propose Noxes [25] which is a client-side, Microsoft Windows based personal web application proxy. Noxes provides *fine-grained* control over the incoming connections to the users so that they can set XSS filter rules without relying on web application provider. Noxes assumes that users are trained and security aware and can set filtering rules, which is not the case often and at the same time it requires considerable amount of effort from the users. Noxes does not consider HTML injection and only Windows based.

Omar Ismail et al. [26] propose a client-side solution for the detection of XSS. The solution, which is user-side proxy, works by manipulating the client request or server response. The solution works in two modes *request change mode* and *response change mode* and also requires servers (i.e., collection/detection and database server). As authors stated in the paper that the proposed solution can affect performance because of extra request in *request change mode*. At the same time in *response change mode*, proxy assumes that the parameter with length greater than 10 characters should contain XSS script, which is not the case often. Last but not the least, solution is not automatic and requires considerable amount of effort from the developer because it requires manual insertion of scripts used for XSS detection.

Vogt et al. also propose a client-side solution [29] for the mitigation of XSS attacks. The proposed solution track flow of sensitive information inside the Mozilla Firefox browser and alert user if information starts flowing towards third-party. The proposed solution is a good protection layer against XSS but as authors stated that it requires considerable engineering effort to modify the Firefox browser.

Mozilla proposed Content Security Policy (CSP) for the mitigation of XSS attacks [31]. At the time of writing, mobile browsers do not support[3] W3C CSP 1.0 specifications[4]. At the same time, CSP requires great amount of effort from developers to modify sites because of no `inline-JavaScript` support. We have also compared our XSS filter with some industry proposed XSS filters (see Sect. 7).

Our Solution. In this paper, we present a simple, optimized, light-weight and black-list client-side XSS filter for mobile applications (see Sect. 4). Our XSS filter is based on a set of regular expressions and can cope with code obfuscation. We have chosen regular expressions because (if implemented correctly) they are computationally fast compared to any equivalent string manipulation operation (see Sect. 6.2) and easy to maintain. Our set of regular expressions can be deployed in server-side filters (e.g., in firewall), or as a client-side JavaScript function.

---

[3] Flip the pref to turn on the CSP 1.0 parser for Firefox for Android: https://bugzilla.mozilla.org/show_bug.cgi?id=858780.

[4] http://www.w3.org/TR/CSP/

Our solution is not intended for desktop based web applications because of complex nature of web applications and significant use of AJAX. Our filter may harm the performance of the rich internet application and it requires more changes from the developers perspective, and may not be able to deal with highly complex XSS vectors available there. From now on, we will only consider mobile version of web application that are simple in nature.

Regular expressions based XSS filters are very common e.g., the Firefox NoScript[5] and the XSS filter implemented in Internet Explorer use regular expressions. In this paper, we leverage the idea of regular expressions from Gary Wassermann et al.'s work [1]. Wassermann et al. have proposed static detection of XSS vulnerabilities using tainted information flow and string analysis. They have developed a function named `stop_xss` that uses regular expressions to capture malicious input from the user-supplied string. The function `stop_xss` has three categories of regular expressions to deal with different types of XSS vectors.

1. A regular expression category that deals with `script` tag based XSS vectors, e.g., `<script>alert(1)</script>`. We call it Category 1.
2. A regular expression category that deals with XSS vectors making use of event handlers like `onerror`, `onload` etc, e.g., `<body onload="alert(1)">`. We call it Category 2.
3. A regular expression category that deals with XSS vectors making use of JavaScripts URIs, e.g., `<p style="background:url(javascript:alert(1))">`. We call it Category 3.

For client-side deployment, we have implemented the XSS filter as a JavaScript function (see Sect. 5). To integrate our filter, sites simply have to *inlcude or link* the JavaScript XSS filter code at the top of their web page. This is very common practice and it can even be observed on the mobile sites especially when sites include the jQuery mobile JavaScript library[6] (see Sect. 2.3). Sites may call our filter function on HTML form's (`<form>` tag) *onsubmit* event handler, e.g., "onsubmit=xssfilter()".

For server-side deployment, sites may use our filtering rules in Firewall or as *server-side reverse proxy*. Apache's `mod_proxy` module provides functionality to set up reverse proxy and then proxy decides how to deal with the incoming requests according to the rules [35]. We have contributed an implementation of our XSS detection rules to the world most widely deployed firewall engine – ModSecurity – (around 1,000,000 deployments[7]), and the filter is now part of OWASP ModSecurity Core Rule Set (CRS) (see Sect. 6.3). In this paper, we focus only on the client-side deployment. We have also tested our filter against a large set of XSS vectors (see Sect. 5.2) and have evaluated our client-side implementation by adding support in two popular open-source (Wordpress and Drupal) mobile applications (see Sect. 6).

---

[5] http://noscript.net/
[6] http://jquerymobile.com/
[7] https://www.trustwave.com/modsecurity-rules-support.php

Contributions. The paper makes the following contributions:

- It presents a survey of 100 mobile sites and found XSS vulnerabilities in 81 of them. The complete list of mobile sites that are vulnerable to XSS vulnerabilities is available at http://pastebin.com/AHJbjJsy.
- It proposes a XSS filter for mobile versions of web applications based on regular expressions and blacklisting. We have contributed our XSS detection rules to the ModSecurity firewall engine, and have implemented it as a Javscript function for client-side deployment.
- The proposed XSS filter was tested against five publicly available XSS vector lists, and no vector was able to bypass the current version of the XSS filter.
- The feasibility of our approach was shown by adding our XSS filter as a JavaScript function in two open-source mobile applications, with reasonably small overhead (client-side), and by the integration into ModSecurity after intensive testing by the OWASP Modsecurity team (server-side).

2 Survey

In this section, we present the results of our survey[8] and discuss these results briefly. To the best of our knowledge, this is the first survey on mobile web applications. All quantitative overviews on XSS we are aware of are related to desktop version of web applications. During the survey of 100 popular mobile version of web applications, we found reflective XSS vulnerabilities in 81 sites, including web sites like Nokia, Intel, MailChimp, Vodafone, Dictionary, Ebay, Answers, HowStuffWorks, Statcounter and Slashdot etc.

2.1 Methodology of Testing Websites

We manually injected a commonly used XSS vector (i.e., `"><img src=x onerror=prompt(1);>`) in the input fields available on the mobile-version of web applications. In order to open mobile versions of websites, we have used Mozilla Firefox browser on Windows 7, running on DELL Latitude E6420ATG (Intel Core i7 processor). In 74 out of 81 XSS vulnerable websites we found HTML forms (`<form>` tag). Similar to the desktop versions, on mobile versions we also found usage of the `<form>` tag for *search*, *feedback* and *log-in* functionality. For the remaining 7 sites we have injected the XSS vector directly in URL being retrieved (in the query string of the URL). The reason for this large amount of XSS vulnerabilities seems to be the total *lack of input validation* on client and server side.

One could argue that this lack of filtering could be intentional, since there is probably no attractive target for attackers amongst mobile web applications. This is however not the case: e.g., Pinterest (http://m.pinterest.com) has an XSS vulnerability (see http://i.imgur.com/sJUQdwt.jpg) and this site has millions of

---

[8] The complete list of surveyed mobile sites is available at http://pastebin.com/MabbJWWL.

unique users[9]. We have also found other examples of attractive targets on the mobile side like MailChimp's log-in form[10], Jobmail's Employer login form[11], Moneycontrol's (India's #1 financial portal) registration form[12] and Mobiletribe personal detail form[13], Homes' login form[14] and many others etc. Attacker can steal users' credentials by exploiting the XSS flaw.

2.2   Ethical Considerations

Regarding our findings, we are acting ethically and have informed some sites about the XSS vulnerability and in the process of contacting others. Some of the XSS issues have been fixed and some are in progress. Sites like Nokia and Intel have reacted promptly and now in both cases XSS (see http://i.imgur.com/ FTVFlpm.png and http://i.imgur.com/Qzp7bhJ.jpg) has been fixed by their security teams and at the same time they have also acknowledged[15] our work. We believe that our survey will help raise awareness about XSS problems on mobile sites. Table 3 (see Appendix) shows top site names along with its Alexa rank at the time of writing.

2.3   Stripped-Down Versions of Desktop Web Applications

HTML Usage on Mobile Sites: Our manual source code analysis of mobile web sites showed that they contain significantly less HTML code as compared to the desktop version of the same application. To be precise, we found an average of 69 % less HTML code on mobile variants of web application. Figure 1 shows the difference in number of lines of HTML code on mobile and desktop sites.

JavaScript Usage on Mobile Sites: Our survey results show that 79 sites out of 100 are using JavaScript on mobile version of their web application. The other 21 sites do not use JavaScript at all. However, most of this code is JavaScript-based third-party tracking. We found 62 sites are using JavaScript tracking code provided by different ad-networks (41 sites are using *Google Analytics* JavaScript code). According to recent report by Ghostery, *Google Analytics* is the most widespread tracker on web [20]. Our survey has found that *Google Anayltics* is the also widespread tracker on mobile[16].

We also found that 33 sites are using jQuery mobile library[17]. The jQuery mobile library allows developers to build mobile applications that can run across

---

[9] http://en.wikipedia.org/wiki/Pinterest

[10] XSS is now fixed, see http://i.imgur.com/oWwpc1e.jpg

[11] http://www.jobmail.co.za/mobile/employerLogin.php

[12] http://m.moneycontrol.com/mcreg.php

[13] http://portal.motribe.mobi/signup

[14] http://m.homes.com/index.cfm?action=myHomesLogin#signin

[15] Nokia has sent us Nokia Lumia 800 Phone as a part of appreciation and responsible disclosure.

[16] For interested readers, we will soon publish a technical report titled — *"A Footprint of Third-Party Tracking on Mobile Web"*.

[17] http://jquerymobile.com/

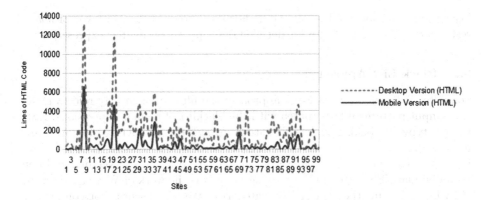

Fig. 1. Comparison of HTML lines of code on Mobile and Desktop versions.

the various mobile web browsers and provide same or at least a similar user interface [21]. Unfortunately, we have found only *one* (out of 79) client-side input validation JavaScript library[18]. We were able to break that validation library using the following cross-domain XSS vector: `"><iframe src=//0x.lv>`[19]. The input field has constraint on length and that's why, in this case, we have used this vector. The remaining 78 sites have no sort of server side filtering also.

3   Overview of XSS Filtering Approach

The goal of an XSS filter is to filter potentially malicious input from the user-supplied string. To achieve maximum protection, we use a blocking approach: as soon as the XSS filter detects malicous input, we immediately block the sending (client side) or processing (server side) of the corresponding `GET` or `POST` request. The idea of completely blocking the `GET` or `POST` request is e.g., implemented by the IE XSS filter's block mode [2]. The Internet Explorer XSS filter supports `X-XSS-Protection: 1; mode=block` which means that when the IE XSS filter detects the malicious outbound HTTP requests and mode value has been set to block, then IE stops rendering the page and only renders # sign. Blocking is a safe way to achieve maximum security and at the same time it helps in avoiding introduction of filter based vulnerabilities in web applications [24], but it may break some of the more complex web applications. Since mobile versions are much simpler than their desktop equivalents, blocking seems to be an adequate method to solve the XSS problem.

3.1   Regular Expressions

A regular expression is a pattern for describing a match in user-supplied input string. Table 4 (see Appendix), briefly describes the syntax related to the regular

---

[18] http://m.nlb.gov.sg/theme/default/js/validate.js
[19] The url 0x.lv has been developed by Eduardo Vela of Google.

expressions that are used in our filter. For interested readers, in favor of space restriction, we refer to [7–10] for detailed descriptions on regular expressions.

3.2   Black-List Approach

Our filter is based on a black-list approach: the filter immediately rejects malicious input patterns if they match with the blacklist of regular expressions. XSS vectors typically belong to specific categories and the number of categories are finite; in our filter we cover every known category of XSS vectors. Our focus during the development of this filter was thus on categories of XSS vectors, and not on individual XSS vectors. Our starting point was the work of Wasserman et. al [1], which contains the idea of XSS categories. We will discuss shortcomings of Wasserman et al.'s regular expressions' categories (see Sect. 3.5). We have carefully analyzed publicly available XSS vector lists to group them into different categories. The figure available at http://i.imgur.com/C0sihbg.jpg shows that the large number of XSS vectors belong to three main categories (i.e., Category 1,2 and 3 – see Sect. 3.5). There are some other categories of XSS vectors and we will discuss in Sect. 4.4.

3.3   Community-Input

In order to cover all possible edge cases and for hardening the filter, we have announced an XSS challenge based on our filter rules. The challenge was announced on Twitter and security researchers as well as professional penetration-testers from around the world have actively participated in the challenge. We have received around 10K XSS vectors from participants and found only three types of bypasses (i.e., <form> tag based XSS vector, <isindex> tag based XSS vector and IE9 specific bypass). In IE9 "vertical tab i.e., **U+000B** " can be used as an alternative of white-space character in between tag name and attribute and IE9 renders the XSS vector. We have added support of bypasses in the filter. The challenge was also intended to get *state-of-the-art* XSS vectors. After extensive testing against publicly available XSS vectors, *state-of-the-art* XSS vectors[20] and internal testing by OWASP Modsecurity team, we can however say that our filter in its current form is hard to bypass and can be used as an additional layer of security (see Sect. 4.5).

3.4   Threat Model

This section describes the capabilities of an attacker that we assume for the rest of this paper. In XSS, an attacker exploits the trust a user has for a particular web application by injecting arbitrary JavaScript on the client-side. A *mobile web application attacker model* is similar to the standard web attacker threat model, proposed by Adam Barth et al. in [30]. In *mobile web application attacker threat*

---

[20] We have collected a list of some of the state-of-the-art XSS vectors here http://pastebin.com/BdGXfm0D.

model, attacker has a mobile server under his control, and has the ability to trick the user into visiting his mobile web application. We do not consider a case where input could originate, for example, as URL encoded parameter via link from another web site.

3.5   Limitations of Regular Expressions Used in Wassermann et al.'s stop_xss Function

In this section we briefly discuss the limitations of Wassermann et al.'s regular expressions and the respective bypasses found. We have mentioned earlier that Wassermann et al. used three categories of regular expressions.

Category 1: The regular expression in this category handles XSS vectors making use of the script tag. The regular expression is:

<code><script[^>]*>.*?</script></code>

The regular expression above can correctly capture XSS vectors like the following:

- `<script src="http://www.attacker.com/foo.js"></script>`[21]
- `<script>alert(1)</script>`

Now we discuss limitations of this regular expression along with XSS vectors that are able to bypass the regular expression:

- The regular expression does not consider "**space**" before the closing angular bracket in the closing `script` tag like: `<script>alert(1)</script >` and this is a valid XSS vector that shows an alert box[22]. Valid means an XSS vector that causes alert window to show up.
- The regular expression does not consider "**space**" along with junk values before the closing angular bracket in the closing `script` tag like: `<script>alert(1)</script anarbitarystring>`[23].
- The regular expression does not consider the absence of a closing angular bracket in the closing `script` tag like: `<script>alert(1)</script` Modern browsers render this vector and display an alert window[24].
- The regular expression does not consider "**new line**" in the script tag like:

```
<script>
        alert(1)
</script>
```

---

[21] http://jsfiddle.net/Nz5ad/

[22] http://jsfiddle.net/dDBdP/

[23] http://jsfiddle.net/dDBdP/1/

[24] http://jsfiddle.net/dDBdP/2/

Modern browsers also render[25] the above XSS vector. An attacker can use this type of vector if sites allow input in a `<textarea>` tag. The `<textarea>` tag is a multi-line input control and sites widely used it to ask for user-comments.

- The regular expression does not consider any obfuscation (base64[26], URL encoding[27], Hex entities[28] and Decimal entities[29]) of XSS vectors as described in http://pastebin.com/a4WSVDzf in favor of space restrictions. In order to convert XSS vectors into obfuscated form, attacker can use publicly available utilities like http://ha.ckers.org/xsscalc.html.
- The regular expression also does not consider the complete absence of a closing `script` tag like: `<script>alert(1)` e.g., following is a valid vector in the Opera browser[30]:

```
<svg><script>alert(1)
```

Category 2: The regular expression in this category matches XSS vectors making use of event handlers like `onload`, `onerror` etc. The regular expression is:

```
/([\s"']+on\w+)\s*=/i
```

The regular expression above can correctly captures XSS vectors like:

- `<body onload="alert(1)">`
- `<img src= /" onerror=alert(1)>`
- `<img src="http://www.google.com/logos/classicplus.png" alt="Img Not Found" onerror=alert(1)>`
- `<img src='x' onerror=alert(1) >`

Now we discuss limitations of this regular expression along with XSS vectors that are able to bypass this regular expression:

- The regular expression does not consider forward slash (/) before an eventhandler e.g., `<svg/onload=prompt(1)>`. All modern browsers render this XSS vector[31].
- The regular expression does not consider a back-tick symobol ' before eventhandler e.g., `<img src='xx:xx'onerror=alert(1)>`. This is a valid XSS vector which is rendered by the Internet Explorer (IE)[32].
- The regular expression does not match an equal sign "=" if present before the eventhandler e.g., IE specific XSS vector[33]: `<script FOR=window Event =onunload>alert(2)</script>`

---

[25] http://jsfiddle.net/dDBdP/3/
[26] http://jsfiddle.net/7aUu8/
[27] http://jsfiddle.net/GPPB6/
[28] http://jsfiddle.net/h2XWN/1/
[29] http://jsfiddle.net/xsrDj/
[30] http://jsfiddle.net/F58Zd/
[31] http://jsfiddle.net/JMEFE/
[32] http://jsfiddle.net/5X6E6/
[33] http://jsfiddle.net/KmQUF/

- The regular expression also fails to capture malicious input if semi-colon sign ";" is present before the eventhandler name e.g.,[34]

  ```
  <iframe src=javascript:/&lt;img&#32;src=1&#32;onerror=
  [alert(1)]&gt/.source>
  ```

- Finally, the regular expression also does not consider any obfuscations like:

  (a) `<iframe src="data:text/html,<body %6fnload=alert(1)>">`
      `</iframe>`

  (b) `<iframe src="data:text/html;base64,PGJvZHkgb25sb2FkPWFsZXXJ`
      `OKDEpPg=="></iframe>`

  (c) `<object data=data:text/html;base64,PHN2Zy9vbmxvYWQ9YWxlcnQ`
      `oMik+ ></object>`

In **(a)**, the attacker used the URL encoding of letter the "o", i.e., %6f. In **(b)**, the base64 obfuscated value (`PGJvZHkgb25sb2FkPWFsZXXJOKDEpPg==`) is equivalent to `<body onload=alert(1)>` and in **(c)**, base64 obfuscated value (`PHN2Zy9vbmxvYWQ9YWxlcnToMik+`) is equal to `<svg/onload=alert(2)>`

Category 3: The regular expression in this category matches XSS vectors making use of JavaScript URIs. The regular expression is:

```
/(=|(U\s*R\s*L\s*\(\))\s*("|\')?[^>]*\s*S\s*C\s*R\s*I\s*P\s*T\s*:/i
```

The regular expression above can correctly capture XSS vectors like:

- `<a href=javascript:alert(1)>Click Me`
- `<p style="background:url(javascript:alert(1))">`
- `<iframe src="jaVAscRipT:alert(1)">`
- `<form><button formaction="javascript:alert(1)">X</button>`

But the main limitation of regular expression is that it can not handle obfuscations like:

  (a) `<img src=x onerror=javascri&#x70;t:alert(1)>`
  (b) `<iframe src=JaVascrIPt&#x3A;alert(1)>`
  (c) `<iframe src=java&#115;cript:prompt(1)>`

In **(a)**, an attacker used hex encoding of the letter "p" in order to bypass the filter. Similarly, in **(b)**, an attacker used hex encoding of colon (:) and in **(c)**, the vector uses decimal encoding of letter "p". Modern browsers render all these XSS vectors, including modern mobile browsers.

4   XSS Filter

In this section, we present our XSS filter and also discuss set of regular expressions that we have added along with the improved versions of Wassermann et al.'s regular expressions categories.

---

[34] http://jsfiddle.net/Cm7JT/

4.1   Category 1 Improvements

In this section, we discuss our version of regular expressions that deals with XSS vectors making use of `script` tag. It is also available at http://jsfiddle.net/8JCF5/1/. Wassermann et al.'s regular expression is:

```
<script[^>]*>.*?</script>
```

Our improved form of above regular expression is:

```
1) /<script[^>]*>[\s\S]*?/i.test(string) ||
2) /%[\d\w]{2}/i.test(string) ||
3) /&#[^&]{2}/i.test(string) ||
4) /&#x[^&]{3}/i.test(string) ||
```

The first improvement that we have added in the regular expression is the use of \s\S class instead of . operator. Dot operator does not handle new line. \s\S gives better coverage by matching any whitespace and non-whitespace characters. We have used the "or" operator of JavaScript in order to combine different categories of regular expressions. The second regular expression covers URL encoding of the XSS vector like `<iframe src="data:text/html,%3Cscript%3Ealert(1)%3C/script%3E"></iframe>`. The regular expression matches the attacker's XSS vector and captures it if regular expression observe % sign and after % sign there is a digit or word in exactly next two characters. This regular expression also works if attacker completly obfuscates the vector in URL encoded form like: `<iframe src="data:text/html,%3C%73%63%72%69%70%74%3E%61%6C%65%72%74%28%31%29%3C%2F%73%63%72%69%70%74%3E"></iframe>`.

The third regular expression covers decimal encoded XSS vectors like: `<a href="data:text/html;blabla,&#60&#115&#99&#114&#105&#112&#116&#62&#97&#108&#101&#114&#116&#40&#49&#41&#60&#47&#115&#99&#114&#105&#112&#116&#62">X</a>`. The regular expression matches the XSS vector if it observes &# signs together and after &# signs there is no & symbol in next two characters.

The last and the forth regular expression above deals with hex encoded XSS vectors like: `<a href="data:text/html;blabla,&#x3C;&#x73;&#x63;&#x72;&#x69;&#x70;&#x74;&#x3E;&#x61;&#x6C;&#x65;&#x72;&#x74;&#x28;&#x31;&#x29;&#x3C;&#x2F;&#x73;&#x63;&#x72;&#x69;&#x70;&#x74;&#x3E;">X</a>`. The regular expression matches the XSS vector if it observes &#x signs together and after &#x signs there is no & symbol in next three characters.

4.2   Category 2 Improvements

This section discusses our improvements of Wassermann et al.'s regular expression that deals with XSS vectors make use of event handlers like `onerror`, `onload` etc. The regular expression is:

```
/([\s"']+on\w+)\s*=/i
```

Our improved version is:

1) `/[\s"\'';\/0-9\=\x0B\x09\x0C\x3B\x2C\x28]+on\w+`
   `[\s\x0B\x09\x0C\x3B\x2C\x28]*=/i.test(string) ||`
2) `/%[\d\w]{2}/i.test(string) ||`
3) `/&#[^&]{2}/i.test(string) ||`
4) `/&#x[^&]{3}/i.test(string)`

In the first regular expression we have added support of back-tick (')
symbol, semi-colon (;), forward slash (/), = symbol, digits (0-9), control characters (U+000B, U+0009, U+000C), U+003B, U+002C and U+0028. The second, third and fourth regular expressions (already discussed in previous section)
deals with obfuscation of vectors like <iframe src="data:text/html,<svg
%6F%6Eload=alert(1)>"></iframe>, <iframe src="data:text/html,<svg
onload=alert(1)>"></iframe> and <iframe src="data:text/
html,
<svg onload=alert(1)>"></iframe>.

4.3 Category 3 Improvements

In this section we discuss the improved form of regular expression that matches
XSS vectors making use of JavaScript URIs. The Wassermann et al.'s regular
expression is:

`/(=|(U\s*R\s*L\s*\())\s*("|\')?[^>]*\s*S\s*C\s*R\s*I\s*P\s*T\s*:/i`

Our improved form is:

1) `/(?:=|U\s*R\s*L\s*\()\s*[^>]*\s*S\s*C\s*R\s*I\s*P\s*T\s*:/i`
   `// Removed: ("|\')? -- The reason is it is an unnecessary capturing group`
   `                    and [^>] will match optional quote anyway.`

The regular expression looks for the following in sequence:

- = or the four characters URL(, in a case insensitive way because of ignore-case
  flag i.e., /i, optionally with one or more whitespace characters following any
  of the characters.
- Any number of characters other than >.
- The characters SCRIPT: in a case insensitive way, optionally with one or more
  whitespace characters following any of the characters.

The regular expression therefore matches all the following if present in user-
supplied input:

- =script:
- "VBScript:
- url('javascript:
- u r l (s c r i p t :

In order to support obfuscation, we have used the regular expressions that we
have already discussed above.

4.4 Miscellaneous Additions

In this section, we briefly discuss some of the miscellaneous classes of regular expressions that we have added in order to cover XSS vectors that do not belong to the above categories. Along with regular expression, we give one example of corresponding XSS vector (See Table 5 in Appendix). The complete set of regular expressions can also be found in Appendix A.

4.5 Limitations

The XSS filter is not meant to replace input validation and output encoding completely. XSS filter rather provide an additional layer of security to mitigate the consequences of XSS vulnerabilities. Our filter does not support DOM[35] and Stored[36] XSS but due to simple nature and significantly less AJAX-style interaction on mobile web applications, the chances of DOM based XSS is very low.

5   Implementation and Testing

This section reports on our implementation and testing of our XSS filter.

5.1 Implementation

We implemented our XSS filter in the form of JavaScript function. On the client side, sites may call our filter function (consists of few lines of JavaScript code) on an HTML form (*<form>* tag) *onsubmit* event handler, e.g. "onsubmit= xssfilter()". The use of HTML *<form>* tag is very common on mobile-side as we have discussed earlier (see Sect. 2.1). The complete code of the filter is available in Appendix A.

5.2 Testing

First we manually tested the performance of our final version of the filter against large number of XSS vectors available in the form of five resources ranging from old to the new ones. To the best of our knowledge, no XSS vector is able to bypass the filter, at the time of writing of this paper. Our regular expression based XSS filter has correctly matched all XSS vectors, if present in the user-supplied input. The five resources we used to test our filter are:

1. XSS Filter Evasion Cheatsheet available at https://www.owasp.org/index. php/XSS_Filter_Evasion_Cheat_Sheet
2. HTML5 Security Cheatsheet available at http://html5sec.org/
3. 523 XSS vectors available at http://xss2.technomancie.net/vectors/

---

[35] https://www.owasp.org/index.php/DOM_Based_XSS
[36] http://en.wikipedia.org/wiki/Cross-site_scripting

4. Technical attack sheet for cross site penetration tests at http://www.vulner-ability-lab.com/resources/documents/531.txt.
5. @XSSVector Twitter Account https://twitter.com/XSSVector. It has 130 plus latest XSS vectors.

Second, the creator[37] of one of the above resources has developed an automated testing framework[38] for us in order to test the filter against sheer volume of XSS vectors. Even with the help of an automated testing framework we were unable to find XSS vector that is able to bypass XSS filter.

6 Evaluation

This section briefly presents the results of the evaluation of our XSS filter. We have added support of the XSS filter in two open-source mobile applications i.e., Wordpress and Drupal. Developers of the sites who wish to include our filter (which is available in the form of JavaScript function) in their web applications has to do minimum amount of effort. Table 1 shows the amount of changes we have to do in order to add support in Wordpress and Drupal respectively. Figure available at http://i.imgur.com/OynTbDT.jpg shows our XSS filter correctly matching the user-supplied malicious input in the Wordpress comments section. Wordpress and Drupal frameworks already have bulit-in server-side validation mechanisms and the reason to choose these frameworks is, that we want to make a point that sites can use our filter in addition to the input checking they are already using and this will help in mitigating XSS consequences and will add additional security layer.

6.1 Evaluation in Terms of Time and Memory

We also wanted to see how our XSS filter performs in terms of time and memory usage because on the mobile-side web applications present a simplified and optimized version of their desktop variant. Table 2 reports on XSS filter on the two subjects (Wordpress and Drupal) in terms of memory and time. We show the average time (in milliseconds) by repeating the process of loading Wordpress and Drupal page, with and without our XSS filter support, 50 times. Direct debugging on mobile devices is not possible due to the lack of support for developer tools. As a consequence, we have used the "Remote Debugging[39]" feature provided by Google for Android.

6.2 Execution Time of XSS Filter JavaScript Function

In order to check Regular Expression Denial of Service (REDoS) [15], we have also measured the execution time of XSS filter JavaScript function. As we have

---

[37] Galadrim https://twitter.com/g4l4drim
[38] http://xss2.technomancie.net/suite/47/run   and   http://xss2.technomancie.net/suite/48/run
[39] https://developers.google.com/chrome/mobile/docs/debugging

discussed before, our filter is based on regular expressions. We prove that our regular expressions' approach is not vulnerable to REDoS attack and is computationally cheap. We have validated our regular expressions in the REDoS benchmark suite available at [14].

Table 1. Statistics on subjects' files

Subject	Files	Lines per file	Total lines
Wordpress	3	1	3
Drupal	1	2	2

Table 2. Statistics in terms of memory and time

Subject	Memory in KB	Avgerage time with filter (ms)	Avgerage time without filter (ms)
Wordpress	1.53	331	243
Drupal	1.17	375	251

REDoS attack exploits the backtracking (*when regular expression applies repetition to a complex subexpression and for the repeated subexpression, there exists a match which is also a suffix of another valid match* [15]) matching feature of regular expressions and in our set of regular expressions backtracking is not used in matching. REDoS benchmark uses the following code to measure the JavaScript time [11,12]:

```
var start = (new Date).getTime(); // Returns Time in millisecond
// XSS Filter Code i.e., Regular Expressions here
var timeelapsed = (new Date).getTime() - start;
```

We have measured the time by passing 100 different XSS vectors that belongs to different categories of regular expressions to the function and the average processing time we have observed is 1 ms.

6.3 Adoption

Our XSS detection rules have been adopted by most popular web application firewall engine i.e., Modsecurity. The XSS filter is now part of OWASP ModSecurity Core Rule Set (CRS)[40]. OWASP ModSecurity Core Rule Set (CRS) provides *generic protection* against vulnerabilities found in web applications [34].

7 Comparison to Other Approaches

In this section we compare our filter with the closely related proposals on the mobile-side.

---

[40] https://github.com/SpiderLabs/owasp-modsecurity-crs/tree/master/base_rules

NoScript Anywhere (NSA): NoScript (http://noscript.net/), is the popular security add-on for Mozilla Firefox. Its mobile form is called NoScript Anywhere (NSA) and is also based on regular expressions. Recently, Mozilla has abandoned support of XML User Interface Language (XUL) architecture for Firefox mobile in order to gain performance benefits and security issues [18]. This architectural change has made NSA useless overnight because of compatibility issues [19]. At the time of writing of this paper, NSA is no more compatible with Firefox mobile [13]. NSA's highly experimental form for testing purpose is available but for Firefox Nightly versions. Before this incompatibility issue, we have observed that NSA lacks update cycle compared to NoScript for desktop systems. NSA has another limitation in a sense that it is only available for Firefox users. Our XSS filter is available in the form of JavaScript function and is compatible with every modern browser. NSA has also usability issues because of blocking the scripts and this is not the case with our filter. Our filter captures malicious string at the time of user-supplied input.

Internet Explorer XSS Filter: Windows phone 7.5 has browser integrated support of XSS filter. The problem with the IE XSS filter is that it does not stop injections like: `<a href=''attackercontrolleddomain''>ClickMe</>`. With this type of injection, attacker can present victim with spoofed log-in page with a goal to steal credentials. Our filter correctly captures the above injection vectors. IE integrated XSS filter can also be bypassed if attacker is able to control two input parameters. IE's integrated XSS filter is only available to IE users while our filter is browser independent.

8   Conclusion

In this paper, we presented XSS filter for the mobile versions of web applications. We gave a survey of 100 popular mobile-version of web applications and found XSS in 81 of them. We have tested our filter against five publicly available XSS vector lists and found not even a single vector that is able to bypass the filter. We have also evaluated our filter by adding support in Wordpress and Drupal for mobiles. We hope that this paper will raise awareness about the XSS issue on mobile-side.

Acknowledgements. The authors would like to thank @0x6D6172696F, @insertScript, @ryancbarnett, @garethheyes, @mal, @avlidienbrunn, @mathias, @secalert, @g4l4drim and many more from Twitter *"infosec community"* for their help and anonymous reviewers for their comments. This work has been supported by the Ministry of Economic Affairs and Energy of the State of North Rhine-Westphalia (Grant 315-43-02/2-005-WFBO-009).

A   Appendix

```
function test(string) {
 var match = /<script[^>]*>[\s\S]*?/i.test(string) ||
 /%[\d\w]{2}/i.test(string) || /&#[^&]{2}/i.test(string) ||   /&#x[^&]{3}
/i.test(string) ||
 /[\s"\'`;\/0-9\=\x0B\x09\x0C\x3B\x2C\x28]+on\w+[\s\x0B\x09\x0C\x3B\x2C
\x28]*=/i.test(string)||
 /(?:=|U\s*R\s*L\s*\(\)\s*[^>]*\s*S\s*C\s*R\s*I\s*P\s*T\s*:/i.test(string)
|| /&colon;/i.test(string) || /[\s\S]src[\s\S]/i.test(string) ||
 /[\s\S]data:text\/html[\s\S]/i.test(string) || /[\s\S]xlink:href[\s\S]/
i.test(string) ||
 /[\s\S]!ENTITY.*?SYSTEM[\s\S]/i.test(string) || /
  [\s\S]pattern(?=.*?=)[\s\S]/i.test(string)||
 /[\s\S]base64[\s\S]/i.test(string) || /[\s\S]xmlns
  [\s\S]/i.test(string) ||
 /[\s\S]xhtml[\s\S]/i.test(string) ||   /[\s\S]href[\s\S]/i.test(string)
```

Table 3. Top sites whose mobile-version are vulnerable to XSS

Site name and URL	Alexa rank
Intel http://m.intel.com/content/intel-us/en.touch.html	1107
Nokia http://m.maps.nokia.com/# action=search&params=%7B%7D&bmk=1	568
StatCounter http://m.statcounter.com/feedback/?back=/	188
The New York Times http://mobile.nytimes.com/search	112
MTV http://m.mtv.com/asearch/index.rbml?search=	1168
HowStuffWorks http://m.howstuffworks.com/s/4759/Feedback	2882
SlashDot http://m.slashdot.org/	2267
Pinterest http://m.pinterest.com/	38
Dictionary http://m.dictionary.com/	182
MapQuest http://m.mapquest.com/	525

Table 4. Regular expression (RE) syntax description [7].

RE Construct	Regular expression (RE) syntax Description
\s	Matches any white-space character
\S	Matches any non-white-space character
|	Matches any one element separated by the vertical bar character
*	Matches the previous element zero or more times
?	Matches the previous element zero or one time
^	The match must start at the beginning of the string or line
/i	Makes the match case insensitive
.	Matches any character except newline
\	Escape Character
[^...]	Matches every character except the ones inside brackets

Table 5. Miscellaneous regular expression (RE) classes along with respective XSS vectors.

Regular expression (RE) classes and examplary XSS vector	
RE Construct	XSS Vector
/:/i	`<form><button formaction=javascript&colon; alert(1)>CLICKME`
/[\s\S]src[\s\S]/i	`<iframe src="http://jsfiddle.net/t846h /">`
/[\s\S]xlink:href[\s\S]/i	`<math><a xlink:href="//jsfiddle.net/ t846h/">click`
/[\s\S]base64[\s\S]/i	`<object data=data:text/html;base64, PHN2Zy9vbmxvYWQ9YWxlcnQoMik+ ></object>`
/[\s\S]href[\s\S]/i	`<a href="http://jsfiddle.net/ t846h">Click Me</a>`
/[\s\S]@import[\s\S]/i	`<style>@import 'http://attacker.com/evilcssfi le.css';</style>`

```
|| /[\s\S]style[\s\S]/i.test(string) ||   /[\s\S]formaction[\s\S]/i.test
   (string) ||
/<style[^>]*>[\s\S]*?/i.test(string) ||   /[\s\S]@import[\s\S]/i.test
   (string) ||
/<applet[^>]*>[\s\S]*?/i.test(string) ||  /<meta[^>]*>[\s\S]*?/i.test
   (string) ||
/<object[^>]*>[\s\S]*?/i.test(string) ||  /<embed[^>]*>[\s\S]*?/i.test
   (string) ||
/<form[^>]*>[\s\S]*?/i.test(string) || /<isindex[^>]*>[\s\S]*?/i.test
   (string);
 return match ? true : false;
} function inputValidation() {
     var string = document.getElementById("searchfield").value;
     if (test(string)){ alert('Filter has detected malicious input');
  return false;  }
     return true;
}
```

References

1. Wassermann, G., Su, Z.: Static detection of cross-site scripting vulnerabilities. In: ICSE 2008. http://dl.acm.org/citation.cfm?id=1368112
2. Controlling the XSS filter. http://blogs.msdn.com/b/ieinternals/archive/2011/01/31/ controlling-the-internet-explorer-xss-filter-with-the-x-xss-/protection-http-header.aspx

3. Cook, S.: A web developer's guide to cross-site scripting (January 2003). http://www.giac.org/practical/GSEC/Steve_Cook_GSEC
4. WhiteHat Security's Website Security Statistics Report (May 2013). https://www.whitehatsec.com/assets/WPstatsReport_052013.pdf
5. Do mobile and desktop interfaces belong together?. http://mobile.smashingmagazine.com/2012/07/19/do-mobile-desktop-interfaces-belong-together/more-130354
6. Mobile site vs. full site. http://www.nngroup.com/articles/mobile-site-vs-full-site/
7. Regular expression language – quick reference. http://msdn.microsoft.com/en-us/library/az24scfc.aspx
8. Regular expression tutorial. http://www.regular-expressions.info/tutorialcnt.html
9. Regular expressions cheat sheet. http://www.cheatography.com/davechild/cheat-sheets/regular-expressions/
10. Regular expressions. https://developer.mozilla.org/en-US/docs/JavaScript/Guide/Regular_Expressions
11. Measuring time with javascript. http://webdesign.onyou.ch/2010/11/30/measure-time-with-javascript/
12. Accuracy of JavaScript time. http://ejohn.org/blog/accuracy-of-javascript-time/
13. NoScript anywhere. http://noscript.net/nsa/
14. redos.js - JavaScript test program for regular expression DoS attacks. http://www.computerbytesman.com/redos/retime_js.source.txt
15. Regular expression denial of service. http://en.wikipedia.org/wiki/ReDoS
16. Singh, K.: Can mobile learn from the Web? In: W2SP 2012. http://www.w2spconf.com/2012/papers/w2sp12-final13.pdf
17. OWASP top 10 mobile risks. https://www.owasp.org/index.php/Projects/OWASP_Mobile_Security_Project_-_Top_Ten_Mobile_Risks
18. XUL (XML User Interface Language). https://developer.mozilla.org/en-US/docs/XUL
19. Mozilla developer platforms mobile. https://groups.google.com/group/mozilla.dev.platforms.mobile/browse_thread/thread/ff8d89bfa28383bb?pli=1
20. Knowyourelements. http://www.knowyourelements.com/#tab=list-view&date=2013-01-24
21. A complete guide of jQuery mobile for beginners. http://www.webappers.com/2013/03/15/a-complete-guide-of-jquery-mobile-for-beginners/
22. Athanasopoulos, E., Pappas, V., Krithinakis, A., Ligouras, S., Markatos, E., Karagiannis, T.: xJS: practical XSS prevention for web application development. In: Proceedings of the 2010 USENIX Conference on Web Application Development (2010)
23. Bisht, P., Venkatakrishnan, V.N.: XSS-GUARD: precise dynamic prevention of cross-site scripting attacks. In: Zamboni, D. (ed.) DIMVA 2008. LNCS, vol. 5137, pp. 23–43. Springer, Heidelberg (2008)
24. Bates, D., Barth, A., Jackson, C.: Regular expressions considered harmful in client-side XSS filters. In: WWW (2010). http://www.collinjackson.com/research/xssauditor.pdf
25. Kirda, E., Kruegel, C., Vigna, G., Jovanovic, N.: Noxes: a client-side solution for mitigating cross-site scripting attacks. In: Proceedings of the 2006 ACM Symposium on Applied Computing, pp. 330–337. ACM (2006)
26. Ismail, O., Etoh, M., Kadobayashi, Y., Yamaguchi, S.: A proposal and implementation of automatic detection/collection system for cross-site scripting vulnerability. In: AINA (2004)

27. Nadji, Y., Saxena, P., Song, D.: Document structure integrity: a robust basis for cross-site scripting defense. In: NDSS (2009)

28. Robertson, W., Vigna, G.: Static enforcement of web application integrity through strong typing. In: Proceedings of the 18th Conference on USENIX Security Symposium, SSYM'09, pp. 283–298. USENIX Association, Berkeley (2009)

29. Vogt, P., Nentwich, F., Jovanovic, N., Kirda, E., Kruegel, C., Vigna, G.: Cross site scripting prevention with dynamic data tainting and static analysis. In: Proceeding of the Network and Distributed System Security Symposium (NDSS)

30. Barth, A., Jackson, C., Mitchell, J.C.: Securing browser frame communication. In: 17th USENIX Security (2008)

31. Stamm, S., Sterne, B., Markham, G.: Reining in the web with content security policy. In: WWW (2010)

32. Oda, T., Wurster, G., van Oorschot, P., Somayaji, A.: SOMA: mutual approval for included content in web pages. In: CCS (2008)

33. Jim, T., Swamy, N., Hicks, M.: Defeating script injection attacks with browser enforced embedded policies. In: WWW (2007)

34. OWASP modSecurity core rule set project. https://www.owasp.org/index.php/Category:OWASP_ModSecurity_Core_Rule_Set_Project

35. Apache module mod_proxy. http://httpd.apache.org/docs/2.2/mod/mod_proxy.html

Punobot: Mobile Botnet Using Push Notification Service in Android

Hayoung Lee[1], Taeho Kang[1], Sangho Lee[1 (✉)], Jong Kim[2], and Yoonho Kim[3]

[1] Department of CSE, POSTECH, Pohang, Korea
{hayoungie,darktoy,sangho2}@postech.ac.kr
[2] Division of ITCE, POSTECH, Pohang, Korea
jkim@postech.ac.kr
[3] Division of Computer Science, Sangmyung University, Seoul, Korea
yhkim@smu.ac.kr

Abstract. A botnet is a collection of computers compromised by attackers, which is being increasingly used to advance political or financial interests. Recently, mobile botnets that rely on compromised mobile devices are emerging due to their improvements in computation power and communication capability. To cope with mobile botnets, we need to anticipate and prevent their command and control (C&C) channels. In this paper, we explore a new C&C channel for mobile botnets that is based on the push notification service (PNS) of Android: Google Cloud Messaging for Android (GCM). We find that (1) the registration process of the GCM only checks the validity of Gmail address and (2) applications can hide received push messages from users. By exploiting these two vulnerabilities, we evaluate the feasibility of the push notification service-based mobile botnet (Punobot) in several aspects. We show that Punobot is stealthy, energy-efficient, and dangerous. We also recommend remedies that any PNSs should consider to eliminate their security weaknesses.

Keywords: Mobile botnet · Push notification service · Google Cloud Messaging for Android (GCM) · Android

1 Introduction

A botnet is a network of computers that have been compromised by attackers. Unlike stand-alone malware, botnets have command and control (C&C) channels to receive commands from their masters for adaptively performing various attacks including Distributed Denial of Service (DDoS), theft of personal information, and spamming. Internet Relay Chat (IRC) [1] and Hypertext Transfer Protocol (HTTP) [2] are commonly used C&C channels. In the early years of the emergence of botnets, their purposes were mainly to have fun or to demonstrate attackers' capabilities. However, attackers have since utilized botnets to advance political or financial interests.

Y. Kim et al. (Eds.): WISA 2013, LNCS 8267, pp. 124–137, 2014.
DOI: 10.1007/978-3-319-05149-9_8, © Springer International Publishing Switzerland 2014

Nowadays, mobile devices become an important target of attackers for establishing *mobile botnets* because their computing capabilities become higher and they are consistently connected to the Internet via Wi-Fi or cellular networks. Since 2009, several cases of mobile botnets have been reported: SymbOS.Yxes [3] targeted the Symbian OS platform, IKee.B [4] was based on Jailbroken iPhones, and Geinimi [5] operated on the Android platform. All these botnets communicated using the HTTP protocol.

To deal with mobile botnets, several studies have been conducted. Most of them try to predict and prevent new types of mobile botnets before they are realized. Especially, several researchers proposed mobile botnets using SMS as a C&C channel [6–10]. They consider both centralized and decentralized structures for stealthy and robust C&C channels. A Bluetooth-based mobile botnet [11] has also been studied. In their design, the closest bot communicates with the attackers directly and the other bots receive commands via Bluetooth. However, both botnets have limitations because SMS is charged in many countries and the coverage of Bluetooth is restricted.

In this paper, we explore a new type of a mobile botnet that utilizes *a push notification service (PNS)* in Android as a C&C channel. PNSs are for informing users of update messages, real-time news, and game messages. WhatsApp Messenger, BNO News, eBay, and E*Trade Mobile are some applications that take advantage of PNSs. Most mobile operating systems provide PNSs, for example, Android has Google Cloud Messaging (GCM) [12] and iOS has Apple Push Notification Service (APNS) [13]. Unlike SMS and Bluetooth, PNSs are free and have no coverage problem. Moreover, PNSs consume low battery and demand low network traffic. Therefore, if attackers can exploit PNSs as C&C channels, they can establish stealthy and energy-efficient mobile botnets.

To identify the possibility of PNS-based botnets, we investigate the GCM framework and find that it has two serious vulnerabilities: (1) its registration process only demands a valid Gmail address and (2) applications with GCM can hide received push messages from users. Using these two findings and advanced techniques such as domain flux, we design a new mobile botnet, Punobot, which uses GCM as a C&C channel. Evaluation results show that Punobot is a stealthy and energy-efficient mobile botnet. We also present methods to detect and prevent Punobot.

The remainder of this paper is organized as follows. Section 2 introduces the Android's push notification service and Sect. 3 explains Punobot in details. Section 4 presents evaluation results of Punobot. Section 5 discusses strength of Punobot and possible countermeasures. Section 6 introduces related work. Lastly, Sect. 7 concludes this paper.

2 Google Cloud Messaging for Android (GCM)

2.1 Basics

GCM is a lightweight PNS that allows developers to send messages to applications installed on Android devices. With JellyBean (Android 4.1), Google intro-

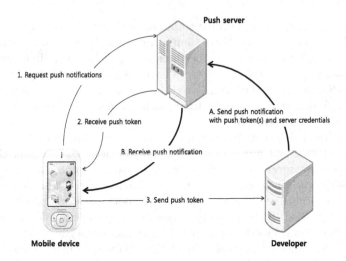

Fig. 1. GCM messaging process

duced GCM, which is a revision of the Android's PNS, in June 2012. Before GCM, Android had a PNS called Cloud to Device Messaging (C2DM). Since GCM is a free service, it helps developers to reduce the cost for messaging in their systems. GCM allows up to 4 KB messages; therefore, it is typically used to send small messages such as update messages or real-time information like weather reports. GCM requires devices running Android 2.2 or higher.

Once a mobile application embedding GCM is installed on a mobile device, the application can receive a push message from a developer, even when the device is turned off or the application has been terminated. Intent broadcast wakes up the mobile application when a push message arrives if the application is set up with proper broadcast receivers and permissions. The mobile device does not need to perform periodic polling to receive the message and consume low network traffic. As a result, a GCM-based mobile application requires only a small amount of battery power.

A developer must compose push messages using JavaScript Object Notation (JSON) format or plain text. The message has an expiration time from zero to four weeks, so a Google push server can conditionally store the message depending on expiration time if a mobile device cannot receive the messages temporarily. GCM does not limit the number of push messages that a developer can transmit.

2.2 Procedures

To utilize the GCM service, three procedures are needed (Fig. 1). First, a developer must register with the GCM service in the Google APIs console page [14] to obtain project ID and API key. A project ID is granted to each Gmail account after the user creates a Google API project and turns the GCM toggle to ON. An API key parameter is also provided if the developer selects the GCM API access function.

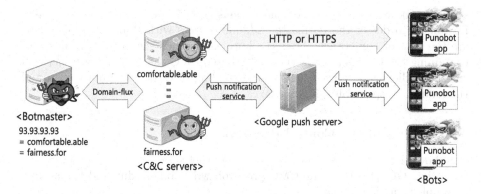

Fig. 2. Architecture of Punobot

Next, after a GCM-based application is installed on a mobile device, the device requests a PNS in the background by transmitting the package name of the application and the developer's project ID to the Google push server. If the request is allowed, the Google push server provides a registration ID to the device for identifying the application on the device. The device needs to deliver the registration ID and corresponding information, such as device ID, to the developer. However, Google does not provide any methods or protocols for this delivery. Therefore, the developer must maintain at least one server to receive the registration IDs using own communication protocol.

Lastly, whenever a developer wants to send a push message to the mobile device, the developer transmits the push message comprising the registration ID of the receiver, API key, and contents to the Google push server. If the message sent is verified as legal, the Google push server delivers the push message to the device. Push messages are transmitted and received using the HTTPS protocol and hence contents cannot be intercepted or modified.

3 Proposed Scheme: Punobot

3.1 Overview

In this section, we delineate a mobile botnet called Punobot that uses GCM in Android as a new kind of a C&C channel (Fig. 2). Before explain it, we introduce two assumptions. We assume that (1) attackers repackage some famous applications to embedding PNS-based malicious codes while applying robust anti-analysis techniques. We call the repackaged application as a Punobot application. We also assume that (2) the Punobot application has already been installed on an end-user mobile device. How to make repackaged applications robust against analysis and how to distribute them to mobile devices are out of scope of this paper.

In our botnet, command servers use domain flux as done by Conficker [15]; i.e., a botmaster is located in the highest level of the overall botnet, and C&C

servers work as proxies between the botmaster and bots. This topology makes it difficult to detect the botmaster. Mobile devices with Punobot applications are the bots of our botnet. After the botmaster sends the bots push messages containing the bot commands via a PNS-based C&C channel, the bots perform specific malicious activities such as the stealing of credential information and the sending of spam/phishing messages.

3.2   Command and Control Protocols

Punobot uses three C&C protocols for the botnet's participants. The PNS protocol (i.e., GCM) is the main C&C protocol, with domain flux and E-mail flux as supplementary protocols.

– *PNS protocol* is utilized by all participants (i.e., botmaster, C&C servers, Google push server, and bots). It is the main actor for delivering push messages containing the botmaster's commands to Punobot applications. In GCM, no predefined rules for decoding and displaying push messages exist. An application that received push messages can solely determine how to handle them. However, if the application does not show any notifications to the user, a malicious activity detector may suspect the application. Therefore, the Punobot application will show a part of the received message to the user while cloaking the botmaster's real intent.
– *Domain flux protocol* is for communication between the botmaster and the C&C servers and the C&C servers and the bots. The domain flux protocol is placed between the C&C servers and the bots primarily because after Punobot receives its registration ID from the Google push server, it must communicate with the C&C servers to send the registration ID. The IP addresses or domain names of the C&C servers must be specified in the Punobot application.
    To evade static analysis, we adopt the domain flux protocol in Punobot. This protocol is used by numerous recent botnets such as Conficker [15] and Kraken [16]. In this protocol, a domain generation algorithm (DGA) is used. Each bot algorithmically generates many domain names and queries each of them until one of them is resolved. The bot then communicates the corresponding IP address used to host the C&C server.
    In our domain flux protocol, we adopt a random word generator and construct domain names using English words with properly matched vowels and consonants.
– *E-mail flux protocol* is positioned in the overall architecture of the botnet. E-mail flux is needed to exploit the vulnerability of the PNS registration. Once a developer creates a project function on the official GCM site, GCM provides one project ID per Gmail address of the developer.
    By exploiting this feature, an attacker can register for the service multiple times using many Gmail addresses so that a mobile device can get many project IDs. Thus, if one registration ID is blocked by Google, the attacker can use other project IDs to obtain other registration IDs.

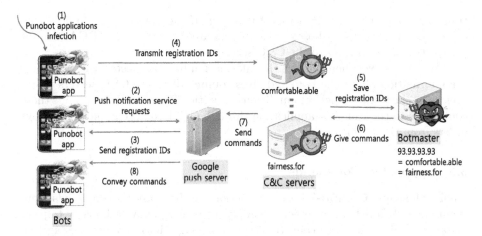

Fig. 3. Attack scenarios of Punobot

3.3 Entities

Our mobile botnet includes three types of entities: bots, attacker servers (a botmaster and C&C servers), and the Google push server.

– *Bots* are mobile devices on which Punobot applications have been installed. A bot is responsible for a PNS request in the background, and for receiving push messages and conducting malicious activities.
– *Attacker servers* consist of a botmaster and C&C servers. The botmaster commands bots and C&C servers, and manages the registration IDs of the bots. The C&C servers act as proxies between a botmaster and bots. If the bots send their registration IDs to the C&C servers, the servers deliver the information to the botmaster. When the C&C servers receive the push messages from the botmaster, the servers deliver the push messages to the bots via the Google push server.
– *Google push server* performs three tasks: issuing of registration IDs to the Punobot applications; identification of developers in the messaging steps; and conveying of push messages from C&C servers to bots.

3.4 Punobot Attack Scenarios

We will explain the attack scenarios utilized by Punobot (Fig. 3). As assumed in Sect. 3.1, the Punobot application is obfuscated before it is distributed in the Android markets and is installed on many user devices. After installation, the bot sends the developer's project ID and the package name of the application to request a PNS in the background.

The Google push server confirms whether the received information is correct. If the information is appropriate, the Google push server issues a registration ID that is used to identify the target application on the mobile device. The bot then transmits its registration ID to a C&C server. If the bot succeeds in accessing one of the C&C servers, whose domain names are generated using DGA, the bot passes its registration ID to the C&C server.

The C&C server then conveys the information to a botmaster who maintains the information about the bots and gives commands to the C&C servers whenever he or she wants to perform malicious activities. The C&C server sends these commands to the Punobot application through GCM and the application obeys orders from the botmaster.

3.5   Supported Commands

Push Message Composition. To conceal the botmaster's commands from the users and Google push server, we apply a steganography technology to push messages. This technology converts original messages into different messages so people who do not know the exact stegnography scheme used cannot extract the meaning of messages.

In Punobot, push messages should look like normal ones. Normal PNS-based applications usually receive push messages for informing announcements, such as "Big Bargain Sale." We select contents from several often-used announcements and connected the commands to the contents. By combining this message with a malicious function, a nefarious activity can be performed in the background without users' noticing.

Malicious Activities. Punobot supports the following four malicious activities.

- *Leakage of device-specific information:* A botmaster can obtain device-specific information such as the International Mobile Equipment Identity (IMEI), International Mobile Subscriber Identity (IMSI), phone number of the mobile device, and Android SDK version. IMEI gives information about the manufacturer and the model name of the device. By combining IMEI and IMSI, attackers can make illegal copies of mobile devices. Android SDK version can be used for secondary attacks such as virus infection or rooting which are based on the vulnerabilities of a certain Android SDK version.
- *Leakage of end-user information:* Information on mobile device users can be extracted via Punobot. The information can be contact information, SMS history, and stored files such as photos.
- *Sending spam and phishing messages:* Since an attacker can obtain information about the user of the mobile device, including phone numbers and E-mail addresses, the attacker can send spam and phishing messages via SMS or E-mail for financial benefits.
- *DDoS attack:* Punobot operates at the application level; hence, it is not affected by distance. Therefore, it can perform DDoS attacks using numerous PING or SYN packets from mobile devices.

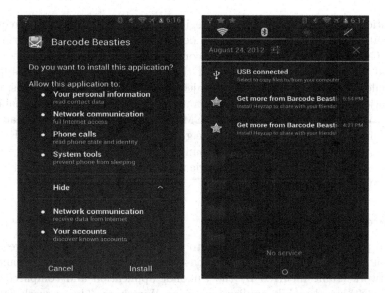

Fig. 4. Installation and messaging of Punobot application

4   Evaluation

To assess the feasibility and level of danger posed by Punobot, we conducted four evaluations: functionality test, stealthiness test, abuseability test, and comparisons to other botnets.

4.1   Experimental Settings

An attack server was set up using an Intel Core i7-2630M CPU and 4 GB memory. Punobot applications were set up on an Android emulator and commercial smartphones of Samsung Galaxy S I and II (Android 2.3), LG Optimus 2X (Android 2.3), and Motorola Atrix (Android 4.0).

4.2   Functionality Test

We performed a functionality test whether the supported commands worked normally in Punobot (Fig. 4). Punobot was able to carry out malicious activities: stealing of mobile-device-specific information; stealing of end-user information; sending of spam and phishing messages; and the carrying out of DDoS attacks.

4.3   Abusability Test

We evaluated whether the Google push server can identify abnormal activities carried out by Punobot. First, the Punobot application requested a GCM service numerous times to check whether the request was denied. In our experiment, the application succeeded in obtaining a registration ID for 10,000 GCM requests for about 3 min. Next, we changed the developer's project IDs to confirm that a new GCM request could still be accomplished with difference project IDs. Without altering the package name of the Punobot application, the application could request GCM even when project IDs had been changed. Thus, if the registration ID is blocked, a new registration ID can be acquired by making a new GCM request. Lastly, we made GCM requests using the package names of famous malicious mobile applications (e.g., com.google.ssearch of DroidKungFu and com.test of AnserverBot). We encountered no errors when using such package names, which implies that the Google push server does not maintain a blacklist for malicious applications.

4.4   Stealthiness Test

We also performed a stealthiness test to determine the difference between the Punobot application and normal PNS-based mobile applications. We monitored the network traffic incurred by the Punobot application and compared it to normal PNS-based mobile applications using Wireshark. The network flow for Punobot (Fig. 5) consisted of traffic from four entities: a bot, two Google push servers (A and B), and an attacker server. The distinguishing characteristic was that this network flow includes two Google push servers: server A was responsible for PNS requests and server B delivered push messages.

The bot requested a PNS from server A through port 443 on HTTPS (Fig. 5a). When server A accepted the service, the bot received its registration ID. The bot then transmitted the registration ID to the attacker's server in the background (Fig. 5b). To order a bot to commit malicious activities, the botmaster sent a push message containing commands to the Google push server B and the bot received the push message from server B (Fig. 5c).

Packets of the push messages are encrypted; therefore, detection schemes that are based on the contents of network packet cannot be applied to detect Punobot. Furthermore, the network flow of normal PNS-based mobile applications was the same as that of the Punobot application. Therefore, Punobot is a stealthy mobile botnet.

4.5   Comparisons to SMS-Based and E-mail-Based Botnets

We also compared Punobot to SMS and E-mail bots. First, we modified Power-Tutor [17] to measure the power consumption of each bot's message from zero to seven messages (Fig. 6). Among the three bots, Punobot consumed the least power. As the number of received messages increased, the difference between Punobot and the other bots increased and power changes were the smallest for Punobot. In addition, when 5 % and 10 % of the entire power were consumed, the number of PNS messages was approximately twice that of SMS messages, and five times greater than that of E-mail messages (Fig. 7).

Next, we measured the total network packet sizes for E-mail bot and Punobot. For the receipt and confirmation of an E-mail containing 360 characters, the total

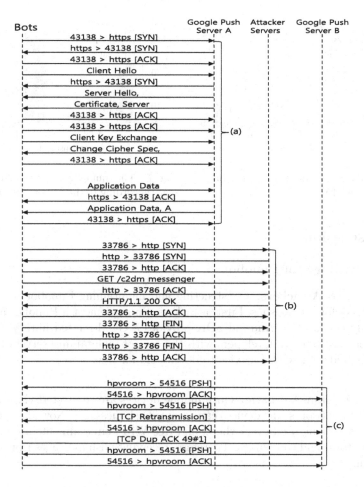

Fig. 5. Network flow of Punobot application

average size of a network packet was 3,882 B. However, a PNS message containing the same amounts of characters only consumed 664 B. Therefore, detecting Punobot using detection approaches based on excessive network traffic may prove difficult.

Lastly, we compared the cost of Punobot to that of an SMS bot. PNS messaging is performed via cellular network or Wi-Fi, the cost of Punobot is almost zero. In contrast, the cost of sending SMS is about US$ 0.02 per message [18]. In conclusion, for reasons of management cost, attackers may prefer Punobot to an SMS bot.

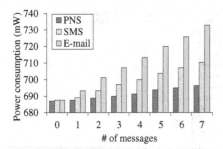
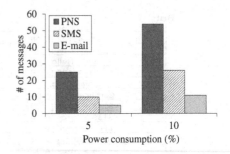

Fig. 6. Power consumption according to the number of messages

Fig. 7. The number of receivable messages according to the power consumption

5   Discussion

5.1   Advantages of Punobot

Favorable to Attackers. Constructing and maintaining Punobot is valuable for attackers for two reasons. First, attackers can implement a Punobot application easily because the Android SDK provides a GCM-related library. Second, GCM does not burden developers with the cost of maintaining servers because Google provides the GCM service to developers for free.

Communication-Agnostic. Once mobile devices are connected via the cellular or Wi-Fi networks, the devices can receive push messages. Nowadays, cellular networks are being used everywhere, and free Wi-Fi environments are provided by many stores and companies. Therefore, receiving push messages from attackers is simple.

Guaranteed Messaging. PNS guarantees the arrival of push messages. Messages from a botmaster can arrive eventually even if mobile devices are turned off or the Punobot application is terminated. Moreover, most of the push messages are also retransmitted if packet delivery fails. For these reasons, attackers can order the bots to carry out malicious activities at any time.

Low Bandwidth and Battery Power Consumption. Punobot consumes very little bandwidth and battery power because of two characteristics of PNS: small overhead in each message and devices do not need to be activate to receive messages. These performance aspects make Punobot efficient for attackers.

5.2   Prevention and Detection

We propose prevention and detection approaches for Punobot.

Vulnerabilities should be Fixed. To prevent Punobot, Google should revise its PNS to eliminate vulnerabilities; i.e., no support for built-in user interfaces and weak PNS request process in the service website.

First, Google only provides push messaging delivery, and does not provide a graphic user interface (GUI). Developers are forced to implement GUI to show push messages to device users. The developers usually use status notifications, pop-up notifications, or icon notifications. By exploiting this weakness, attackers can secretly send push messages the bot. To solve this problem, Google should modify GCM to force that received push messages should be shown to users as they are.

Second, developers can utilize the GCM service once they have Gmail accounts. To decrease the chance of a developer abusing the GCM service, Google should ask for more information such as the IP addresses or domain names of developers.

Data Tracking-Based Approach. Unlike many normal PNS-based applications, Punobot sends sensitive information to the botmaster in the background. Therefore, outgoing data by applications on a mobile device should be monitored and a warning should be issued to users if sensitive information is being sent. The research on monitoring data out such as TaintDroid [19] can be applied.

Permission-Based Approach. In this approach, permissions are checked prior to the GCM service being used. Android applications must declare permissions to utilize specific functions in mobile devices. To use the GCM service, developers must specify the following permissions:

- com.google.android.c2dm.intent.RECEIVE
- com.google.android.c2dm.intent.REGISTRATION
- com.google.android.c2dm.permission.RECEIVE
- com.google.android.c2dm.permission.SEND
- ⟨package name⟩.permission.C2D_MESSAGE
- android.permission.INTERNET

To detect Punobot, the bot detector may use static analysis to check the above permissions. However, this approach is restricted because normal PNS-based applications can also have the permissions. Nevertheless, this feature can reduce the volume of applications being monitored, and is thus useful for bot detectors. In addition, combining this with other detection schemes will improve the performance of the bot detector.

6   Related Work

PNS-Based Mobile Botnet. Recently, we found that Zhao et al. [20] have studied a PNS-based mobile botnet overlapped with our study period. The interesting characteristic of their botnet is that they use each mobile device as a server for sending push messages to exchange commands and registration IDs. No direct communications from bots to a botmaster to deliver registration IDs bring the robustness against detection. However, since several bots share the same API key, Google can easily notice malice: accessing the same API key from diverse IP addresses and geographical locations. To solve this problem, attackers need a large number of API keys, which brings a scalability problem. Since Punobot uses domain flux to cloak the IP addresses of C&C servers, it does not share such a problem. In addition, they only show spam attacks but we implemented private data stealing, spam, and DDoS attacks.

Abusing Notification Service. A notification service is a method to display push messages and other events to users. Xu and Zhu [21] exploit this service to show fraudulent notifications to users for phishing and spam attacks.

7   Conclusion

In this paper, we introduced a new mobile botnet called Punobot that utilizes GCM, which is an official PNS in Android, as a C&C channel. Punobot is based on GCM's two vulnerabilities: (1) the registration process is vulnerable and (2) applications can hide received messages from users. Without the changes in GCM, Punobot can perform malicious activities, unnoticeably. Therefore, we need to prepare countermeasures before such botnets evolve.

Acknowledgements. This research was supported by World Class University program funded by the Ministry of Education, Science and Technology through the National Research Foundation of Korea (R31-10100) and the MSIP (Ministry of Science, ICT & Future Planning), Korea, under the ITRC (Information Technology Research Center) support program supervised by the NIPA (National IT Industry Promotion Agency) (NIPA-2013-H0301-13-3002). A poster version of this paper was presented at [22].

References

1. F-Secure: Agobot. http://www.f-secure.com/v-descs/agobot.shtml
2. Symantec: Peacomm. http://www.symantec.com/security_response/writeup.jsp?docid=2007-011917-1403-99
3. Apvrille, A.: Symbian worm Yxes towards mobile botnets. http://www.fortiguard.com/papers/EICAR2010_Symbian-Yxes_Towards-Mobile-Botnets.pdf
4. Porras, P., Saïdi, H., Yegneswaran, V.: An analysis of the iKee.B iPhone botnet. In: Schmidt, A.U., Russello, G., Lioy, A., Prasad, N.R., Lian, S. (eds.) MobiSec 2010. LNICST, vol. 47, pp. 141–152. Springer, Heidelberg (2010)
5. Lookout: Security alert: Geinimi, sophisticated new Android trojan found in wild. http://blog.mylookout.com/blog/2010/12/29/geinimi_trojan/
6. Mulliner, C., Seifert, J.: Rise of the ibots: Owning a telco network. In: International Conference on Malicious and Unwanted Software (Malware) (2010)

7. Geng, G., Xu, G., Zhang, M., Yang, Y., Yang, G.: An improved SMS based hetero-geneous mobile botnet model. In: IEEE International Conference on Information and Automation (ICIA) (2011)
8. Hua, J., Sakurai, K.: A SMS-based mobile botnet using flooding algorithm. In: Ardagna, C.A., Zhou, J. (eds.) WISTP 2011. LNCS, vol. 6633, pp. 264–279. Springer, Heidelberg (2011)
9. Weidman, G.: Transparent botnet command and control for smartphones over SMS. In: Shmoocon (2011)
10. Zeng, Y., Shin, K.G., Hu, X.: Design of SMS commanded-and-controlled and P2P-structured mobile botnets. In: ACM Conference on Security and Privacy in Wire-less and Mobile Networks (WiSec) (2012)
11. Singh, K., Sangal, S., Jain, N., Traynor, P., Lee, W.: Evaluating bluetooth as a medium for botnet command and control. In: Kreibich, C., Jahnke, M. (eds.) DIMVA 2010. LNCS, vol. 6201, pp. 61–80. Springer, Heidelberg (2010)
12. Android Developers: Google cloud messaging for Android. http://developer.android.com/google/gcm/index.html
13. Apple: Apple push notification service. http://developer.apple.com/library/mac/documentation/NetworkingInternet/Conceptual/RemoteNotificationsPG/ApplePushService/ApplePushService.html
14. Google: Google APIs console. https://code.google.com/apis/console
15. Porras, P., Saidi, H., Yegneswaran, V.: An analysis of conficker's logic and ren-dezvous points (2009)
16. Royal, P.: Analysis of the Kraken botnet (2008)
17. Dong, M., Zhong, L.: Self-constructive, high-rate energy modeling for battery-powered mobile systems. In: International Conference on Mobile Systems, Appli-cations and Services (MobiSys) (2011)
18. Twilio: Twilio SMS price reduced - now $0.02 per message. http://www.twilio.com/blog/2010/11/twilio-sms-price-reduced-now-002-per-message.html
19. Enck, W., Gilbert, P., Chun, B.G., Cox, L.P., Jung, J., McDaniel, P., Sheth, A.N.: TaintDroid: an information-flow tracking system for realtime privacy monitoring on smartphones. In: USENIX Symposium on Operating Systems Design and Imple-mentation (OSDI) (2010)
20. Zhao, S., Lee, P.P.C., Lui, J.C.S., Guan, X., Ma, X., Tao, J.: Cloud-based push-styled mobile botnets: A case study of exploiting the cloud to device messaging service. In: Annual Computer Security Applications Conference (ACSAC) (2012)
21. Xu, Z., Zhu, S.: Abusing notification services on smartphones for phishing and spamming. In: USENIX Workshop on Offensive Technologies (WOOT) (2012)
22. Lee, H., Kang, T., Kim, J.: Design and detection of mobile botnet using push noti-fication service (poster). In: Conference on Information Security and Cryptology-Summer 2012 (CISC-S12) (2012)

Bifocals: Analyzing WebView Vulnerabilities in Android Applications

Erika Chin[✉] and David Wagner[✉]

University of California, Berkeley, USA
{emc,daw}@cs.berkeley.edu

Abstract. WebViews allow Android developers to embed a webpage within an application, seamlessly integrating native application code with HTML and JavaScript web content. While this rich interaction simplifies developer support for multiple platforms, it exposes applications to attack. In this paper, we explore two WebView vulnerabilities: *excess authorization*, where malicious JavaScript can invoke Android application code, and *file-based cross-zone scripting*, which exposes a device's file system to an attacker.

We build a tool, Bifocals, to detect these vulnerabilities and characterize the prevalence of vulnerable code. We found 67 applications with WebView-related vulnerabilities (11 % of applications containing WebViews). Based on our findings, we suggest a modification to WebView security policies that would protect over 60 % of the vulnerable applications with little burden on developers.

Keywords: Security · Smartphones · Mobile applications · Static analysis

1 Introduction

Mobile devices and platforms are a rapidly expanding, divergent marketplace. Application developers are forced to contend with a multitude of Android mobile phones and tablets; customized OS branches (e.g., Kindle Fire, Nook Tablet); and a score of competing platforms including iOS and Windows Phone. Android developers are responding to the challenge of supporting multiple platforms through the use of WebViews, which allow HTML content to be displayed within an application. At a high level, WebViews provide the same functionality as a web browser, but allow full customizability with respect to how and what content is displayed (e.g., navigation UIs, full screen, etc). These in-application browsers allow developers to write code in platform-neutral HTML and JavaScript that can be displayed by any device and version. Furthermore, application updates become simple. Developers merely update the HTML content downloaded by an application.

While convenient, these customized browsers can also pose a threat to application security, as allowing web content to interact with the application increases

Y. Kim et al. (Eds.): WISA 2013, LNCS 8267, pp. 138–159, 2014.
DOI: 10.1007/978-3-319-05149-9_9, © Springer International Publishing Switzerland 2014

the application's attack surface. We show in this paper that these problems are real.

One feature of Android is that it provides a way for JavaScript in a WebView to invoke Android application code, if this is enabled by the application. In particular, the application developer can register an interface (an API to the mobile application) that can be called by the JavaScript. This allows the web page to access functionality and data exposed by the application. This may seem safe, as typically developers use WebViews to display trusted websites. However, it introduces a new risk [29]. If the user navigates the WebView to an untrusted malicious website, the malicious page may receive access to potentially sensitive application data. Similarly, if the application loads a page over HTTP and if the user is using an insecure WiFi network, a man-in-the-middle could inject malicious content into the page and mount a similar attack. Allowing JavaScript to invoke application code breaks traditional browser security models.

In this work, we detail various WebView-based attacks and present our vulnerability identification tool, Bifocals. We ran the tool on a data set of 864 applications. Among the 608 applications that contain WebViews, we find that over 20 % of applications have the potential to give websites access to code. Of these applications, we find 54 % allow a user to navigate to malicious JavaScript that could access application code.

Based on our findings, we recommend modifications to Android to address these risks. Our experiments suggest that these modifications would protect more than 60 % of the vulnerable applications.

We make the following contributions:

- We build a tool to identify vulnerable WebViews.
- We measure the prevalence and impact of vulnerable WebViews.
- We suggest and evaluate solutions to mitigate these vulnerabilities.

2   Application and Web Interaction

To understand vulnerabilities in WebViews, we must first understand the features provided by WebViews. The WebView class allows developers to display data from web pages and files within the confines of the application, seamlessly integrating web and application content. Through the WebView, not only can developers set the content to be displayed, but they can also specify the layout and behavior of the WebView (e.g., display the address bar, track the browsing history, allow searches, etc.). Essentially, the WebView class allows a developer to create their own custom, embedded web browser.

Alternatively, web content can be displayed by sending a request to a browser application to load the content. We will focus on the WebView approach to displaying web content as customizations in a WebView can lead to security problems, while browsers are separate applications outside of an application's security boundary.[1]

---

[1] We use the term "web browser" to specifically reference a device's default web browsing application and "WebView" to refer to developer customized views.

Table 1. Select list of API calls used to customize WebView behavior

API call
`setWebViewClient(WebViewClient client)`
`addJavascriptInterface(Object object, String name)`
`getSettings().setJavaScriptEnabled(...)`

We discuss how WebViews are created and how they can be customized in detail.

2.1   WebView API

The WebView API allows developers to display content in various formats. Web-Views can load (1) web content using the HTTP or HTTPS protocols, (2) files from the file system via "file://," and (3) HTML via "data://." By default, a basic WebView does not execute JavaScript nor can the web content interact with the application in any way. If the user clicks on a link within the Web-View, the application is exited and the URI is loaded by the device's default web browser.

2.2   WebView Customizations

We discuss relevant WebView customizations that can be made by the developer. We list the APIs in Table 1.

WebSettings (Javascript and File Access). Each WebView contains its own WebSetting. The Android WebSettings class manages the settings of a WebView:

- Javascript execution in a webpage can be enabled by calling `setJavaScript-Enabled()` on the WebSetting. By default, JavaScript execution is off.
- Access to the local file system (e.g. loading a file in a WebView) is enabled by calling `setAllowFileAccess()`. By default, WebViews have file system access.[2]
- Access to files by JavaScript running in the context of a file scheme URI is enabled by calling `setAllowFileAccessFromFileURLs()`. By default, Web-Views grant this access for API versions prior to Jelly Bean.
- Access to content from any origin by JavaScript running in the context of a file scheme URI is enabled by calling `setAllowUniversalAccessFromFile-URLs()`. By default, WebViews grant this access for API versions prior to Jelly Bean.

WebViewClient (Navigation Ability). A WebView may or may not have an associated WebViewClient. The Android WebViewClient class is an event

---

[2] Regardless, access to an application's assets and resources (located at `file:///android_asset` and `file:///android_res`) is always granted within each application.

Table 2. How navigation events are handled, based on properties of the WebViewClient (WVC)

Has WVC?	shouldOverride()?	Loaded in:
No	N/A	Browser
Yes	Default	WebView
	Returns false	WebView
	Returns true	Depends on impl.

handler that allows developers to specify how content is rendered. By subclassing this client, the developer can specify what actions should be taken when the page finishes loading, a resource is loaded, an error is received, etc. Most notably, it allows the developer to specify the navigation behavior of the WebView (i.e., what action should be taken when the user clicks on a link in the WebView.) By overriding the default `shouldOverrideUrlLoading()` method, the developer can take different actions based on the contents of the URI. For example, a developer may specify that the URI be loaded in the WebView if it is on a specific domain, otherwise it launches the URI via web browser.

The default behavior of the WebView when the user clicks on a link in the WebView depends on the WebViewClient. We show this in Table 2. A WebView without a WebViewClient launches the web browser. If the WebView has a WebViewClient, the behavior depends on the `shouldOverrideUrlLoading()` method. If the method is not overridden or it returns `false`, then URIs are launched in the WebView. Otherwise, the behavior depends on the implementation of the method.

Interfaces (Code Access). Developers can also give web content access to the application's internal Java code. By calling `addJavascriptInterface(Object object, String name)`, the developer provides a handle to an application's interface to be used by JavaScript in loaded pages. For example:

```
WebView wv = new WebView();
wv.getSettings().setJavaScriptEnabled(true);
wv.addJavascriptInterface(new MyClass(), "mycls");
wv.loadURL("http://www.foo.com");
```

The above code creates a WebView where its web contents can invoke methods in `MyClass`. Any webpage in the WebView can invoke the methods with this JavaScript:

```
<script>
    mycls.someMethod1();
    mycls.someMethod2();
</script>
```

WebViews provide a way to meld applications with web content. Developers can allow JavaScript to invoke registered application methods, potentially enabling application state to be altered on the fly; and they control how a user may navigate pages. These can be powerful mechanisms towards providing a rich, interactive user experience. However, they can also introduce security vulnerabilities.

3   Attacks

The use of WebViews exposes applications to a larger attack surface. We discuss two types of vulnerabilities we identified: excess authorization and file-based cross-zone scripting, and the relevant threat model for attackers to exploit these vulnerabilities.

3.1   Threat Model

We assume developers are not malicious, though they may have varying levels of expertise in developing on the Android platform. While the application itself is trusted, web content and the open network it passes over should not be. We will discuss this in greater detail as we explain each vulnerability.

3.2   Excess Authorization

When a developer enables JavaScript execution and registers interfaces to a WebView, JavaScript content in the WebView can invoke the registered interfaces. If malicious third-party JavaScript gets loaded in the page, then it too can invoke the application's registered Java code. As authorization is actually granted to more web content than intended, we call this an excess authorization vulnerability. This general attack was introduced by Luo [29]. We develop variations and design and conduct a large-scale measurement study to understand the prevalence of this vulnerability.

Repercussions. Access to the application's Java code can lead to a variety of security implications depending on the functionality of the Java code. Information injection and leakage can occur if the invoked methods receives and returns information, respectively. Malformed input parameters may be able to crash the application, corrupt data, or otherwise launch a denial of service. Privilege escalation can occur if the methods require privileges that are owned by the applications [22,24]. Malicious JavaScript, in combination with other application vulnerabilities such as inter-application messaging vulnerabilities [17], can lead to attacks on other applications installed on the device. These are just a few of the ways an attacker can wreak havoc on an application.

Attackers. We consider two threat models:

Malicious Third-Party Content. There are many ways malicious JavaScript can appear in a WebView. Usually, the first-party content on the first page loaded is trusted. However, this page could also contain ads. Malicious ads containing JavaScript have appeared on popular advertising networks such as Google, Yahoo, and The New York Times [5, 6, 13]. Another way third-party content can be embedded in the page is through the use of frames. Finally, the user may navigate to third parties via links (if allowed by the WebView's settings). If any of this third-party content is malicious, it could invoke the application interfaces in ways the developer might not have anticipated.

Network Attacker. Another variation on this vulnerability is if the device is on an insecure network. If any page or resource is loaded over an unencrypted connection (i.e., over HTTP), then a man-in-the-middle attacker could inject any page of his choosing as a response to the request and thereby inject malicious JavaScript into the WebView.

Other Threats not Considered in this Paper. Even supposedly "trusted" websites can present a threat. First, trusted parties may purposely include what they think to be benign, third-party JavaScript. Nikiforakis et al. have shown that over 88 % of websites include at least one remote JavaScript library [30]. Malicious JavaScript could be included and could invoke the Android application's interface.

Additionally, "trusted" websites may also contain a cross-site scripting (XSS) vulnerability that allows an attacker to load malicious JavaScript in the page [18, 20, 27]. Over 75 % of web applications are estimated to be vulnerable to cross-site scripting [33]. If a page loaded in the WebView is vulnerable to XSS, an attacker may be able to exploit the XSS vulnerability to introduce malicious JavaScript into the page and then attack the mobile application.

For the purposes of this study, we focus on malicious third-party content and network attackers. Vulnerabilities in trusted websites can be inferred by assuming that 75–88 % of websites may also pose a threat due to remote script inclusion or XSS.

3.3   File-Based Cross-Zone Scripting

The Android WebView renderer treats everything loaded via a "file://" URL as being in the same origin. This allows any content loaded via a "file://" URL to read any file on the filesystem that the application can, including application internal storage (which is not accessible to any other application) and, if the application has permission, any file stored on the SD card. If the application loads static content via a "file://" URL, and this content includes third-party, untrusted JavaScript (or includes JavaScript over an unencrypted HTTP connection), this JavaScript gains the ability to read all the files in the filesystem that the application can.[3]

---

[3] Caveat: In the latest release of Android, the Android OS was modified to require developers to explicitly enable access to "file://" URLs, reducing the opportunity for attack. For applications prior to Jelly Bean and for applications that do not set the minimum OS version to Jelly Bean, access to files is still granted by default.

If the JavaScript is requested over an insecure connection, a man-in-the-middle attacker can inject malicious JavaScript. If the JavaScript is requested over HTTPS, but from an external, potentially untrusted source, the JavaScript itself could be malicious. Once malicious JavaScript is loaded, it can read files, create a network connection, and send the contents back to the attacker.

The exposed surface for this attack is admittedly smaller than the excess authorization attack. Only loaded files provide access to the vulnerability, and once the user navigates away from the "file://" scheme, the attack can no longer be launched. Similarly, the attack cannot be launched through a non-file frame. As we find in our measurement study, file-based cross-zone scripting vulnerabilities are fortunately fairly rare.

4   Bifocals

We present a tool, Bifocals, which closely examines two aspects of WebView interaction, the application and the web content, to automatically identify WebView vulnerabilities in Android applications. In Sect. 4.1, we describe how we analyze Android applications to identify at-risk WebViews. In Sect. 4.2, we describe how we crawl and analyze the web pages loaded into WebViews, to determine whether an attacker may be able to inject malicious Javascript into the WebView. In Sect. 4.3, we describe how we put these parts together to determine the potential impact of an attack.

4.1   Application Analysis

The first step of the tool is to detect potential WebView vulnerabilities.

Policy. If a WebView enables JavaScript, registers a JavaScript interface, and loads a URI, then it may be vulnerable to an excess authorization attack (depending on the content loaded). WebViewClient settings determine whether a user can navigate away from the page while staying within the confines of the WebView. This increases the potential for attack because every page a user navigates could also contain malicious JavaScript, as opposed to just the initial landing page.

Implementation Details. Applications for the Android platform are comprised of Dalvik executable (DEX) files that run on Android's Dalvik Virtual Machine. We first disassemble application DEX files and extract XML content and file resources packaged with the application using the publicly available Dedexer [31] and Baksmali tools [12].

Bifocals statically analyzes the disassembled output. Static analysis is a common approach for bug finding [16,28,37]. Bifocals specifically performs flow-sensitive, interprocedural static analysis. For optimization purposes, we limit the method invocation tracking to a nesting depth of three. Experimentally, we have not seen any cases where WebView information is propagated more than three levels deep. Bifocals tracks the state of WebViews (and WebView subclasses), WebViewClients (and WebViewClient subclasses), strings, numbers, and any relevant fields, parameters, and return values.

For each method that uses WebViews, Bifocals determines:

1. Whether JavaScript execution has been enabled for the WebView
2. If it allows JavaScript, what interfaces are made accessible to the JavaScript
3. The URI that is being loaded
4. Whether a user can navigate to other webpages within the WebView (by evaluating the implementation of any methods that override `WebViewClient.shouldOverrideUrlLoading()`)

In most cases, these properties are determined by tracking information to the WebView (string value, numbers, classes, etc.). Determining the fourth property requires a little more explanation. In addition to implicitly setting a navigation policy via the presence of the WebViewClient or using the default behavior of the `WebViewClient.shouldOverrideUrlLoading()` method, developers may also apply a policy for navigation behavior through code in the `WebViewClient.shouldOverrideUrlLoading()` implementation. We apply a heuristic to infer navigability. If the implementation of this method returns `false`, then users can navigate within the WebView. If the code for this method (or any methods called within the code for this method) contains a load URI call, then users can navigate within the WebView, *unless* it also contains a message invocation to launch the web browser. In that case, the developer has set a hybrid policy (e.g., loading the page in the WebView if the domain is `mysite.com` and launching the browser otherwise), and we conservatively consider that any new URIs will launch the browser (limiting the navigability, and thus, the attack opportunity).

These vulnerable WebViews and the URIs loaded into them are passed to the web analysis portion of the tool.

4.2   Web Analysis

The second stage analyzes the URIs (websites, files, and data) that are being accessed to determine whether they might embed or navigate to third-party content.

Policy. For each URI, Bifocals examines the page for potentially malicious third-party content. We focus specifically on attack scenarios where malicious JavaScript may be included in the WebView via website content, insecure networks, and user navigation and not via the exploitation of XSS vulnerabilities. Although third-party content can encompass many forms of content (e.g., images, scripts, frames, etc.), we limit the definition of potentially malicious third-party content to content that can lead to the execution of untrusted script. We classify ads and frames that load third-party sites as potentially malicious. Ads can be supplied by anyone and can contain JavaScript. Similarly, frames that load external content are considered untrusted. We ignore third-party images and other content that does not contain or execute script. We also ignore non-ad-related JavaScript (e.g., non-ad `<script src=...>`) unless it is embedded in a third-party page. Many webpages include popular, trusted third-party JavaScript, such as Google Analytics, Facebook's "Like" button, etc., and we assume these are intentional and we do not treat them as potentially malicious.

If a WebView is navigable, we apply the same evaluation to all pages transitively linked from the landing page (to a depth of three). Additionally, if the user can navigate to a third-party page (via links) in the WebView, we classify it as potentially malicious.

We assume that the primary website being visited and sites within the same domain are trustworthy, as well as anything belonging to the same second-level domain (the domain directly below the top-level domain in the DNS). For example, suppose a WebView loads `http://mysubdomain.mysite.com`. The domain `mysubdomain.mysite.com`, its second-level domain (SLD) `mysite.com`, and other subdomains of it (e.g., `myothersubdomain.mysite.com`) are most likely under the same jurisdiction and therefore we treat them all as trustworthy. This trust is similar to the implicit trust of cookie setting between a subdomain and its parent domain [4]. In the case of domains with country codes, we take the third-level domain (e.g., `http://blogs.telegraph.co.uk`'s trusted domain would be `telegraph.co.uk`.).

Implementation Details. To perform this analysis, we build on a basic web crawler built as a Firefox extension [25]. Given a URI, this crawler invokes Firefox, loads the page, and returns redirect information and the HTML source (including the frame source). We modified the extension to also log links, frames, and links within frames.

To identify ad content, we incorporated and modified the Adblock Plus extension [1]. Adblock Plus is a browser extension that parses pages and identifies and removes ads. For every network request required to load a page, it invokes a JavaScript function `shouldLoad()` that returns whether that content is an ad and should be loaded. We modified Adblock Plus in two ways. First, we modified the `shouldLoad()` function to log the content type (e.g., script, image, document, subdocument, etc. [9]), request origin, and target location. Second, we always allow the content to be loaded but log when an ad is identified.

To simulate a mobile browser, we modify the Firefox preference file (prefs.js) to set the user-agent string to the user-agent of an Android browser. This way, the web behavior returned by the request is the mobile behavior, not the desktop browser behavior.

Finally, we modify URIs before loading. For URIs that load data, we prepend the HTML with `data:text/html,` so that the browser loads the data string as a data URI. For URIs that load data with a relative base URI, we prepend the HTML with `data:text/html,<base href=''` + theBase + `">` to ensure that the browser renders the data and resolves all relative references.

The crawler then crawls the URIs that could be loaded into the WebView. If a vulnerability is identified or the WebView that the URI is from is not navigable, the crawling for that URI ends. Otherwise, the crawler repeats the page analysis for all links in the page and frames with the same SLD as the original URI or its redirects. We limit the crawling link depth to three for feasibility reasons.

Results from the crawler and the application analysis are then combined to identify WebViews that are fully vulnerable to the excess authorization attack.

We identify file-based cross-zone scripting attacks by checking if any of the loaded file URIs (regardless of whether interfaces are registered) contain third-party JavaScript.

4.3 Impact Analysis

There are many ways to examine the impact of a vulnerability. As discussed in Sect. 3.2, an attack on a WebView could result in information leakage, information injection, DoS, etc. One way to measure impact is to examine how many privileged resources an attacker would gain access to. We do this by analyzing the code invoked by the interface and determining the permissions required to execute that code.

We built a tool to determine what Android APIs a registered interface transitively grants access to (through invocation) and the permissions they correspond to. Given an interface, we analyze all methods that can be accessed in that interface (namely, all public methods and any superclasses' public methods). We assume that the attacker can determine public methods via reflection or direct analysis of the target application.

For each of the directly accessible methods, we recursively analyze the methods invoked by the method and the Android API calls made in the method. If an interface method returns an object of a different class, we analyze that object's public methods as well. We apply an Android API-to-permission map [21] to determine the set of permissions used by the reachable code. To determine the permissions used by non-API calls, Android message passing, Android databases, and code invoked via Java reflection, we modify Felt et al.'s Stowaway tool [21] to identify and output the methods in which these permissions are used. If those methods are reachable, then we add the corresponding permissions to the permission set. We include both normal and dangerous permissions in the set of permissions used.

4.4 Limitations and Discussion

Platforms. There are alternatives to using Firefox extensions to perform a web crawl. We could have used a command-line tool (e.g., `wget`), however this has limitations on the information received from the page. We chose a full-featured web browser which allowed us to leverage the existing Adblock extension, parse the loaded DOM in real-time, and fully render the content.

We chose to run this on a desktop computer with modifications to the browser preferences to spoof a mobile browser, as Firefox is more robust and efficient in crawling pages at scale. Given the massive amounts of meta-data produced from the crawl (from a large data set), performing the crawl on a mobile device would present challenges of dealing with a less robust, memory- and space-limited operating system. While it is possible for websites to rely on fields other than user-agent to determine whether it is running on a mobile device (and change content accordingly), user-agent is by far the most commonly used field.

In fact, we investigated the possibility of alternate indicators (e.g., JavaScript's `Navigator.platform` or `Navigator.appName`), but we observed only the user-agent being used in the websites we crawled. Even if websites were modified based on different Navigator fields, it is more likely to change the layout, not the nature of the content (frames, ads, etc.), and therefore it would not impact our results.

Ad Networks. Although we identify ads as potentially malicious, some ad networks may prohibit JavaScript from advertisers. We did not further classify ad networks based on whether a third-party advertiser could include JavaScript.

Crawling. One of the limitations of our crawling approach is the possibility of false negatives. Web content is dynamic. An ad or other third-party JavaScript may not always appear on a given page. To address this, we crawled each page three times.

Another potential source of false negatives is the inability to crawl all content. We limited the crawl depth to three links, but untrusted JavaScript may be on a page that our tool did not crawl. Websites might prevent our crawler from seeing the content behind a pay-wall or login-wall. In this case, our crawler will only analyze the login page. To address this, we would have to manually create accounts, log in, and crawl the page.

Due to these limitations, our tool reports a lower bound on vulnerable applications. On the other hand, mobile applications change less frequently than web content, and we can use the number of potential WebView vulnerabilities from the application analysis to estimate an upper bound on the number of actual vulnerable WebViews.

Static Analysis. A limitation to our static analysis approach is the risk of not deriving the full URI. If a URI is comprised of strings that are obtained from dynamic messages (Intents), from an API call that we do not handle, or from system state (e.g., getting the device ID, getting accelerometer data), then static analysis may fail to infer the full URI loaded into the WebView. Crawling an invalid URI could result in a redirect to a different page. In most cases, we believe that the redirected page would also be representative of the content that the page would have displayed (in terms of using ads and linking to third-parties). We additionally supplement missing data by substituting logical default values for substrings that cannot be derived. For example, if float value that we do not track is included in the URI, then a "1.0" is inserted in its place. Our tool also does not attempt to handle implicit control flow or resolve Java reflection of the WebView API, and this could lead to false negatives. Our tool, however, does resolve Java reflection for the impact analysis which is more likely to contain reflection. (Developers are unlikely to reflectively call the WebView API as the API is already publicly accessible.)

We considered a dynamic analysis approach to Bifocals as an alternative to our static approach. A dynamic analysis tool would be able to accurately determine dynamically set variables and state. It would also be able to confirm a vulnerability by exploiting it at run-time. However, it would be challenging to explore the full application state space to traverse all WebViews and to generate valid input for malicious JavaScript. Additionally, some Android UIs cannot be explored without user input (e.g., applications with logins). We chose a static approach because it achieves better code coverage, increasing the possibility of discovering vulnerabilities that may not have been exposed at runtime. We leave the possibility of a combined static and dynamic approach to leverage the benefits of both techniques for future work.

5   Evaluation

We ran Bifocals on 864 popular Android 2.2 applications to identify the prevalence of WebView vulnerabilities. The dataset consists of the 100 most popular paid applications, 764 most popular free applications, and 100 recently added free applications from the Android Market (as of Oct. 2010). After removing duplicate applications, applications that only consisted of keys to unlock paid features for free applications, and applications used for tool development and testing, we were left with a set of 864 applications for analysis.[4]

5.1   Characterizing the Use of WebViews

Developer Use of WebViews. We first analyzed these applications to better understand their use of WebViews. We found that 608 of the 864 applications (70.4 %) contained at least one WebView in the application. Of these 608 applications, 433 (71.2 % of applications with WebViews, 50.1 % of all applications) contained at least one WebView in the core functionality of the application. Also, 351 applications (57.7 % of applications with WebViews, 40.6 % of all applications) contained at least one WebView displayed by an ad library in the application.[5] This suggests that use of web content in Android applications is common.

The web content displayed in a WebView can be hosted remotely or locally. We analyzed all WebViews in these applications to identify what URI is initially loaded into the WebView. In Table 3, we summarize the schemes used by these applications. Overall, many applications load content over HTTP or via the data scheme. Use of SSL is much less common.

Exposure of Interfaces. We further examined how many applications allow JavaScript to invoke application code (by registering interfaces). We call these *authorized WebViews*. As indicated in Table 4, of the 608 applications with Web-Views, we find that one-fifth of these applications have at least one authorized WebView. Furthermore, one-fifth of applications have authorized, core

---

[4] We wanted to analyze both free and paid applications in order to avoid biases that might be present in free applications. Therefore, we reused an existing dataset rather than buying the applications a second time. It would be interesting to see if the results differ if we were to repeat the same experiments on current applications.

[5] In the rest of the section, we may shorten the phrases "WebView in the core functionality of the application" to "core WebView" or "core application" and "WebView in an ad library in the application" to "ad WebView" or "ad application."

Table 3. The types of URIs loaded into WebViews

Content loaded via:	# of apps	%
HTTP or HTTPS	345	56.7%
http://	335	55.1%
https://	15	2.5%
Local static content (file/data)	374	61.5%
file://	103	16.9%
data: (e.g., <html>...)	323	53.1%

Table 4. Breakdown of applications that grant JavaScript code access by whether the WebView is in the core application or ad library

	Total	Core	Ad
Apps with WebViews	608	433	352
Apps with auth'ed WVs	120	85	38
%	19.7%	19.6%	10.8%

WebViews, while 10.8% of applications have authorized, ad WebViews.[6] This suggests that many developers do use WebView APIs to grant web content access to application content. The 38 applications with authorized ad WebViews can be attributed to three distinct ad providers: Millennium Media [8], AdMarvel [2], and Medialets [7].

In Table 5, we further break these authorized WebViews down by the scheme of the URI initially loaded in the WebView. Unsurprisingly, many of these Web-Views load content over the HTTP protocol, and very few use SSL. The distribution of schemes for these types of WebViews closely mirrors that for all Web-Views, except that fewer of the applications loading content via data schemes expose an interface (10% vs. 16%; $p = 0.025$, Fisher's exact test).

Among the 85 applications that expose interfaces to core WebViews, 34 applications (40%) have WebViews where the user can navigate within the WebView, while 51 applications (60%) have WebViews that limit navigation (by launching subsequent URLs in a browser application). This is promising, as it shows that a majority of the applications have reduced their potential attack surface. However, restricting navigation does not fully eliminate the risk if the first page includes third-party frames or JavaScript.

5.2 Automated Analysis

In summary, Bifocals found 67 applications (11.0% of applications with Web-Views, and 55.8% of applications with authorized WebViews) that are vulnerable to at least one of the attacks presented. The high rate of vulnerabilities suggests that the Android WebView interface is error-prone and exposing APIs to web content is particularly risky.

---

[6] The sum of the applications with core and ad WebViews exceed the 120 applications as some applications have both core WebViews and ad WebViews.

Table 5. Breakdown of authorized applications by the URI scheme used

Authorized WVs by URI scheme	# of Apps
http://	57 (47.5 %)
https://	2 (1.7 %)
file://	19 (15.8 %)
data:	32 (26.7 %)

Table 6. The number of vulnerable apps found by Bifocals

Vulnerability	Core	Ad	Total
Network attack	32	33	65
Web attack	18	33	51
Total	33	33	66

Excess Authentication Vulnerabilities. We summarize the number of vulnerable applications in Table 6. We evaluate ad and core WebViews separately, as vulnerabilities in ad libraries can only be fixed by the ad provider, while vulnerabilities in the core application can be fixed by the application developer. Also, patching one ad library could secure multiple applications while patching vulnerabilities found in core WebViews must be done individually by each affected developer.

Network Attacker. We found 65 applications (54.1 % of applications that register interfaces) that are vulnerable to an excess authorization attack if used while connected to an insecure network.

The impact of these vulnerabilities varies. For 18 (56.2 %) of the 32 applications with this type of vulnerability in a core WebView, a network attacker gains access to API calls that use one or more Android permissions available to the application. Thus, the attacker may be able to take actions that would not be available to arbitrary web content. None of the ad libraries' WebViews give access to API calls that require permissions, so those vulnerabilities may have lower impact. It is important to note that access to permissions is only one metric to measure impact. Several other attacks may be possible even on applications whose API does not use any special permissions.

Web Attacker. Bifocals found 51 applications (42.5 % of applications that register interfaces) that are vulnerable to attack through malicious websites.

Many of these vulnerabilities grant a malicious website abilities that we would not expect web content to receive. 13 (72 %) of the 18 applications containing a core WebView that is vulnerable to a web attack give the web attacker the ability to invoke an API that uses one or more of the application's Android permissions. In contrast, none of the ad-based vulnerabilities allow attackers to invoke code that uses permissions.

File-Based Cross-Zone Scripting Vulnerabilities. Our tool identified two applications that load files with remote JavaScript. One of these is vulnerable to a network attack. The other makes requests over SSL from a trusted site, making it resistant to attack.

Upon further inspection, we find that many files loaded into a WebView are simple HTML pages with no need for JavaScript. For example, files may contain EULAs, Terms of Service, and FAQ pages.

5.3   Manual Analysis

We randomly selected 10 applications (of the 18 applications with a web-based excess authorization vulnerability in a core WebView) and manually analyzed these applications to determine the false positive rate of Bifocals. For each selected application, we examined the code, the loaded websites, and application as installed on an Android phone. For each reported vulnerability, we confirmed that Bifocals correctly inferred the APIs registered, URIs loaded, and navigation capability of the WebView. For each loaded URI, we confirmed the crawler result: that an ad, external frame, or site was found within the navigation constraints of the WebView. We did not build an exploit. We manually analyzed 19 vulnerable WebViews across 10 applications and found no false positives suggesting that Bifocals's false positive rate is likely below 5–10 %.

We now discuss a few applications and the vulnerabilities we discovered.

Alive. Alive is an application that displays Japanese cartoon images. It has a feature that allows a user to browse for other applications to install. This content is displayed in a WebView, and the landing page and linked pages contain ads. The registered interface provides code to download and install an application. The expected use case is that a user can select an application and click "download" which will download content at a specified URL and save it the SD card. The user is then asked whether they want to install the application. If they accept it, the code launches Android's application installation process.

This introduces multiple risks. One possible attack is that a network attacker or malicious advertisement could save arbitrary files to the SD card, by invoking the registered API with a URL pointing to a site controlled by the attacker. Also, an attacker could trick the user into installing a malicious application, if the attacker launches her attack when the user is browsing an application they are likely to install, or possibly through some other social engineering attack.

The Alive application has two other WebViews with vulnerabilities that allow web content to be downloaded to the internal data folder instead of the SD card.

AIM. The AOL Instant Messaging application contains a vulnerable WebView that accesses the READ_PHONE_STATE permission. The application provides an interface to handle successful logins. An attacker (network or web) can use this interface to control the values of the authentication token, session key, screen name, profile URL, and icon URL. This data goes into an "IdentityPreference" data structure which gets used throughout the application, making the application vulnerable to information injection and potentially a CSRF login attack.

Ad Libraries. We also manually examined two of the three ad libraries with potential vulnerabilities: Millennial Media and AdMarvel. The third, Medialets, was obfuscated. Millennial Media and AdMarvel are advertising services that offer rich media ads. Both have registered interfaces that allow the web content to modify the look and feel of the WebView (e.g., view size or layout settings). While neither of these libraries' interfaces invoke protected resources, an attack can still be mounted. An attacker can resize the WebView to take up the whole screen, increasing the chance that the user clicks on it.

Our tool was unable to determine the URLs for these WebViews (due to complexities with URL generation), so we manually confirmed the vulnerability and blacklisted the two libraries. It is possible that the obfuscated library, Medialets, is also vulnerable, but we conservatively leave that out of our analysis. Only 5 applications use Medialets.

Evaluation of the Tool. We find that our tool is able to correctly determine the URL loaded for each WebView in most cases. In both cases, the missing portion of the URL was a value for the URL query string. Ultimately, these query parameters did not affect the landing page, therefore the result from the crawler was correct.

In two cases, the website no longer existed, and in its place were squatter and GoDaddy pages, respectively. Our crawler crawled these pages and found potential vulnerabilities. We believe this to be the correct result as the squatting page would be displayed to the user, making the WebView vulnerable. In fact, this may present a larger threat, as an attacker can easily gain access to the user's application by purchasing the domain.

5.4   Limitations

One limitation of our study is that our data set is two years old. It would be interesting to evaluate Android 4.2 applications. We do not know how the results would differ. (We suspect the results may not change significantly. First, Web-Views have increased in popularity, potentially increasing the number of applications exposed to these vulnerabilities. Second, all vulnerabilities still exist in the current platform API. Only one change was made to the JavaScript interface for Android 4.2, which was to require explicit annotations to JavaScript accessible methods (announced on Feb. 14, 2013 [11]). This modification is only applied to applications that set Android 4.2 as the minimum or targeted API. As of Feb. 4, only 1.4 % of Android devices operate on Android 4.2 [3], and it is unlikely that many developers have set their applications to restrict distribution to the Android 4.2 platform.)

6   Suggested Improvements

6.1   Current Shortcomings

The core of the excess authorization problem is that *any* content loaded in the WebView is able to invoke application code, making it very easy for developers to unintentionally grant untrusted sources the ability to invoke application code. We conjecture that many of the vulnerabilities we found may be attributable to developer confusion with the WebView system. In particular, we observed three significant pitfalls for developers:

1. WebViewClients transparently change navigation behavior. If a WebView-Client is added, the WebView is implicitly made navigable. A developer who adds a WebViewClient to alter some non-navigation feature will make their WebView navigable, and thus may introduce an excess authorization vulnerability without realizing.
2. We have observed confusion with what the `shouldOverrideURLLoading()` method means and does. Stack Overflow contains many questions on what the method should do [36]. Most commonly, we have observed implementations of the overridden method that load a URL and then return `true`. This is the equivalent of not overriding the method at all or simply returning `false`.
3. A third potential source of confusion is that developers just may not be aware that *everything* loaded in the page or navigated to can invoke the application code.

6.2   Recommendations for Developers

In light of these pitfalls, we suggest ways a developer can reduce their attack exposure:

- **Disable Javascript.** Developers can turn off JavaScript if they do not need it.
- **Restrict Navigability.** Developers can restrict the WebView's navigability. This, however, only limits content loaded via links and does not limit content in the document (e.g., frames or JavaScript). Consequently, it is not a complete defense.
- **Limit APIs.** Third, developers can limit the exposure to the API by only registering necessary interfaces. Functionality that should not be made available to web content should be separated out into a different class.
- **Use New Android Mechanisms.** Android recently announced a new requirement for accessible interface methods to be annotated with `@JavascriptInterface` for Android 4.2 [11]. Developers should opt in to this by setting the minimum (or targeted) SDK version to Android 4.2. One caveat, however, is that while this may reduce accidental over-inclusion of accessible methods, it does nothing to prevent JavaScript from invoking intentional interface methods. Another caveat is that this approach does not exist for devices running versions older than 4.2. Also, it may take years for Android 4.2 to be used by a majority of phones, and developers may not want to limit their application's user base by targeting 4.2 for a while.

While these do not wholly prevent a vulnerability, they may limit the attack surface.

6.3 Recommendations for the Android Platform

To reduce the risk of unintentional excess authorization, we recommend that the Android platform be modified so that access to an exposed interface is granted only to specified domains instead of all content loaded in a particular WebView. For example, if a WebView loads foo.com, only foo.com should be allowed to invoke the interface. Other domains should not get access to the interface. Third-party web content loaded via frames should not get access to application code.

Specifically, we propose a policy that limits access by the second-level domain (SLD). The policy maintains a list of allowed SLDs for each WebView, and authorizes all content from such an SLD to invoke any interface registered with that WebView. By default, the list of allowed SLDs is initialized with the SLD of the URL initially loaded in the WebView. If this triggers a redirect, we automatically add the SLD of the target as well. This list can be supplemented by an optional developer-supplied whitelist of acceptable SLDs for each WebView (a WebView-level whitelist).

This approach provides an automated way to secure WebViews, lowering developer burden, while providing flexibility for developers to override the policy if they intentionally want specific third-party content to access the application.

Developer Effort. We evaluated this approach based on the amount of developer effort that would be required to comply with it. We found that 100 % of core applications that give access to code are handled automatically by our default policy and do not require any developer effort or other changes.

Effectiveness. Our approach would patch vulnerabilities due to frames and links. It would not patch vulnerabilities due to third-party JavaScript included directly on the landing page as they would obtain the domain of the page.[7]

We find that of the 18 vulnerable core applications, 11 of the landing pages (61 %) would be patched by our proposed policy. The remaining applications load ads directly on the landing page. Our estimate, however, may be an underapproximation of the number of patched pages. Adblock flags actual ads as well as ad providers' JavaScript (such as the Google script that generates the ad). It is possible that the JavaScript subsequently loads the ad content in a frame, in which case our solution would patch the vulnerability; however, this case is not included in our count of patched applications.

7   Related Work

WebViews. We are inspired by the work of Luo et al., which identifies the potential for WebView attacks [29]. They give examples for how webpages can attack applications, how applications can attack webpages, and introduce the excess authorization vulnerability. They perform a brief, primarily manual analysis of the possibility of these vulnerabilities in applications. We extend their work by

---

[7] Our approach also would not mitigate attacks via a XSS vulnerability (which is outside the scope of this work).

identifying variations on the basic code exposure attack and enumerating threats from different attackers, including the network attacker and attacks via remote script inclusion and XSS threats. Also, in contrast to their small-scale, manual investigation, we perform a large-scale measurement study and build an automated analysis tool to detect these vulnerabilities.

Saltzman blogged about a WebView-related attack in file-sharing applications [10]. File-sharing applications, such as DropBox, often save files to the application's internal file directory and can be displayed in a WebView. Assuming a malicious file gets saved, this file would then gain access to other files, potentially sending them to the attacker. We present a file-based cross-zone scripting attack that is a more general form of this attack, which can occur in any application. A trusted internal file, as opposed to a malicious file, can load external JavaScript, giving it access to the file system.

Static Analysis Tools for Android. Researchers have developed static analysis tools to identify other security properties in Android applications. For vulnerability detection, Grace et al. and Felt et al. apply CFG-based static analysis techniques to detect capability leaks across application boundaries [22,24]. Felt et al. and Au et al. build static analysis tools examine permission overprivilege in Android applications [14,21]. AdDroid examines overprivilege due to permissions only required by ad libraries [32].

Other static analysis tools focus on the identification of grayware or malicious applications. SCanDroid takes a data-centric approach to reasoning about the consistency of security specifications concerning permissions and databases [23]. Their tool, however, takes Java source code as input. Kim et al. present a bytecode-level static analysis tool to detect privacy leaks. They track location info, IDs (IMEI, IMSI, ICC-ID), audio and video eavesdroppers [26]. Batyuk et al. and Schmidt et al. similarly propose static analysis techniques to identify malicious Android applications [15,35]. To our knowledge, no tools have been created to analyze Android and web interaction.

In contrast to building static analysis tools from scratch, Scandariato et al. apply the COTS tool, Fortify Source Code Analyzer, to open-source Android applications and use code metrics to infer the likelihood of vulnerabilities [34]. Enck et al. also take advantage of Fortify's SCA but avoid dataset limitations of open source applications by creating a decompiler called *ded* to generate Java source code from an application binary. They examine security properties such as IMEI leakage and resource abuse [19].

8   Conclusion

While WebViews facilitate the creation of rich, interactive applications, they also introduce the potential for attack if developers are not careful. We examine vulnerabilities of WebViews and present Bifocals, which analyzes both Android applications and web content to identify vulnerabilities in applications. We discovered 67 applications that are vulnerable to attack through WebViews.

Excess authorization arises due to a mismatch in authorization expectations. A developer may intend to give code access to a specific website, but in actuality access is granted to anything loaded in the WebView. We propose changes to WebViews to grant code access based on the domain and not the WebView, thereby limiting the opportunity for exposure to malicious JavaScript. Our solution patches 60 % of the vulnerabilities we found and requires very little developer effort.

Acknowledgments. This research was supported by Intel through the ISTC for Secure Computing. Any opinions, findings, conclusions, or recommendations expressed in this publication are those of the authors and do not necessarily reflect the views of Intel.

References

1. Adblock plus. http://adblockplus.org/
2. AdMarvel. http://www.admarvel.com/
3. Dashboards: Platform versions. http://web.archive.org/web/20130205234427/ http://developer.android.com/about/dashboards/index.html
4. HTTP state management mechanism RFC. http://www.rfc-editor.org/rfc/rfc6265. txt
5. Malware delivered by Yahoo, Fox, Google ads. http://news.cnet.com/8301-27080_3-20000898-245.html
6. Malware-infected WinRAR distributed through Google AdWords. http://www.zdnet.com/blog/security/malware-infected-winrar-distributed-through-google-adwords/2405
7. Medialets. http://www.medialets.com/
8. Millennial media. http://www.millennialmedia.com/
9. nsIContentPolicy. https://developer.mozilla.org/en-US/docs/XPCOM_Interface_Reference/nsIContentPolicy
10. Old Habits Die Hard: Cross-Zone Scripting in Dropbox & Google Drive Mobile Apps. http://blog.watchfire.com/wfblog/2012/10/old-habits-die-hard.html
11. Security Enhancements in Jelly Bean. http://android-developers.blogspot.com/2013/02/security-enhancements-in-jelly-bean.html
12. Smali and baksmali. http://code.google.com/p/smali/
13. Times web ads show security breach. http://www.nytimes.com/2009/09/15/technology/internet/15adco.html
14. Au, K.W.Y., Zhou, Y.F., Huang, Z., Gill, P., Lie, D.: Short paper: a look at smartphone permission models. In: Proceedings of the 1st ACM Workshop on Security and Privacy in Smartphones and Mobile Devices (2011)
15. Batyuk, L., Herpich, M., Camtepe, S. A., Raddatz, K., Schmidt, A., Albayrak, S.: Using static analysis for automatic assessment and mitigation of unwanted and malicious activities within Android applications. In: Proceedings of the 6th International Conference on Malicious and Unwanted Software (MALWARE) (2011)
16. Chess, B., McGraw, G.: Static analysis for security. IEEE Security & Privacy. **2**(6), 76–79 (2004)
17. Chin, E., Felt, A.P., Greenwood, K., Wagner, D.: Analyzing inter-application communication in Android. In: Proceedings of the Annual International Conference on Mobile Systems, Applications, and Services (2011)

18. Di Lucca, G.A., Fasolino, A.R., Mastoianni, M., Tramontana, P.: Identifying cross site scripting vulnerabilities in web applications. In: Proceedings of the 6th IEEE International Workshop on Web Site Evolution (WSE) (2004)

19. Enck, W., Octeau, D., McDaniel, P., Chaudhuri, S.: A study of Android application security. In: Proceedings of the 20th USENIX Security Symposium (2011)

20. Endler, D.: The evolution of cross site scripting attacks. Whitepaper, iDefense Incorporation (2002)

21. Felt, A.P., Chin, E., Hanna, S., Song, D., Wagner, D.: Android permissions demystified. In: Proceedings of the ACM Conference on Computer and Communications, Security (2011)

22. Felt, A.P., Wang, H., Moshchuk, A., Hanna, S., Chin, E.: Permission re-delegation: Attacks and defenses. In: Proceedings of the 20th USENIX Security Symposium (2011)

23. Fuchs, A.P., Chaudhuri, A., Foster, J.S.: SCanDroid: Automated security certification of Android applications. Technical report, University of Maryland (2009)

24. Grace, M., Zhou, Y., Wang, Z., Jiang, X.: Systematic detection of capability leaks in stock Android smartphones. In: Proceedings of the 19th Annual Symposium on Network and Distributed System, Security (2012)

25. Kanich, C., Chachra, N., McCoy, D., Grier, C., Wang, D.Y., Motoyama, M., Levchenko, K., Savage, S., Voelker, G.M.: No plan survives contact: Experience with cybercrime measurement. In: Proceedings of the 4th Conference on Cyber Security Experimentation and Test (2011)

26. Kim, J., Yoon, Y., Yi, K., Shin, J., Center, S.: ScanDal: Static analyzer for detecting privacy leaks in Android applications. In: Proceedings of the MoST (2012)

27. Kirda, E., Kruegel, C., Vigna, G., Jovanovic, N.: Noxes: A client-side solution for mitigating cross-site scripting attacks. In: Proceedings of the 2006 ACM Symposium on Applied, Computing (2006)

28. Livshits, V.B., Lam, M.S.: Finding security vulnerabilities in Java applications with static analysis. In: Proceedings of the 14th Conference on USENIX Security Symposium (2005)

29. Luo, T., Hao, H., Du, W., Wang, Y., Yin, H.: Attacks on WebView in the Android system. In: Proceedings of the 27th Annual Computer Security Applications Conference (2011)

30. Nikiforakis, N., Invernizzi, L., Kapravelos, A., Van Acker, S., Joosen, W., Kruegel, C., Piessens, F., Vigna, G.: You are what you include: Large-scale evaluation of remote JavaScript inclusions. In: Proceedings of the ACM Conference on Computer and Communications, Security (2012)

31. Paller, G.: Dedexer. http://dedexer.sourceforge.net/

32. Pearce, P., Felt, A.P., Nunez, G., Wagner, D.: AdDroid: Privilege separation for applications and advertisers in Android. In: Proceedings of AsiaCCS (2012)

33. SC Magazine. WhiteHat: 90 percent of websites vulnerable to attack. http://www.scmagazine.com/whitehat-90-percent-of-websites-vulnerable-to-attack/article/58066/

34. Scandariato, R., Walden, J.: Predicting vulnerable classes in an Android application. In: Proceedings of the 4th International Workshop on Security Measurements and Metrics (2012)

35. Schmidt, A.-D., Bye, R., Schmidt, H.-G., Clausen, J., Kiraz, O., Yuksel, K.A., Camtepe, S.A., Albayrak, S.: Static analysis of executables for collaborative malware detection on Android. In: Proceedings of International Conference on Communications (ICC) (2009)

36. Stack Overflow. Developer sites contradict each other regading webview-shouldoverrideurlloading. http://stackoverflow.com/q/10865788
37. Wagner, D., Foster, J.S., Brewer, E.A., Aiken, A.: A first step towards automated detection of buffer overrun vulnerabilities. In: Proceedings of Network and Distributed System Security Symposium (2000)

Network Security

We Are Still Vulnerable to Clickjacking Attacks: About 99 % of Korean Websites Are Dangerous

Daehyun Kim[✉] and Hyoungshick Kim

Department of Computer Science and Engineering, Sungkyunkwan University,
Seoul, Republic of Korea
{dan.0901,hyoung}@skku.edu

Abstract. *Clickjacking* is an attack that tricks victims into clicking on invisible elements of a web page to perform an unintended action that is advantageous for an attacker. To defend against clickjacking, many techniques have already been proposed, but it is still unclear whether they are effectively deployed in practice. We study how vulnerable Korean websites are to clickjacking attacks by performing real attacks on top 100 popular Korean websites as well as all the financial websites. Our results are quite significant: almost all Korean websites (about 99.2 %) that we looked at are vulnerable to clickjacking attacks. Extending our observation to mobile websites, we can also obtain similar results.

1 Introduction

A web framing attack, called *clickjacking* [4], uses a transparent `iframe`[1] to hijack users' clicks. In a typical clickjacking attack scenario, a malicious web page is constructed by an attacker so that the attacker tricks victims into clicking on elements of the web page within an invisible iframe to perform an unintended action that is advantageous for the attacker.

Recently, clickjacking attacks have been considerable interest and many prevention techniques (e.g., *frame busting* [12]) have been proposed [6]. However, it is still questionable whether the defence mechanisms are indeed effectively deployed in practice. Our work is originally motivated by this question.

In this paper, we present an empirical study on analyzing the feasibility of clickjacking attacks by intensively testing the 100 most popular and all 36 financial institution websites, respectively, in Korea (the total of 130 unique Korean websites). Our experimental results show that 129 out of 130 websites (about 99.2 %) are vulnerable to clickjacking attacks. The `Citi Bank` website (http://www.citibank.co.kr/) is the only website that was not vulnerable to clickjacking attacks. We also extend our analysis to mobile web pages and then obtain the almost same results: all of the 100 most popular websites, when browsed through mobile phones, were also vulnerable to clickjacking attacks. Our key contributions can be summarized as follows:

---

[1] `iframe` is the HTML tag to specify an inline frame which is used to embed another document within the current HTML document.

Y. Kim et al. (Eds.): WISA 2013, LNCS 8267, pp. 163–173, 2014.
DOI: 10.1007/978-3-319-05149-9_10, © Springer International Publishing Switzerland 2014

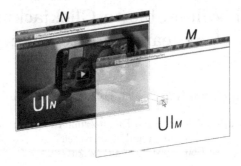

Fig. 1. An example of clickjacking attacks. An invisible web page (M) with a button (UI$_M$) to run a malicious action is put on top of what appears to be a normal web page (N) with a video clip (UI$_N$). A victim can see the play button on the video clip, but cannot see the button in a transparent web page. When the victim click on the play button, the victim actually click on the button in the transparent web page to trigger a malicious action such as downloading malware.

- As far as we are aware, this is the first empirical study of clickjacking attacks for the regional websites in a country. Our results show that the most popular Korean websites (96 out of 96 websites – 100 %) are much more vulnerable to clickjacking attacks compared with global websites (62 out of 100 websites – 62 %). We also extend our analysis to mobile web pages and then obtained the same results (read Sect. 3.1 and 3.2).
- Second, we examine the feasibility of clickjacking attacks for all the financial institution web pages in Korea and demonstrate that they are also vulnerable to clickjacking attacks (35 out of 36 websites – about 97.2 %). Five websites have used defence codes against clickjacking, but three websites among them can be easily bypassed by disabling JavaScript with a simple HTML tag; one website can be vulnerable to an attacker who controls a domain with the victim's server domain as a substring (read Sect. 3.3).
- Third, we discuss the possible reasons why Korean websites are still vulnerable to clickjacking attacks and suggest reasonable solutions to fix the problems (read Sect. 4).

In the rest of this paper, we will present the above results in detail. First, we will explain how clickjacking attacks work in practice to provide a better understanding of our study and then demonstrate this empirically on Korean websites.

2 What Is Clickjacking?

Clickjacking is a web-based attack that was reported by Jeremiah Grossman and Robert Hansen in 2008 [4]. It is a technique to attract users to click an element of a web page which is designed by an attacker [12]. The attacker uses the HTML tag called `iframe` to specify an inline frame which is used to embed an HTML document inside another HTML document. Figure 1 illustrates an example of

```
<html>
<title>An example page</title>
<body>

<style>
iframe { filter:alpha(opacity=0); opacity:0; }
</style>

<iframe src="./FakePage.html" border="0" scrolling="no">
</iframe>

</body>
</html>
```

Fig. 2. A HTML document with a transparent inline frame. An element in the HTML document can be hidden by making the inline frame's CSS opacity value zero. In addition, an attack can specify the option for scrolling to remove the scroll bar from the inline frame. This document shows that clickjacking attacks can be easily implemented.

clickjacking attacks. Figure 2 also shows how to create such a transparent inline frame. We can see that an invisible **iframe** can be simply made by setting the Cascading Style Sheet (CSS) property to control the opacity of HTML elements.

To generalize clickjacking attacks, we use N to represent a normal web page (e.g., web-portal, banking, social networking services) with an innocuous UI element UI_N. An attacker creates a malicious web page M with an element UI_M to perform a malicious action (e.g., downloading malware, sending an email message to the attacker, liking the attacker's website) by transparently overlaying UI_M on top of UI_N. Hence, when a victim tries to click on UI_N within N, the victim indeed clicks on UI_M within M to trigger an unintended action instead of UI_N. Clickjacking attacks can also be more sophisticated than simply hiding the target element as follows:

- Using the CSS cursor property, attackers can hide the default cursor and programmatically draw a fake cursor elsewhere [7], or alternatively set a custom mouse cursor icon to a deceptive image that has a cursor icon shifted several pixels off the original position [3].
- Attackers can use JavaScript – a single click can be changed into a double click which can click on UI_N as well as UI_M at the same time. Unless the intended action is performed by clicking on UI_N, careful users suspect that the visiting web page might be strange or deceptive.
- Clickjacking can be used with another attack such as Cross-Site Request Forgery (CSRF) which is a widely exploited website vulnerability whereby unauthorized commands are transmitted from a user that the website trusts [10] (see, for example, http://seclab.skku.edu/csrf_daum.avi).

```
if (top.location != self.location)
       { top.location = self.location }
```

Fig. 3. A simple frame busting code. This code is typically used to for preventing framing by another website.

Note that clickjacking attacks don't make use of bugs (e.g. a failure to properly sanitize the user input) in web browsers or applications unlike other common web vulnerabilities such as SQL injection and cross site scripting. They are consequences of a misuse of some HTML/CSS features (e.g., the ability to manipulate opacity of inline frames), combined with the way in which the web browser allows users to interact with invisible, or barely visible, elements [1] and thus anyone who knows basic HTML/CSS can easily implement clickjacking attacks.

3   Feasibility of Clickjacking Attacks for Korean Websites

We evaluated the feasibility of clickjacking attacks for the 100 most popular websites in Korea and their corresponding mobile websites. We also examined all Korean financial institutions since these are obviously high-risk targets.

In our adversary model, the goal of an adversary is to embed a target website within the adversary's website so that the embedded website can be used to lure victims to trigger an action (e.g., downloading malware) that is advantageous for an attacker. We here assume that the target website is not compromised.

3.1   Results for the Most Popular Websites in Korea

We used the top 100 websites (including web portals, online shopping, search engines, social networks, banks, online media, and games listed on Rankey (http://www.rankey.com/) which provides information about websites ranking to show the feasibility of clickjacking attacks for Korean websites.

To test whether clickjacking attacks can be successfully achieved, we used the five different web browsers (Internet Explorer, Chrome, Firefox, Safari, and Opera) which run on a Windows PC since the attack and defence implementations might perform differently on some web browsers. The reason why we chose these browsers is that they are the most popular in Korea[2]; we also used Internet Explorer 8 between different Internet Explorer versions for the same reason.

To defend against clickjacking attacks, some websites have used frame busting codes which intend to prevent the web pages from being loaded within an inline frame. A simple example code is shown in Fig. 3. A common frame busting code is made up of a conditional statement (e.g., `top.location != self.location`) and a counter action (e.g., `top.location = self.location`) [12].

---

[2] http://gs.statcounter.com/#browser-KR-monthly-201204-201304

```
<iframe src="http://www.kbstar.com" security="restricted"
    sandbox></iframe>
```

Fig. 4. An example code to bypass the frame busting code used for Korean websites: KB bank (http://www.kbstar.com). We can also bypass the codes for Nonghyup (http://www.nonghyup.com) and Hana bank (http://www.hanabank.com) in the same manner.

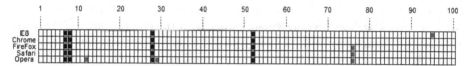

Fig. 5. Experimental results for the 100 most popular websites with five web browsers (Internet Explorer 8, Chrome, Firefox, Safari, and Opera – which are sorted in descending order of their traffics in Korea) on a Windows PC. The numbers represent the ranks of websites based on their traffics. Black boxes indicate that the websites are secure against our clickjacking attacks; gray boxes indicate that the websites do not support the tested web browser.

We found that seven websites have only used frame busting codes which rely on JavaScript to detect framing and prevent it, but can easily be bypassed by disabling JavaScript HTML attributes; if JavaScript is disabled in the context of `iframe`, their frame busting codes might not be working properly against clickjacking attacks. Therefore we tried to restrict use of the JavaScript with the attribute `security`="restricted" for Internet Explorer 8 and `sandbox` for Chrome, Firefox, and Safari. Figure 4 shows how to bypass the frame busting codes used for the three Korean websites (KB bank, Nonghyup, and Hana bank). Their frame busting codes can be easily framed by using simple HTML tags.

For each combination of a website S in the list and a web browser B, we tested whether the website S can be successfully framed by our website which can be assumed as the attacker's malicious website M and then still normally work. The visualization in Fig. 5 provides an overall view of the clickjacking distributions for the tested web browsers. In this figure, black boxes indicate that the websites are secure against our clickjacking attacks; gray boxes indicate that the websites do not support the tested web browser.

Surprisingly, in Fig. 5, we can see that all websites are vulnerable to our clickjacking attacks except for the four ones (Google, Facebook, YouTube, and Twitter). Interestingly, all these are not Korean websites. This is because global websites such as Google and Facebook might have already experience such attacks [13] more intensively than the Korean websites. To see the difference between Korean websites and global websites, we also evaluated the top 100 global websites selected from the Alexa Top-500 Global Sites (http://www.alexa.com/topsites) in the same manner. 62 out of the tested global websites can be effectively framed by our clickjacking attacks; this proportion (62 %) is significantly less than the 100 % attack success with the most popular Korean websites. To verify this statistically, we performed the one-tailed, two-proportion Z test with 95 % confidence and then obtained the results of $z = 6.7271$ and $p < 0.05$. This shows that Korean websites are significantly weaker against clickjacking attacks compared with global websites.

In the analysis for the top 100 global websites, we found that 18 out of the 38 websites that cannot be framed by clickjacking are in the US (the total of 53 websites); 4 out of the 38 websites are in Russia (the total of 5 websites). This shows that clickjacking attacks may appear to be relatively popular in some countries such as US and Russia rather than the other countries. Also, we surmise that companies with higher rewards for finding security bugs are more secure against clickjacking; 25 out of the 38 websites (about 66 %) are owned by the companies (Google, Facebook, and PayPal) which run a bug bounty program for cash (see the list of representative bug bounty programs in http://bugcrowd. com/list-of-bug-bounty-programs/).

All web browsers show almost the same results except for a few websites that do not support Internet Explorer, Firefox, Safari, and Opera, respectively. For example, Hyundai card (http://www.hyundaicard.com/) with the 95th rank requires a plug-in but Internet Explorer 8 has failed to install the required plug-in unlike the other web browsers. Since the Opera web browser doesn't support the sandbox attribute, the approach to disable JavaScript is not effective in the 12th and 29th websites with the Opera web browser.

3.2   Results for Mobile Web Pages

We extend our empirical analysis to also investigate the feasibility of clickjacking attacks on mobile web pages. We visited the 100 most popular Korean websites again with the two mobile devices: Samsung Galaxy Note 2 which runs Android Jelly Bean 4.2 and Apple iPad which runs iOS 6.1.3. We tested each website with the ten different web browsers (Android: Android default, Chrome, Opera, Dolfin, Firefox, and iOS: Safari, Chrome, Dolfin, Opera, Mecury), respectively, which are selected based on their popularity (see http://statcounter.com/).

When we visited the websites via the mobile devices, 92 websites served mobile alternatives instead of their original web pages. However, the results for mobile devices are not changed from those which are designed for desktop screens. We cannot observe any obvious difference between browsers and/or platforms as the same as for the desktop system.

The six mobile web pages are only designed to make users to download an app offering services rather than to explore the websites themselves. However, this practice might lead to security risks for mobile users; clickjacking attacks will be a serious concern for such web pages since clickjackers can effectively try to lure users to download malware instead of legitimate apps.

3.3   Results for Korean Banking Websites

We also examined the feasibility of clickjacking attacks for 36 financial institution websites since these are obviously high-risk targets. We classified the financial institutions as monetary and non-monetary financial institutions to see whether monetary financial institutions have much concerned about security compared with non-monetary financial institutions.

For the 18 *monetary* financial institutions, 17 banking websites can be successfully framed by using clickjacking. Although the four banking websites have used codes to detect and disable clickjacking, the three codes among them can be easily bypassed with the HTML attributes of sandbox or security= "restricted". There exists only one monetary financial institution Citi Bank (http://www.citibank.co.kr/) using a sophisticated defence code (see Fig. 6) against clickjacking attack, which is similar to Rysdstedt's recommendation [12]: When a web page is first loaded, the style tag hides all contents on the web page (html{display:none;}). If JavaScript is disabled, the web page will remain blank. Similarly, if the web page is framed, it will either remain blank or it will attempt to frame bust. The script only reveals the document's contents if the web page is not running in a frame.

For the 18 *non-monetary* financial institution websites, all the websites can be attacked by using clickjacking. Since the SinHyup Bank website (http://www. cu.co.kr/) that only uses a defence code to block clickjacking attacks, all the remaining websites can be easily framed with a simple HTML tag.

The defence code (see Fig. 7) used in the SinHyup Bank website seems secure against clickjacking at first glance in that this code uses the property of document.domain which returns the domain name of the server that loaded the current document. However, this web page can be framed by an attacker who

```
<style>
html{display:none;}
<style>

<script>
try{
    if(top.location.host == self.location.host)
    {
        document.documentElement.style.display='block';
    }else{
        top.location = self.location;
    }
}catch(e){ top.location = self.location; }
</script>
```

Fig. 6. The frame busting code used for Citi Bank. This code is almost similar to Rysdstedt's recommendation [12].

```
<script>
if(document.domain.indexOf("openbank.cu.co.kr") > -1) {
     location.href = "https://" + document.domain;
  }else{
     alert("Access Deny");
  }
}
</script>
```

Fig. 7. The frame busting code used for SinHyup Bank. This code checks whether the domain name of the server includes the substring "http://openbank.cu.co.kr"

controls a domain with the substring "http://openbank.cu.co.kr" (e.g., http://kopenbank.cu.co.kr). It shows the limitation in checking the domain name of a server to prevent clickjacking attacks.

Although one *monetary* financial institution website Citi Bank is secure against clickjacking, it is still unclear that *monetary* financial institution websites are overall more secure against clickjacking than *non-monetary* financial institution websites. To verify this statistically, we performed the one-tailed, two-proportion Z test with 95 % confidence and then obtained the results of $z = 1.0142$ and $p = 0.1563$. From this test result, we conclude that they are not significantly different at $p < 0.05$.

4   Discussion

Clickjacking attacks and defences have been intensively studied [6,12] since it was already reported almost five years ago [4]. Interestingly, however, almost Korean websites (about 99.2 %) are still vulnerable to these attacks.

Probably, clickjacking is unpopular in Korea. We can see that the small number (6 out of 130 – about 4.6 %) of websites have only tried to prevent clickjacking attacks. This is because victims from clickjacking attacks have been highly concentrated until now. For example, there have currently been two kinds of widespread clickjacking attacks in the wild: Likejaking [13] and Tweetbomb [9]. Fortunately, Korean websites don't seem attractive targets yet for clickjackers.

A few of Korean websites have used defence codes to detect framing and prevent it, but they are naively implemented and thus impractical. Unlike the global websites (e.g., Google), the Korean websites don't use code obfuscation techniques for their defence codes to make the codes themselves difficult to analyze. To make matters worse, almost frame busting codes used in the Korean websites can be easily bypassed with a simple HTML tag. Perhaps this is another example of "security theatre", which tackles the feeling but not the reality – vendors (or engineers) may demonstrate this perfunctory function to assure their customers (or managers) that their websites are really secure against clickjacking attacks. We have to understand what defences are practically effective.

At the technical level, we recommend that Korean websites have to implement a secure code like the frame busting script used in `Citi Bank` (see Fig. 6) and also use obfuscation techniques to protect their codes. Some manual labor will be required to de-obfuscate clickjacking defences when they are properly obfuscated.

Surely, it is not easy to trace new vulnerabilities in dynamically updated websites over time. The existence of a bounty program for security bugs seems helpful to solve this problem. For example, when a clickjacking vulnerability in Google Docs (http://docs.google.com) was found [8], it was fixed soon within two weeks. In general, companies with higher rewards for finding bugs will become more secure and sustainable.

5   Related Work

The possibility of attacks using transparent frames was first mentioned in a Mozilla bug report [11]. Hansen and Grossman [4] coined the term "clickjacking" in 2008. Clickjacking attacks can be used alone or in combination with other attacks such as Cross-Site Request Forgery (CSRF) [2] which is a technique that allows the attacker to trick a user into performing an action, using her authority and credentials. Targeted attacks were made on Facebook [13] and Twitter [9]. Rydstedt et al. [12] showed that the most frame-busting practices implemented by the Alexa top 500 sites can be circumvented by a simple way such as JavaScript disabling.

There are several clickjacking defence techniques to provide the visual integrity of a web page. One straightforward mitigation is to present a confirmation prompt to users when the target element has been clicked. Unfortunately, this approach gives a poor user experience and is still vulnerable to double-click timing attacks [6]. Another popular approach is to use the UI layout randomization technique [5]; however, this is not the ultimate solution to this problem since the attacker may try to ask the victim to keep clicking until successfully guessing the location of a target UI element [6]. Huang et al. [6] proposed a new defence called "InContext", where websites mark UI elements that are sensitive, and browsers enforce context integrity of user actions on these sensitive UI elements. This technique is very effective against clickjacking attacks but requires the client browsers (or OSes) modification. Rydstedt et al. [12] presented a simple but effective frame-busting code to mitigate clickjacking attacks.

Many client-side defence solutions were also proposed: (1) The removal of all transparency from all cross-origin elements is surely effective to detect clickjacing attacks; however, it can incur a significant visual penalty on benign websites [6]. (2) Heuristic-based techniques (e.g., ClickIDS [1]) decide when to allow rendering transparent frames by detecting whether the clicked cross-origin frame is not fully visible. But, these solutions have not been widely deployed since heuristics will inherently incur false positives and false negatives, and there is always a room for attackers to design their websites to bypass the heuristics that are being checked. They also introduced some compatibility costs for legacy websites, which may hinder browser vendor adoption.

6   Conclusion

We analyzed the feasibility of clickjacking attacks by testing the 100 most popular and all 36 financial institution websites in Korea (the total of 130 unique websites). Our experiments show that 129 out of 130 websites (about 99.2 %) are vulnerable to clickjacking attacks; even Korean websites with clickjacking defences could be easily defeated with a simple HTML tag. A statistical test (the one-tailed, two-proportion Z test with 95 % confidence) shows that Korean websites are significantly more vulnerable compared with global websites (62 out of 100 websites – 62 %).

When we consider that clickjacking defence techniques are clearly understood and fairly easy to implement, the reason why Korean websites are still vulnerable to clickjacking seems rather clear. This is because Korean websites might be unattractive targets for clickjackers until now; the small number (6 out of 130 – about 4.6 %) of websites have only tried to prevent clickjacking attacks but 5 of them failed in practice. However, we need to prepare for forthcoming attacks. So we recommend a secure implementation of frame busting codes and the use of code obfuscation techniques to make the codes themselves difficult to analyze at the technical level. Also, the introduction of a bounty program will be helpful to fix security bugs such as clickjacking quickly; we can see that about 66 % of the secure global websites against clickjacking are owned by the companies (Google, Facebook, and PayPal) which run a bug bounty program.

References

1. Balduzzi, M., Egele, M., Kirda, E., Balzarotti, D., Kruegel, C.: A solution for the automated detection of clickjacking attacks. In: Proceedings of the 5th ACM Symposium on Information, Computer and Communications Security (2010)
2. Barth, A., Jackson, C., Mitchell, J.C.: Robust defenses for cross-site request forgery. In: Proceedings of the 15th ACM conference on Computer and communications security (2008)
3. Bordi, E.: Proof of concept - cursorjacking (noscript). http://static.vulnerability.fr/noscript-cursorjacking.html
4. Hansen, R.: Clickjacking. http://ha.ckers.org/blog/20080915/clickjacking/
5. Hill, B.: Adaptive user interface randomization as an anti-clickjacking strategy (2012). http://www.thesecuritypractice.com/the_security_practice/papers/AdaptiveUserInterfaceRandomization.pdf
6. Huang, L.S., Moshchuk, A., Wang, H.J., Schechter, S., Jackson, C.: Clickjacking: attacks and defenses. In: Proceedings of the 21st USENIX Conference on Security Symposium (2012)
7. Kotowicz, K.: Cursorjacking again. http://blog.kotowicz.net/2012/01/cursorjacking-again.html
8. Kumar, M.: Hacking google users with google's goopass phishing attack (2013). http://thehackernews.com/2013/03/hacking-google-users-with-googles.html
9. Mahemoff, M.: Explaining the "don't click" clickjacking tweetbom (2009). http://softwareas.com/explaining-the-dont-click-clickjacking-tweetbomb
10. Ristic, I.: Apache Security. O'Reilly Media, Sebastopol (2005)

11. Ruderman, J.: Bug 154957 - iframe content background defaults to transparent (2002). https://bugzilla.mozilla.org/show_bug.cgi?id=154957
12. Rydstedt, G., Bursztein, E., Boneh, D., Jackson, C.: Busting frame busting: a study of clickjacking vulnerabilities at popular sites. In: IEEE Oakland Web 2.0 Security and Privacy (W2SP 2010) (2010)
13. SophosLabs: Facebook worm - "likejacking" (2010). http://nakedsecurity.sophos.com/2010/05/31/facebook-likejacking-worm/

Resistance Is Not Futile: Detecting DDoS Attacks without Packet Inspection

Arjun P. Athreya$^{(\boxtimes)}$, Xiao Wang, Yu Seung Kim, Yuan Tian,
and Patrick Tague

Wireless Network and System Security Group,
Carnegie Mellon University, Pittsburgh, USA
{arjuna,xiaowang,yuseungk,yt,tague}@cmu.edu

Abstract. Packets in anonymous networks are fully protected. Therefore, traditional methods relying on packet header and higher layer information do not work to detect Distributed-Denial-of-Service (DDoS) attacks in anonymous networks. In this paper we propose to use observable statistics at routers that need no packet inspection to infer the presence of an attack. We propose packet resistance as a metric to detect the presence of attacks which reduce the availability of channel bandwidth for wireless routers in the core network. Our proposed detection framework is distributed, wherein each router in the network core monitors and reports its findings to an intermediate router. These intermediate routers form a hierarchical overlay to eventually reach a centralized attack monitoring center. The alarm messages are used to construct an attack path and determine the origin of the attack. We present simulation results to demonstrate the effectiveness of our proposed metric.

Keywords: Anonymous networks · DDoS · Intrusion detection

1 Introduction

In many communication applications (email, social networking, peer-to-peer file sharing, sensitive battlefield military communications for example) the end users share sensitive data between them. The data and communication patterns learned from networks sharing such sensitive information leads to privacy and other security breaches [1]. Hence, for reasons such as confidentiality, political restraint evasion or sensitive communications, network anonymity is desired.

Network anonymity protects against traceability of end-hosts of networks even though their data traverses through the network in the presence of adversaries. In a fully anonymized network using services such as Tor [2], all the packet's contents and the packet's meta data are fully protected by cryptographic techniques. These packets offer no flow information, source and destination IP addresses, other IP header details or even higher layer details of the applications being supported. Therefore if attackers inject or flood such networks with garbled or replayed packets, the routers cannot distinguish between flows of

Y. Kim et al. (Eds.): WISA 2013, LNCS 8267, pp. 174–188, 2014.
DOI: 10.1007/978-3-319-05149-9_11, © Springer International Publishing Switzerland 2014

legitimate traffic versus attack traffic. Thus traditional attack detection mechanisms do not work for anonymous networks. This is because traditional network attack detectors monitor network parameters and meta-data of network packets (IP addresses, packet sequence numbers, packet sizes) and then looks for their anomalies in their behavior to raise attack alarms [3–5]. Many of these attack detectors are designed to raise alarms in nearly real-time [6]. Cryptanalysis is one way of breaking cryptographic properties of these fully encrypted messages, but such mechanisms do not always yield plain text information in real time.

Anonymous networks themselves offer no insights of data packet traffic flowing through them. However routers in such networks could offer statistics which are easily observable. Statistics such as packet count, packet dropping rate at a router's interface can be observed without needing packet inspection. Such statistics could reveal the current performance of the attack detection metrics and observe anomalies to detect the presence of an attack. Given that these statistics are observable with no packet inspection needed, attack detectors using such statistics could raise attack alarms in near real-time. Studies and research efforts are still being pursued to de-anonymize users of anonymous networks [7–9], but to our best knowledge designing a real-time DDoS detector for anonymous networks remains to be a hard and unsolved problem.

In this paper we propose a statistical distributed and hierarchical attack detector for anonymous networks using observable statistics at routers in the core network. In this work, our attack model focuses on DDoS attacks which reduce available channel bandwidth to routers in the core network. The attacks either flood the network with data packets or exhaust bandwidth by misbehaving with the medium access control protocols [10].

Our contribution for the proposed statistical DDoS detection is as follows,

- *Packet Resistance* metric for local monitoring: We define packet resistance as the ratio of incoming (receive packet rate) data rate over outgoing (transmit packet rate) data rate. This metric therefore needs no packet inspection.
- Local Analysis on Packet Resistance: We monitor the proposed metric to detect attacks and raise alarms. Packet resistance increases when a router experiences opposition to outgoing traffic on its egress interface. This indicates the presence of an attack.
- Hierarchical decision aggregation: We allow for locally generated alarms to be collected by an overlay of intermediate routers and eventually reach a centralized attack monitoring center.
- We use aggregated alarm data to construct an attack path to determine the possible origin of the attack.
- We simulate our work using the CORE simulator for a network of 50 nodes and present our detection accuracy using the packet resistance metric.

The remainder of the paper is organized as follows. In Sect. 2 we discuss our system assumptions and network model. We propose our statistical attack detection framework in Sect. 3. We discuss local attack monitoring in Sect. 4. Then we study the use of local attack reports to construct attack paths and determine the location of the intruder in Sect. 5. Finally we discuss conclusion and our future work in Sect. 6.

2   Network and Attack Model

We discuss our network and attack model for our work in this section. We describe a network architecture for our work that illustrates the anonymous communications between users of trusted groups.

2.1   Network Model

Our network model comprises end-hosts in various trusted groups communicating with each other via a network core as shown in Fig. 1. The network core comprises several wireless local area network (WLAN) using the IEEE 802.11 communications standard. The routers of a WLAN share the channel bandwidth supported by the wireless communication standard followed in the WLAN. These routers have multiple interfaces and therefore can act as gateways to two or more WLANs. The packets leaving the trusted groups are anonymized by the group's gateway. The core network in this work is a fully wireless network deployed by trusted groups or trusted organizations (for example: military or private corporations). We assume that the hardware and software on these routers are tamper-proof and trustworthy. Each of the routers deployed have attack detection sensors on them which can monitor and report the metric's performance.

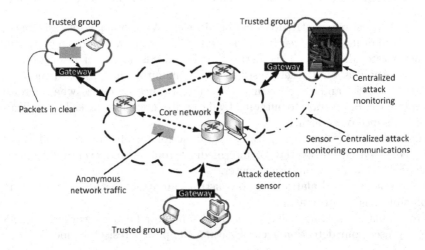

Fig. 1. We illustrate anonymous communication in the core network supporting communications between end-hosts in trusted groups. The attack detection sensors in the core report to centralized attack monitoring centers in the trusted groups.

2.2   Attack Model

Our attack model involves launching a Distributed-Denial-of-Service (DDoS) attack in the core network. The DDoS attack in our work affects channel bandwidth of the WLAN in the core network. We consider two ways in which this DoS can be launched. First, the target router is attacked in such a way that the net incoming rate on all its ingress interfaces exceeds its forwarding rate on the egress interface. For example, in the IEEE 802.11 standard the maximum data rate is 54 Mbps. If a router has two ingress interface receiving at 40 Mbps each and one egress interface, it can only send at a maximum data rate of 54 Mbps while its net incoming data rate is 80 Mbps. We consider this as an instance of flooding the router to create the DoS on the egress link of the target router. Second, available bandwidth for a router is exhausted by through medium access misbehavior [10]. Thus both these attacks render the target router to lower its forwarding rate in the WLAN.

Our attack model is distributed in the sense that the flooding could be initiated by multiple attackers located distributed in the core network. Specific links could be targeted by attackers distributed in the network as demonstrated in the Coremelt Attack [11]. Hence this leads to a DDoS attack framework.

We consider three attack traffic models: bursty, periodic and random. The bursty attack floods the victim (target) router occasionally such that there is a sudden surge in data traffic at the router. For bursty traffic, we allow the attacker to periodically flood the network with high volume traffic but with very short duration and then send no traffic during other times. We set the duration of the pulse to 5 s. The periodic attack exhibits the same attack pattern as bursty attack, but does it periodically. Finally, the random attack injects attack traffic at random instances of time. The volume of attack traffic and the length of attack can be varied.

3   DDoS Detection in Anonymous Wireless Networks

We take a top-down approach to describe our attack detection framework for anonymous networks. Our framework has two primary components: local analysis of network performance statistics at each router and aggregation of alerts or decisions using hierarchy. In what follows, we describe these two components and the associated challenges.

3.1   Local Analysis of Router Statistics

In anonymous networks, the packets reveal nothing about the services generating these packets nor the source and destination hosts in trusted groups. This makes it difficult to distinguish the attack traffic packets from legitimate network traffic packets in real-time which otherwise would have helped in detecting an attack at such routers. In order to determine the presence of attacks which affect the channel bandwidth, we observe the aggregate packet statistics such as received packet counts, transmitted packet counts at each router over periodic time intervals that help illustrate the trend of the forwarding rate at the respective router.

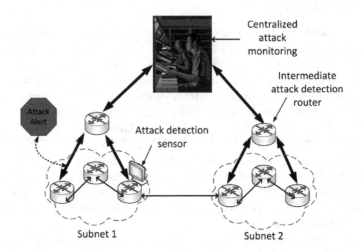

Fig. 2. We illustrate an example of scalable hierarchical attack detection system. Intermediate attack detection sensors collect alarm messages from a group of routers and report the alarms to a central attack monitoring center.

If a router experiences drops in its forwarding rate while its incoming rate is still the same, then it raises an alarm. At this instance the router raises an attack alarm which conveys the interface it is experiencing the attack. We allow each router to raise an alarm when it experiences such a phenomenon and thereby multiple alarm messages could be used to understand the attack's effect in the core network.

3.2 Hierarchical Decision Aggregation

Practical deployments of anonymous networks comprise a large number of routers [12]. This makes all routers directly reporting to one centralized attack detection monitoring center not feasible. A hierarchical attack detection model is thus desired to allow for scalability and improving accuracy. It is possible when local monitoring reports be outliers which are errors in detecting the attack. However, when reports from several routers are aggregated, the error in falsely detecting attacks can be reduced by observing the reports from other adjacent routers. In a hierarchical attack detection model, a set of routers report the alarms to a gateway router of a subnet of routers. These routers could make local decisions at a subnet level or forward all the alarms to its supervising attack detection node which could be monitoring several other subnets. With this, a hierarchy of attack monitoring routers could create a logical overlay in a larger network to eventually report to a central attack detection center as shown in Fig. 2.

3.3 Challenges with Aggregate Statistics

The attack detection metrics based on observable and aggregated statistics while being non-invasive also pose challenges in attack detection in anonymous networks. Aggregated statistics are easy to collect at routers and statistical operations such as deviations or variances do indicate the changes in metric with time. Particularly for wireless networks, operations on aggregated statistics do not always provide straight forward intuitions of attack's existence. Bandwidth consumption is not constant in wireless networks even when there are no attacks. The stochastic nature of the wireless channel imposes large variations in the metric. The stochastic nature of wireless channels could result from factors such as changes in propagation environment, mobility and different propagation models. Hence, the variance of metrics about its mean will not be small as could be seen in wired networks which can capture certain instances of flooding attacks with relatively good accuracy [11,13]. Metric variation could also result due to higher layer performance optimization such as TCP. Traffic could surge until TCP starts to back off and during this brief period of time, it is possible that the metric shoots beyond the ideal value leading to an alarm being raised. This leads to the fact that false alarms could be raised by attack detectors in anonymous networks which rely on raw aggregated statistics for attack detection.

4 Local Attack Monitoring Using Packet Resistance

To demonstrate the use of our statistical DDoS detection framework, we propose a specific router statistic that can easily observed in anonymous networks, yet promising detection capabilities. In what follows, we propose the *packet resistance* metric, discuss its practical aspects and provide an experimental study.

4.1 Packet Resistance

To determine the increase in opposition to outgoing traffic at a router, there are two ways to observe this phenomenon at routers. One is to observe the rate at which incoming packets arrive and monitor the packet queue at routers. This however is tied to the fact that different routers could have different upper bounds on the queue lengths and thereby setting global thresholds to detect the presence of an attacker is not possible. However, we can monitor both the incoming and outgoing packet rates at a router. Thus we can detect an attack if a router sends out packets at a rate lower than it receives.

In device physics, *resistance* of a conductor is defined as the opposition to the passage of electric current through it. In our work we define *packet resistance* of a router as the opposition to its packet transmission. In a sampling interval of t_s seconds at router i, reception of rx_i packets and subsequent forwarding of f_i packets can be interpreted as a *packet resistance* (PR) of $R_i = rx_i/f_i$, which is a unitless measure.

The PR metric measures the resistance faced by a router when the outgoing link is being attacked. For example, if the router is able to transmit packets nearly at the rate it receives them, then the average value of the metric should be 1.0 with very little variance. When the incoming packet rate exceeds the outgoing packet rate during the sampling interval, then the metric overshoots

1.0. While higher layer services such as TCP changes the rate at which packets are delivered to the network layer, the attackers may not follow such traffic control techniques and sustain their traffic which our metric can capture.

Other advantages of packet resistance metric are multiple fold. First, the metric is based on commonly available and easily observable statistics at routers. It needs no inspection of packets and makes no distinction between various flows of the data traffic, even including the attack traffic. The alarm is thus based on aggregate statistics observed at a router. Second, the metric needing no packet inspection means that the metric can be computed in near real-time and presents very minimal computation overhead at the router. Finally, since a wireless medium is shared by network routers, affecting one link could affect multiple other links in the network, thus there will be variations in the metric's performance on other network routers.

Metric Smoothing. To mitigate false alarms resulting from bursty and stochastic behavior of network traffic or traffic control mechanisms of higher layer services such as TCP, we propose a smoothing technique for the packet resistance metric. The smoothing technique is implemented in each router and takes only the PR metric's history as its input. The output will be used to help decide if the observed fluctuations in the metric is an indication of an attack or a genuine burst in the traffic.

The traffic at an interface of a router is sampled in intervals of t_s seconds and computes the metric for this time period. The router then maintains a historic average of the metric that gets reset at time intervals very large compared to t_s. This refresh interval for the historic average can be decided by network administrators based on traffic behavior over time. This historic average of the metric is our notion of measurement history on the interface of a router, assuming that it is serving the same network and connected to the same set of adjacent routers. This historic average of the metric at a router i is defined as $\overline{R_i}$.

If the router sounds an alarm every time the metric during the t_s interval overshoots a threshold T_r, the metric flags the measurement instance as an instance of flooding attack. If this is due to a genuine burst in traffic from an end-host, then we are capturing these bursts as *false positive* alarms. In order to mitigate the occurrences of false positives, we introduce a smoothing function for the proposed metric. While the interface samples the traffic at t_s seconds, we allow the router to observe the traffic for a time period of t_o seconds which we call as the observation interval. For simplicity purposes, we allow the t_o to be integer multiples of t_s. The t_o is a moving window which progresses after every t_s interval by 1 s. We define a function which has two input parameters, first, the deviation of the samples computed with respect to the historic average and second, the t_o. Let $t_o = k \cdot t_s$ and the value of the metric in k^{th} interval can be $R_i^{(k)}$. The deviation is computed as

$$D = \frac{\sqrt{\sum_{i=1}^{k} (R_i^{(k)} - \bar{R}_i)^2}}{k}. \tag{1}$$

During t_o, if the metric average $\overline{R_i^{(k)}}$ during t_o exceeds a threshold T_r and its deviation D exceeds a threshold T_o, then we treat this as a possibility of an attack at the router.

However, the smoothing interval and the thresholds can be learned by the attacker over time. Hence, the attacker could get away by not flooding the link for the duration which will not be seen as a genuine burst in traffic. Such an instance is an example of a *false negative* alarm. In order to mitigate the instances of false negatives in our detection, we define t_d in seconds as the attack detection interval. We let t_d be a time window being integer multiples of t_o which progresses after every t_s seconds. During this larger time interval, we can count the number of instances ($Count$) where $\overline{R_i^{(k)}}$ and D overshot the thresholds T_r and T_o respectively during the t_o intervals within t_d. If PR and D overshot their respective thresholds during majority of the observation intervals within a t_d, then the router will raise an alarm to indicate that an attack is detected as shown in Fig. 3. We set T_d as two-thirds the number of t_o in t_d to indicate a majority.

Statistical Attack Detection
```
 1  R̄_i ← 0
 2  while R_i
 3      for each t_d
 4          for each t_o
 5              Count ← 0
 6              for each k ∈ t_s
 7                  R_i^(k) ← rx_i / f_i
 8              Update R̄_i
 9              Compute D
10              if R(k)_i ≥ T_r AND D ≥ T_o
11                  then Count ← Count + 1
12          if Count ≥ T_d
13              then Raise Alarm
```

Fig. 3. We illustrate our statistical attack detection mechanism for detection DDoS in anonymous networks.

4.2   Experiment Setup

We implemented the attack methods and proposed detection techniques using the Common Open Research Emulator (CORE) [14]. Our network comprises 50 routers and use the OSPFv2 routing protocol to establish routes. The bandwidth for each link is 54 Mbps per the IEEE 802.11 standard. Since each router may have multiple radios, the total incoming traffic for a router can go above 54 Mbps with an upper bound of number of ingress interface times 54 Mbps. The routers were configured to report the attack alarms to a server managed by the trusted groups. For this setting we allowed for one server, while multiple such reporting servers could be setup for demonstrating a hierarchical detection framework. The attacker targets a router and introduces traffic flows at higher data rates to ensure the flooding is effective. We launched the attack traffic using *iperf* and set the attack traffic to be UDP and of constant rate during each sampling interval [15]. Our sampling interval was set to 3 s, which was the lowest possible due to the constraints set by the simulator.

We chose various smoothing parameters to analyze the detection performance. We chose these parameters to vary the ratio between the evaluation interval and the detection interval. We selected 6 pairs of (t_o, t_d) parameter tuples for evaluation purpose: (1, 3), (3, 3), (3, 6), (6, 6), (10, 6) and (10, 10). Since we are constrained by space, we show the results observed at one router for the parameter tuples (1, 3), (6, 6) and (10, 10) as similar results were seen at other affected routers in the core network. The T_r was set to 1.0 and T_o was set to 0.1.

4.3   Results and Analysis

We evaluate the effectiveness of the proposed packet resistance metric to detect the presence of attackers who launch bandwidth consumption attacks.

In Figs. 4, 5 and 6 we illustrate the proposed metric for the three attack traffic models for the parameter tuple (1, 3). In each of the Figs. 4, 5 and 6, sub-figure (a) illustrates the variation of the packet resistance metric and sub-figure (b) shows corresponding change in attacker traffic.

In Figs. 4(a), 5(a) and 6(a), as the attack traffic floods a link of a target router, our initial observation was that the metric overshoots the threshold value of 1.0 as the outgoing traffic rate at the affected router is reduced. We further observe that there is a delay in decision making of about 1–2 s due to processing of the observed data to make a decision at the end of decision interval. Our metric also captured the surge of outgoing traffic when the attacker traffic stops. This phenomenon is due to the fact that the router clears queued traffic at the router when its outgoing link is affected, which means the residue traffic has to be queued. Thus once the bandwidth frees up, the router makes an attempt to transmit the data at a rate higher than the incoming data rate, which leads to the metric value dropping below 1.0.

To analyze the detection performance, we use the false alarm rate, miss rate and accuracy. We first calculate the true positive (TP), true negative (TN), false positive (FP) and false negative (FN) occurrences in our detection results for all parameter tuples and attack traffic models. True positive detection instances are those where the detector raised an alarm when there was actually an attack. True negative detection instances are those when the detection raised no alarm when there was no attack. False positive detection instances are those where the detector raised an alarm when there was no attack. Finally, false negative detection instances are those when the detector raised no alarm when there

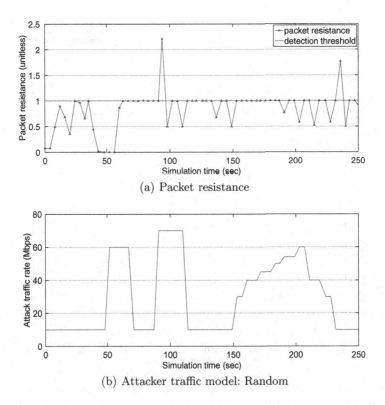

(a) Packet resistance

(b) Attacker traffic model: Random

Fig. 4. We demonstrate (a) the resulting packet resistance due to (b) random attack traffic with detection parameter $(1, 3)$. Our results suggest that the packet resistance metric can reflect the dynamics in attack traffic.

was attack. False alarm rate refers to the ratio of false positive instances over instances when there are no attacks (false alarm rate = FP / (FP + TN)). Miss rate refers to the ratio of false negative instances over instances when there are actually attacks (miss rate = FN / (FN + TP)). Accuracy is given by the ratio of true detection instances over all instances (accuracy = (TP + TN)/(TP + TN + FP + FN)).

For all the three attack traffic models and the parameter tuples in Table 1, we observed that the attack detection accuracies by using a readily observable technique needed observation intervals longer than just one sampling interval. We see that the average prediction accuracy for all three attacker traffic models when observation interval t_o set to the sampling interval t_p is 75 %. The false alarm rate is from 4 % to 24 %, depending on the attack traffic type. The miss rate hits 0 for tuple (6, 6) and (10, 10), but goes up to 96 % for the tuple (1, 3).

For other observation intervals greater than the sampling interval, the average detection accuracy is 98 %. This shows that observing the traffic for duration longer than sampling interval allows us to capture the instant bursts in traffic

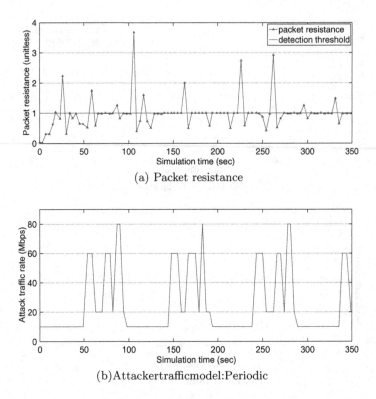

(a) Packet resistance

(b) Attacker traffic model: Periodic

Fig. 5. We demonstrate (a) the resulting packet resistance due to (b) periodic attack traffic with detection parameter $(1, 3)$. We observe that with short observation interval, the metric was able to detect the attack on 90 % of the times when the periodic attacker traffic was in the network.

either due to medium stochastic nature or due to the traffic bursty nature while higher layer protocols such as TCP converge. Additionally, for the detection interval which is several sampling intervals facilitates the monitoring of traffic for longer intervals of time. This allows for the natural bursts in traffic to normalize, while still being able to capture the presence of persistent attack traffic. We clearly observe that needing an observation interval greater than sampling interval improved detection accuracy for the periodic and bursty attack traffic. However for the random attack traffic, the tuple $(1, 3)$ is sensitive to traffic changes which results in high miss rate which should have yielded higher false positives instead of false negatives. But this is a trend which needs further investigation as this bias could be due to measurement error or lack of enough metric samples. While we observe these trends, it still remains to be an interesting question as to what is the optimal detection interval for a chosen observation interval to maximize the detection accuracy.

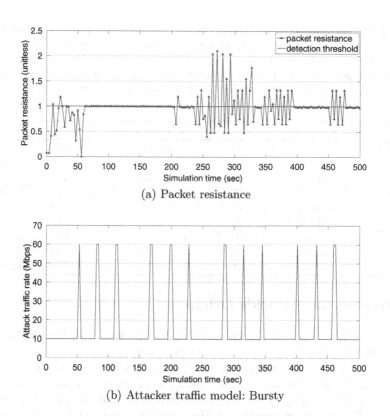

(a) Packet resistance

(b) Attacker traffic model: Bursty

Fig. 6. We demonstrate (a) the resulting packet resistance due to (b) bursty attack traffic with detection parameter $(1, 3)$. Though the attacker introduced short interval traffic bursts into the network and remained offline for remainder of the time, even with the observation interval equal to one sampling period, the metric captured the presence of attack with close to 90 % accuracy.

From the detection results in Table 1 and the visual illustration of the metric behavior for various attack traffic models, we show that statistical attack detection using purely observable metrics yields good attack detection accuracy for anonymous networks. Additionally, these detections were made in near real-time needing a few seconds of delay for processing and decision making. Thus we need not break the cryptography to learn about the presence of intruders who are able to attack the core network bandwidth. We are not claiming this metric to always detect local attacks with such high detection accuracy since our simulation setup and data sample set is small. However, when local monitoring alarms are used by a hierarchical attack detection system with lower accuracy, then the attack detection accuracy of the for the whole system will be high due to aggregation of larger number of attack reports.

Table 1. We illustrate the detection accuracy for our proposed statistical attack detection framework using packet resistance metric. The detection accuracy are shown for 3 types of attack traffic models and various detection parameter tuples. The parameter tuple comprises the observation interval which is integer multiples of the sampling interval and the detection interval which is integer multiples of the observation interval.

Attacker traffic	Parameter	TP	TN	FP	FN	False alarm rate	Miss rate	Accuracy
Random	$(1,3)$	1	41	2	25	0.0465	0.9615	0.6087
	$(6,6)$	2	81	0	0	0.0000	0.0000	1.0000
	$(10,10)$	2	83	3	0	0.0349	0.0000	0.9656
Periodic	$(1,3)$	3	77	9	3	0.1047	0.5000	0.8696
	$(6,6)$	9	69	0	0	0.0000	0.0000	1.0000
	$(10,10)$	2	51	2	0	0.0377	0.0000	0.9636
Bursty	$(1,3)$	61	364	115	0	0.2401	0.0000	0.7870
	$(6,6)$	6	69	2	0	0.0282	0.0000	0.9740
	$(10,10)$	71	226	0	0	0.0000	0.0000	1.0000

5   Tracing the Attack's Origin

In Fig. 7, we illustrate the procedure to infer the source of flooding attacks in an anonymous network. When an attack is locally detected at each router, each router sends an alarm with the wireless network interface where the attack happens. In the wireless network we model, each router detects an attack when the amount of outgoing traffic exceeds the assigned bandwidth at each wireless interface. The receiving network interface, on the other hand, always receives the amount of traffic less than or equal to the assigned bandwidth. In Fig. 7, R_3, R_4, R_7, and R_8 report the flooding alarm with their respective detected network interface to the centralized attack detection center. In this example, the attack is detected at all egress interfaces of routers. The centralized attack detection center can make a decision on the source of flooding attack by reconstructing the attack path. Since the number of paths (between routers) via each wireless network interface is different, the centralized attack detection center can first include all the paths used by the reported network interface in the set of candidate attack paths. In this example, the set will have the path element R_3-R_5, R_3-R_4, R_4-R_7, R_7-R_6, R_7-R_8, and R_8-$Victim$. Then, the centralized attack detection center gets rid of the paths to the router that no alarm is reported (e.g., R_3-R_5 and R_7-R_6). Consequently, the attack path will be conjectured as R_3-R_4-R_7-R_8-$Victim$.

We note that one attack flow might not generate alarms on all other routers on a given path. But with each router locally monitoring the attack raises an alarm based on independently occurring attacks. As the routers have no global network knowledge, the extent of attack propagation will not be known to the individual routers. Hence, using the alarms and aggregating them at the centralized attack monitoring center allows for the use of locally generated alarms from possibly different phenomenons to construct a global view of the various routes under attack as shown in Fig. 7.

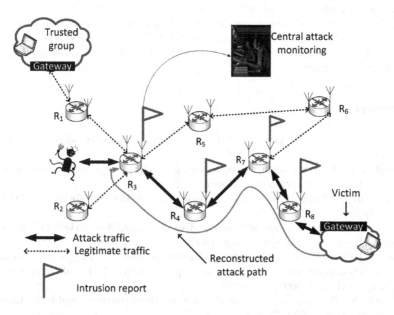

Fig. 7. We illustrate the mechanism to trace the source of the flooding attack in an anonymous network. Each router locally raises an alarm and informs the centralized attack monitoring center about the interface it is experiencing the attack. The attack path is constructed starting at the last node to report the attack and then the source is traced as R_3-R_4-R_7-R_8-$Victim$ for this example.

6   Conclusion and Future Work

With ubiquitous network access, users in trusted groups seek network anonymity for a variety of applications. Anonymous networks are still prone to network attackers who can disrupt communications. When attackers flood the network with packets, the routers of anonymous networks cannot distinguish flows of an attacker from the legitimate users. This makes traditional attack detection systems unusable for anonymous networks. In this work we designed a statistical distributed and hierarchical attack detection system for the anonymous networks using a readily observable metric. We proposed *packet resistance* as the metric which detected the presence of bandwidth attackers by observing the resistance to outgoing traffic at a router. The routers locally monitored for attack and raised alarms by indicating the interface they are experiencing a flooding attack's instance. These were collected by a centralized monitoring system to reconstruct the attack path and infer the attack's origin.

In our future work, we will design a larger experimental setup to demonstrate the effectiveness of the hierarchical decision aggregation using local statistical analysis at routers. We will then formalize our attack path reconstruction mechanism at the centralized attack monitoring center using alarms collected by aggregating the hierarchical decisions.

Acknowledgments. This research was supported through the Northrop Grumman Cybersecurity Research Consortium. The views and conclusions contained here are those of the authors and should not be interpreted as necessarily representing the official policies or endorsements, either express or implied, of Northrop Grumman or Carnegie Mellon University.

References

1. Lee, W., Stolfo, S.J.: Data mining approaches for intrusion detection. Defense Technical Information Center (2000)
2. Dingledine, R., Mathewson, N., Syverson, P.: TOR: The second-generation onion router. Technical report, DTIC Document (2004)
3. Northcutt, S.: Network intrusion detection: an analyst's hand-book. EDPACS **27**, 1–2 (2000)
4. Ferguson, P.: Network ingress filtering: Defeating denial of service attacks which employ IP source address spoofing (2000)
5. García-Teodoro, P., Díaz-Verdejo, J., Maciá-Fernández, G., Vázquez, E.: Anomaly-based network intrusion detection: techniques, systems and challenges. Comput. Secur. **28**, 18–28 (2009)
6. Paxson, V.: Bro: a system for detecting network intruders in real-time. Comput. Netw. **31**, 2435–2463 (1999)
7. Wondracek, G., Holz, T., Kirda, E., Kruegel, C.: A practical attack to de-anonymize social network users. In: 2010 IEEE Symposium on Security and Privacy (SP), pp. 223–238 (2010)
8. Murdoch, S., Danezis, G.: Low-cost traffic analysis of tor. In: 2005 IEEE Symposium on Security and Privacy, pp. 183–195 (2005)
9. Back, A., Möller, U., Stiglic, A.: Traffic analysis attacks and trade-offs in anonymity providing systems. In: Moskowitz, I.S. (ed.) IH 2001. LNCS, vol. 2137, pp. 245–257. Springer, Heidelberg (2001)
10. Kyasanur, P., Vaidya, N.: Selfish MAC layer misbehavior in wireless networks. IEEE Trans. Mobile Comput. **4**, 502–516 (2005)
11. Studer, A., Perrig, A.: The coremelt attack. In: Backes, M., Ning, P. (eds.) ESORICS 2009. LNCS, vol. 5789, pp. 37–52. Springer, Heidelberg (2009)
12. Tor: Tor metrics portal: graphs. https://metrics.torproject.org/graphs.html
13. Kang, M.S., Lee, S.B., Gligor, V.D.: The crossfire attack. In: 2013 IEEE Symposium on Security and Privacy (SP), pp. 127–141 (2013)
14. Ahrenholz, J.: Comparison of CORE network emulation platforms. In: IEEE MILCOM Conference, pp. 864–869 (2010)
15. iperf: http://iperf.sourceforge.net/

SoK: Lessons Learned from SSL/TLS Attacks

Christopher Meyer[✉] and Jörg Schwenk

Horst Görtz Institute for IT-Security, Ruhr-University Bochum, Bochum, Germany
{christopher.meyer,joerg.schwenk}@rub.de

Abstract. Since its introduction in 1994 the *Secure Socket Layer (SSL)* protocol (later renamed to *Transport Layer Security (TLS)*) evolved to the de facto standard for securing the transport layer. SSL/TLS can be used for ensuring data confidentiality, integrity and authenticity during transport. A main feature of the protocol is flexibility: Modes of operation and security aims can easily be configured through different cipher suites. However, during the evolutionary development several flaws were found. This paper presents an overview on theoretical and practical attacks of the last 17 years, in chronological order and four categories: Attacks on the Handshake protocol, on the Record and Application Data Protocols, on the PKI infrastructure and various other attacks.

We try to give a short "Lesson(s) Learned" at the end of each paragraph.

1 Introduction

In 1994, *Netscape*[1] addressed the problem of securing HTTP traffic by introducing the Secure Sockets Layer protocol version 2. Over the decades SSL gained improvements, security fixes and from version 3.1 on a new name - *Transport Layer Security*[2]. A key feature of SSL/TLS is the layered design with mainly two blocks:

Handshake Protocol. This is an Authenticated Key Exchange (AKE) protocol for negotiating cryptographic secrets and algorithms.

Record Protocol. This is an intermediate MAC-then-PAD-then-Encrypt layer positioned between the application and the TCP layer.

In addition, error messages are bundled in the **Alert Protocol**, and the one-message **ChangeCipherSpec Protocol** which signalizes activation of the pending state (e.g. switch from unencrypted to encrypted mode).

Due to space limitations a comprehensive introduction to SSL/TLS is skipped, but the specifications of SSL 2.0 [1], SSL 3.0 [2], TLS 1.0 [3], TLS 1.1 [4] and TLS 1.2 [5] are available online[3]. Additionally, a detailed overview on SSL/TLS is e.g. provided by Eric Rescorla in [6]. For convenience, complete communication example illustrating the handshake phase finally leading to the application data phase is given in Fig. 1.

---

[1] http://www.netscape.com

[2] http://datatracker.ietf.org/wg/tls/

[3] SSL version 1.0 was never published.

Y. Kim et al. (Eds.): WISA 2013, LNCS 8267, pp. 189–209, 2014.
DOI: 10.1007/978-3-319-05149-9_12, © Springer International Publishing Switzerland 2014

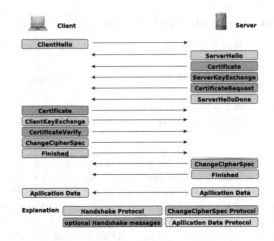

Fig. 1. SSL/TLS communication example

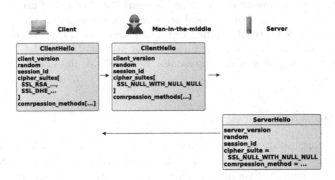

Fig. 2. Cipher-suite rollback attack - *based on:* [7]

2   Attacks on the Handshake Protocol

2.1   Cipher Suite Rollback

The cipher-suite rollback attack, discussed by Wagner and Schneier in [7] aims
at limiting the offered cipher-suite list provided by the client to weaker ones or
NULL-ciphers. A Man-in-the-middle (Mitm) attacker may alter the ClientHello
message and strips of unwanted cipher-suites or replaces the whole cipher-suite
list. The server has no real choice - it can either reject the connection or accept
the weaker cipher-suite. An example is given in Fig. 2.

The problem was fixed with the release of SSL 3.0 by authenticating *all
messages of the Handshake Protocol.* A hash value of all handshake messages sent
and received by the client (the server, resp.) was included into the computations
of the Client Finished (Server Finished, resp.) message[4].

---

[4] However, this hash value explicitly excludes messages of the Alert and
ChangeCipherSpec protocols, leaving room for future attacks.

Lesson learned. Authenticate what was sent and received. Theoretically, this idea was put forward in [8] with the concept of *matching conversations*.

2.2 ChangeCipherSpec Message Drop

This simple, but effective attack by Wagner and Schneier in [7] was feasible in SSL 2.0 only. During the handshake phase the cryptographic primitives are determined. For their activation it is necessary for both parties to send a ChangeCipherSpec message. This messages informs that the following communication will be secured by the previously agreed parameters. An attacker acting as Mitm could drop the ChangeCipherSpec messages and causes both parties to never activate the pending state.

According to Wagner and Schneier the flaw was independently discovered by Dan Simon and addressed by Paul Kocher. The author's recommendation is to ensure that a ChangeCipherSpec message is received before accepting the Finished message. RFC 2246 [3] (TLS 1.0) enforces exactly this behaviour.

Lesson learned. See Sect. 2.1.

2.3 Key Exchange Algorithm Confusion

Another flaw pointed out by Wagner and Schneier in [7] is related to temporary key material. SSL 3.0 supports the use of temporary key material during the handshake phase (RSA public keys or DH public parameters) signed with a long term key. A problem arises from a missing type definition of the transferred material. Each party implicitly decides, based on the context, which key material is expected and decodes accordingly. This creates the surface for a type confusion attack. This attack is strictly theoretical at time of writing.

Figure 3 sketches an attack where a client is fooled in establishing an RSA based key agreement while at the same time performing DHE[5] with the server.

Lesson learned. This attack highlights the need for context-free message structures: Misinterpretation of a received message should be avoided by providing explicit information on the content.

2.4 Version Rollback

Wagner and Schneier described in [7] an attack where a ClientHello message of SSL 3.0 is modified to look like a ClientHello message of SSL 2.0. This would force a server to rollback to the more vulnerable SSL 2.0.

As a countermeasure (proposed by Paul Kocher), the SSL/TLS version is also contained in the PKCS encoded PreMasterSecret of the ClientKeyExchange message (when RSA-based cipher suites are used). The countermeasure is sufficient, since SSL 2.0 only supports RSA-based key exchange.

---

[5] Ephemeral Diffie-Hellman Key Exchange.

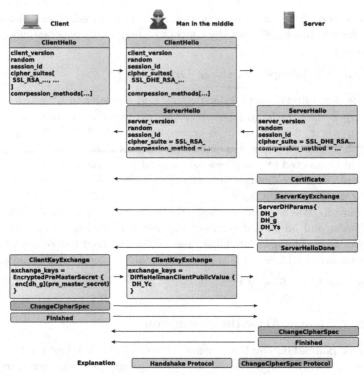

Fig. 3. Key exchange algorithm confusion attack - *based on:* [7]

Lesson learned. Backward compatibility is a serious security threat: The countermeasure described in Sect. 2.1 against modification of single messages is of no help, since it was not present in Version 2.0!

2.5 Bleichenbacher's Attack on PKCS#1

In 1998, Daniel Bleichenbacher presented in [9] an attack on RSA based cipher suites. Bleichenbacher utilized the strict structure of the PKCS#1 v1.5 format and showed that it is possible to decrypt the `PreMasterSecret` in a reasonable amount of time. The `PreMasterSecret` in an RSA based cipher suite is a random value generated by the client and sent (encrypted and PKCS #1 formatted) within the `ClientKeyExchange`. An attacker eavesdropping this (encrypted) message can decrypt it later on by abusing the server as a decryption oracle.

Bleichenbacher's attack is based on (a) the fixed structure of PKCS#1 and (b) a known weakness of RSA to *Chosen Ciphertext Attacks* (cf. [10]). The idea is to *blind* the original ciphertext, pass it to the decrypter and finally separate the blinding value. Depending on the validness of a received PKCS structure the processing at server side differs. In particular, SSL specified different error messages for e.g invalid padding and invalid MAC. With this information one can build an oracle as given in Fig. 4.

$$\mathcal{O}_{PKCS}(x) = \begin{cases} \text{true, if } x \text{ is PKCS conforming} \\ \text{false,} \qquad \text{otherwise} \end{cases}$$

Fig. 4. PKCS oracle

By the use of this oracle it is possible to decrypt the `PreMasterSecret` by continuously blinding the eavesdropped, encrypted message. Based on the oracle's responses the attacker adjusts the blinding value.

Lesson learned. Apparently negligible pieces of information such as distinguishable errors, can leverage an attacker to break security. It is necessary to reveal as little information as possible on the internal processing[6].

2.6 The Rise of Timing Based Attacks

Brumley and Boneh outlined in [11] a timing attack on RSA based SSL/TLS. The attack extracts the private key from a target server by observing the timing differences between sending a specially crafted `ClientKeyExchange` message and receiving an `Alert` message inducing an invalid formatted `PreMasterSecret`. Even a relatively small difference in time allows to draw conclusions on the used RSA parameters. The attack is only applicable in case of RSA based ciphersuites. Additionally, the attack requires the presence of a fine resolutive clock on the attacker's side. OpenSSL was successfully attacked - the problem was caused by performance tweaks made by the OpenSSL library that could, under special circumstances, leverage timing differences during processing. The attack was significantly improved in 2005 by Aciicmez, Schindler and Koc in [12].

As a countermeasure the authors suggest the use of RSA blinding.

Lesson learned. Brumley and Boneh demonstrated that designers have to take special care on building implementations with nearly equal response times for each conditional branch of message processing.

2.7 Improvements on Bleichenbacher's Attack

Klíma, Pokorny and Rosa not only improved Bleichenbacher's attack (cf. Sect. 2.5) in [13], but were able to break a countermeasure for Bleichenbacher's attack.

Breaking the countermeasure. A countermeasure against Bleichenbacher's attack is to generate a random `PreMasterSecret` in any kind of failure and continue with the handshake until the verification and decryption of the `Finished` message fails due to different key material (the `PreMasterSecret` differs at client and server side). Additionally, the implementations are encouraged to send no distinguishable error messages. These countermeasures are regarded as best-practice. Moreover, because of a different countermeasure concerning

---

[6] Especially error messages are a valuable source for information.

$$\mathcal{O}_{BadVersion}(x) = \begin{cases} \text{true, if version number is valid} \\ \text{false,} \qquad \text{otherwise} \end{cases}$$

Fig. 5. Bad version oracle

version rollback attacks (cf. Sect. 2.4) the encrypted data includes not only the `PreMasterSecret`, but also the major and minor version number of the negotiated SSL/TLS version. Implementations should check for equality of the sent/received and negotiated protocol versions. In case of version mismatch some implementations returned distinguishable error messages to the sender (e.g. `decode_error` in case of OpenSSL). An attacker could build a new (bad version) oracle from this, as shown in Fig. 5.

By the use $\mathcal{O}_{BadVersion}$ Klíma, Pokorny and Rosa were able to mount Bleichenbacher's attack, in spite recommended countermeasures are present.

Lesson learned. Countermeasures against one vulnerability (cf. Sect. 2.4) may lead to another.

2.8   ECC Based Timing Attacks

At ESORICS 2011 Brumley and Tuveri [14] presented an attack on ECDSA based TLS connections. Only OpenSSL seemed to be vulnerable.

The problem arose from the strict implementation of an algorithm to speed up scalar multiplications[7]. From a formal point of view, the algorithm is timing resistant, but from an implementational point of view it contained a timing side-channel. Brumley and Tuveri combined this side-channel with the lattice attack of Howgrave-Graham and Smart [17] to recover secret keys.

ECDSA signatures are generated in TLS/SSL when `ECDHE_ECDSA` cipher-suites are used and rely on scalar multiplications. The authors measured the time between the `ClientHello` message and the arrival of the `ServerKeyExchange` message, which contains an ECDSA signature. As this signature can only be created on-the-fly, and not in advance, an adversary is able to measure runtime of the scalar multiplication function and draw conclusions on the input parameters.

Lesson learned. Side channels may come from unexpected sources.

2.9   Even More Improvements on Bleichenbacher's Attack

In [18] Bardou, Focardi, Kawamoto, Simionato, Steel and Tsay significantly improved Bleichenbacher's attack (cf. Sect. 2.5) far beyond previous improvements (cf. Sect. 2.7). The algorithm was fine-tuned to perform faster and with lesser oracle queries. Additionally, the results were combined with previous improvements.

---

[7] Montgomery power ladder [15] (with improvements by López and Dahab [16]).

$$\mathcal{O}_{Padding}(C) = \begin{cases} \text{true, if } C \text{ is correctly padded} \\ \text{false,} \qquad \text{otherwise} \end{cases}$$

Fig. 6. Padding oracle

Lesson learned. Attacks improve and adjust as time goes by. It is necessary to observe research on attacks - even if they are patched.

2.10 ECC-Based Key Exchange Algorithm Confusion Attack

In [19] Mavrogiannopoulos, Vercauteren, Velichkov and Preneel showed that the key exchange algorithm confusion attack (cf. Sect. 2.3) can be applied to ECDH. According to the authors, it is not feasible yet due to computational limitations.

Lesson learned. See Sect. 2.3.

3 Attacks on the Record and Application Data Protocols

3.1 MAC Does Not Cover Padding Length

Wagner and Schneier pointed out in [7] that SSL 2.0 contained a major weakness concerning the Message Authentication Code (MAC) used for ensuring integrity. The MAC covered only data and padding, but left the padding length field unprotected. This may lead to message integrity compromise.

Lesson learned. Not only since the introduction of padding oracles by Vaudenay (cf. Sect. 3.2) each single bit of information should be considered useful for an attacker. Thus, data should be integrity protected and authenticated to keep the attack vector as small as possible.

3.2 Weaknesses through CBC Usage

Serge Vaudenay introduced a new attack class - *padding attacks* - and forced the security community to rethink on padding usage in encryption schemes (cf. [20]). These attacks rely on the fact that block encryption schemes operate on blocks of fixed length, but in practice most plaintexts have to be *padded* to fit the requested length (a multiple of the block length). After padding, the input data is passed to the encryption function, where each plaintext block (of length of the block size) is processed and chained[8]. This allows to directly influence the decryption process by altering the successive blocks.

---

[8] Mostly according to the Cipher Block Chaining Mode (CBC) scheme which chains consecutive blocks so that a subsequent block is influenced by the output of its predecessor.

In the case of SSL/TLS the receiver may send a `decryption_failure` alert, if invalid padding is encountered. The padding oracle is defined in Fig. 6.

With such an oracle and clever changes to the ciphertext an attacker is able to decrypt a ciphertext without knowledge of the key. The optional MAC of SSL/TLS, ensuring message integrity, does not hinder this attack, since padding is not covered by the `MAC`.

As a solution, SSL/TLS defines equal error messages for padding and decryption errors. But there still remains room for timing attacks (cf. Sect. 3.13).

Lesson learned. Although the attack is not directly applicable to standard SSL/TLS (since *Fatal* errors immediately invalidate the session and accordingly the key material), it is applicable to DTLS (cf. Sect. 3.11).

3.3   Information Leakage by the Use of Compression

In [21] Kelsey described a side-channel based on compression. SSL/TLS offers message compression as an optional feature. If compression is used it is possible to correlate output bytes of the compression to (guessed) input bytes. This uses the fact that compression algorithms, when applied to plaintext, reduce the size of the input data - if the guess for a plaintext is right the message size should decrease. With this side-channel, it is possible to draw conclusions on the plaintext. Rizzo and Duong used this observation to attack SSL/TLS (cf. 3.12). Kelsey advices that compression may also cause timing side-channels.

Lesson learned. Performance optimizations can lead to side-channels.

3.4   Intercepting SSL/TLS Protected Traffic

In [22] Canvel, Hiltgen, Vaudenay and Vuagnoux extended Vaudenay's attack (cf. Sect. 3.2) to decrypt a password from an SSL/TLS secured IMAP session. They suggested three additional attack types:

Timing Attacks. The authors concluded that a successful MAC verification needs significantly more time compared to an abortion caused by invalid padding.

Multi-Session Attacks. This type requires a critical plaintext to be present in each TLS session (e.g. a password). The attacker checks if a given ciphertext ends with a specific byte sequence instead of trying to guess the whole plaintext.

Dictionary Attacks. Leveraged by the previous type this attack checks for byte sequences included in a dictionary.

As a recommendation the MAC should also cover the padding, which implies the order PAD-then-MAC-then-Encrypt.

Lesson learned. The order of processing makes a big difference.

3.5   Chosen-Plain-Text Attacks on SSL

Gregory Bard observed in [23] that in a CBC Mode secured connection only the Initialization Vector (IV) of the first plaintext is chosen randomly. All subsequent IVs are simply the last block of the previous encrypted plaintext. This is contrary to cryptography best-practice. An attacker can easily verify if a particular block has a guessed value. Bard recommended as a fix the use of pseudo random IVs or completely dropping CBC[9]. The practicability of the attack was proven by Bard two years later (cf. Sect. 3.6).

Bodo Möller discovered this vulnerability at the same time[10]. Möller described a fix which was later used by the OpenSSL project: Prepending a single record with empty content, padding and MAC, to each message.

Lesson learned. Ignoring security best-practices for the sake of simplicity may lead to vulnerabilities.

3.6   Chosen-Plain-Text Attacks on SSL Reloaded

Bard revisited the attack of Sect. 3.5 in 2006 [24]. He addressed the same topics as before, but provided an attack sketch how to exploit this problem by the use of a Java applet executed on the victim's machine. As already discussed, the vulnerability was fixed with TLS 1.1, since it dictates the use of explicit IVs.

Rizzo and Duong proved Bard's attack scenario to be applicable, but in a slightly different implementation (by using JavaScript instead of Java applets). The described attack was adopted in their B.E.A.S.T. tool (cf. Sect. 3.8).

Lesson learned. Not only the protocol has to be considered when evaluating security - the interplay between different layers and applications is relevant, too.

3.7   Traffic Analysis of TLS

George Danezis highlighted in an unpublished manuscript [25] ways how an attacker may use the obvious fact that minimal information, despite the connection is TLS protected, remain unencrypted to analyze and track traffic.

The fields `type`, `version` and `length` of each TLS Record always remain unencrypted - even in an encrypted record. In [7] the authors already criticized the presence of such unauthenticated and unencrypted fields. RFC 2246 [3] is also aware of this information leak and advices to take care of this. Danezis identified the following information leaks:

- Requests to different URLs may differ in length which results in SSL/TLS records of different size.
- Responses to requests may also differ in length, which again yields to SSL/-TLS records of different size.

---

[9] TLS 1.1 follows the first recommendation by introducing an explicit IV field.

[10] http://www.openssl.org/~bodo/tls-cbc.txt

- Different structured documents may lead to a predictable behavior of the client's application (e.g. a browser normally gathers all images of a website - causing different requests and different responses).
- Content on public sites is visible to everyone, thus linking (e.g. by size) is possible.

Moreover, an attacker could also actively influence the victim's behavior and gain information by providing specially crafted documents with particular and distinguishable content lengths, structures, URLs or external resources.

The author provides some hints on how the surface of the attack can be limited, but the practicability of the recommended measures remains questionable.

- URL padding - all URLs are of equal length
- Content padding - all content is of equal size
- Contribution padding - all send data is of equal size
- Structure padding - all sites have an equal structure

This flaw was also discussed by Wagner and Schneier in [7] who credited Bennet Yee as the first one describing traffic analysis on SSL. As a counter-measure Wagner and Schneier suggested random length padding not only for block cipher mode, but for all cipher modes. The attack feasibility was proven by Chen, Wang, Wang and Zhang in [26].

Lesson learned. Attackers may find ways to use every obtainable part of information for further attacks. More sophisticated attacks are possible if fields are left unauthenticated. Protocol designers and developers should be aware of this fact and sparely disclose *any* information.

3.8   Practical IV Chaining Vulnerability

Rizzo and Duong presented in [27] a tool called B.E.A.S.T. that is able to decrypt HTTPS traffic (e.g. cookies). The authors implemented and extended ideas of Bard [23,24], Möller and Dai[11]. Rizzo and Duong created a decryption oracle based on the precondition that the IVs used by CBC (the last encryption block of the preceding encryption) are known to the attacker.

To decrypt ciphertexts byte-wise, the authors propose a new kind of attack named *block-wise chosen-boundary attack*. It requires an attacker who is able to move a message before encryption in its block boundaries. This means an attacker may prepend a message with arbitrary data in such a way that it is split into multiple blocks of block-size of the cipher. Based on this, it is possible to split a message of full block-size into two blocks: the first one consisting of arbitrary data and the first byte of the original block and the second block consisting of the remaining bytes and a single free byte. So prefixing a message with an attacker defined amount of data shifts the message (if necessary into a new block). An attacker is absolutely free to prepend any data of her choice and length. An example is given in Fig. 7.

---

[11] http://www.weidai.com/ssh2-attack.txt

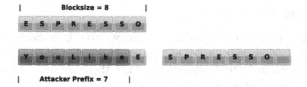

Fig. 7. Example boundary shifting

Full message decryption. To decrypt a full message the attacker adjusts the amount of random prefix data so that the next *unknown* byte is always the last byte in a block. This means that the message is shifted in such a way, that the scenario illustrated in Fig. 7 applies to the next unknown byte. The unknown byte becomes the last and only byte of a single block unknown to the attacker. Finally, this leads to a byte by byte message decryption.

Rizzo and Duong demonstrated how B.E.A.S.T. could be used to decrypt HTTPS secured cookies. Due to this massive vulnerability, migration to TLS Version 1.1 has been recommended since by IETF.

Lesson learned. Theoretical only vulnerabilities can turn into practice.

3.9   Short Message Collisions and Busting Length Hiding

In [28] Paterson, Ristenpart and Shrimpton outlined an attack related to the MAC-then-PAD-then-Encrypt scheme in combination with short messages. In particular, their attack is applicable if all parts of a message (message, padding, MAC) fit into a single block of the cipher's block-size. Under special preconditions the authors described the creation of different ciphertexts leading to the same plaintext message.

The surface for this attack is limited, since the preconditions (message, padding and MAC have to fit into a single block) are quite strong.

Lesson learned. MIN/MAX lengths for input and output data of cryptographic algorithms are beneficial.

3.10   Message Distinguishing

Paterson et al. extended in [28] the attack described in Sect. 3.9 enabling an attacker to distinguish between two messages. The attack is based on clever modification of the eavesdropped ciphertext so that it either passes the processing or leads to an error message. Based on the outcome (error/no error) it is possible to determine which content was send. The attack works only if the possible contents are of different, short length. At least, the attack remains unexploitable (until the day of writing) due to the fact that it is only possible for 80 bit truncated MACs.

Lesson learned. See Sect. 3.9 and always remember Sect. 3.8.

3.11   Breaking DTLS

In [29] AlFardan and Paterson applied Vaudenay's attack (cf. Sect. 3.2) to DTLS. DTLS is a slightly different version of regular TLS adjusted to unreliable transport protocols, such as UDP. Compared to TLS, there are two major differences:

1. Complete absence of Alert messages
2. Messages causing protocol errors (bad padding, invalid MAC, ...) are simply dropped, instead of causing a connection abort invalidating the session keys

Vaudenay's attack works on DTLS since bad messages do not cause session invalidation. But with the lack of error messages there is no feedback whether the modified messages contained a valid padding or not. The authors adjusted Vaudenay's algorithms to use a timing oracle.

OpenSSL and GnuTLS were analyzed, both vulnerable to a timing oracle enhanced version of Vaudenay's attack. According to the authors, it was necessary to disable the protocol's *anti-replay* option, which is enabled by default.

Lesson learned. The authors recommend that defining standards only by specifying differences to other standards should be avoided.

3.12   Practical Compression Based Attacks

In 2012, Rizzo and Duong presented the *C.R.I.M.E.* attack tool which targets HTTPS and is able to decrypt traffic, enabling cookie stealing and session takeover. It exploits a known vulnerability caused by the use of message compression (cf. Sect. 3.3). The attack requires compression to be enabled in an SSL/TLS session.

Basically, an attacker prefixes the secret with guessed subsequences and observes if it leads to compression (by observing the resulting ciphertext length). A decreased ciphertext length implies redundancy, so it is very likely that the guessed, prefixed subsequence caused redundancy in the plaintext. This implies that a guess, having something in common with the secret, will have a higher compression rate leading to a shorter output. When such an output is detected the attacker knows that the guess has something in common with the secret.

Lesson learned. See Sect. 3.8.

3.13   Timing Based Side-Channels Strike Back

In February 2013, AlFardan and Paterson introduced the *Lucky Thirteen* attack [30]. The attack enables plaintext recovery against TLS and DTLS by exploiting the already discussed MAC-then-PAD-then-Encrypt design of the protocols. The author's tamper with the padding data and measure the time needed for MAC calculation on server side. By cleverly choosing the padding values it is possible to distinguish valid from invalid paddings, leaking information about the plaintext. Basically, the time required for MAC computation is of significance - the decryption oracle is based on these timing differences. The attack can be enhanced when combined with techniques of the B.E.A.S.T. attack (cf. Sect. 3.8).

Lesson learned. Weaknesses may turn into practice and get even worse when combined with known attacks.

3.14   RC4: A Vulnerable Alternative

The stream cipher RC4 is often proposed as a countermeasure to Padding Oracle Attacks (cf. Sect. 3.2). Unfortunately, RC4 is known to have vulnerabilities and weaknesses[12]. In 2013, Isobe, Ohigashi, Watanabe and Morrii identified in [32] biases in the initial bytes of RC4 keystreams that can be used to perform plaintext recovery of encrypted ciphertexts (similar results have been discussed independently[13], but are not yet published) and thus break SSL/TLS encryption.

Lesson learned. Take known weaknesses seriously!

4   Attacks on the PKI

4.1   Weak Cryptographic Primitives Lead to Colliding Certificates

Lenstra, Wang and de Weger described in 2005 how an attacker could create valid X.509 certificates with collinding MD5 hash values [33]. With that it is possible to impersonate clients or servers - this enables hard to detect attacks.

The practicality of the attack was demonstrated in 2008 by Sotirov, Stevens, Appelbaum, Lenstra, Molnar, Osvik and de Weger[14] who were able, through clever interaction between certificate requests from a legal CA and a massively parallel search for MD5 collisions, to create a valid CA certificate for TLS.

Lesson learned. As long as user agents accept MD5 certificates, the surface still exists. Weak algorithms may lead to complete breach of the security.

4.2   Weaknesses in X.509 Certificate Constraint Checking

In 2008, US hacker Matthew Rosenfeld, better known as Moxie Marlinspike, published a vulnerability report [34] affecting the certificate basic constraint validation of Microsoft's Internet Explorer (IE). IE did not check if certificates were allowed to sign sub-certificates. Any valid certificate, signed by a trusted CA, was allowed to issue sub-certificates for *any* domain.

The tool `sslsniff`[15] provides a proof of concept implementation with the attacker acting as Mitm, issuing certificates for a requested domain on the fly.

Lesson learned. The attack relies on a specific implementation bug and has been fixed. However, certificate validation is a critical step. This again stresses the need for well-written specifications sketching all security related processing steps in detail and, in turn, obligates developers to implement exactly as outlined.

---

[12] That, in the past, lead to the decline of e.g. WEP [31].

[13] http://www.isg.rhul.ac.uk/tls/

[14] http://www.win.tue.nl/hashclash/rogue-ca/

[15] http://www.thoughtcrime.org/software/sslsniff/

4.3   Attacks on Certificate Issuer Application Logic

Attacks on the PKI by exploiting implementational bugs on CA side were demonstrated by Marlinspike in [35], who was able to trick the CA's issuance logic by using specially crafted domain strings. Marlinspike gained certificates for arbitrary domains, issued by trusted CAs.

Marlinspike made use of the encoding of X.509 - ASN1. ASN1 supports multiple String formats, all leading to slightly different PASCAL String representation conventions. PASCAL and C store strings differently, the first: length prefixed, and the other: NULL terminated.

This prepares the way for the NULL-Prefix attack: A sample domain name which could be used in a Certificate Signing Request (CSR) is the following www.targetToAttack.com\0.example.com, assuming that the attacker is the owner of example.com. The attack works, because the CA logic only checks the TLD (example.com). The leading NULL-byte (\0) is valid because of ASN1's length-prefixed representation (where NULL-bytes within the payload String are valid). When the prepared domain String is presented to common application logic (mostly written in languages representing Strings NULL-terminated), such as e.g. most browsers, the String is prematurely terminated. As a result only the String afore the NULL byte (www.targetToAttack.com) is being validated.

A specialization of the attack are wild-card certificates. The asterisk (*) can be used to create certificates, valid - if successfully signed by a trusted CA - for **any** domain (e.g., *\0.example.com).

Lesson learned. Certification authorities should be prepared to deal with different encodings and security issues related to this.

4.4   Attacking the PKI

Marlinspike described in [36] an attack that aims at interfering the infrastructure to revoke certificates. By the use of the Online Certificate Status Protocol (OCSP) a client application can check the revocation status of a certificate. The response contains a field responseStatus which is not protected by a signature.

An attacker acting as Mitm could respond to every query with tryLater. Due to lack for a signature the client has no chance to detect the spoofed response. Thereby, a victim is not able to query the revocation status of a certificate.

Lesson learned. Every sensitive message parts should be integrity protected and authenticated. If necessary, encryption should additionally be used for confidential data. If real-time checks on a PKI are required, unsigned responses should lead to a halt in protocol execution.

4.5   Wildcard Certificate Validation Weakness

Moore and Ward published a Security Advisory [37] concerning wildcard (*) usage when IP addresses are used as CN URI in X.509 certificates. According to RFC 2818 [38] wildcards are not allowed for IP addresses. The authors found multiple browsers treating IP addresses including wildcard characters as certificate CN as valid and matching. The authors could fool browsers to accept issued certificates with CN="*.168.3.48". This certificate was treated as valid for any server with a ".168.3.48" postfix.

Lesson learned. Certificate validation is challenging.

4.6   Conquest of a Certification Authority

In March 2011 the *Comodo CA Ltd.* Certification Authority (CA) was successfully compromised [39]. An attacker used a reseller account to issue 9 certificates for popular domains. Except rumors, the purpose of the attack remains unclear.

Lesson learned. Certification authorities have to protect their critical infrastructure with strong security mechanisms.

4.7   Conquest of Another CA

Soon after the attack on Comodo, a Dutch Certification Authority - *DigiNotar* - was completely compromised by an attacker [40]. In contrast to the Comodo impact, the attacker was able to gain control over the DigiNotar infrastructure. The attack discovery was eased by Google's Chrome web browser who complained about mismatching certificates for Google-owned domains. The browser stores hard coded copies of the genuine certificates for Google and thus was able to detect bogus certificates.

Lesson learned. Beside the lesson learned from Sect. 4.6, it can be seen that mechanisms like malware and intrusion detection must be present in CA systems.

4.8   Risks of Unqualified Domain Names

The risks of unqualified domain names such as e.g. `mail`, `exchange` or `wiki` were discussed in a blog entry by Chris Palmer [41].The author used the EFF SSL Observatory[16] to identify certificates with unqualified domain names, issued by trusted CAs. This could leverage Man-in-the-middle attacks.

Lesson learned. Only rely on fully qualified domain names.

4.9   CA's Issuing Weak Certificates

DigiCert Malaysia was blamed for issuing 22 certificates with weak 512-bit RSA keys and no certificate revocation extensions[17]. As a consequence *Entrust* revoked *DigiCert Malaysia*'s intermediate CA certificate.

Lesson learned. Strong algorithms and key lengths are of major importance.

---

[16] https://www.eff.org/observatory

[17] http://www.entrust.net/advisories/malaysia.htm

4.10   Attacks on Non-browser Based Certificate Validation

Georgiev et al. [42] uncovered that widespread libraries for SSL/TLS suffer from vulnerable certificate validation implementations. As major causes for these problems bad and misleading API specifications, lacking interest for security concerns at all and the absence of essential validation routines were identified.

Especially, the following security tasks and robustness of the libraries' code responsible for these tasks are considered:

– Certificate chaining and verification
– Host name verification
– Certificate revocation checks
– X.509 extension handling and processing

Exploiting these vulnerabilities may lead to Mitm and impersonation attacks.

Lesson learned. Clean, simple and well documented APIs are important.

4.11   Mis-Issued Certificates

A flawed business process at *TURKTRUST* accidently issued 2 intermediate CA certificates [43]. The issue was discovered by Google's Chrome Browser when it recognized bogus certificates for *.google.com.

Lesson learned. Means for the detection of illegal certificates are needed.

5   Various Attacks

5.1   Random Number Prediction

In January 1996, Goldberg and Wagner published an article [44] on the quality of random numbers used for SSL connections by the Netscape Browser. The authors identified striking weaknesses in the algorithm responsible for random number generation. The algorithm's entropy relied on a few, predictable values.

Lesson learned. Good (pseudo) random number generators (PRNGs) are essential for cryptography (cf. Sect. 5.2).

5.2   Weak Random Numbers

In 2008, Luciano Bello [45] observed during code review that the PRNG of Debian-specific OpenSSL was predictable, due to an implementation bug. A Debian-specific patch removed two very important lines in the libssl source code responsible for providing adequate entropy[18]. limited without these code lines.

Lesson learned. Developers should comment security critical parts of source code, exactly explain the intention and highlight the consequences when altered. Beyond this, test cases targeting the critical code lines should be provided.

---

[18] http://anonscm.debian.org/viewvc/pkg-openssl/openssl/trunk/rand/md_rand.c?
p2=%2Fopenssl%2Ftrunk%2Frand%2Fmd_rand.c&p1=openssl%2Ftrunk%2Frand%2Fmd_
rand.c&r1=141&r2=140&view=diff&pathrev=141

5.3   Denial of Service Enabled by Exceptions

In [46] Zhao, Vemuri, Chen, Chen, Zhou and Fu provided attacks on the TLS handshake which leads to an immediate connection shutdown.

– The first attack targets the Alert protocol of TLS and makes use of the fact that, due to yet missing cryptographic primitives during the handshake phase, all `Alert` messages remain strictly unauthenticated and thus spoof-able. This enables an obvious, but effective attack: Spoofing *Fatal* `Alert` messages which cause immediate connection shutdowns.
– The second attack simply confuses a communication partner by sending either misleading, replayed or responding with wrong messages according to the expected handshake flow.

Lesson learned. Even obvious and self-evident weaknesses have to be discussed and focus of research.

5.4   Renegotiation Flaw

Ray and Dispensa discovered in [47] a serious flaw induced by the renegotiation feature of TLS. The flaw enables an attacker to inject data into a running connection without destroying the session. The attacker gets no authentication cookie in plaintext, but her request is constructed to be concatenated on server side in a special way - the attacker is at no time able to decrypt traffic. *Anil Kurmus* proved the flaw to be practical[19] by stealing confidential data from Twitter sessions. The attack was slightly modified (an unfinished `POST` request was used), but the idea remained the same.

Lesson learned. When switching security contexts it needs to be guaranteed that there is no pending data left.

5.5   Disabling SSL/TLS at a Higher Layer

In February 2009, Marlinspike released `sslstrip`[20] a tool which disables SSL/-TLS at a higher layer. As a precondition it is necessary for an attacker to act as Mitm. To disable SSL/TLS the tool sends `HTTP 301` - permanent redirection - responses and replaces any occurrence of `https://` with `http://`. This causes the client to move to the redirected page with SSL/TLS turned off. Finally, the attacker opens a fresh session to the (requested) server and passes-through or alters any client and server data. The attack sketch is outlined in Fig. 8.

Lesson learned. Proper visualization of secured connections in the user agents is necessary.

---

[19] http://www.securegoose.org/2009/11/tls-renegotiation-vulnerability-cve.html
[20] http://www.thoughtcrime.org/software/sslstrip/

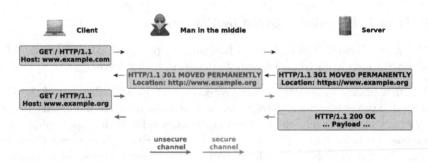

Fig. 8. Example scenario for a SSL stripping attack

5.6 Computational Denial of Service

In 2011, the German Hacker Group *The Hackers Choice* released a tool called THC-SSL-DoS[21], which creates huge load on servers by overwhelming the target with SSL/TLS handshake requests. Assuming that the majority of computation during a handshake is done by the server, the attack creates more system load on the server than on the own device - leading to a Denial of Service.

Lesson learned. When dealing with DoS attacks, cryptography is part of the problem, not a solution.

6   Conclusion

Summarizing the lessons learned leads to some basic hints:

1. Theoretical attacks can turn into practice
2. Side channels may appear at different layers in different situations
3. Reliable cryptographic primitives are important
4. Processes must leak as little information as possible
5. Specifications have to be implemented without own improvements
6. Critical parts in specifications and source code have to be highlighted
7. Specifications have to be verbose, unambiguous and technically detailed
8. Details on requirements and preconditions are necessary
9. Data has to be protected (authenticated, integrity ensured, encrypted, etc.)
10. The interplay between different layers must be part of the security analysis
11. Flexibility mostly means additional risks
12. Always be careful and alarmed

DoS attacks remain a future problem. Means to lower the attack surface emerged to be of increased relevance.

---

[21] http://www.thc.org/thc-ssl-dos/

References

1. Hickman, K.: The SSL Protocol. Internet Draft, April 1995
2. Freier, A., Karlton, P., Kocher, P.: The secure sockets layer (SSL) protocol version 3.0. RFC 6101, August 2011
3. Dierks, T., Allen, C.: The TLS protocol version 1.0. RFC 2246 (Proposed Standard), January 1999
4. Dierks, T., Rescorla, E.: The transport layer security (TLS) protocol version 1.1. RFC 4346 (Proposed Standard), April 2006
5. Dierks, T., Rescorla, E.: The transport layer security (TLS) protocol version 1.2. RFC 5246 (Proposed Standard), August 2008
6. Rescorla, E.: SSL and TLS: Designing and Building Secure Systems. Addison-Wesley, Reading (2001)
7. Wagner, D., Schneier, B.: Analysis of the SSL 3.0 protocol. In: The Second USENIX Workshop on Electronic Commerce Proceedings (1996)
8. Bellare, M., Rogaway, P.: Entity authentication and key distribution. In: Stinson, D.R. (ed.) CRYPTO 1993. LNCS, vol. 773, pp. 232–249. Springer, Heidelberg (1994)
9. Bleichenbacher, D.: Chosen ciphertext attacks against protocols based on the RSA encryption standard PKCS #1. In: Krawczyk, H. (ed.) CRYPTO 1998. LNCS, vol. 1462, pp. 1–12. Springer, Heidelberg (1998)
10. Davida, G.: Chosen signature cryptanalysis of the RSA (MIT)public key cryptosystem. Technical report (1982)
11. Brumley, D., Boneh, D.: Remote timing attacks are practical. In: Proceedings of the 12th Conference on USENIX Security Symposium, SSYM'03, vol. 12. USENIX Association, Berkeley, June 2003
12. Aciicmez, O., Schindler, W., Koc, C.: Improving Brumley and Boneh timing attack on unprotected SSL implementations. In: Proceedings of the 12th ACM conference on Computer and communications security. ACM, November 2005
13. Klíma, V., Pokorný, O., Rosa, T.: Attacking RSA-based sessions in ssL/TLs. In: Walter, C.D., Koç, C., Paar, C. (eds.) CHES 2003. LNCS, vol. 2779, pp. 426–440. Springer, Heidelberg (2003)
14. Brumley, B.B., Tuveri, N.: Remote timing attacks are still practical. In: Atluri, V., Diaz, C. (eds.) ESORICS 2011. LNCS, vol. 6879, pp. 355–371. Springer, Heidelberg (2011)
15. Montgomery, P.L.: Speeding the Pollard and elliptic curve methods of factorization. Math. Comp. **48**, 243–264 (1987)
16. López, J., Dahab, R.: Fast multiplication on elliptic curves over GF (2m) without precomputation. In: Koç, C., Paar, C. (eds.) CHES 1999. LNCS, vol. 1717, pp. 316–327. Springer, Heidelberg (1999)
17. Howgrave-Graham, N.A., Smart, N.P.: Lattice attacks on digital signature schemes. Des. Codes Crypt. **23**, 283–290 (2001)
18. Bardou, R., Focardi, R., Kawamoto, Y., Simionato, L., Steel, G., Tsay, J.-K.: Efficient padding oracle attacks on cryptographic hardware. In: Safavi-Naini, R., Canetti, R. (eds.) CRYPTO 2012. LNCS, vol. 7417, pp. 608–625. Springer, Heidelberg (2012)
19. Mavrogiannopoulos, N., Vercauteren, F., Velichkov, V., Preneel, B.: A Cross-protocol attack on the TLS protocol. In: Proceedings of the 2012 ACM Conference on Computer and Communications Security, CCS '12. ACM, October 2012

20. Vaudenay, S.: Security flaws induced by CBC padding - applications to SSL, IPSEC, WTLS. In: Knudsen, L.R. (ed.) EUROCRYPT 2002. LNCS, vol. 2332, pp. 534–545. Springer, Heidelberg (2002)

21. Kelsey, J.: Compression and information leakage of plaintext. In: Daemen, J., Rijmen, V. (eds.) FSE 2002. LNCS, vol. 2365, pp. 263–276. Springer, Heidelberg (2002)

22. Canvel, B., Hiltgen, A.P., Vaudenay, S., Vuagnoux, M.: Password interception in a SSL/TLS channel. In: Boneh, D. (ed.) CRYPTO 2003. LNCS, vol. 2729, pp. 583–599. Springer, Heidelberg (2003)

23. Bard, G.V.: The vulnerability of SSL to chosen plaintext attack. IACR Cryptology ePrint Archive 2004, May 2004

24. Bard, G.V.: A challenging but feasible blockwise-adaptive chosen-plaintext attack on SSL. In: SECRYPT 2006, Proceedings of the International Conference on Security and Cryptography, INSTICC Press, August 2006

25. Danezis, G.: Traffic analysis of the HTTP protocol over TLS (Unpublished manuscript)

26. Chen, S., Wang, R., Wang, X., Zhang, K.: Side-channel leaks in web applications: a reality today, a challenge tomorrow. In: Proceedings of the 2010 IEEE Symposium on Security and Privacy, SP '10. IEEE Computer Society, May 2010

27. Rizzo, J., Duong, T.: Here come the XOR ninjas, May 2011

28. Paterson, K.G., Schuldt, J.C.N., Stam, M., Thomson, S.: On the joint security of encryption and signature, revisited. In: Lee, D.H., Wang, X. (eds.) ASIACRYPT 2011. LNCS, vol. 7073, pp. 161–178. Springer, Heidelberg (2011)

29. AlFardan, N., Paterson, K.: Plaintext-recovery attacks against datagram TLS. In: Network and Distributed System Security Symposium (NDSS 2012), February 2012

30. AlFardan, N., Paterson, K.: Lucky thirteen: breaking the TLS and DTLS record protocols. In: Proceedings of the 2013 IEEE Symposium on Security and Privacy, SP '13. IEEE Computer Society, February 2013

31. Fluhrer, S.R., Mantin, I., Shamir, A.: Weaknesses in the key scheduling algorithm of RC4. In: Vaudenay, S., Youssef, A.M. (eds.) SAC 2001. LNCS, vol. 2259, pp. 1–24. Springer, Heidelberg (2001)

32. Ohigashi, T., Isobe, T., Watanabe, Y., Morii, M.: Full plaintext recovery attack on broadcast RC4. In: Proceedings of the 20th International Workshop on Fast Software Encryption (FSE 2013), March 2013

33. Lenstra, A., Wang, X., de Weger, B.: Colliding X.509 certificates. Cryptology ePrint Archive, Report 2005/067, March 2005

34. Rosenfeld, M.: Internet explorer SSL vulnerability, May 2008

35. Rosenfeld, M.: Null prefix attacks against SSL/TLS certificates, February 2009

36. Rosenfeld, M.: Defeating OCSP with the character '3', July 2009

37. Moore, R., Ward, S.: Multiple browser wildcard certificate validation weakness, July 2010

38. Rescorla, E.: HTTP over TLS. RFC 2818, May 2000

39. Comodo CA Ltd.: Comodo report of incident - comodo detected and thwarted an intrusion on 26-MAR-2011. Technical report, March 2011

40. Asghari, H.: Fox-IT: Black Tulip - Report of the investigation into the digiNotar. Certificate Authority Breach. Technical report, August 2012

41. Palmer, C.: Unqualified names in the SSL observatory, April 2011

42. Georgiev, M., Iyengar, S., Jana, S., Anubhai, R., Boneh, D., Shmatikov, V.: The most dangerous code in the World: Validating SSL certificates in non-browser software. In: ACM Conference on Computer and Communications Security (2012)

43. Langley, A.: Enhancing digital certificate security, January 2013
44. Goldberg, W.: Randomness and the netscape browser. Dr. Dobb's Journal, January 1996
45. Weimer, F.: DSA-1571-1 openssl - predictable random number generator, May 2008
46. Zhao, Y., Vemuri, S., Chen, J., Chen, Y., Zhou, H., Fu, Z.: Exception triggered DoS attacks on wireless networks. In: Proceedings of the 2009 IEEE/IFIP International Conference on Dependable Systems and Networks, DSN 2009, June 2009
47. Ray, M., Dispensa, S.: Renegotiating TLS. PhoneFactor, Inc. Technical report, November 2009

Looking Future

Foundational Security Principles
for Medical Application Platforms
(Extended Abstract)

Eugene Y. Vasserman[✉] and John Hatcliff

Kansas State University, Manhattan, USA
eyv@ksu.edu

Abstract. We describe a preliminary set of security requirements for safe and secure next-generation medical systems, consisting of dynamically composable units, tied together through a real-time safety-critical middleware. We note that this requirement set is not the same for individual (stand-alone) devices or for electronic health record systems, and we must take care to define *system-level requirements* rather than security goals for components. The requirements themselves build on each other such that it is difficult or impossible to eliminate any one of the requirements and still achieve high-level security goals.

1 Introduction

This position paper is a first step in deriving and elucidating security properties needed for safe operation of next-generation medical systems – sets of medical devices and health information systems, dynamically composable as needed. and enabled by **medical application platforms**. MAPs are safety- and security-critical real-time *open computing platforms* for (a) integrating *heterogeneous devices*, medical information systems, and information displays via a communication infrastructure and (b) hosting application programs (clinical logic and/or workflow automation) that provide medical utility via the ability to both acquire information from, and update/control integrated devices, IT systems, and displays [1]. A MAP can be implemented in a number of ways and environments such as clinical, home-based, mobile, or distributed.

While security alone cannot guarantee safety, it is unlikely that we will be able to achieve safety without security. Current safety evaluation and verification and validations techniques are designed primarily to deal with environmental failures and stand-alone devices or collections of devices that are integrated by a single manufacturer. For medical systems that do include some form of limited dynamic integration and reconfigurability of components such as central station monitors, current safety approaches often dictate that each combination of components requires evaluation as a complete system. This implies that for

Position paper

Y. Kim et al. (Eds.): WISA 2013, LNCS 8267, pp. 213–217, 2014.
DOI: 10.1007/978-3-319-05149-9_13, © Springer International Publishing Switzerland 2014

a system with interchangeable constituents, the manufacturer must gain regulatory approval for every possible permutation of constituent devices forming the composite medical system (which has been termed "pair-wise" approval).[1] For example, if a new type of medical device is added to the central station monitoring system, then the entire system must be reevaluated. Security is rarely taken into account, dismissed with blanket statements of precautions such as usage of antivirus software on desktops and intrusion detection/prevention in networks. Note that we are referring to the security of medical *platforms* as a whole rather than individual devices. Device security is vital [3,4], but *does not capture the all security requirements for a system of interoperating devices.*

Experience in consumer electronics with interoperability standards such as USB, WiFi, etc. has shown the success of the "component-wise" certification approach: manufacturers submit their products to third-party certification organizations that verify that the products conform to interfacing and communication standards. These components are then integrated into larger systems/configurations with high degrees of confidence and without the need to verify each possible combination of components. Of course, the challenges in the area of safety/security-critical medical systems are much greater. However, in the critical systems space, Integrated Modular Avionics [5] and the MILS Security architecture [6] are examples where standards-based architectures and interfaces are being used to encourage the development of a commodity market of safety-critical components, taking security into account explicitly. We believe that lessons learned in these frameworks can help in constructing standards that will allow medical systems to be verified and receive safety evaluations in a component-wise, as opposed to a pair-wise, fashion.

2   Unique Security Challenges

Medical systems are a unique instance of cyber-physical systems (CPS). They often require real-time guarantees which are more strict than other CPSes such as the smart grid. Avionics, power plant control systems, and other industries with federal safety regulations come to mind as the closest analogs, but these systems are *closed* to the outside and physically protected from tampering. Hospitals and other care facilities, on the other hand, rarely incorporate physical access control except for controlled substances, and individual devices are almost never tamper-resistant. Several additional quirks make medical applications unique within the CPS realm. One is the regulatory *requirement for emergency override* – human caregivers must be able to disable safeguards that are designed to ensure safety and security but may, in an emergency, inhibit delivery of needed care. *Medical systems themselves are assumed to be unreliable in determining when such an emergency is taking place.* Therefore, security controls must be subject to disabling – termed "break-glass," [7] such as when pulling a fire alarm breaks a glass rod before activating. Security is especially challenging to implement when it can be disabled. Further, while we cannot rely on authentication during

---

[1] Details of issues with the current pair-wise regulatory approach can be found in [2].

emergencies – it may slow down emergency response – we must maintain (in fact, increase) accountability and logging to ensure that post-hoc event reconstruction and auditing is possible.

3 Minimal Requirements

We suggest a list of security properties (for component-wise evaluated systems) that must be enforced in order to ensure:

- no harm can come to the patient through deliberate tampering with data;
- confidential patient data is not obtained by unauthorized parties;
- regulatory authorities and medical system operators can be confident that only components that are authorized for use are incorporated; and
- in case of an adverse incident, authorities have sufficient information available to support audits to determine the root cause(s) of the incident.

These properties are inspired by, and partially draw from, Anderson's model of clinical information systems [8], but encompass individual composable devices as well as middleware/support system architecture rather than focusing on databases of patient health records or individual devices.

1. **Integrity** to prevent unauthorized alteration of data or code[2] in transit[3] or at rest, and prevent unauthorized physical modification.
2. **Authenticity** for trustworthy *identification* of principals.
3. **Authorization** to codify the actions that an entity is allowed to perform.
4. **Attribution** to allow unambiguous identification of proximal causes of events or sources of data.
5. **Provenance** to record the original source *and chain of possession* of data (i.e., series of attributions). This should be securely and reliably logged.
6. **Availability** to guarantee that the system is reliable for predefined (possibly very small) periods of time.
7. **Timeliness** and transparency of system availability state, i.e., messages are delivered in a timely fashion[4] or not at all, and exposure to the components of the status of the system – whether or not it is *currently* available/reliable.
8. **Confidentiality** to ensure data is not readable by anyone who does not have the correct cryptographic credentials.
9. **Privacy**, which is broader than confidentiality, and is meant to partially control information leakage and inference.

Figure 1 shows property dependencies, but they may differ depending on the point of view. Moving from the bottom up, **provenance** (and secure logging of data and metadata) achieves accountability of original source *as well as intermediate entities*, providing full traceability of data custody and alteration.

---

[2] Code can include "virtual" software-only "devices".

[3] Data left its producer but has not yet arrived at the final consumer (destination).

[4] As defined by the receiving component.

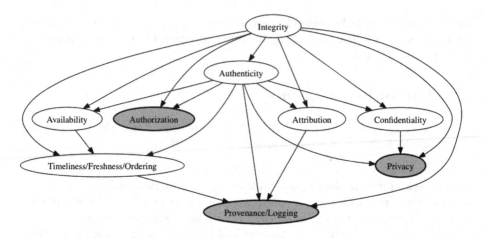

Fig. 1. Requirement interdependencies. Children depend on parents.

This can only be achieved by systems providing **attribution** of data to its previous custodian. Attribution in turn relies on the **authenticity** and **integrity** of the data and the device that authored it. Note that **authorization**, while requiring **authenticity** and **integrity**, is somewhat orthogonal, since actions may be allowed under certain circumstances without prior authorization (such as break-glass), as long as they are logged and can later be audited and their provenance traced. **Confidentiality** and **privacy** are likewise orthogonal, since in most cases they are not required for safe operation (although they are required by law in some jurisdictions to protect private health information [9,10]). **Availability** and **timeliness** of events are both required, but not to the same extent in all systems. Not all medical interactions require full real-time guarantees and continuous connectivity, but these properties must be taken into account: **availability** because the system must be functional at least part of the time, even if only long-enough for initial programming and a "start" command, and **timeliness** or temporal ordering awareness because in cases where real-time control is needed, we must reliably notify communicating components when that property has been lost, so they can engage their fallback failsafe states. Certainly temporal ordering is also required for logging, in order to allow for accurate forensic reconstruction of events [11,12].

4   Conclusion

The properties enumerated above are required for effective component-wise clearance, and eliminating each one presents a problem for technical operation, regulatory approval, or both. Some properties build upon others, and their requirements can be traced to the desirability of the "top-level" property. For instance, if we want **provenance** information as part of a log, we must also have **attribution**, which requires **authenticity** and **integrity**.

Acknowledgments. This work was supported by National Science Foundation grants CNS 1239543, and CNS 1224007, and National Institutes of Health grant 1U01EB012470-01.

References

1. Hatcliff, J., King, A., Lee, I., MacDonald, A., Fernando, A., Robkin, M., Vasserman, E.Y., Weininger, S., Goldman, J.M.: Rationale and architecture principles for medical application platforms. In: Proceedings of the International Conference on Cyber-Physical Systems (ICCPS) (2012)
2. Goldman, J.M.: CIMIT/TATRC symposium on developing a plug-and-play open networking standard for the operating room of the future (May 2005)
3. Burleson, W.P., Clark, S.S., Ransford, B., Fu, K.: Design challenges for secure implantable medical devices. In: Proceedings of the Design Automation Conference (DAC) (June 2012)
4. Clark, S.S., Fu, K.: Recent results in computer security for medical devices. In: Nikita, K.S., Lin, J.C., Fotiadis, D.I., Arredondo Waldmeyer, M.-T. (eds.) Mobi-Health 2011. LNICST, vol. 83, pp. 111–118. Springer, Heidelberg (2012)
5. Conmy, P., Nicholson, M., McDermid, J.: Safety assurance contracts for integrated modular avionics. In: Proceedings of the 8th Australian Workshop on Safety Critical Systems and Software (SCS) (2003)
6. Objective Interface Systems, Inc.: Multiple independent levels of security (MILS) — technical primer. http://www.ois.com/Products/mils-technical-primer.html (2011)
7. Brucker, A.D., Petritsch, H.: Extending access control models with break-glass. In: Proceedings of the ACM Symposium on Access Control Models and Technologies, New York, NY, USA, pp. 197–206. ACM (2009)
8. Anderson, R.J.: A security policy model for clinical information systems. In: Proceedings of the IEEE Symposium on Security and privacy, pp. 30–43 (1996)
9. United States Congress: Health Insurance Portability and Accountability Act, Privacy Rule. 45 CFR 164 (1996)
10. United States Congress: Gramm-Leach-Bliley Act, Financial Privacy Rule. 15 USC §6801–§6809
11. Accorsi, R.: Safe-keeping digital evidence with secure logging protocols: state of the art and challenges. International Conference on IT Security Incident Management and IT Forensics, pp. 94–110 (2009)
12. Arney, D., Weininger, S., Whitehead, S.F., Goldman, J.M.: Supporting medical device adverse event analysis in an interoperable clinical environment: design of a data logging and playback system. In: International Conference on Biomedical Ontology (ICBO) (July 2011)

Network Iron Curtain: Hide Enterprise Networks with OpenFlow

YongJoo Song[1]($\boxtimes$), Seungwon Shin[2], and Yongjin Choi[1]

[1] Atto Research, Seoul, Korea
{yongjoo.song,yongjin.choi}@atto-research.com
[2] Korea Advanced Institute of Science and Technology, Daejeon, South Korea
claude@kaist.ac.kr

Abstract. In this paper, we propose a new network architecture, NETWORK IRON CURTAIN that can handle network scanning attacks automatically. NETWORK IRON CURTAIN does not require additional devices or complicated configurations when it detects scanning attack, and it can confuse scanning attackers by providing fake scanning results. When an attacker sends a scanning packet to a host in NETWORK IRON CURTAIN, NETWORK IRON CURTAIN detects this trial and redirects this packet to a honeynet, which is installed with NETWORK IRON CURTAIN. The honeynet will respond to this scanning packet based on the predefined policy instead of the original target host. Therefore, the attacker will have fake information (i.e., false open port information). We implement a prototype system to verify the proposed architecture, and we show an example case of detecting network scanning.

Keywords: Software-Defined Networking · OpenFlow · Network security · Scanning attack

1 Introduction

Nowadays, networks are facing many network threats, such as denial of service attacks, network intrusion attacks, and network scanning attacks. Among them, network scanning attacks are the most basic and critical threat, because they are the starting point of following threats. For example, if an attacker wants to infect a host in a network, he needs to discover some candidate hosts for infection. To do this, he should first find a host that can be reached through a network and has some vulnerabilities by sending network packets for scanning.

Likewise, an attacker will start his malicious operations by scanning a network, and thus, network administrators try to defend their networks from this network scanning attack. In this context, to detect network scanning attacks, many approaches have been proposed so far, and TRW [17] and RBS [8] algorithms are good examples. They have been implemented in real detection systems (e.g., Bro network intrusion detection system [1]), and used in real world networks.

Y. Kim et al. (Eds.): WISA 2013, LNCS 8267, pp. 218–230, 2014.
DOI: 10.1007/978-3-319-05149-9_14, © Springer International Publishing Switzerland 2014

However, current detection approaches have some limitations. First, it usually requires steps for determining some configuration variables (e.g., threshold values) for detection. This limitation has been pointed out by the previous work [20], and it denotes that detection rates of the popular network scanning detection approaches (e.g., TRW [17], RBS [8], and MRW [22]) are various according to the threshold values. Second, they may not detect some stealthy scan trials. Stafford et al., mentions that one network scan trial per every 10 s can avoid most detection approaches [20]. Third, most detection approaches only provide ways of detection, and they do not provide some methods to handle scan trials.

To address these issues, in this paper, we propose a new network architecture, NETWORK IRON CURTAIN that can detect network scanning trials and handle them automatically. To detect and handle scanning trials without additional devices or programs, we employ a new network technology - OpenFlow [11,14], and it helps us dynamically monitor and control network flows. With the help of this technology, we can detect network scanning trials by simply adding network applications running on the OpenFlow controller[1]. In addition, we do not need to concern about the configurations for detection systems, because the proposed network architecture will automatically handle suspicious flows (i.e., flows that can be considered as scanning trials). Moreover, this architecture will provide fake information to a network scanning attackers, and it ultimately hides our networks from attackers.

The contributions from this work can be summarized as follows:

- We propose a new network architecture - NETWORK IRON CURTAIN - that can detect network scanning trials automatically, and the architecture does not need to consider additional devices or complicated configurations
- Our approach can confuse attackers by providing fake information of our network,
- We implement a prototype system with Software-Defined Networking technology (i.e., OpenFlow), and we show example working cases to verify our approach.

2   OpenFlow

In this section, we describe what is OpenFlow and how it works. OpenFlow (OF) represents an interface between the data plane and the control plane to support SDN functions. It specifies the functions of network devices (e.g., switch), and it also defines the protocol between network devices and a controller that conducts the function of control plane. Thus, the OpenFlow specification itself does not cover all functions of SDN. However, we usually use OpenFlow and SDN *interchangeably* because the OpenFlow specification [14] is the key part of SDN technology. OpenFlow enabled network devices (i.e., data plane) are commonly cooperated with network controllers (i.e., control plane) such as NOX [7], Floodlight [5], and POX [16]. A simple OpenFlow enabled network architecture is shown in Fig. 1.

---

[1] We provide more information about OpenFlow in the next section.

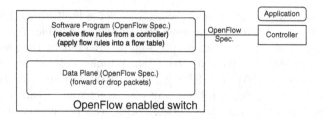

Fig. 1. High-level overview of OpenFlow switch architecture.

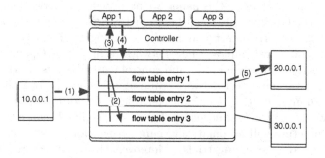

Fig. 2. A simplified OpenFlow network

How OpenFlow/SDN works: To demonstrate how a typical OpenFlow/SDN network works, we create a simplified scenario as shown in Fig. 2. This network consists of three hosts, an OpenFlow enabled switch, a controller, and three applications running on the controller.

Unlike a legacy network device, which makes packet handling decision by itself, an OpenFlow network device handles network flows based on the flow rules sent by a controller (and an application), as illustrated in Fig. 2. (1) A new packet arrives. (2) The OF device first checks its flow table. If there is an existing rule for this flow, it simply follows the rule. (3) Otherwise, it will ask the controller. (4) The controller application makes a decision and sends a flow rule back. (5) Finally, the device uses the receive flow rule to handle the packet. It is worth noting that the OF device only needs to contact the controller for a new flow that does not have corresponding rule yet, i.e., this operation happens only for the first packet of a new flow.

3   Design

At a high level, our system checks whether an incoming packet is toward a closed port or an unused port or corrupted[2]. If it is, our system considers the packet as

---

[2] We consider that the packet is corrupted if it does not follow the network protocol standard. For example, if a TCP session is initiated by a TCP RST packet, then we regard that the RST packet is corrupted.

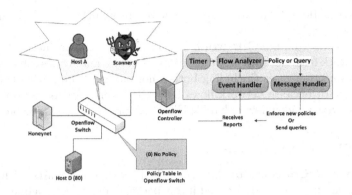

Fig. 3. Simplified network architecture and OpenFlow controller diagram

a network scanning trial. If the incoming packet is considered as a network scan trial, this packet and the following packets from the same source (i.e., from the same source IP address) will be redirected to our honeynet system. Then, our honeynet first reacts to the scanning packet based on the predefined policies. In addition, the honeynet system keeps maintaining the connection, and it tries to capture more information (e.g., malware binary download) from an attacker.

3.1 Overall Operation

To explain how NETWORK IRON CURTAIN operates and detects network scanning trials clearly, we use a simplified OpenFlow based network architecture shown in Fig. 3. In this architecture, there is a host (Host D), which opens network port 80 and connected to an OpenFlow enabled switch , and a honeynet is connected to the switch as well. This OpenFlow switch is controlled by a controller in the Figure. A network policy table, which will be used to control network flows, is in the OpenFlow switch, and there is no policy for handling network flows at this time. Two hosts (Host A and Scanner S) in the Internet are connected to the OpenFlow switch, and they can contact Host D through the OpenFlow switch.

Figure 3 also shows the four modules for realizing NETWORK IRON CURTAIN functions. These four modules are located in the OpenFlow controller; (i) event handler, which receives reports from the OpenFlow switches about new network flows or statistical information of flows, (ii) flow analyzer, which analyzes reports from the OpenFlow switches and decides new policies, (iii) message handler, which delivers messages of queries or new policies to the OpenFlow switches, and (iv) timer, which notifies timing events to the flow analyzer.

These operations are similar with the dynamic firewall, that can detect and block the malicious client. The major strong point of NETWORK IRON CURTAIN is that all switches can be the dynamic firewall without any firewall devices. The location of a firewall is the problem, especially in cloud network [18].

So, NETWORK IRON CURTAIN is a better solution than the several dynamic firewall devices in a large network.

Now, we describe how NETWORK IRON CURTAIN handles network flows to hide a network from network scanning trials. Here, we mainly describes the cases of TCP connection cases (including both a normal TCP connection trial and a scanning trial), because network flows for TCP covers most of network traffic. We also provide an idea how to handle UDP network flows to harden our system.

3.2   TCP Connection Case

TCP Normal Connection: A normal TCP connection starts with a SYN flagged packet from an initiator, and if this packet is delivered to a open network port, which serves network services based on TCP protocol, a SYN/ACK packet will be answered from the port. And finally, the initiator finishes a connection set-up by sending an ACK packet (i.e., TCP 3-way handshake).

When a TCP 3-way handshaking happens, NETWORK IRON CURTAIN works as shown in Fig. 4: (1) Host A sends a TCP SYN packet to the OpenFlow switch, (2) Since there is no matching policy in the policy table, the switch reports the information of this packet to the OpenFlow controller. (3) The event handler in the controller receives this report and delivers to the flow analyzer. The flow analyzer investigates the packet and it sees the SYN flag in the packet and sets a timer[3], and finally it enforces a new policy, which is forwarding a packet from the Host A to port 80 in the Host D, to the switch through the message handler. (4) The switch receives the policy and stores the policy into the policy table. (5) The switch forwards the packet to port 80 in the Host D. (6) Since the port 80 of the Host D is open, Host D responds with a SYN/ACK packet. (7) The packet from the Host D (i.e., the SYN/ACK packet from the Host D to the Host A) does not match any policy in the policy table, thus the switch reports this to the controller. (8) The controller observes a SYN/ACK flag in the packet, release the timer for this flow, and enforces a new policy, which is a forwarding packets from Host A to Host D and from Host D to Host A (i.e., bi-directional policy). (9) The switch stores the new policy into the policy table. (10) Finally, the switch forwards the SYN/ACK packet to Host A.

TCP SYN Scanning to Closed Ports: When the Scanner S tries to scan this network, he is likely to contact closed network ports instead of open ports, because he usually does not know which port is open, and thus he may choose some random ports. In our test scenario, we assume that the Scanner S contacts port 445 for scanning.

When a TCP SYN scanning trial happens, our system performs as shown in Fig. 5: (1) Scanner S sends a TCP SYN packet to the Openflow switch. (2) Since there is no matching policy in the policy table, the switch reports the information of this packet to the Openflow controller. (3) The flow analyzer in the controller investigates the packet, sees the SYN flag and sets the timer, and

---

[3] This timer will be used to detect TCP SYN scanning trials. We will show how the controller uses this timer in the following case.

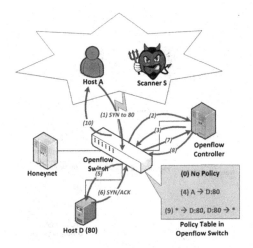

Fig. 4. Normal TCP connection

finally enforces a new policy, which is forwarding a packet from the Scanner S to port 445 in the Host D. (4) The switch receives the policy and stores the policy into the policy table. (5) The switch forwards the packet to port 445 in the Host D. (6) At this time, since Host D does not open port 445, it responds differently from the normal case. There are two cases in the response of the Host D based on its network stack implementation or its security policy. It responds with a RST packet to tear down the connection or it does not reply with any packet. (7) Here we have two cases (i) if the Host D replies with the RST packet, the switch reports this to the controller because there is no matching policy. The flow analyzer observes that there is a RST flag in the packet thus it knows that the port is closed *(scan detection)*. (ii) If the Host D does not reply, the switch will not receive any packet and it will not report anything to the controller. Thus, the timer for this flow in the controller will be expired thus the flow analyzer knows the port is closed *(scan detection)*. (8) The flow analyzer enforces a new policy. At this time, the policy is to redirect packets from the Scanner S to the Honeynet. (9) The switch stores the new policy into the policy table. (10) The switch redirects the any following scanning packets from the Scanner S to the Honeynet (i.e., a scanner will send more than one packet to a target network). (11) Finally, the Honeynet will respond to the Scanner S to confuse him (i.e., the Scanner S may receive some response packets from the honeynet, and he regards that he can successfully scan the host D).

TCP FIN/NULL/X-MAS Scanning: Beside a TCP SYN scanning, the Scanner S can employ other techniques such as FIN and X-MAS scanning. In these cases, the main difference between these and the TCP SYN scanning is that whether there is a SYN flag in the first packet for connection or not. These cases can also be detected by NETWORK IRON CURTAIN easily.

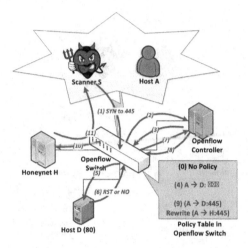

Fig. 5. TCP SYN scanning trial to a closed network port

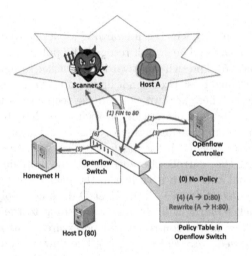

Fig. 6. TCP Non-SYN scanning trial

When this scanning trial happens, our system operates as shown in Fig. 6: (1) a Scanner S sends a TCP FIN packet to the OpenFlow switch, (2) Since there is no matching policy in the policy table, the switch reports the information of this packet to the OpenFlow controller, (3) The flow analyzer investigates the packet and it sees the FIN flag. However, this is the first packet for a TCP connection, thus any other flags except SYN are not allowed. From this, the flow analyzer understands that it is a scanning trial. The flow analyzer enforces a new policy, which is to redirect packets from the Scanner S to the Honeynet. (4) The switch stores this policy into the policy table. (5) The switch will redirect the packet to the Honeynet. (6) The Honeynet will response with a RST packet to the Scanner

S. The other scanning trials such as a X-MAS scanning could be also handled by the same approach shown here.

3.3 UDP Connection Trials

Since there is no pre-defined connection set-up (i.e., 3-way handshaking in TCP protocol) in UDP protocol, we can not employ the previous approach for UDP protocol. However, we expect that most UDP connections operate as a request-and-reply manner. For example, in the case of a DNS service, if a client sends a query (i.e., DNS Q query using UDP protocol) to a DNS server, the server will respond (i.e., DNS A query using UDP protocol). It also can be applicable to network scan attackers because they will expect some responses from a port in order to understand whether the port is open or not.

Based on this intuition, we use the approach used in the previous case (i.e., TCP protocol case), but the approach for UDP protocol differs in that we only investigate suspicious connections based on timer. In the case of TCP protocol, to know whether a packet is for a scan attack or not, we parse the packet to investigate whether there are flags which denote success/failure of the connection (i.e., SYN, SYN/ACK, RST, and FIN flags) or we check a timer. Since UDP protocol does not have these flags, we only use a timer to find a scan attack. If there is a packet to an UDP port but no reply within certain time value, we consider that the packet is for network scanning. Thus, the overall operation is the same as shown in Fig. 5 (only considering timer).

The attack using one-way UDP streams is out of scope in this paper. Since the one-way UDP stream does not issue any reply, it is not a scanning attack but a kind of DoS attack. (Using the SDN statistics like the incoming packet per seconds, we can block DoS attack too.)

3.4 Honeynet

If we detect scan packets, we redirect them and successive packets of them (in the same flow) to a honeynet. The honeynet consists of multiple honeypots and each honeypot emulates possible vulnerable network services. The attacker mistakes the honeynet for the original one. In addition to confusing network scanner, the honeynet can collect the attack information. The collected attack pattern can be very useful to prevent and detect the another attack. At this time, we can have two different strategies to confuse network scanners; (i) all-alive network, and (ii) phantom network. These two approaches are only different from each other in some configurations, thus we can easily apply any case that we want.

All-Alive Network: In this case, our honeypots open all network ports even there are no popular network services. Current honeypot programs open some networks ports to emulate network services but they may not emulate all possible network services. Thus, we simply run a simple network program to cover all other network ports which are not covered by honeypot programs. For example, if a honeypot program opens network port 80, 445, and 8080, out program will open other network ports from 1 to 65545 (except 80, 445, and 8080) and wait network requests. However, this program does not emulate network services, it only reply with simple predefined data.

Phantom Network: Network scanning attackers may think that it is not common that most (all) network ports are open. They may understand that there is an approach to confuse themselves. To deceive network scanning attackers more effectively, we can make fake network environments. We randomly select some network services and let honeypots only open network ports for them. It looks like another network environment, but its configuration is totally different from original one which we want to protect from network scanning attacks.

4   Implementation and Evaluation

In this section, we describe how we have implemented the proposed system, and we explain the evaluation environment and results.

4.1   Prototype Implementation and Evaluation Environment

We have implemented a prototype system for NETWORK IRON CURTAIN to verify our proposal. Our prototype has been implemented as an application program running on POX controller [16]. In this application, we have implemented four modules explained in Fig. 3.

We have used mininet [12] to evaluate our prototype Iron Curtain. Using the typical mininet virtual machine and configuration [12], we have simulated the simplified network environment shown in Fig. 3. There is one OpenFlow enabled switch controlled by NETWORK IRON CURTAIN, and the switch has 3 physical ports that are connected with 3 virtual hosts. These ports are connected to a client (Host A in Fig. 3) that act as a benign client or a network scanning attacker, a server (Host D in Fig. 3), and a honeynet.

4.2   Evaluation Results

Figures 7 and 8 shows the start-up of mininet simulator and POX controller with NETWORK IRON CURTAIN. Figure 7 shows that we add 3 hosts (h1, h2, and h3 in line 6) and a switch (s1 in line 8), and it also shows that each host is connected to a switch (in line 10). Here, we use the host h1 as a normal client or a scanning attacker (i.e., Host A), and the host 3 is regarded as a honeynet. The created virtual switch (i.e., s1) in this mininet network is connected to the POX controller, and it is presented in Fig. 8 (in line 8).

First, we test the normal flows in Fig. 4. To do this, we run a simple TCP echo server on the host h2 and run a TCP echo client on the host h1. Figure 9 shows that a new flow set up for the SYN packet and the other new flow also set up for the reply packet. This Figure presents that a TCP SYN packet is delivered from the host h1 (line 2), and the packet is forwarded to the host h2

```
 1 mininet@mininet-vm:~$ sudo mn --topo single,3 --mac --switch ovsk --controller remote
 2 *** Creating network
 3 *** Adding controller
 4 Unable to contact the remote controller at 127.0.0.1:6633
 5 *** Adding hosts:
 6 h1 h2 h3
 7 *** Adding switches:
 8 s1
 9 *** Adding links:
10 (h1, s1) (h2, s1) (h3, s1)
11 *** Configuring hosts
12 h1 h2 h3
13 *** Starting controller
14 *** Starting 1 switches
15 s1
16 *** Starting CLI:
17 mininet> xterm h1 h2 h3
18 mininet>
```

Fig. 7. Console screen for launching a test network environment with mininet

```
 1 mininet@mininet-vm:~/pox$ ./pox.py log.level --DEBUG misc.iron_curtain
 2 POX 0.1.0 (betta) / Copyright 2011-2013 James McCauley, et al.
 3 DEBUG:core:POX 0.1.0 (betta) going up...
 4 DEBUG:core:Running on CPython (2.7.3/Sep 26 2012 21:51:14)
 5 DEBUG:core:Platform is Linux-3.5.0-17-generic-x86_64-with-Ubuntu-12.10-quantal
 6 INFO:core:POX 0.1.0 (betta) is up.
 7 DEBUG:openflow.of_01:Listening on 0.0.0.0:6633
 8 INFO:openflow.of_01:[00-00-00-00-00-01 1] connected
 9 DEBUG:misc.iron_curtain:Controlling [00-00-00-00-00-01 1]
```

Fig. 8. Console screen for launching NETWORK IRON CURTAIN on the POX controller

```
 1 DEBUG:misc.iron_curtain:Controlling [00-00-00-00-00-01 1]
 2 DEBUG:misc.iron_curtain:TCP Packet from 1: [TCP 49889>50000 seq:1213458478 ack:0 f:S]
 3 DEBUG:misc.iron_curtain:      Mod Normal flow
 4 DEBUG:misc.iron_curtain:      --> forward to 2: [TCP 49889>50000 seq:1213458478 ack:0 f:S]
 5 DEBUG:misc.iron_curtain:TCP Packet from 2: [TCP 50000>49889 seq:1972446336 ack:1213458479 f:SA]
 6 DEBUG:misc.iron_curtain:      Mod Normal flow
 7 DEBUG:misc.iron_curtain:      --> forward to 1: [TCP 50000>49889 seq:1972446336 ack:1213458479 f:SA]
```

Fig. 9. Console message for showing a normal TCP connection set up

```
 1 DEBUG:misc.iron_curtain:Controlling [00-00-00-00-00-01 1]
 2 DEBUG:misc.iron_curtain:TCP Packet from 1: [TCP 49894>50000 seq:1791507265 ack:0 f:S]
 3 DEBUG:misc.iron_curtain:      Mod Normal flow
 4 DEBUG:misc.iron_curtain:      --> forward to 2: [TCP 49894>50000 seq:1791507265 ack:0 f:S]
 5 DEBUG:misc.iron_curtain:TCP Packet from 2: [TCP 50000>49894 seq:0 ack:1791507266 f:AR]
 6 DEBUG:misc.iron_curtain:      --> Detect Scanning Trial to a Closed Network Port
 7 DEBUG:misc.iron_curtain:      Mod flow to HoneyNet
 8 DEBUG:misc.iron_curtain:      Mod flow from HoneyNet
 9 DEBUG:misc.iron_curtain:      --> forward to 3: [TCP 49894>50000 seq:1791507265 ack:0 f:S]
```

Fig. 10. Console message for detecting a TCP scanning trial

(line 4). A TCP SYN/ACK packet from the host h2 (line 5) is forwarded to the host h1 (line 7).

Second, we test a network scanning trial to a closed network port case in Fig. 5. At this time, the Host D does not run a echo server, and we run a simple scanner at the host A to scan a network port for a TCP echo service in the Host D. However, since the Host D does not open this port, the Host D will return a TCP RST packet to the scanner. Figure 10 shows the detection of this scanning trial. NETWORK IRON CURTAIN first detects this scanning trial when it finds a TCP RST packet (line 6), and it forwards this packet to the honeynet (line 7). Finally, the honeynet will return a fake packet to confuse the scanning attacker (line 9).

5   Related Work

There are some previous studies to defend a network from network scanning attacks. TRW [17], RBS [8], and MRW [22] are good example techniques for this. They are different from our work in that they require additional monitoring devices or network mirroring techniques. In addition, they just focus on detection, and they do not provide an way of handling detected scanning packets.

Recently, some research based on OpenFlow technique has been proposed to hide networks from network scanning. FRESCO [19] provides an way of implementing reflector network, and Random host mutation technique [9] has been suggested to hide a network from scanning trials. Our work is different from them in that the goal is different (proposing a new network architecture vs. a framework for developing security applications) and the approach is different (detecting network scanning and remove the effect vs. varying the IP address of hosts in a network).

Some approaches without using OpenFlow have been proposed to hide a network. Gu et al., propose an approach of whitehole technique [6] to hide a network from scanning trials. Although its goal is similar to our approach, it requires additional devices that can modify network packets, and it is not easy to deploy in a real world network. The idea of tarpit has been proposed to reduce the effect of computer worm [10], and this idea can also be used to reduce the effect of network scanning. However, this approach is clearly different from our work in that it requires complicated configurations of software or hardware.

6   Limitation and Discussion

Although NETWORK IRON CURTAIN can detect network scanning trials and remove the effects of scanning, it has some limitations. First, it can delay the performance of overall network throughput. Since NETWORK IRON CURTAIN needs to monitor all possible TCP sessions, it should control network flows in a fine-grained way. However, we believe that it is the common problem for most Software-Defined Networking architecture, and the it only adds delays to network packets for connection setup. Once a connection has been established, NETWORK IRON CURTAIN does not affect the performance. The performance of the controller is a common concern in the SDN studies. Tootoonchian et al. shows that the controller with the common PC server can endure enough traffic [21]. The DoS attack to the SDN contoller is also an important research issue [2,23].

Second, it is possible that there are some false positives when NETWORK IRON CURTAIN redirects suspicious packets to a honeynet. If a benign client contacts a closed port by mistake, following packets from this client could be considered as suspicious packets. To address this issue, we can hire some reputation technology to investigate whether a host is really malicious or not. There are several studies that try to detect network scanning attacks or web based attacks and Dshield [3] and FIRE [4] are good examples of them. Dshield [3] provides information to detect hosts or ASes sending suspicious network scanning/attacking packets, and FIRE [4] lists malicious ASes by measuring their reputation. Clearly speaking, NETWORK IRON CURTAIN can maintain some history information for scanning trials from each host. Although NETWORK IRON CURTAIN detects a failed TCP session from a host, it does not simply redirect all future packets to a honeynet (but investigates more), if a host sends benign packets in the past (normal TCP connections).

Third, NETWORK IRON CURTAIN needs OpenFlow-enabled devices, although it does not need any security devices. The switching cost to the OpenFlow-enabled network would be a entry barrier. But the application area of OpenFlow does not only focus on the security [13,15], and some are already applied into realworld network environments [24]. The SDN technology is already spreading widely.

7 Conclusion and Future Work

In this paper, we propose a new network architecture - NETWORK IRON CURTAIN - to hide a network from network scanning trials. The proposed network architecture employs the functions of OpenFlow technology, and it can performs its operations without adding third-party devices or programs. In the near future, we will deploy the proposed network architecture in a real network environment. In addition, we will test more diverse network scanning cases to verify the proposed network architecture.

References

1. Bro: Network security monitor. http://www.bro.org
2. Curtis, A.R., Mogul, J.C., Tourrilhes, J., Yalagandula, P., Sharma, P., Banerjee, S.: Devoflow: scaling flow management for high-performance networks. ACM SIG-COMM Comput. Commun. Rev. 41, 254–265 (2011)
3. DSHIELD: Cooperative network security community. http://www.dshield.org/
4. FIRE: Finding rogue networks. http://maliciousnetworks.org/
5. FloodLight: Open sdn controller. http://floodlight.openflowhub.org/
6. Gu, G., Chen, Z., Porras, P., Lee, W.: Misleading and defeating importance-scanning malware propagation. In: Proceedings of the 3rd International Conference on Security and Privacy in Communication Networks (SecureComm'07), September 2007
7. Gude, N., Koponen, T., Pettit, J., Pfaff, B., Casado, M., McKeown, N., Shenker, S.: NOX: towards an operating system for networks. Proc. ACM SIGCOMM Comput. Commun. Rev. 38(3), 105–110 (2008)
8. Jung, J., Milito, R.A., Paxson, V.: On the adaptive real-time detection of fast-propagating network worms. In: Hämmerli, B.M., Sommer, R. (eds.) DIMVA 2007. LNCS, vol. 4579, pp. 175–192. Springer, Heidelberg (2007)

9. Haadi Jafarian, J., Al-Shaer, E., Duan, Q.: Openflow random host mutation: transparent moving target defense using software defined networking. In: Proceedings of the First Workshop on Hot Topics in Software Defined Networks, HotSDN '12 (2012)
10. Liston, T.: Tom liston talks about labrea. http://labrea.sourceforge.net/Intro-History.html
11. McKeown, N., Anderson, T., Balakrishnan, H., Parulkar, G., Peterson, L., Rexford, J., Shenker, S., Turner, J.: Openflow: enabling innovation in campus networks. SIGCOMM Comput. Commun. Rev. **38**, 69–74 (2008)
12. Mininet: An instant virtual network on your laptop (or other pc). http://mininet.org
13. Nayak, A., Reimers, A., Feamster, N., Clark, R.: Resonance: dynamic access control for enterprise networks. In: Proceedings of WREN (2009)
14. OpenFlow: OpenFlow swtch specification version 1.1.0. Technical report (2011). http://www.openflow.org/documents/openflow-spec-v1.1.0.pdf
15. Popa, L., Yu, M., Ko, S.Y., Stoica, I., Ratnasamy, S.: Cloudpolice: taking access control out of the network. In: Proceedings of the 9th ACM Workshop on Hot Topics in Networks, HotNets (2010)
16. POX: Python network controller. http://www.noxrepo.org/pox/about-pox/
17. Schechter, S.E., Jung, J., Berger, A.W.: Fast detection of scanning worm infections. In: Jonsson, E., Valdes, A., Almgren, M. (eds.) RAID 2004. LNCS, vol. 3224, pp. 59–81. Springer, Heidelberg (2004)
18. Shin, S., Gu, G.: Cloudwatcher: network security monitoring using openflow in dynamic cloud networks (or: how to provide security monitoring as a service in clouds?). In: 2012 20th IEEE International Conference on Network Protocols (ICNP), October 2012
19. Shin, S., Porras, P., Yegneswaran, V., Fong, M., Gu, G., Tyson, M.: Fresco: modular composable security services for software-defined networks. In: Proceedings of the 20th Annual Network and Distributed System Security Symposium (NDSS'13), February 2013
20. Stafford, S., Li, J.: Behavior-based worm detectors compared. In: Jha, S., Sommer, R., Kreibich, C. (eds.) RAID 2010. LNCS, vol. 6307, pp. 38–57. Springer, Heidelberg (2010)
21. Tootoonchian, A., Gorbunov, S., Ganjali, Y., Casado, M., Sherwood, R.: On controller performance in software-defined networks. In: USENIX Workshop on Hot Topics in Management of Internet, Cloud, and Enterprise Networks and Services (Hot-ICE) (2012)
22. Sekar, V., Xie, Y., Reiter, M.K., Zhang, H.: A multi-resolution approach for worm detection and containment. In: Proceedings of the International Conference on Dependable Systems and Networks (DSN), June 2006
23. Wang, R., Butnariu, D., Rexford, J.: Openflow-based server load balancing gone wild. In: Proceedings of the 11th USENIX Conference on Hot Topics in Management of Internet, Cloud, and Enterprise Networks and Services, p. 12. USENIX Association (2011)
24. Wired: Going with the flow: Googles secret switch to the next wave of networking. http://www.wired.com/wiredenterprise/2012/04/going-with-the-flow-google/

Towards a Methodical Evaluation
of Antivirus Scans and Labels
"If You're Not Confused, You're Not Paying Attention"

Aziz Mohaisen[1]([✉]), Omar Alrawi[2], Matt Larson[3], and Danny McPherson[1]

[1] Verisign Labs, Reston, USA
amohaisen@verisign.com
[2] Qatar Foundation, Cambridge, USA
[3] Dyn, Manchester, USA

Abstract. In recent years, researchers have relied heavily on labels provided by antivirus companies in establishing ground truth for applications and algorithms of malware detection, classification, and clustering. Furthermore, companies use those labels for guiding their mitigation and disinfection efforts. However, ironically, there is no prior systematic work that validates the performance of antivirus vendors, the reliability of those labels (or even detections), or how they affect the said applications. Equipped with malware samples of several malware families that are manually inspected and labeled, we pose the following questions: How do different antivirus scans perform relatively? How correct are the labels given by those scans? How consistent are AV scans among each other? Our answers to these questions reveal alarming results about the correctness, completeness, coverage, and consistency of the labels utilized by much existing research. We invite the research community to challenge the assumption of relying on antivirus scans and labels as a ground truth for evaluating malware analysis and classification techniques.

Keywords: Malware · Labeling · Automatic analysis · Evaluation

1 Introduction

Antivirus (AV) companies continuously evolve to improve their products. AV products provide users with an added protection from malware threats, but they are not a complete solution. Malware evolves at a much faster rate than AV products, which then forces AV companies to innovate and improve approaches for malware detection. AV products provide two major functionalities: first and more importantly, detecting malicious software and secondly, labeling malware based on a family association. Labeling is an important problem to AV vendors because it allows them to filter known malware and focus on new malware families or variants of similar malware families. Labeling also allows the AV vendors to track a malware family and its evolution.

Y. Kim et al. (Eds.): WISA 2013, LNCS 8267, pp. 231–241, 2014.
DOI: 10.1007/978-3-319-05149-9_15, © Springer International Publishing Switzerland 2014

The AV market is very diverse and provides much room for competition, allowing new companies to build AV products and compete for a share of the market. This diversity of AV software vendors creates disorganization in the AV market characterized by a lack of standards for information sharing, malware family naming, and transparency. For example, each AV company has its own way of naming malware families as they are discovered. Malware names are usually created by analysts who study new malware samples, by utilizing artifacts within the malware to derive the given names. Some malware is so popular in underground forums, like SpyEye, Zeus, ZeroAccess, DirtJumper, etc., that AV vendors use those names given to the malware by the authors or the malware market. Other smaller and less prominent malware is usually named independently by each AV company. For example, targeted malware, which is known as advance persistent threat (APT), is low key malware that AV vendors name and track independently.

Malware naming and labeling has many useful applications in the security field. Security practitioners have an interest in identifying a malware by a family name so that they can mitigate the threat for their organization. AV vendors can use labels to filter out insignificant malware and focus only on high priority malware families. Researchers in academia have benefited from detections and labeling of malware provided by AV vendors in many ways. For example, researchers in the fields of malware analysis, detection, and classification have benefited from AV scans and labels in establishing baselines to compare their designs against. In fact, there exists a large body of academic literature that relies on AV labels to verify methods and techniques, including [2,3,6,12,13,16,20,22,23] (a survey of those works is in [15]).

However, the use of AV labels for validating classification research—while creating a ground truth for comparing different works to each other— has many shortcomings and pitfalls. First, oftentimes malware samples collected by researchers are not necessarily represented in their entirety within a single malware scanning engine. Accordingly, researchers tend to use multiple engines to cover their datasets, despite inconsistencies in labeling and naming conventions used by those engines. Those inconsistencies are resolved by translating names from one AV vendor to another, although—as we mentioned earlier—different AV vendors may use different names to refer to the same family. Even worse, different families may have the same name in different AV detections—for example "generic" and "trojan" are used by many vendors as an umbrella label [9].

1.1 The Origins of Inconsistency and Implications

The AV inconsistencies arise because of the methods used by the AV vendors for detection. The primary goal for an AV vendor is detect malicious code, hence making labeling a secondary priority. Most AV vendors use a combination of static and heuristic-based methods to identify and label malware. Static signatures are insufficient because malware authors use obfuscation techniques, which quickly outdates a static signature. A heuristic signature, on the other hand, allows detection based on the behavior of the unknown software. A heuristic signature can consist of several behavior conditions that will trigger the signature. For example, if a piece of unknown software listens on a port for incoming connections, injects code into privileged processes, and hooks specific Windows APIs, then a heuristic signature is triggered and an alert is generated. These heuristic rules are loosely designed to detect malicious code, hence they are not suitable for labeling due to their generic labeling schemes.

Those inconsistencies create inefficiencies in the industry and could prevent stakeholders from benefitting from a common standard for malware family naming and information sharing. For example, if a user of an AV engine A_i detects a malware with label ℓ_1, the user might have a mitigation plan for that malware family. On the other hand another AV vendor, A_j, detects the same malware as ℓ_2, then the user of A_j will not be able to use an existing mitigation plan for the same malware. This inefficiency can cost organizations millions of dollars in intellectual property theft or reputation damage. Understanding the size of the damage caused by this issue is nontrivial, since companies are conservative in revealing information about the compromise of their systems and exfiltration of their users' or proprietary data, and only insiders are aware of this threat and its cost. However, there has been recent public information that support, highlight the trend, and put good figures on that cost and pervasiveness of such phenomena; examples include the hacking of LinkedIn [18], Ubisoft [4], LivingSocial [17], and most famously Nissan [10].

An even worse problem related to those inconsistencies is when the same AV engine detects the same malware family with different labels due to an evasion technique used by the malware. For example, if a malware is initially detected using a static signature, then later—due to its polymorphism technique—heuristically using a generic malicious behavior, the AV vendor will give it another label. This will create an inconsistent label within the same AV vendor's labeling schema. These inconsistencies and shortcomings may not have a direct implication on the malware detection provided by the AV scanner, although they impact applications that use AV labeling. For example, mislabels may propagate error throughout an experiment that relies on those labels as a ground truth. In the literature, researchers widely accepted AV labels as a ground truth of malware family membership, including applications of classification, clustering, and alternative detection techniques.

Motivated by our recent work on cross-validating AV labels against highly-accurate expert-vetted and labeled malware samples, we pursue the study of systematically understanding those inconsistencies and reveal several interesting insightful remarks that greatly affect the way applications based on AV provided labels (or even detections) work. Our study to address the problem, while inspired by the work in [2], is the first of its type to go at length to systematically evaluate those labels and detections. We do this by considering one popular malware family, the Zeus banking Trojan, thus giving AV scanners many benefits of the doubt. The Zeus banking Trojan is a famous banking Trojan that is used by cyber criminals to run a botnet to steal money, credentials, and system resources from the infected victims. In particular, the Zeus source code was leaked in 2011 and since then there has been numerous variants that have surfaced [7]. Our samples are used so that their detection in our system is old enough to make sure that they are populated in those AV scanners. The popularity of the studied malware family makes it a good candidate to evaluate detections and labels, because one would expect this family to be well researched in the AV community, thus reducing inconsistencies in labels and detections across different AV vendors.

1.2   Contribution

The contribution of this study is twofold. We provide metrics for evaluating AV detections and labeling systems. Second, we use a highly-accurate and manually-vetted dataset for evaluating the detections and labelings of a large number of AV engines using the proposed metrics. The dataset, scripts, and AV scans will be all made available publicly to the community to use and contribute to problem at hand. To the best out our knowledge, there is no prior systematic work that explores this direction at the same level of rigor we follow in this paper (for the related work, see Sect. 4). Notice that we disclaim any novelty in pointing out the problem. In fact, there has been several works that pointed out problems with AV labels [2,3], however those works did not systematically and quantitatively study the performance of AV scanners and the accuracy of their labels. This, as mentioned before, is in part because of the lack of datasets with solid ground truth of their label[1].

1.3   Organization

The organization of the rest of this paper is as follows. In Sect. 2 we provide an overview of the dataset we used in this study and the method we use for obtaining it. In Sect. 3 we review the measurements and findings of this study: we first introduce evaluation metrics for AV vendors, and then use those metrics to evaluate 48 vendors and their performance on our dataset. In Sect. 4 we review the related work, followed by concluding remarks, open directions, and the future work in Sect. 5.

2   Datasets

To evaluate the different AV vendors based on a common ground of comparison, we use the Zeus banking trojan, which has been identified manually by analysts. Our dataset consists of 1,000 samples, which is large enough to derive meaningful insights into the problem at hand and small enough to be manually vetted for correct results[2]. To identify the label of this family, we used forensic memory signatures to identify a set of possible Zeus samples from our malware repositories,

---

[1] Ironically, some of those works pointed out the problem and yet used AV-provided labels for validating their malware clustering algorithms [3,15].

[2] We use malware samples accumulated over a period of a year (mid 2011 to 2012). As we will see later, this would give the AV vendors an advantage and might overestimate their performance compared to more emerging threats (APT).

then we manually vetted the set to ensure our final data set is clean of malware families that might falsely trigger our memory signatures. More details on this method for vetting malware samples is described in [9]. For the evaluation of our data set we used VirusTotal [1] signatures for 48 AV engines to test several evaluation measures. We discarded all engines that provided detections for only less than 10 % of our dataset.

VirusTotal is a multi-engine AV scanner that accepts submissions by users and scans the sample with multiple AV engines. The results from VirusTotal have much useful information, but we only use the AV vendor name and their detection label. VirusTotal will provide more AV results when a malware sample has been submitted in the past. The reason for this is that AV engines will provide an updated signature for malware that is not previously detected by their engines but was detected by other engines. Hence, malware samples that have been submitted multiple times for a long period of time will have better detection rates. However, because no researchers have had an alternative to the labels the AV scanners provide, so far the completeness, consistency, and correctness—the three comparison and evaluation measures we study in Sect. 3—of AV labels and scans were not challenged. Implications of those metrics of an AV scan were overlooked in the literature.

3 Measurements

3.1 Evaluation Metrics

In this work we use several evaluation metrics, namely completeness, consistency, and correctness, and coverage. The metrics are defined as follows:

- Completeness: For our references dataset $\mathcal{D}$, we compute the *completeness* of the scans of an AV vendor $\mathcal{A}_i$ as the number of detections returned by $\mathcal{A}_i$ normalized by the size of the dataset, $|\mathcal{D}|$.
- Consistency: The *consistency* is computed as the agreement (or disagreement) in detections between $\mathcal{A}_i$ and the rest of AV vendors we tested. For that, we use the Jaccard distance which captures the number of samples consistently detected or undetected by two vendors $\mathcal{A}_i$ and $\mathcal{A}_j$ and results in $n - 1$ consistency values for $\mathcal{A}_i$.
- Correctness: Given our reference dataset $\mathcal{D}$, we compute the *correctness* of an AV vendor $\mathcal{A}_i$ as the number of detections matching our reference detection normalized by the size of the reference dataset, $|\mathcal{D}|$.
- Coverage: We define the *coverage* as the number of the AV scans (list of detections and labels, respectively) required for achieving a correct and complete scan. This is, as various AV scans will provide partial correctness and completeness scores for the reference dataset, this measure would determine how many AV vendors one needs to utilize to get a perfect score for both measures.

3.2   Results and Analysis

Completeness. For completeness, and as explained above, we use the ratio of detections out of our 1,000 sample set per an AV engine. For example, if an AV engine A_i has 950 detections for the 1,000 sample dataset then AV engine A_i has a 0.95 completeness regardless to what labels that are returned by the named AV. Figure 1 plots the completeness of all AV engines that were used in the evaluation. The results show a detection rate as low as 0.15 for our dataset and as high as 0.94 for the given AV engines. Roughly 45 % of the AV engines in our study have a less than 70 % detection rate (0.7 completeness score).

While the completeness scores given to AV scanners are not surprising, the high diversity in the score and large range are. Thus, the result has many interesting implications. Most importantly, given that no AV scanner provided a completeness of one, we cannot establish consistency over a labeling based on a single reference AV vendor. Furthermore, we cannot establish a consensus on what different AV providers mean by their labels for the entire dataset. Second, even the most widely used AV scanners are do not provide sufficient results: among the most widely used AV vendors in the academic community for validation of studies are Avira (Antivir), Kaspersky, Symantec, McAfee, Microsoft, AhnLab, AVG, and ClamAV. While they are among the most complete AV scans for the reference dataset (with completeness scores ranging from 0.76 to 0.94), we notice that the small "incompleteness" of scans is problematic to the application for which the scans are used. While researchers strive to achieve 99 % of accuracy in their classification of malware samples [3], a 6 % of incompleteness is an overlooked margin of error, and it is unclear how this margin is considered in the total performance measures in the literature. Even worse, the completeness of a scan does not guarantee a correctness of a detection.

Correctness. We define the correctness as the ratio of detections with a correct label per AV engine for all of our dataset. In our study we considered three labels to be acceptable for correctness, "Zbot," "Trojan," and "Generic." Although those labels might be anticipated to yield high results, especially for generic labeling (Generic) the results show otherwise. Figure 2 illustrates two plots of the correctness evaluation. The bar chart is color coded differently for

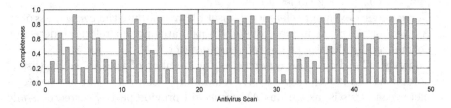

Fig. 1. Completeness of detections by 48 AV vendors. Popular AV scans used in the literature include Avira (Antivir), Kaspersky, Symantec, McAfee, Microsoft, AhnLab, AVG, and ClamAV, which are bars numbers: 27, 18, 11, 4, 36, 40, 47, and 17, respectively. (in all figures)

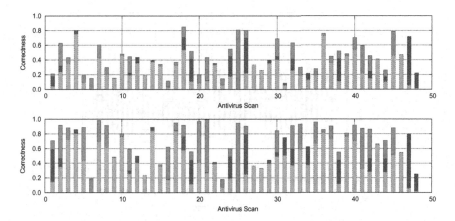

Fig. 2. Correctness of detections by 48 vendors. Color code: green is precise detection (Zbot), red and violet are translated detections (generic and trojan). Upper figure is normalized by 1000 (incorporates the completeness score), while the lower figure is normalized by number of detections of the given AV scan (Color figure online).

each label mentioned above, green is "Zbot," red is "Generic," and violet is "Trojan" (the height of the bar is inclusive of all detections and variants). The difference between the two bar charts is the normalization value used for both. While the first bar chart is normalized based on the size of our dataset of 1,000 samples to incorporate the completeness score, the second bar chart is normalized by the number of detections for the given AV engine. We observe that the majority of AV engines label the malware "Zbot" less than 50 % (0.5 of correctness) of the time per detection. We also observe that the "Zbot" label is used by almost all of the AV engines. Note that the correctness score for each AV engine is lower than the completeness score because other labels are used by the AV engine to label our dataset, which vary outside the three major labels we chose.

This evaluation measure of AV scans has perhaps the most critical implication. In short, this measure says that, even when an AV provides a complete scan for a malware dataset, it is still not guaranteed that the same scanner will provide a correct label, and thus a labeling provided by an AV vendor cannot be used as a certain ground truth for labeling.

Consistency. We define the consistency as an AV engine detecting a malware sample alongside other AV engines. The consistency is determined per sample and is compared across all AV engines. We observed on average an AV engine is about 50 % consistent with other AV engines, meaning that given a malware sample detected by $\mathcal{A}_i$, 50 % of the time it is also detected by $\mathcal{A}_j$ as malicious. Figure 3 illustrates the consistency of each AV engine across all other engines using box plots (min, first quartile, median, third quartile, and max). The figure clearly displays a median of approximately 50 % for all AV engines. This finding further raises the question of how many AV scanners it would take to get a consistent detection for a given dataset.

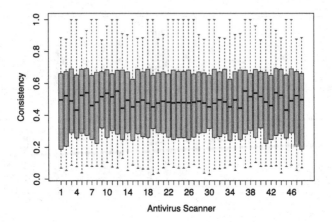

Fig. 3. Consistency of detections by 48 vendors.

Coverage: How many AV scanners? For completeness and correctness we pose the following question: What is the least number of scanners it takes to get a complete (or correct) scan of our reference dataset? This question stems from the fact that many researchers in the literature combined more than one AV vendor's results to get a better coverage of labels for their experiments. Answering this question is not as easy as it sounds: the problem is the optimization version of the set-cover problem, which is known to be NP-hard. Thus, we consider heuristics to answer the question.

Again, we use the same scans we used for plotting the previous figures of the completeness and correctness scores. We use two strategies for each score, namely l/s and s/l, as shown in Fig. 4. For l/s, we start by considering potential

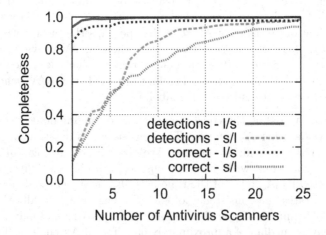

Fig. 4. Completeness (per detections and correct detections) when using largest to smallest and smallest to largest scan to accumulate the entire dataset.

scans to obtain the required completeness from large to small, add them to the list of final scans, increase the number of AV scanners by one for each, and recompute the completeness (correctness) score respectively. The s/l strategy does the opposite. We use the strategies as extremes, and don't consider the best strategy[3]. As expected, we notice that it takes fewer scanners to achieve a completeness of 1 than it takes to achieve correctness of 1, even with the better-performing strategy. Numerically, we observe that while 5 scans are required to achieve completeness of 1, 22 AV scans give only 0.97 of correctness. Indeed, even 48 AV scanners (the total) were able to achieve only 0.99 of correctness.

4   Related Work

Ironically, while the use of AV-provided labels has been widely employed in the literature for training algorithms and techniques utilized for malware classification and analysis[2,3,5,8,9,11–14,19,20,23], there is less work done on understanding the nature of those labels. Recent works, like [13,15] only pointed out the problem of AV-provided labels without any measurements or evaluation.

To the best of our knowledge, the only prior work dedicated to systematically understanding AV-provided labels is due to Bailey et al. [2]. However, our work is different from that work in several aspects highlighted as follows:

- While our work relies on a set of manually-vetted malware samples for which we know the accurate label and family, the work in [2] relies on an AV vendor as a reference and compares other vendors to it. In particular, the authors use McAfee as the presumed complete and accurate reference of detection and labeling and compare a handful other vendors to it. Our technique avoids this issue by relying on a manually inspected reference set against which the performance of many AV vendors is tested.
- Our study considers the largest set of AV-vendors studied in the literature thus far for a comparative work. We do that by relying on the largest number of manually-vetted malware samples as well. As shown in the study, even when certain AV providers are consistent among each other, they still don't provide perfect results with respect to the ideal ground truth.
- Finally, given that we rely on a solid ground truth, we develop several metrics of AV scans evaluation that are specific to our study: the correctness, completeness, and coverage. On the other hand, the prior work considers all results provided by the reference AV scan to be correct and compares other AV scans to them.

5   Conclusion and Future Work

In this work, we unveil the danger of relying on incomplete, inconsistent, and incorrect malware labeling systems provided by AV scanners and using them

---

[3] The greedy strategy, by adding the AV scan with least overlap to the current set, is the best known approximation [21].

in the research community for validating malware analysis and classification techniques. Our study shows that one needs many independent AV scanners to obtain complete and correct labels. Our study has many limitations to it, and does not try to answer many questions that are either out of its scope or beyond our resources and capabilities. First of all, our study cannot be used as a generalization on how AV vendors would perform against each other in other contexts, because we don't use every hash in every given AV scanner. Similarly, the same generalization cannot be used for the Zeus malware family, since we didn't use all samples known to be Zeus against the AV scanners. Our study is, however, meaningful in answering the limited context's questions it poses for 1000 malware samples. Furthermore, our study goes beyond the best known work in the literature in the problem by not relying on AV-provided vendors as reference for comparing other vendors.

To this end, in the future we will try to answer those questions with more manually-vetted malware samples belonging to different families, and by studying better ways of obtaining consensus over AV-provided labels, ways that can tolerate many inconsistencies among vendors. We see a solution to the problem by enabling information sharing, so one of our future works is to explore how this sharing would enable better use of indicators for better malware labeling. We will release all datasets used in this study (AV scans, hashes, and scripts used for comparison), to help pursue alternatives. We hope this note will trigger further investigation and attention in the community to this crucial issue.

Acknowledgement. We would like to thank Andrew West for proofreading this work, and Allison Mankin and Burt Kaliski for their feedback. We would like to further thank Trevor Tonn, Ryan Olson, Brandon Dixon, Leo Fernandes, and Blake Hartstein for sharing with us the dataset and for their valuable feedback.

References

1. VirusTotal - Free Online Virus, Malware and URL Scanner. https://www.virustotal.com/en/ August 2013
2. Bailey, M., Oberheide, J., Andersen, J., Mao, Z.M., Jahanian, F., Nazario, J.: Automated classification and analysis of internet malware. In: Kruegel, C., Lippmann, R., Clark, A. (eds.) RAID 2007. LNCS, vol. 4637, pp. 178–197. Springer, Heidelberg (2007)
3. Bayer, U., Comparetti, P.M., Hlauschek, C., Krügel, C., Kirda, E.: Scalable, behavior-based malware clustering. In: NDSS (2009)
4. Kerr, D.: Ubisoft hacked; users' e-mails and passwords exposed. http://cnet.co/14ONGDi July 2013
5. Kinable, J., Kostakis, O.: Malware classification based on call graph clustering. J. Comput. Virol. **7**(4), 233–245 (2011)
6. Kong, D., Yan, G.: Discriminant malware distance learning on structural information for automated malware classification. In: Proceedings of the 19th ACM SIGKDD Conference on Knowledge Discovery and Data Mining (2013)
7. Kruss, P.: Complete zeus source code has been leaked to the masses. http://www.csis.dk/en/csis/blog/3229 March 2011

8. Lanzi, A., Sharif, M.I., Lee, W.: K-tracer: a system for extracting kernel malware behavior. In: NDSS (2009)
9. Mohaisen, A., Alrawi, O.: Unveiling zeus: automated classification of malware samples. In: WWW (Companion Volume), pp. 829–832 (2013)
10. Mozzherina, E.: An approach to improving the classification of the New York Times annotated corpus. In: Klinov, P., Mouromtsev, D. (eds.) KESW 2013. CCIS, vol. 394, pp. 83–91. Springer, Heidelberg (2013)
11. Park, Y., Reeves, D., Mulukutla, V., Sundaravel, B.: Fast malware classification by automated behavioral graph matching. In: CSIIR Workshop, ACM (2010)
12. Perdisci, R., Lee, W., Feamster, N.: Behavioral clustering of http-based malware and signature generation using malicious network traces. In: USENIX NSDI (2010)
13. Rieck, K., Holz, T., Willems, C., Düssel, P., Laskov, P.: Learning and classification of malware behavior. In: Zamboni, D. (ed.) DIMVA 2008. LNCS, vol. 5137, pp. 108–125. Springer, Heidelberg (2008)
14. Rieck, K., Trinius, P., Willems, C., Holz, T.: Automatic analysis of malware behavior using machine learning. J. Comput. Secur. 19(4), 639–668 (2011)
15. Rossow, C., Dietrich, C.J., Grier, C., Kreibich, C., Paxson, V., Pohlmann, N., Bos, H., van Steen, M.: Prudent practices for designing malware experiments: status quo and outlook. In: IEEE Symposium on Security and Privacy (2012)
16. Sharif, M.I., Lanzi, A., Giffin, J.T., Lee, W.: Automatic reverse engineering of malware emulators. In: IEEE Symposium on Security and Privacy (2009)
17. Shaw, A.: Livingsocial hacked: cyber attack affects more than 50 million customers. http://abcn.ws/15ipKsw April 2013
18. Silveira, V.: An update on linkedin member passwords compromised. http://linkd.in/Ni5aTg July 2012
19. Strayer, W.T., Lapsley, D.E., Walsh, R., Livadas, C.: Botnet detection based on network behavior. In: Lee, W., Wang, C., Dagon, D. (eds.) Botnet Detection. Advances in Information Security, vol. 36. Springer, New York (2008)
20. Tian, R., Batten, L., Versteeg, S.: Function length as a tool for malware classification. In: IEEE MALWARE (2008)
21. Vazirani, V.V.: Approximation Algorithms. Springer, Heidelberg (2004)
22. Yan, G., Brown, N., Kong, D.: Exploring discriminatory features for automated malware classification. In: Rieck, K., Stewin, P., Seifert, J.-P. (eds.) DIMVA 2013. LNCS, vol. 7967, pp. 41–61. Springer, Heidelberg (2013)
23. Zhao, H., Xu, M., Zheng, N., Yao, J., Ho, Q.: Malicious executables classification based on behavioral factor analysis. In: IC4E (2010)

Privacy

Assured Supraliminal Steganography in Computer Games

Anton Mosunov[1], Vineet Sinha[1], Heather Crawford[2], John Aycock[1(✉)], Daniel Medeiros Nunes de Castro[1], and Rashmi Kumari[1]

[1] Department of Computer Science, University of Calgary,
2500 University Drive NW, Calgary, AB T2N 1N4, Canada
{asmosuno,vsinha,aycock,dmncastr,rkumari}@ucalgary.ca
[2] Harris Institute for Assured Information, Florida Institute of Technology,
150 W. University Blvd., Melbourne, FL 32901, USA
hcrawford@cs.fit.edu

Abstract. While there is some work on supraliminal steganography, its definition makes it problematic in several respects. We deconstruct and sharpen the definition to create *assured* supraliminal steganography. The taxonomy and definition of assured supraliminal steganography are illustrated by hiding messages in computer games. We discuss four steganographic computer game implementations, and present the results of an experiment needed to ascertain whether or not a supraliminal method is actually assured supraliminal steganography. The results showed that it was possible to embed assured supraliminal messages into the four game implementations, and extract the messages with no or minimal errors.

1 Introduction

Most steganography research relies on subliminal techniques, hiding information by making unobtrusive changes to some cover object like a data file. But what if the "hidden" information is hidden in plain sight? The techniques for doing this are far less studied. We present novel techniques for hiding information in plain sight in computer games.

In the field of information hiding, the Prisoners' Problem [27] is a common method of describing steganographic channels. Alice and Bob have been put in jail and would like to communicate an escape plan to each other. The warden, who is often called Wendy, will allow Alice and Bob to exchange messages provided that she does not suspect they are hiding escape plans in innocuous messages. If she discovers that they are passing secret messages, she will eliminate all communication. Wendy can be one of three types of warden: passive, active, or malicious. A passive warden simply watches the messages as they pass between Alice and Bob – she cannot change or delete the messages, nor spoof either Alice or Bob to the other, nor can she inject new messages into the message stream. An active warden is allowed to change a small amount of data in

---

Heather Crawford – Work done while at the School of Computing Science, University of Glasgow, UK.

Y. Kim et al. (Eds.): WISA 2013, LNCS 8267, pp. 245–259, 2014.
DOI: 10.1007/978-3-319-05149-9_16, © Springer International Publishing Switzerland 2014

each message (one bit in 100 has been suggested as a suitably small amount [3]) but cannot add or delete messages to the message stream. A malicious warden can change all or part of a message, delete or add new message and also spoof Alice to Bob and vice versa. This last type of warden is not considered in this work because supraliminal channels are only defined using an active warden [3].

Supraliminal steganography uses a perceptually significant channel to transmit a secret message [3]. The goal is to convince Wendy that the secret message is innocuous, such as noise in a still image.[1] *Subliminal* steganography, on the other hand, occurs when the message is hidden in perceptually *in*significant parts of the channel, such as changing the value of the least significant bit (LSB) of an image or audio file [6,23]. The basic tenets of a supraliminal channel are that it must be robust in that making small changes to the channel will not eradicate the message; the channel must be inconspicuous, which means that knowledge of the channel must not imply knowledge of the existence of the message; finally, the channel must be blatant, meaning that the message must be available to anyone who has access to the channel [3]. Furthermore, Wendy may only be an active and not a malicious warden, which means that she can only make small changes to the image. This restriction is valid because it is unlikely that Wendy would be able to make significant changes to each image under the assumption that a large number of images are exchanged between Alice and Bob.

Deconstructing supraliminal. The original definition of supraliminal steganography is due to Craver [3], but problems arise in practice when trying to pin down what constitutes "supraliminal."

First, the level of interpretation must be defined. For example, a bit conveyed by the presence or absence of a teacup in a digital picture may be easily seen as supraliminal in terms of a human viewing the rendered image. Such semantic interpretation of the teacup's existence in the image is known as *content–aware* steganography [1]. However, there is also a representation of that teacup in the image file that is unseen directly by the human, so it can be argued to also be subliminal from that level of interpretation. Indeed, we conjecture that *all* digital supraliminal messages must have some subliminal component.

Second, the very terms "subliminal" and "supraliminal" are linked to (human) perception. In some cases, it is clear that a steganography technique is subliminal because of what is known about human physiology. Beyond those cases, and especially as we consider supraliminal steganography, we think that there is a spectrum of perceptibility, and in many instances user studies are warranted to ascertain whether a steganographic technique is truly supra- or subliminal to a human. Such user studies are not a typical feature in steganography, though.

Third, the limits on the warden's possible actions with respect to the channel must be well defined in the same way as security research defines threat models. This is necessary to understand, when we claim a channel is "robust," what it is robust with respect to.

---

[1] We use images as examples initially due to their familiarity; we turn to games later in this section.

Application to computer games. In the remainder of this paper, we illustrate how supraliminal messages may be conveyed in even simple computer games. To address the issues mentioned above, we strengthen Craver's original definition to create what we call *assured* supraliminal steganography. This inherits the original properties – that the channel be robust, blatant, and inconspicuous – but adds the proviso that we assure the channel is human-perceptible (and therefore supraliminal in the true sense) because a human is able to see enough to extract the message manually, if necessary. We do not preclude the human being a trained operator; recall that trained humans once routinely sent and received Morse code. Furthermore, historical accounts of early steganographic techniques such as the tattooed slave's head [16] required a trained operator to both embed and retrieve the message.

The level of interpretation (for both the intended message receiver and the warden) is the game interface as used by a human playing the game. A message may or may not be extractable by looking at network packets or a browser-based game's JavaScript code, but that lies outside our threat model.

Finally, the warden may actively make changes on the recipient's end in order to impede or destroy any steganographic channel, but gameplay cannot be altered as a result.

Assured supraliminal steganography in games has a natural taxonomy that we follow in this paper, that derives from how a human extracts a message. If the message may be perceived in its entirety initially without starting to play the game, we call such a steganographic method *static*. If, on the other hand, the message may only be perceived (in whole or part) while the human is actively playing the game, this is a *dynamic* method. Note that a static method does not imply a limited number of bits conveyed, because a message can be split statically across multiple games or levels.

Section 2 discusses related work; Sects. 3 and 4 present our implementations of static and dynamic assured supraliminal steganography, respectively; Sect. 5 concludes.

2   Related Work

As mentioned, supraliminal steganography was proposed by Craver et al. in 1998 [3]; the same authors proved that the concept is viable in a video application [4] (with some limitations), and a wireless device application [14]. Furthermore, it was shown that audio files can contain supraliminal channels [5].

Online gaming has become increasingly popular with the advent of social networking applications that allow physically distant participants to participate in a single game. The communication channels that exist within such games have inadvertently provided a covert channel that may be used for communication during gameplay. The communication, while generally covert, is used to collude with other players with the intention of winning the game [20].

Research into using games as covert channels has spanned the depth and breadth of available games. Combinatorial games, which are those games where chance does not play a role and the player has perfect information about possible moves, have seen particular focus. Hernandez-Castro et al. used the combinatorial game of Go to test a general methodology for embedding messages in games [10]. Similarly, Ritchey and Rego used the game Tic-Tac-Toe as the basis for a steganographic combinatorial game [25].

Many of these successful steganographic methods passed messages relating to strategy and collusion between team members, although not always in a digital representation of the game. Examples of research into collusion in a digital game exist; Murdoch and Zieliński embedded messages into an online game of Connect Four, with the intention of colluding with team members in order to win an online tournament [20]. Shirali-Shahreza and Shirali-Shahreza used a Sudoku puzzle sent via SMS to hide messages [15]; this shows that the digital game need not be combinatorial nor multiplayer. Online first–person shooter games were the cover for Zander et al.'s steganographic method [28]. They embedded the message bits within slight variations of a game character's movements, which has the possibility of being perceived by a human, although this possibility was not addressed in their paper.

The majority of the research mentioned thus far has assumed that the parties exchanging messages must play the game in order to communicate – our definition of dynamic methods encompasses these games. Several examples for our definition of static methods (i.e., those that do not require gameplay to embed or extract the message) exist within current research. Lee et al. embedded messages in a maze with hidden walls [12]. The maze is displayed on the screen, with hidden walls containing the message bits, and once so displayed, the message can be retrieved (electronically) without solving the maze.

The related work cited here does not allow for human extraction of the messages in the cases of messages that have been digitally encoded into the game. Furthermore, many of the examples here have assumed a multiplayer paradigm in which collusion for the purposes of winning has been the main goal. Our work focuses on generic messages from one person to another in all game modalities, not simply multiplayer. Furthermore, we allow for human extraction of the message. In the following sections, we present cases in which both static and dynamic gaming methods may be used to hide a message that can be extracted by a human without using digital methods.

3   Static Methods

Aspects of the definition of assured supraliminal steganography are brought out by examining two of the static methods we implemented, for Breakout and two types of Solitaire.

3.1   Breakout

Our first example, Breakout, is illustrative of several points in our definition of assured supraliminal steganography.

SS Breakout

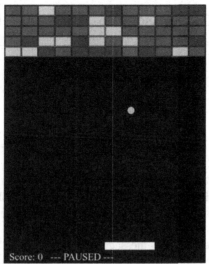

Fig. 1. Breakout with a hidden message

Breakout originally appeared in 1976 [7] and has had many clones and descendants. The game is straightforward: a player, using a ball that they keep in play using a paddle, tries to hit (and thereby remove) all the colored blocks arranged in lines on the far end of the screen (Fig. 1). Once all the colored blocks are removed, the player progresses to the next level.

Our embedding method encodes a message using the color of blocks.[2] With $C = 4$ colors, a small number of colors to allow easy discernment by a human, we can represent the bytes of a message M as base C numbers, meaning we need $\lceil \log_C 256 \rceil$ blocks to represent each byte of M. M_C denotes M as a base C number. The colors are read from left to right, top to bottom; red, green, blue, and yellow represent the values 0 through 3, respectively. A level in our game has $NR = 5$ rows, where each row is of length $|R| = 12$.

The embedded message E is preceded in each level by a random nonce N, where $|N|$ and $|R|$ are relatively prime to try to avoid obvious repeating patterns. N serves to ensure that a message will appear differently even if the same message is embedded in different levels. The ith digit of E (in base C), where i indexes digits of a number from left ($i = 0$) to right, is encoded as $E_C[i] = (M_C[i] + N[i \bmod |N|]) \bmod |C|$.

Figure 1 contains the message "Hello world" using the encoding in Table 1. The randomly chosen nonce value, 2011 2231 1311 1101, occupies the first 11 blocks. The next four blocks, green-red-yellow-green, correspond to 1031;

---

[2] Our browser-based JavaScript implementation is based on [26].

Table 1. (Partial) Breakout message encoding; underlining indicates where the nonce value starts being reused

Character	ASCII, Base 4	Base 4 Encoding with Nonce (Colors)
H	1020	2011 (BRGG)
e	1211	2231 (BBYG)
l	1230	131<u>1</u> (GYG<u>G</u>)
l	1230	1101 (GGRG)
o	1233	1033 (GRYY)
⋮	⋮	⋮

subtracting the first four nonce values from each digit modulo 4, respectively, gives us 1020, which is the base 4 representation of ASCII "H." The last five blocks are unneeded to encode the message and their colors are selected randomly.

As described, an embedded message could be altered or destroyed by the warden. So long as the colors are decorative only, the warden could change them arbitrarily. To counter this, our version of Breakout makes each block color worth a different number of points; changing the colors would thus change gameplay and is outside the scope of what the warden can do.

Breakout also illustrates a static method that can convey an unlimited number of bits. Although a single level only has $NR \times R - |N|$ blocks available for encoding, a longer message can be split across multiple levels. The message on each level can be read off by a human without active gameplay, making this static assured supraliminal steganography.

3.2 Solitaire

Solitaire computer card games are well known to Windows users, and there are an enormous number of variants: PySolFC 2.0, the Python-based solitaire game we modified to add steganographic capability, boasts over 1000 solitaire games [24].

We consider single-deck (i.e., 52-card) games here.[3] The exact layout of the cards is immaterial; for our purposes, all that matters is that there are zero or more cards face-up (implying their suit and rank are visible) on the layout, and that any leftover cards unused in the layout are kept in a *stock* pile that may be revealed in a controlled manner by the player. This varies by game. For example, Freecell has all 52 cards face-up in the layout, and no stock; Klondike has seven cards face-up, with 24 cards in the stock that can be revealed one by one.[4]

Our encoding scheme only considers cards that are face-up or ones that may be revealed from the stock; the number of these cards is denoted N in this section. While hidden cards in the layout may be revealed through play, there

---

[3] We follow card terminology and Solitaire rules given in [18].

[4] At least in the variant we consider here.

are often multiple moves that a player can make in Solitaire at any given time; choosing the "wrong" move would render the hidden message unextractable.

We use the permutation of the N cards as the basis for encoding, and given that there are $N!$ permutations, this allows us $\lfloor \log_2 N! \rfloor$ bits per game. This is 225 bits for Freecell, 112 bits for Klondike. For reference, 224 bits is the minimum key size for elliptic curve cryptography recommended by NIST until the year 2030 [21].

Assigning each suit a number ($0 = \clubsuit, 1 = \spadesuit, 2 = \heartsuit, 3 = \diamondsuit$), we can calculate a unique numerical value for each card by computing $suit \times 13 + rank$. Reading the N cards in a known order (e.g., for Freecell, from left to right, top to bottom of the layout) thus gives us a sequence of unique numbers that may be interpreted as a permutation. Assuming that there is some way to order all possible permutations, the message M as a number would then identify a specific permutation of cards. On the recipient's side, the N cards' values can clearly be read by a human, and the card layout cannot be changed on that end by the warden without affecting gameplay, making this assured supraliminal steganography. We list this as a static method, but in fact the static/dynamic classification actually depends on the exact Solitaire variant: Freecell is static, but Klondike requires the player to play and cycle through the stock cards.

The only issue is how to convert a number to a permutation, and vice versa. Following an observation by Lehmer [13], one made much earlier by Laisant [11], we convert M to its equivalent value $M_!$ in a factorial number system. The digits of $M_!$ can be read to identify a specific permutation of cards. In reverse, the cards' permutation is used to find $M_!$, which can be converted to M.

This is best illustrated with an example. If $M = 43$, then $M_! = 1\,3\,0\,1\,0$, because $43 = (1 \times 4!) + (3 \times 3!) + (0 \times 2!) + (1 \times 1!) + (0 \times 0!)$ or, equivalently, each digit of $M_!$ has a different base, so $43 = 1_5\,3_4\,0_3\,1_2\,0_1$. Conversion is a minor variation on normal base-to-base conversion; we omit the details. Given the cards $(4\clubsuit, A\spadesuit, 3\heartsuit, Q\heartsuit, 9\diamondsuit)$, these correspond to the ordered sequence of numbers $(3, 13, 28, 37, 47)$. Reading the digits of $M_!$ from left to right gives us indices into this ordered sequence (numbered from $0 \ldots 4$) to arrive at a permutation. The first digit of $M_!$, 1, selects and removes 13 from the sequence; 3 selects and removes 47 (which is now at index 3); 0 selects/removes 3; 1 yields 37, and finally 0 trivially selects 28. The permutation for M is thus $(A\spadesuit, 9\diamondsuit, 4\clubsuit, Q\heartsuit, 3\heartsuit)$. The reverse process can convert the card permutation into $M_!$, knowing the original ordered sequence, and from there to M.

Applications of permutations in *sub*liminal steganography already exist, e.g. [2,8,9], but our implementation highlights how permutations may be used to provide assured supraliminal steganography.

Finally, we observe that the unpermuted cards need not be in sorted order, so long as Alice and Bob agree on the same unpermuted order. We found this steganographic method gave the best results in terms of appearing to be a random deal when the unpermuted deck was shuffled to begin with.

4   Dynamic Methods

Moving to dynamic assured supraliminal steganography, we present methods we implemented for Pong and Pac-Man before showing the results of an experiment to determine if these methods met our assured supraliminal steganography definition.

4.1   Pong

Pong, released by Atari in arcade format in 1972 [7], was one of the first video games. Based on the physical game of table tennis, or ping-pong, there are four game elements (Fig. 2): two paddles, one per player, where each player can move their paddle up and down vertically; a ball that bounces back and forth and must be kept in play; a board, divided in half by a line indicating the net. It is interesting that, even in so rudimentary a game, there are several possibilities for conveying hidden messages.

Our Java implementation of Pong is played across the network via TCP. Recall that the level of interpretation here is at the game interface, not the network level.

For steganographic purposes, the sender's paddle is divided into three areas. The ball hitting the top of the paddle indicates a 1 bit, the bottom of the paddle indicates a 0 bit, and the middle is used to convey that a message is starting or stopping. Each message begins with the preamble mid-mid-mid-mid-top-bottom and terminates with mid-mid-mid-mid-bottom-top. On the sender's end, the message M to transit is entered in a text box, at which point the sender's paddle becomes automated and moves such that M is transmitted. The only problem is if the sender's paddle hits the end of the board and is unable to send the appropriate value; we simply ignore ball contact when the paddle is in this position. The length of M is unlimited, at least in theory, because continued gameplay can send any number of bits (in practice, we concede that Pong's novelty value likely makes it suitable only for small values of $|M|$).

The need to have a human interpret the hidden message is really a limiting factor in Pong, with the few game elements there are to commandeer for steganographic purposes. An earlier version we had a much higher bit rate, by using the difference in y coordinates between the ball and the paddle to send information,

Fig. 2. Pong

but this value is too fine-grained for a human to discern during gameplay, and automatic extraction was required in that earlier version.

4.2 Pac-Man

There are few video games that truly can be called iconic, and Pac-Man is one of them. The goal is for the Pac-Man to clear each level of dots, whilst avoiding the four non-player characters, who are better known as the ghosts. While each of the ghosts chases Pac-Man differently, their behavior is deterministic, and this lack of randomness led players to memorize patterns so that Pac-Man could completely avoid ghosts during the game [22]. Future Pac-Man sequels, such as Ms. Pac-Man, remedied this with 'less evidently deterministic' ghost movement [17, page 77].

In our Java implementation, based on Ms. Pac-Man 2010 [19], we hide a message M into ghost movement. Variation from deterministic ghost movement would be fairly easy to spot, of course. Fortunately, whenever Pac-Man eats a so-called *power pill* and the ghosts get scared, they start to move randomly, to make it more challenging for Pac-Man to catch them. In our version, whenever ghosts get scared, they start transmitting M. A ghost transmits a bit whenever it reaches an intersection with three or more paths, where it has a choice of two or more directions to go to.

Suppose that a ghost reaches an intersection and would like to transmit a single bit. Such an intersection must have at least three paths leading to it, and the ghost must choose a direction in which to continue. Note that in the original game the ghost cannot move back in the direction where it came from. We define *1-direction* as the direction where the ghost transmits a 1 bit, and *0-direction* as the direction where the ghost transmits a 0 bit. For each intersection type, the 1-direction is unique, and is dependent on where the ghost came from (Fig. 3). The 0-direction is any direction that is not a 1-direction. For an intersection of three paths, the 0-direction is unique, whereas every intersection of four paths has two 0-directions.

Each intersection might have four possible directions: up, right, down, and left. To find a 1-direction, starting from the up direction, the 1-direction is the first direction in clockwise order that (a) exists for a particular intersection; and

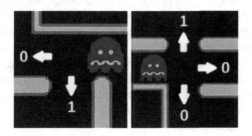

Fig. 3. Finding 1- and 0-directions in Pac-Man

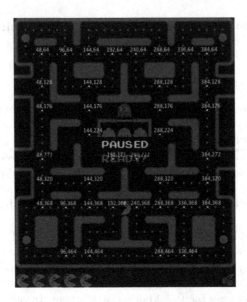

Fig. 4. Pac-Man maze overlaid with the pixel tracker

(b) is not a direction where the ghost came from. Note that according to this definition, left cannot be a 1-direction, and up can never be a 0-direction.

In Fig. 3, on the left, the up direction does not exist, and the ghost itself comes from the right, making the 1-direction downwards. In the rightmost image, no such complications exist, and the 1-direction is upwards, with the other two paths 0-directions.

As for the drawbacks of this approach, the most significant one is the low embedding rate. The scared mode does not last for long, and gets shorter as the player progresses through the levels. Furthermore, the Pac-Man maze has only four power pills in it. Multiple levels are obviously needed to transmit any substantive message and, apart from Pac-Man savants, multiple games are also likely necessary. Correspondingly, our implementation recalls how much of the message is transmitted, so it can resume at that point during the next game. Although gameplay strategy is outside the scope of assured supraliminal steganography for games, a player receiving a message should not interfere with transmission, and thus must avoid scared ghosts rather than eat them for bonus points. This strategy might seem unusual to an outside observer.

While the ultimate goal is manual message extraction, and certainly the player can see the ghosts transmitting the message, manually following two or more ghosts is challenging. This is especially obvious when it comes to ordering: when multiple ghosts reach intersections almost at the same time, which is transmitting first? Furthermore, the more ghosts we are able to have transmitting, the greater the embedding rate.

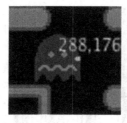

Fig. 5. A ghost overlapping a spy point

To try to address this and explore the limits of manual extraction, we developed a program we call a *pixel tracker* as a tool to assist with manual extraction.[5] We start the Pac-Man game, pause it, then carefully position the pixel tracker's transparent window over the Pac-Man maze and unpause the game. In other words, the pixel tracker is completely independent of the Pac-Man game. Figure 4 shows the maze overlaid with the pixel tracker window. The pixel tracker will highlight an intersection where a ghost appears by pointing to it with a mouse cursor arrow ($\nwarrow$). Where several ghosts reach intersections at the same time, the arrow will jump back and forth rapidly between those intersections. The arrows remain in place until a different intersection needs highlighting, i.e., they only signal ghosts arriving, not leaving.

The pixel tracker works by leveraging observations about color. The ghosts are normally brightly colored. Whenever ghosts get scared, they turn blue; when the power pill's effect expires, the ghosts flash gray. The pixel tracker's transparent window contains what we call a *spy* at each intersection of the maze. The spy is a single pixel located within an intersection. The locations must be chosen carefully to avoid false positives, because when not scared, the ghosts' eyes are blue and the eyelids are gray. Also, some of the bonus objects appearing on the maze periodically, like cherries, use gray as well. A different pixel tracker overlay is needed for each different Pac-Man maze. Figure 5 shows a ghost overlapping a spy.

4.3 Experiments

For the static assured supraliminal steganography methods in Sect. 3, it was clear that a human could see the elements used to convey the hidden message: the colors in Breakout and the card values in Solitaire were plainly visible. The same is not as obvious for dynamic methods. For these methods to be considered supraliminal, as we stated earlier, we must be able to show that a human can extract the message. We are not interested here in whether or not *all* humans can extract it, although that would be an interesting follow-on study. Instead, we just aim to see if human extraction is possible at all; it is sufficient to show that there exists a human who can extract the message with high accuracy.

---

[5] Note that, as our results show, this tool is not necessary for extraction.

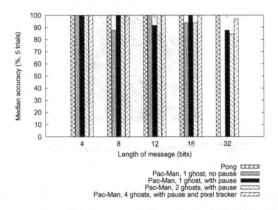

Fig. 6. Median extraction accuracy of dynamic methods using trained operators

In keeping with historical precedents mentioned before, we employ what amount to trained operators for our experiments, the people who developed the dynamic stego-games (AM, VS).[6] Strings of bits were chosen randomly and transmitted, and the trained operators recorded the bits they saw; they could also record the fact that they knew a bit was transmitted, but that they didn't know what it was. Random bitstrings of 4, 8, 12, 16, and 32 bits were used, and the experiment for each length was repeated five times, using a different random bitstring each time. There is no data for the 32-bit "one ghost, no pause" case for Pac-Man; for reasons described below, the effort to extract the bits would take an onerous amount of time. Also, there were some instances in Pac-Man where two bits were read correctly, but their order was unclear, and we have treated those as errors.

The median extraction accuracy from our experiments is shown in Fig. 6. The Pong accuracy was flawless in all cases; the operator noted that distinguishing the top and bottom hits on the paddle was not difficult, but definitely took a while for longer bitstrings – 32 bits may require up to three minutes depending on the ball's angle.

The median Pac-Man results, while not perfect, are perhaps more interesting. The median extraction accuracy is very high for all of them, and for bitstrings of length 4, 8, 12, and 16, there were always extraction trials having 100 % accuracy. Of the three 32-bit extraction strategies (more on this below), one had a perfect trial, and the other two had trials with at most a single-bit error. This suggests that human extraction of longer messages is feasible, although perhaps in combination with an error-correcting code. Figure 7 shows the *lowest*-accuracy trial for each technique for comparison, and even there some of the Pac-Man strategies fared tolerably well. The operator noted that trials with more errors

---

[6] As they are co-authors and we are reporting on our own performance rather than gathering data from other human subjects, no ethics approval is required from our institution.

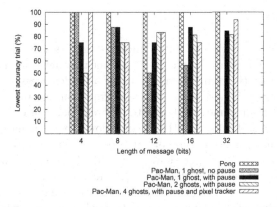

Fig. 7. *Lowest* extraction accuracy of dynamic methods using trained operators

would often correspond to eating a pill at the wrong time with respect to the ghosts' position.

Given these results, it is fair to say that both our Pong and Pac-Man methods for hiding messages qualify as assured supraliminal steganography methods. For Pac-Man, however, the results indicate that a combination of further training for the operator, improved extraction strategies, and coding to compensate for any errors are required to make it more practical.

More needs to be said on the Pac-Man extraction strategies, though. One significant difference between Pong and Pac-Man is that Pac-Man allows the game to be paused, meaning a Pong message must be extracted in real time, but one dimension of Pac-Man extraction strategy may involve repeated pausing of the game to interpret the ghost movement. Another dimension is how many ghosts are carrying the message, which is a tradeoff: more ghosts may be more complicated to track, but allow for transmitting more bits. With one ghost, the four pills in a Pac-Man maze yield 8–10 bits, after which the operator must deliberately die and restart the game, gaining another four pills to work with. Two ghosts boost this amount to 16–28 bits per level, or 4–7 bits per pill; with all four ghosts, it increases to 28–32 bits per level (7–8 bits per pill). We emphasize that tracking four ghosts was only possible with the pixel tracker, which the operator noted was very helpful for extraction.

Apart from the pixel tracker, the key to extraction seemed to be having the ghost(s) in a known location when a pill is eaten. A strategy that worked for two ghosts with pausing, variants of which were used for the other extraction methods, provides a useful example. The red ghost is the first to leave its "home" location in the center of the maze and moves towards the upper right-hand corner. The operator would wait until the red ghost reached this corner, which is far from any intersections, then eat a pill. While the red ghost is moving towards an intersection, the pink ghost will have left home, and the pink ghost's bits can be recorded before turning attention back to the red ghost and the bits it is transmitting.

5   Conclusion

We have refined the notion of supraliminal steganography to create assured supraliminal steganography, where "assured" means that a human can actually perceive and extract the elements transmitting a hidden message. This has been applied to computer games, where we have implemented assured supraliminal steganography in four games to illustrate different parts of our static/dynamic taxonomy. Some classification subtleties come down to particulars of a game variant, and even within a single type of game (e.g., Solitaire) static and dynamic variants may coexist. Verifying that a method of message hiding is, in fact, dynamic assured supraliminal steganography means verifying that a (possibly trained) human is able to extract a hidden message. We performed this verification with a number of experiments using trained operators; while experiments involving humans are not the norm in steganographic research, they make sense as a practical measure of what is truly sub- and supraliminal.

Acknowledgments. The authors' work is supported in part by grants from the Natural Sciences and Engineering Research Council of Canada (JA), and the Scottish Informatics and Computer Science Alliance (HC). Thanks to Melissa Aycock for translating [11].

References

1. Bergmair, R., Katzenbeisser, S.: Content-aware steganography: about lazy prisoners and narrow-minded wardens. In: Camenisch, J.L., Collberg, C.S., Johnson, N.F., Sallee, P. (eds.) IH 2006. LNCS, vol. 4437, pp. 109–123. Springer, Heidelberg (2007)
2. Chakinala, R.C., Kumarasubramanian, A., Manokaran, R., Noubir, G., Rangan, C.P., Sundaram, R.: Steganographic communication in ordered channels. In: Camenisch, J.L., Collberg, C.S., Johnson, N.F., Sallee, P. (eds.) IH 2006. LNCS, vol. 4437, pp. 42–57. Springer, Heidelberg (2007)
3. Craver, S.: On public-key steganography in the presence of an active warden. In: Aucsmith, D. (ed.) IH 1998. LNCS, vol. 1525, pp. 355–368. Springer, Heidelberg (1998)
4. Craver, S., Li, E., Yu, J., Atakli, I.: A supraliminal channel in a videoconferencing application. In: Solanki, K., Sullivan, K., Madhow, U. (eds.) IH 2008. LNCS, vol. 5284, pp. 283–293. Springer, Heidelberg (2008)
5. Crawford, H., Aycock, J.: Supraliminal audio steganography: audio files tricking audiophiles. In: Katzenbeisser, S., Sadeghi, A.-R. (eds.) IH 2009. LNCS, vol. 5806, pp. 1–14. Springer, Heidelberg (2009)
6. Cvejic, N., Seppanen, T.: Increasing the capacity of LSB-based audio steganography. In: 2002 IEEE Workshop on Multimedia Signal Processing, pp. 336–338 (2002)
7. Dillon, R.: The Golden Age of Video Games. CRC Press, Boca Raton (2011)
8. Eidenbenz, R., Locher, T., Wattenhofer, R.: Hidden communication in P2P networks: steganographic handshake and broadcast. In: IEEE INFOCOM, pp. 954–962 (2011)

9. Forest, K., Knight, S.: Permutation-based steganographic channels. In: 4th International Conference in Risks and Security of Internet and Systems, pp. 67–73 (2009)

10. Hernandez-Castro, J.C., Blasco-Lopez, I., Estevez-Tapiador, J.M., Ribagorda-Garnacho, A.: Steganography in games: a general methodology and its application to the game of go. Comput. Secur. 25(1), 64–71 (2006)

11. Laisant, C.-A.: Sur la numération factorielle, application aux permutations. Bulletin de la Société Mathématique de France 16, 176–183 (1888)

12. Lee, H.-L., Lee, C.-F., Chen, L.-H.: A perfect maze based steganographic method. J. Syst. Softw. 83(12), 2528–2535 (2010)

13. Lehmer, D.H.: Teaching combinatorial tricks to a computer. In: 10th Symposium in Applied Mathematics of the American Mathematical Society, pp. 179–193 (1960). Symposium was actually held in 1958

14. Li, E., Craver, S.: A supraliminal channel in a wireless phone application. In: 11th ACM Workshop on Multimedia and Security, pp. 151–154 (2009)

15. Shirali-Shahreza, M.H., Shirali-Shahreza, M.: Steganography in SMS by sudoku puzzle. In: IEEE/ACS International Conference on Computer Systems and Applications, pp. 844–847 (2008)

16. Macaulay, G.C.: (trans.) The History of Herodotus, vol. 2. Macmillan, London (1890)

17. Montfort, N., Bogost, I.: Racing the Beam: The Atari Video Computer System. MIT Press, Cambridge (2009)

18. Morehead, A.H., Mott-Smith, G. (eds.): Hoyle's Rules of Games, 3rd edn. Penguin Putnam Inc, New York (2001). Revised by Morehead, P.D.

19. Ms. Pac-Man. http://meatfighter.com/mspacman2010/ 2010. Accessed 21 May 2013

20. Murdoch, S.J., Zieliński, P.: Covert channels for collusion in online computer games. In: Fridrich, J. (ed.) IH 2004. LNCS, vol. 3200, pp. 355–369. Springer, Heidelberg (2005)

21. National Institute of Standards and Technology: Recommendation for Key Management - Part 1: General (revised), 800–857 edn. NIST Special Publication, Berhampur (2007)

22. Pittman, J.: The Pac-Man dossier. http://home.comcast.net/~jpittman2/pacman/pacmandossier.html. Accessed 16 June 2011

23. Pooyan, M., Delforouzi, A.: LSB-based audio steganography method based on lifting wavelet transform. In: IEEE International Symposium on Signal Processing and Information Technology, pp. 600–603 (2007)

24. PySolFC: a Python solitaire game collection. http://pysolfc.sourceforge.net/. Accessed 21 May 2013

25. Ritchey, P.C., Rego, V.J.: Covert channels in combinatorial games. In: 5th International ICST Conference on Simulation Tools and Techniques, pp. 234–241 (2012)

26. Shankar, A.R.: HTML5 game development tutorial: breakout part I - introduction to Canvas. http://www.adityaravishankar.com/2011/10/html5-game-development-tutorial-breakout-i-introduction-to-canvas/, 11 October 2011. Accessed 21 May 2013

27. Simmons, G.J.: The prisoners' problem and the subliminal channel. In: Advances in Cryptology, Proceedings of CRYPTO '83, pp. 51–67 (1984)

28. Zander, S., Armitage, G., Branch, P.: Covert channels in multiplayer first person shooter online games. In: 33rd IEEE Conference on Local Computer Networks, pp. 215–222 (2008)

A Cloud and In-Memory Based Two-Tier Architecture of a Database Protection System from Insider Attacks

Cheolmin Sky Moon[1], Sam Chung[1,2(✉)],
and Barbara Endicott-Popovsky[2]

[1] Computer Science and Systems, Institute of Technology,
University of Washington Tacoma, Tacoma, USA
{mtm0riah, chungsa}@uw.edu
[2] Center for Information Assurance and Cybersecurity,
University of Washington, Seattle, USA
endicott@uw.edu

Abstract. As a response of emerging insider attacks targeting on database, we are proposing architecture of database protection system from insider attacks. Existing pattern matching approach to detect insider attacks cannot provide perfect solution because of false positive and true negative ratios. Accordingly, we still need reasoning by a human at the last decision to declare that the insider is malicious or not using analysis on history of transaction logs performed by the insider. To construct a system with the consideration above, the system needs to satisfy following requirements: (1) effective monitoring and analysis on large amount of log data (2) scalable system depending on increase or decrease of the log data, and (3) prompt analysis even though the amount of the log data is large enough. We propose a two-tier, distributed, cloud, and in-memory computing based architecture. The proposed architecture brings several benefits such as managing a large amount of log data, distributing analysis workload over multiple nodes, being scalable on big log data, and supporting real-time analysis of big log data.

Keywords: Insider attacks · Database audit logs · File system audit logs · Monitoring · Cloud computing · In-memory database

1 Introduction

By the definition of insider attacks provided by Computer Emergency Response Team (CERT) program in Carnegie Mellon University, it is the threats performed by a malicious insider who is a current or previous employee, or business partner having authorized access to the system or data, but intentionally used the authority to harm the system or information [1]. Insider attacks would be treated as much important as external attacks. According to the 2010/2011 Computer Security Institute (CSI) Computer Crime and Security Survey, 40.9 % of respondents believe that the loss of their data is from malicious insiders [2]. Another survey conducted by the U.S. Secret Service, the CERT Insider Threat Center, 43 % of respondents experienced at least

Y. Kim et al. (Eds.): WISA 2013, LNCS 8267, pp. 260–271, 2014.
DOI: 10.1007/978-3-319-05149-9_17, © Springer International Publishing Switzerland 2014

one malicious insider attack in 2010, and 46 % of the respondents think the damage caused by the insider attacks was more dangerous than one from outsider attacks [1].

There are several papers suggesting comprehensive insider attack detection models in high level [3–5]. These papers are beneficial to grab the general idea of how the architecture of the insider attack detection systems are supposed to look like, but those models in these papers are not much helpful to understand how to implements the each component of the suggested whole systems in low level.

One of the critical components of the each systems mentioned in the three papers is a monitoring component [3–5]. Greitzer and Hohimer [4] mentioned many different kinds of the cyber data which are meaningful to perform insider attack analysis on them. One of the cyber data mentioned by Greitzer is database server logs. There are also some papers claiming the importance of auditing and analyzing database server log and proposing the auditing and log processing mechanism to detect insider attacks [6–9].

Chagarlamudi et al. [6] pointed out that the potentiality of insider attacks to the database is greater than external threats: the more the legitimate insider knows about the database systems, the greater possibility of threats. Liu and Huang [7] said that according to more legitimate employees such as database administrator, system administrator, application developers, HR, etc. are getting database accesses in the enterprise, there are more possibility of intentional or unintentional data corruptions. For that reason, those employees having the authorization to access critical infor-mation in the database should be closely monitored.

We assume that database systems could be internally accessed and managed by two groups: a system administrator and a database administrator group. We decided to more focus on protecting the database system from a malicious database administrator group rather than a system administrator group because it is technically too difficult to protect a system from the administrators having full controls over the system without significant changes of the operation system structure. System administrators can detour any kinds of monitoring in the system. Accordingly, we want to start building the database protection system based on the assumption that the system administrator group is trustworthy. With the assumption, this paper will focus on the insider attack detection on database systems, and come up with a two-tier architecture of the insider attack detection systems that monitors activities of the legitimate users and database administrators (DBAs), detects abnormal behaviors, and reports them to the security team in the organization: one is running on multiple local systems to monitor short-term user behaviors, and the other is running on the cloud to store processed tre-mendous amount of database logs and monitor long-term user behaviors. Furthermore, we use In-Memory Database (IMDB) in the system running in memory, not disk, to speed up the analysis speed of the long-term user behaviors.

2 Previous Work

There were many papers mentioning the insider threat detection systems, but only a few papers focus on the insider threat detection targeting on database. However, general intrusion detection on database is lively researched. They usually not only focus on database intrusion detection, but also concern about the intrusion by insiders, and discuss about the solutions. For that reason, we will provide not only the research about database insider threat detection system in specific, but also the researches about general insider threat detection systems and database auditing systems on insider attacks.

Table 1 shows a comparison of four approaches that will be discussed. Chagarlamudi et al. [6] suggested insider threat prevention system on database. The mechanism to detect threats in the system is based on a set of predefined tasks for each user. The assumption of the system is that there are multiple applications performing tasks. Each task consists of multiple transactions partially ordered with Petri Nets. Since the applications predefine the transactions, no user can add, remove, or modify the transactions. Whenever a user performs a task, the system checks whether the task is in the set allocated to the user and the order of transactions to perform the task follows the predefined Petri net for each task. This approach is meaningful to suggest a solution to detect abnormal behaviors. However, the application of this approach is very limited because it can only detect the insider attacks performed by applications. It is not able to provide solutions to detect the insider attacks performed by the user having broader capabilities: system administrator, database administrators, etc. Additionally, the test sets of the research are too small to simulate enterprise environment.

Doss and Tejay [3] suggested a high level architecture that detects general insider attacks. A survey data is collected on a large government enterprise having more than

Table 1. A comparison of previous approaches

	Chagarlamudi et al. [6]	Doss and Tejay [3]	Rathod et al. [8]	Liu and Huang [7]
Providing an architectural model	Y	Y	Y	Y
Providing a prototype	Y	N	Y	Y
Focusing on insider attack detection	Y	Y	N	N
Focusing on attacks in database	Y	N	Y	Y
Considering database accesses through an application layer	Y	N/A	Y	Y
Considering database accesses without any intermediate layer	N	N/A	Y	Y
Considering all routes to access points to the database	N (only through application)	N/A	Y	N (only through network)
Preprocessing the raw log data to be analyzed	Y (A Petri Net based model)	N/A	Y (Transaction signature based)	N
Considering the management of large amount of log data	N	N	N	N
Distributing analysis workload over multiple nodes	N	N	N	N
Being scalable on big log data	N	N	N	N
Supporting real-time analysis of big log data	N	N	N	N

20,000 employees and 30,000 computer systems. Based upon the grounded theory analysis [13] on the data, an architecture that has four components, monitoring, threat assessment, insider evaluation, and remediation, is proposed. The monitoring process is divided into two sub-processes: short-term (30 min–4 h) and long-term (one day - several months) monitoring processes. The short-term monitoring is used to detect immediate insider attacks, and the long-term monitoring to analyze the collected user behaviors and find anomaly. However, they do not provide enough specifications of each component to implement them.

Rathod et al. [8] suggested intrusion detection in database based on transaction signature. He claimed that intrusion should be detected by not only wrong authorization but also misuse detection and anomaly detection. Rathod suggested an architecture that consists of three phases. The first phase is a learning phase - teaching the machine with offline log data. The second phase is a signature generation phase - a user's signature is generated by a transaction performed by the user. The third phase is a response phase - the trained machine compares the user signature with the legitimate transaction sets. The limitation of this approach is that it stores log files and trains the machine locally. It did not consider how fast the log data can be filed up in an enterprise system. Also, the approach could not fit to distributed systems having databases in multiple locations.

One of the main problems of the database auditing using DBMS auditing tool is that it drops the performance of the database up to 54.40 % [11]. A framework for database auditing which does not affect the performance of the database was suggested by Liu and Huang [7]. It captures network packet and parses it to extract the SQL transaction commands from each packet. In other word, the auditing is done by outside of the database, so it does not affect the performance of the database. However, it could not be used to detect a malicious insider who has the ability to directly access the machine having database. It did not also mention about how to deal with the audit logs for distributed systems.

Although it was not included in Table 1, a multi-perspective auditing approach was suggested by Raissi-Dehkordi and Carr [9]. Database auditing is done in terms of three views: user, file and database metrics. A different Support Vector Machine (SVM) is located for each view to train the machines. The user behavior analysis done by three SVMs goes to the aggregate detection module to analyze the three views together. They also considered a malicious event performed by the aggregation of the multiple normal events performed by group of malicious users. It was a good idea to analyze the user behaviors in multiple perspectives using three components, but it lacks the explanation of how to classify the attributes in each component to generate the profile metrics. This multi-perspective auditing approach will be considered in our design.

3 A Cloud and In-Memory Based Architecture

We propose a two-tier, distributed, cloud, and in-memory computing based architecture to build a database protection system. The architecture focuses on insider attack monitoring and detection using large amount of log data analysis in distributed way considering all entry points to the database. Raw transaction log data is pre-processed to reduce the log data size. Analysis system is located in the cloud to make the infrastructure of the system be easily scaled up and down. We also use an in-memory database to boost up the analysis speed on the insider transactions.

3.1 Assumption

First of all, the system administrators in the system are trustworthy. Second, a database server (DS) should have an access control mechanism (e.g. Linux), so the database administrators or users cannot directly access to the file of the database system and modify the configuration file to turn off the database monitoring or copy the whole or parts of database. Third, a DS and insider behavior analysis server (IBAS) both should be protected by firewall and secure socket layer connection between the DS and IBAS.

3.2 Two-Tier Architecture and IMDB

Figure 1 shows the two-tier architecture, in which a database server (DS) at the log processing tier is connected to an insider behavior analysis server (IBAS) at the insider behavior analysis and attack detection tier. The log processing tier runs on multiple local database servers to monitor preprocessing of file changes and transaction logs, and the insider behavior analysis and attack detection tier runs in the cloud with an IMDB.

Figure 2 shows the names of components composing a Database Server (DS) at the log processing tier. A DS is a part of the whole system in an organization targeted by an insider.

- DBMS: The asset to be protected from insider attacks
- DBMS Audit Logs: It logs all the transactions performed by database user accounts (not application account) into log files or tables created by DBMS audit features.
- File Change Audit Logs: It logs all changes of all files and folders related to the databases in the DBMS.
- File and Database Log Preprocessor (DLP): DLP preprocesses the log data and sends it to the insider behavior analysis server.

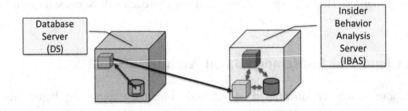

Fig. 1 A proposed two-tier architecture using cloud and IMDB for a DB protection system

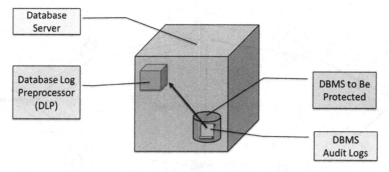

Fig. 2 Database server (DS)

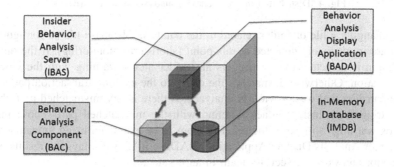

Fig. 3 Insider behavior analysis server (IBAS)

Figure 3 shows each component of an Insider Behavior Analysis Server (IBAS) at the insider behavior analysis and attack detection tier. The IBAS collects transaction histories of each insider in the IMDB, matches an incoming transaction of the insider to a set of analyzed patterns of the insider, detects a threat, and updates the insider's pattern set.

- Inside Behavior Analysis Server (IBAS): One or more IBASs compose the insider behavior analysis server in the cloud.
- In-Memory Database (IMDB): IMBD significantly reduces the analysis time on the database to accomplish real time detection of insider attacks. SAP HANA[1] in-memory database will be used for our implementation. IMDB in each IBAS has a data set to recognize a short-term attack, but the data set for an insider patterns are distributed.
- Behavior Analysis Component (BAC): BAC analyzes short/long-term behaviors of insiders (short-term: 30 min – 4 h and log-term: one day - several months). First, it exams the incoming insider behavior whether it has obvious violation to the database. For example, unauthorized access try, storing a result of the query into a

---

[1] SAP HANA, http://www.saphana.com/welcome

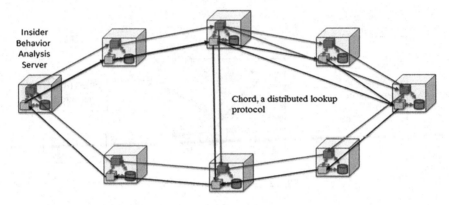

Insider Behavior Analysis Server

Chord, a distributed lookup protocol

Fig. 4 Distributed insider behavior analysis system (DIBAS)

file, changing a file or folder related to the database (database file or configuration file) are immediately detected at this point (short-term monitoring). If the obvious violation is detected, then it triggers an insider attack warning with the violation information. Otherwise, it matches the query to the existing transaction pattern set of the insider that was previously analyzed. If there is any mismatched part, then it also triggers an insider attack warning with the mismatched part. Those insider attack warnings will go to the security team to be examined using human sense.

- Behavior Analysis Display Application (BADA): BADA displays the results of the behavior analysis to a security team in an organization.

3.3 Distributed Architecture

Multiple IBASs make up a DIBAS to distribute the workload of insider behavior analysis from multiple DSs. A system of an organization would have more than one database servers. Furthermore, all DBs would have one to hundreds legitimate insiders having access to the databases. For that reason, distributing the workload will be a critical part to accomplish real time insider attack detection. Figure 4 displays the Distributed Insider Behavior Analysis System (DIBAS) using a distributed lookup protocol, Chord.

Chord protocol will be used to build an easily scalable, and restorable distributed system from some IBASs failure [12]. Each IBAS only needs to generate and maintain log *N* number of the location information in the route table, and makes backup data for its successor IBASs, where *N* denotes the number of servers [12].

3.4 Cloud Computing

In Fig. 5, we put all the components that we have mentioned into the cloud (Amazon Elastic Compute Cloud (EC2)[2] server) to achieve scalability of the insider attack

---

[2] Amazon Elastic Compute Cloud (EC2), http://aws.amazon.com/ec2/.

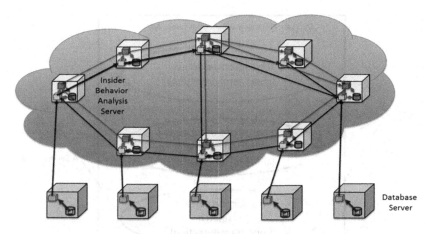

Fig. 5 A cloud and in-memory computing based two-tier architecture

detection system and reduce the maintenance cost. If we use a cloud infrastructure service, we can not only easily add and remove a server depending on the workload of the insider behavior analysis in remote, but also reduce the cost from running and maintaining servers in local. The usage of the servers would be fluctuated by day or month, so we can also save the cost from running an idle IBAS.

4   Case Study – Insider Threat Detection

4.1   Scenario

We start with a use case scenario that shows how insiders can attack the system: One of the database administrators of a big IT company A, John, has been working for the company for three years. Since the company did not treat John well and poorly paid him, he has recently been looking for a chance to leave the company and find a better place to work. Meanwhile, he thought company A's proprietary design data would be attractive to a company B which is a competitor of the company B, and the data would help him to get a good position in the company B. Accordingly, John turns out as a malicious insider. He accessed a database that has the data and executed a batch of queries to extract the data then put them into a thumb drive. A few minutes later, he left his room. However, at that moment, a security officer in a security team in the company came to catch him and investigated his malicious behavior.

The reason why the security team could detect John's malicious behavior was that the company A has used an insider attack detection system. The system immediately detects all of the unauthorized access trials and extracting files from the databases in the company. Then the system preprocesses all the transactions on the databases performed by the database insiders and send them to the insider behavior analysis system in the cloud. The insider behavior analysis system stores all the transaction history from the insiders, and generates a set of patterns of the insiders. If the insider's current transaction is different from the pattern set, then it warns a security team in the

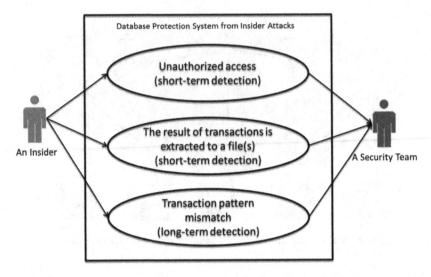

Fig. 6 Use case diagram

company with the mismatched part. Then the security team examines the part using human sense (e.g. to contact a manager of the department in the company which mainly deals with the part of data the suspicious insider unusually accessed to and performed unusual transactions on) to double check that the insider is really attacking the system.

For that reason, at the moment John executed the batch of queries on the data sets which he has not usually done, the first warning was triggered from the mismatched behaviors from his previous pattern set. Then when he extracts the result of the queries into a file, the second warning was triggered. Accordingly, the security team realized that they need to stop John.

Figure 6 shows a use case scenario in Unified Modeling Language (UML)[3] use case diagram. There are three kinds of behaviors triggering a short-term insider attack detection warning and one case triggering a long term insider attack detection warning.

Each use case is described below:

- Unauthorized Access (short-term detection): An insider does not have authority to access the database (for example, it can be shown as multiple time password failures).
- The result of a transaction is extracted to a file (short-term detection): A file having a result of a database query should be dealt very carefully. After the result is extracted into a file, it will not be traceable any longer
- A current transaction is mismatched from his previous transaction patterns (long-term detection): Every transaction from an insider will be compared with a set of

---

[3] Unified Modeling Language (UML), http://uml.org/.

the transaction patterns of the insider to detect insider attack. If there is no mismatch more than the pre-decided threshold, then update the existing patterns.

Based upon the use case diagram, we can show how the system using the two-tier, distributed, cloud, and IMC based architecture works in Fig. 7.

1. A malicious insider accesses a DS, then either extracts data from the database or executes queries which are not usually performed by the insider.
2. Logs of the changes on files or unusual queries are passed to the DLP to pre-process them.
3. The logs passed from 2 are preprocessed to reduce the file size and only meaningful information is extracted. After the preprocessing, the DS sends the processed logs to an IBAS.
4. BAC in the IBAS detects an insider attack using the short-term and the long-term analyses, then write down the attack on IMDB.
5. BAC also triggers BADA to let the security team know current insider attack.
6. BADA notifies the insider attack to a security team in the organization.
7. The security team checks the warning in detail using BADA.
8. The security team contacts a manager who is mainly dealing with the data set in the databases which was the source of triggering the insider attack warning to ask whether the insider is recently involved in any project which would let the insider execute the unusual transactions.
9. The manager responds to the security team's request.
10. If the response from the manager is negative (the insider does not have any reason to execute the transactions on the data set), then catch the insider. If it is positive, let the insider keep performing the transactions.

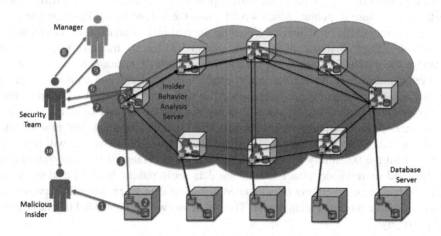

Fig. 7 A cloud and in-memory computing based two-tier architecture with a use case

5 Discussion and Future Work

5.1 Contribution

There are three benefits in proposed architecture. Firstly, it yields prompt results about each monitored transaction of an insider by using two-tier and in-memory computing. If the system took several minutes or hours to analyze the transactions, it would not be applicable because the several minutes are enough time to make something bad happen and damage the organization. Secondly, it is open to the complicated analysis which needs more computing power and takes longer time. Since this architecture is powered by distributed and cloud computing, we can simultaneously scale up while we add more rules to perform more sophisticated analysis on the log data. Lastly, by using the cloud storage, we can easily manage large amount of log data that can be quickly piled up to several terabytes in a month or even several days.

5.2 Future Research

Evaluation part will be the most important to prove how much correctly the system can detect insider attacks. Even though partial order of transactions [6] and signature of legitimate transactions [8] are used to detect insider attacks with the pattern mismatch mechanism in the previous researches, the pattern mismatch itself may or may not be related to the insider attacks. Pattern mismatch can be a start point of insider attack detection, but not more than that. Accordingly, without defining the relation between the pattern mismatches and real insider attacks, any provided system for insider attack detection is actually no more than a pattern mismatch detection system. However, it is almost impossible to access the insider attack data set in public because attacked organizations are reluctant to provide their insider attack log data set in public to keep their reputation. Moreover, providing the data set would reveal their database structure in public, which would cause the second attack from external.

To overcome the limitation of accessing the real insider attack data set and make the insider attack analysis area flourish, we need to have a framework not only to manage the transaction history for each insider in the organization, but also to share the set of transactions having the insider attack history information without revealing the database structure of the organization. After we set this framework up, then we can finally analyze the real insider attack data set provided by multiple organizations, and mine meaningful information from the data set to find insider attack pattern in certain time intervals. With the perspective that we have introduced above, we will research more about the possibility to provide a framework to manage the insider transaction history and share insider attack transaction data set in public. We will also use role-playing bad actors operating on simulated historical data when we build a prototype based upon the proposed architecture. The bad actors will be embedded in a large pool of good guys.

References

1. Silowash, G., Cappelli, D., Moore, A., Trzeciak, R., Shimeall, T., Flynn, L.: Common Sense Guide to Mitigating Insider Threats, 4th edn. Software Engineering Institute, Carnegie Mellon University, Pittsburgh, Technical Report CMU/SEI-2012-TR-012 (2012). http://www.sei.cmu.edu/library/abstracts/reports/12tr012.cfm. Accessed 15 May 2013
2. Richardson, R.: CSI Computer Crime and Security Survey 2010/2011. Computer Security Institute (2010). https://cours.etsmtl.ca/log619/documents/divers/CSIsurvey2010.pdf. Accessed 15 May 2013
3. Doss, G., Tejay, G.: Developing insider attack detection model: a grounded approach. In: Proceedings of IEEE International Conference on Intelligence and Security Informatics (ISI) 2009, (ISI09), pp. 107–112 (2009)
4. Greitzer, F.L., Hohimer, R.E.: Modeling human behavior to anticipate insider attacks. JSS J. Strateg. Secur. 4(2), 25–48 (2011)
5. Nithiyanandam, C., Tamilselvan, D., Balaji, S., Sivaguru, V.: Advanced framework of defense system for prevention of insider's malicious behaviors. In: 2012 International Conference on Recent Trends in Information Technology (ICRTIT) (2012). doi: 10.1109/ICRTIT.2012.6206788
6. Chagarlamudi, M., Panda, B., Hu, Y.: Insider threat in database systems: preventing malicious users' activities in databases. In: Sixth International Conference on Information Technology: New Generations 2009, ITNG '09 (2009). doi: 10.1109/ITNG.2009.67
7. Liu, L., Huang, Q.: A framework for database auditing. In: Fourth International Conference on Computer Sciences and Convergence Information Technology 2009, ICCIT '09 (2009). doi: 10.1109/ICCIT.2009.207
8. Rathod, Y.A., Chaudhari, M.B., Jethava, G.B.: Database intrusion detection by transaction signature. In: 2012 Third International Conference on Computing Communication and Networking Technologies (ICCCNT) (2012). doi: 10.1109/ICCCNT.2012.6395997
9. Raissi-Dehkordi, M., Carr, D.: A multi-perspective approach to insider threat detection. In: Military Communications Conference 2011 - Milcom 2011 (2011). doi: 10.1109/MILCOM.2011.6127457
10. International Data Corporation (IDC): The 2011 digital universe: extracting value from chaos, June 2011. http://www.emc.com/collateral/demos/microsites/emc-digital-universe-2011/index.htm. Accessed 15 May 2013
11. Giuseppe Maxia: MySQL 5.4 Performance with Logging. The Data Chamber. http://datacharmer.blogspot.com/2009/04/mysql-54-performance-with-logging.html. Accessed 16 May 2013
12. Stoica, I., Morris, R., Karger, D., Kaashoek, M.F., Balakrishnan, H.: Chord: a scalable peer-to-peer lookup service for internet applications. SIGCOMM Comput. Commun. Rev. 31(4), 149–160 (2001)
13. Grounded Theory Online; supporting GT researchers. https://sites.google.com/a/groundedtheoryonline.com/www/what-is-grounded-theory. Accessed 20 May 2013
14. Forbus, K.D.: Qualitative reasoning, DRAFT: chapter for the CRC Handbook of Computer Science. http://www.qrg.northwestern.edu/papers/Files/crc7.pdf (1996)

Author Index